Constitution for a Future Country

Also by Martin J. Bailey

DETERRENCE, ASSURED DESTRUCTION AND DEFENSE

MISMEASUREMENT OF ECONOMIC GROWTH

NATIONAL INCOME AND THE PRICE LEVEL: A Study in Macroeconomic Theory

OPTIMAL FULL-EMPLOYMENT SURPLUS

REDUCING RISKS TO LIFE: Measurement of the Benefits

STUDIES IN POSITIVE AND NORMATIVE ECONOMICS

TAXATION OF INCOME FROM CAPITAL (*editor with Arnold C. Harberger*)

Constitution for a Future Country

Martin J. Bailey

with editing by

Nicolaus Tideman
Professor of Economics
Virginia Polytechnic Institute and State University
USA

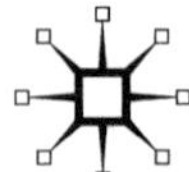

First published 2001 by
PALGRAVE
Houndmills, Basingstoke, Hampshire RG21 6XS and
175 Fifth Avenue, New York, N. Y. 10010
Companies and representatives throughout the world

PALGRAVE is the new global academic imprint of St. Martin's Press LLC Scholarly and Reference Division and Palgrave Publishers Ltd (formerly Macmillan Press Ltd).

ISBN 0–333–71909–3

This book is printed on paper suitable for recycling and made from fully managed and sustained forest sources.

A catalogue record for this book is available from the British Library.

Library of Congress Cataloging-in-Publication Data
Bailey, Martin J.
Constitution for a future country / Martin Bailey ; with editing by Nicolaus Tideman.
p. cm.
Includes bibliographical references and index.
ISBN 0–333–71909–3
1. Common good—Economic aspects. 2. Public interest–
–Economic aspects. 3. Political planning—Economic aspects.
4. Political participation—Economic aspects. I. Tideman, Nicolaus. II. Title.

JC330.15 .B35 2000
362—dc21

00–053068

10 9 8 7 6 5 4 3 2 1
10 09 08 07 06 05 04 03 02 01

Printed and bound in Great Britain by
Antony Rowe Ltd, Chippenham, Wiltshire

Contents

List of Tables

List of Figures

Acknowledgements

We are grateful to Kluwer Academic Publishers for permission to include matter previously published by Martin Bailey in articles in *Public Choice*. In particular, material from 'Toward a Constitution for a New Country' (March 1997) appears in Chapters 1 – 3. Material from 'Implementation of the Thompson Mechanism' (December 1996) appears in Chapter 5. Material from 'The Demand Revealing Process: To Distribute the Surplus' (April 1997) appears in the appendix to Chapter 6. And material from 'Lindahl Mechanisms and Free Riders' (July 1994) appears in Chapter 7. Edward Clarke helped compile the index and provided valuable advice on many points.

Foreword

Martin Bailey had a vision of structure through which a nation could rein in and productively redirect the impulses of citizens to use political processes to promote their selfish interests at the expense of their fellow citizens. This structure is an integration and elaboration of two ideas that were first developed several decades ago: the idea of a government-controlled market for insurance against unfavorable political outcomes, published by Earl Thompson in 1966, and the idea of marginal cost pricing for influence over political outcomes. While this second idea is sometimes called the 'demand-revealing process' or the 'pivotal mechanism', Bailey refers to it primarily as the 'VCG mechanism', in recognition of the independent contributions of three persons to the understanding of how a generalization of marginal cost pricing can improve incentives. William Vickrey described in 1961 how an auction that sold an item to the highest bidder at the price offered by the second highest bidder could induce bidders to make truthful bids. Theodore Groves showed, in a 1973 article from his dissertation, that efficient incentives in teams could be created by giving each member of the team a reward that increased or decreased by a dollar for each dollar increase or decrease in the product of the team's efforts. But it was Edward Clarke's 1971 paper that first showed how the principle of marginal cost pricing could be used to motivate people to report the magnitudes of their demands for public services, and this is the application of marginal cost pricing that Bailey employs in this book. He shows that generalizations of marginal cost pricing can resolve some of the most common problems of the public economy, apart from issues of basic entitlements, in a reasonably satisfactory way.

Bailey presents evidence of the great costs we endure because we lack a structure that generates efficient incentives in government, the details of how such a structure would work, an annotated draft constitution for a nation that wished to implement this structure, explanations of why various alternatives are inadequate, and a variety of theorems regarding the formal properties of the structure. Bailey explains that the potential audience for his book is 'a country with wise leaders and prudent voters, willing and able to take a fresh look at an unorthodox approach to government that offers the best possible prospects for themselves and their descendants.' It is a *tour de force* and essential reading for anyone who wants to understand what economics can contribute to the construction of political processes that come to grips with the selfish impulses that tend to undermine public decision-making.

Martin Bailey brought me into the project when he learned that he had only a few months to live because of a brain tumor. My role was to find a publisher and put the manuscript in final form. I edited the verbal parts of the manuscript very lightly. My main change was in the manner in which the formal results are presented. The Appendix to Chapter 6 was originally four appendices based on four different papers, each with slightly different assumptions and notation. As this seemed potentially confusing, I integrated them into a single appendix with more consistent assumptions and notation, improving on one result and correcting some small errors along the way. So of the errors that remain, some are Martin's responsibility and some are mine.

Nicolaus Tideman

1 The Emerging Country

So two cheers for democracy: one because it admits variety and one because it permits criticism. Two cheers are quite enough: there is no occasion to give three.[1]

1.1 INTRODUCTION

Since World War II many countries have emerged from under alien or tyrannical rule and have faced the problem of writing new constitutions for themselves. Usually there have been clear traditions to follow and strong political forces within each such country that have given the national leadership only limited scope for original thinking about what form government should take. Occasionally, however, a strong national leader may have had considerable leeway and possibly some motivation to try to draft a document that would lead to the best attainable rate of long-term economic growth and would preserve other values of greatest importance to the people.

If we review the results of actual cases in these past few decades, we do not find many constitutions with new and constructive features that would promise unusually strong performance. Nothing remarkably distinctive has emerged. The problems and inefficiencies in the ensuing governments have resembled or, often, caricatured those of older countries. To the extent that they have established a track record, these new countries have in fact seldom performed unusually well. If they have sought advice from scholars especially knowledgeable about constitutional matters, such advice has also not been remarkably distinctive. One may ask, do we really have nothing to offer, based on more than two centuries of experience with several modern forms of citizen sovereignty, that would give distinctly better results than the performance that these modern forms have achieved thus far?

It would seem reasonable to suppose that a deliberative process governed by rules that favor truthful interchange of ideas over partisan, adversarial politics would produce sounder results than those now achieved in the legislative and executive functions of present-day governments. No existing form of government based on citizen sovereignty, however, displays such a deliberative process. The stakes are too high and the clash of interests and beliefs too sharp for calm deliberation to play a significant role in the public drama of politics.

Even where national leaders have recognized the clash of interests and have felt that it needed to be moderated, they have viewed it as virtually inevitable and have failed to find an effective, robust way to deal with it. In the course of the debates over ratification of the U.S. Constitution, for example, Madison wrote a remarkably insightful description of the problem in *Federalist* 10 and argued that the proposed U.S. Constitution offered the best hope of limiting its effects.[2] At the time his claim was very likely true, but within a few decades, if not sooner, his best hopes nevertheless proved to be overly optimistic.

From the perspective of a typical household concerned about its long-term economic prospects, the problem is both tolerable and at the same time much worse than it seems. It is tolerable because governments have on the whole presided over immensely better economic performance than what was possible before the era of organized government. It is worse than it seems because the lost potential for even higher economic performance is not self-evident; it is obscure and difficult to measure.

1.2 ADVANTAGES AND DISADVANTAGES OF GOVERNMENT

First consider the plus side of government. In several of the places where ancient governments arose, there is evidence of murderous conflict in the agricultural villages that preceded them. There is also evidence of violence among the nomadic, nonagricultural peoples in those and other areas.[3] One may reasonably suppose that the earliest chieftain who took the title and authority of king was either a successful nomadic raider or a successful defender against raids. Having established order, the ruler maintained it and protected against raids from outside his domain because such raids reduced taxable capacity and weakened his rule. A partly unexpected side effect of this established order in several places in the ancient world, once it had also established continuity, was a massive increase in total wealth, which supported and protected flourishing civilized arts, such as writing, sculpture, and monumental architecture. That is, in due course it set the stage for the present state of comparative peace, worldly comforts, and security in much of the world. However repugnant it may have been in many ways, from a long-term perspective government in ancient times was better than the alternative, as are its current successors.

While granting that things could be worse, we shall see that things could be better. Government's performance problems seem to arise from an intractable problem of reconciling and coordinating the conflicting interests and concerns of various groups in demographically diverse populations. Modern scholars interested in this problem (and in related matters) have made excellent progress in describing it, but have offered no persuasive new ideas on how to deal with it. When such scholars have advised new governments on constitutional matters, neither the advice nor the results have offered any grounds to expect dramatic improvement. We shall concentrate on the factual evidence and analysis of the problems in the remainder of this chapter. Then in the subsequent chapters we shall turn to the remedies that scholars have begun to develop, together with the lessons of experience that we will put together here as a first attempt to offer a significant improvement.

There is no practical way to measure the harm done in the past by self-serving responses to perverse incentives within and generated by governments. It is difficult to measure this harm in current circumstances anywhere. There are, however, a few insights obtainable here and there.

In 1990, when the Soviet Union and its empire were breaking up, real output per worker in East Germany and the corresponding standard of living were about half that in West Germany. This difference was the result of 45 years of state socialism in East Germany, where the government owned and operated almost the entire economy, in contrast to a much smaller share for the state-controlled sector in West Germany. Similar comparisons applied to other Eastern and Western European countries, and the differences between the two sides were growing. Standards of living were nevertheless higher in Eastern Europe than they had been in the decades prior to World War II and had continued to improve after the rebound during postwar reconstruction. That is, Eastern European peoples continued to enjoy modestly increasing benefits of civilization during those 45 years, despite the gross inefficiencies of socialist rule. They found the inefficiencies to be intolerable, however, when they could see the benefits of more efficient, free societies not far away in Western Europe

1.3 THE COMPARATIVE EFFICIENCY OF GOVERNMENTS

This experience says something both about the losses of wealth arising from suppression of constructive incentives in the private sector and about the inefficiency of government operations. Consider now the data we have from other parts of the world that shed light on each of these losses. Data comparing other economies provide a check on the lessons we can draw from the experiences of Eastern Europe's state socialist countries. These other economies are not always governed by politically liberal representative governments, nor do they generally practice free trade and unfettered laissez-faire capitalism. Nevertheless, their degree of economic freedom compares favorably with that of most countries of the world.

First, the data from the Asian 'tigers' show a clear-cut advantage over almost all other countries, and especially over other developing countries. Table 1.1 shows how well Korea and Singapore did in two postwar periods compared to the average performance of all developing countries. (Data for Taiwan and Hong Kong, where available, are similar to those for Korea and Singapore, but are less accessible and are incomplete.)

Table 1.1 Comparative growth rates of Korea, Singapore, and all developing countries (per cent)

	Korea	Singapore	All Developing Countries
1960-80	8.85	9.19	5.45
1980-93	8.26	8.30	4.03

Sources: For Korea and Singapore, *International Financial Statistics*. For all developing countries, International Monetary Fund, *World Economic Outlook*.

Whereas Korea and Singapore grew at annual rates over 8.0 percent per year in both periods, with a small decline after 1980, the developing countries as a group grew at annual rates about half those of Korea and Singapore, with a more substantial decline after 1980. Through the 1960s and 1970s the developing countries could grow comparatively rapidly by using western technology and 'catching up.' By 1980 some of that opportunity had played out, although they still lagged far behind. Thereafter the weight of state socialism in most of them and severe trade restrictions and other forms of economic regulation in almost all of them produced a severe drag on their growth rates.

Another comparison that gives similar results comes from the data for a small set of countries that liberalized their internal and external trade at a point during the years 1975 to 1983. Table 1.2 shows a group of these that had clear-cut changes of economic policy regimes and for which reasonably good data are available.

The gains from shifting to comparatively open, almost free trade vary from case to case, and must be supposed to reflect other effects in addition to liberalization, such as world economic conditions at the time of the change of policy. However, comparison with the performance of developing countries as a group after 1980, shown in Table 1.1, indicates that these liberalizing countries had been doing worse than other developing countries prior to economic liberalization, but did better than the others afterward. The average improvement of annual growth rate of GDP shown in Table 1.2 is about 2 percentage points, which over a generation would cumulate to a huge difference.

Table 1.2 Some cases of policy liberalization (annual growth rates of real GDP in percent)

	Chile	Ghana	Mauritius	Turkey
Pre-liberalization	2.6	1.5	3.1	5.2
Post-liberalization	4.9	4.5	5.5	5.9
Year of liberalization	1975	1983	1980	1983

Source: International Financial Statistics.

The effects of economic liberalization, moreover, are poorly measured by real GDP. Besides the uncertain distortion due to world economic conditions, there is also an inherent distortion in the growth rate of GDP as a measure of benefits. This measure includes production of exports, but does not show the improvement in what the exports buy for consumers in these countries.

When a country opens up its economy to foreign trade after a long period of extreme protectionist policies, state socialism, and heavy regulation of the private sector, a rush of new consumer goods comes into its domestic market. The benefit of these to consumers could be measured by a proper measure of real national expenditure, which includes imports but not exports. Unfortunately, even the comparatively sophisticated Consumer Price Index of the U.S. fails to capture many effects of this kind, and developing country price indexes are hopelessly poorly designed and unreliable. One can only speculate on how large an effect these goods have on economic welfare and for how long this effect would continue in a proper measure of real national expenditure. My own speculation is that it would add two to three percentage points to measured economic growth for two or three decades, after which the growth rate advantage of liberalization would taper off. A five percentage point annual advantage in the growth rate would double the real standard of living in fourteen years, relative to the alternative. If one takes into account the tapering off of growth in West Germany after enactment of the burdensome social legislation of the early 1970s, this speculative figure for the growth advantage of liberalization reconciles tolerably well with the comparison of East with West Germany mentioned earlier.[4]

1.4 THE INEFFICIENCY OF GOVERNMENT OPERATIONS

The foregoing examples are driven primarily by private-sector performance as a function of economic freedom. A source of insights and of approximate measurement of inefficiencies of government operations themselves is the rich array of cost-benefit and related studies done in the United States, primarily by scholars outside government. These studies range over a wide array of government activities, although they do not cover everything the government does. The results are diverse, but they consistently find that the costs of government programs and projects substantially exceed either the measurable benefits, or the costs of private-sector provision of similar services, or the alternative costs of more efficient programs. We can now review some examples of this excess cost, and then sum up our findings.

Our first example involves expenditures on water quality under the Federal Water Pollution Control Amendments of 1972 and 1977. The 1972 amendments set a technically impossible goal for 1985, namely that there should be 'zero discharge' of pollutants into U.S. lakes and streams. Although this law and subsequent amendments laid heavy requirements on industry, the potentially most costly part has applied to municipal waste disposal. The initial interim standards set for 1983, directly after enactment of the 1972 amendments, were found to cost $468 billion in initial capital cost, (Kneese and Schultze, 1975, p. 70)—almost a quarter of a year's GNP at that time, which in today's dollars would come to more than $1.5 trillion. The annual operating cost worked out at 7.5 percent of GNP.[5] Consequently, the EPA ignored the impossible 1985 goal, scaling back and delaying implementation of these standards for municipal wastes.

Actual spending, public and private, for water quality has lately run at about $38 billion per year, or 0.5 percent of GNP, of which about one-third is by government (U.S. Department of Commerce, May 1995).[6]

Even before the passage of the 1972 amendments, studies of the costs and benefits of clean water programs found that the EPA approach to setting water quality standards resulted in costs substantially higher than the likely benefits. Also, even if the goals were scaled back, the costs of improving water quality in the manner directed by the EPA ran about double what the costs would be of the least-cost way to achieve the scaled-back goal (Kneese and Bower, 1968, pp. 158-64, 224-35). If we suppose that the broad effect of water cleanup during the past two decades has been to maintain most inland waters at fishable quality, rather than being mostly degraded to being usable only for boating, the best available assessment we now have of the consequences of the EPA approach shows benefits of less than $6 billion per year in 1995. (According to these estimates, households would be willing to pay less than $2 billion extra to have water quality further improved to permit swimming in all lakes and rivers.)[7] This $6 billion benefit is less than 16 percent of the $38 billion cost. Inasmuch as government and private spending jointly produce the improved water quality, the ratio of benefit to cost of about 16 cents per dollar overall applies equally to both shares of the expenditure.

Now consider national defense, on which the U.S. government spends about $300 billion annually. That is one-fifth of its total outlays and about 5 percent of GNP. My own research on military weapons procurement has found a persistent pattern of trying to equip all forces with the most expensive, most technically advanced weapons available instead of using a more practical mix of weapons. For example, the U.S. Army buys only the heaviest, most advanced tank available instead of a mix of light, medium, and heavy tanks. Similarly, the Air Force and Navy now buy supersonic aircraft for almost all combat roles, instead of an efficient mix of aircraft of various capabilities. By contrast, in World War II all major combatants used a mix of light, medium, and heavy tanks and a similar mix of aircraft. For the allied side to have followed the present U.S. practice would have been disastrous, because we had barely enough weapons to win when we had a sound, practical mix of weapons. My estimates can be reproduced using published data on costs and forces. They show that a sound, practical mix of weapons during the 1980s would have provided twice as much conventional military power as the U.S. had, for the same conventional-forces budget the U.S. was spending. Equivalently, the U.S. could have had as capable a conventional military force as it had for half the budget.[8]

This estimate took no account of several costly weapons that malfunction and are unmaintainable in the field, or that have no value for strategic reasons. Under post-Soviet conditions, the conclusions of this research would apply with extra cogency.

A third example of the value per dollar of government spending concerns garbage collection and other services that are readily compared with privately provided services of the same kind. A survey of studies of public and private enterprises ranging from garbage collection to airlines in five countries found that in forty of forty-nine comparisons the private service was unambiguously less costly per unit of service. In three comparisons the public service was less costly, but its services were of lower quality than those of the private counterpart. In six comparisons the two types of service were about equally efficient. In the forty cases for which public provision was inefficient and costly, the excess cost or lower efficiency ranged from a few percent to hundreds of percent. A midrange, typical figure for extra cost of the public-sector service was about 50 percent (Borcherding, Pommerehne and Schneider, 1982). Data in the Statistical Abstract of the United States indicate a similar cost excess for public over private schools, but with no adjustment for quality differences or for other non-comparabilities.

The foregoing examples concern direct government provision of services, and do not concern government policies whose specified purpose is to transfer incomes from taxpayers and consumers in general to particular groups. Examples of such transfers are international trade restrictions such as textile quotas, agricultural subsidies and price supports, welfare programs, and Medicare. For these types of programs we will look at efficiency from a narrower viewpoint. We will ask what fraction of the money taken from taxpayers and consumers is a true net increase of income for the targeted recipients. We do not attempt to give an estimate of how much of the aid goes to the 'wrong' people, such as to people who have higher incomes than the income of the typical taxpayer-consumer.

The first example of income transfers is the agricultural income support programs of the U.S. and other advanced industrial countries. These programs all use direct government payments to raise farm incomes, and in addition raise prices to consumers.

In the case of the U.S. agricultural programs, it has long been true that the sum of the costs to taxpayers and consumers is a multiple of the addition to farm incomes due to the programs. A study of the 1950s estimated that the costs were two to five times the gains to farmers (Floyd, 1963). A study in the 1980s estimated that the costs to taxpayers and consumers were over five times the gains to farmers, although an alternative, higher estimate of farmers' gains reduced the ratio to about two to one (U.S. Council of Economic Advisors, 1986, p. 155ff). (The total cost of such U.S. programs, including higher prices to consumers, ran over $20 billion per year in the 1980s but has declined almost by half in recent years.) That is, since World War II U.S. farmers have been getting from 20 cents to 50 cents of increased income per dollar of added cost to taxpayers and consumers.[9]

In the case of agricultural programs in Western Europe and Japan, comparable estimates of the gains to farmers relative to the costs to other citizens appear to be even less favorable. The programs in those countries are generally more extreme and more wasteful than the programs in the United States. In the case of Europe, the total cost of the program to consumers and taxpayers exceeded $150 billion in 1992, as estimated by the OECD. The latest estimate is that the Common Agricultural Policy (CAP) raises European farm incomes by about 11 percent of this cost, or by some $17 billion. The Japanese program is even more outlandish, and the scanty data available indicate a similar inefficiency in the transfer of income (Johnson, 1995, p. 31, 1991 pp. 224-29).

Another example similar to agriculture is that of trade restrictions, such as textile tariffs and quotas. In the case of textiles, the United States and other industrial countries have both. As a result, a consumer pays $20 for a shirt instead of less than $15 for an imported shirt of equal quality, and similarly for other textile goods. Past experience with closings of textile mills in New England and in some areas of the southern United States suggest that textile-mill workers who lose their jobs find higher-paying employment afterward. If this protection had never been provided, it seems that some of the financial capital and labor devoted to textile production would have been at least as well off devoted to other industries. Studies of the elasticity of supply of textiles, however, taking account of adjustment delays when these resources move from one industry to another, given that protection is well established, do show some gains to textile capital and labor resulting from protection. Higher prices, due to trade restrictions on textiles and apparel, cost U.S. consumers in the mid-1990s some $38.4 billion annually, of which $4.4 billion represents gains to capital and labor in those industries and $10.2 billion is a further partial offset due to tariff revenues and other transfers. The remaining $23.8 billion is waste, so that the ratio of the gain to textile producers and labor to net consumer cost works out at just under 16 percent.[10]

The next example is welfare programs in the United States. A case that especially draws attention is the set of income support programs available to those single mothers who qualify for Aid for Families with Dependent Children (AFDC). These recipients may also obtain food stamps, Medicaid, aid for heating fuel, public housing, nutrition assistance, and sometimes miscellaneous other forms of aid. The amount of aid these recipients receive varies widely from state to state, but a recent study shows that in every state of the U.S. they receive more than what a person can earn as take-home income in a food service job or other unskilled job paying about $5 per hour. The median among the state welfare payment levels is equivalent to the take-home pay of a person on an hourly wage of $9.18. This figure works out to be higher than the average starting salary for a secretary (Tanner, Moore and Hartman, 1995; Carroll, 1994).

In assessing these figures, one must take into account not only the cost to taxpayers of benefit payments and administration of the program, but also the loss of national product because of recipients who otherwise would find jobs. Another way to measure this effect is to subtract the induced loss of wage earnings, if known, from the benefits received by welfare recipients to obtain their net gain. Unfortunately, one does not know how big an offset this is. Probably a large part of the huge increase in recent decades of single motherhood can be accounted for by the strong inducement provided by generous welfare payments. If so, the net gain to welfare recipients would be little more than half what the welfare system pays them, and perhaps less than half the costs (including administrative costs) to taxpayers.

Although other factors may need to be accounted for, the high benefit levels undoubtedly help to explain why the data show that since the advent of these programs, poverty has not declined. For example, although welfare and social security programs lifted 46 percent of the otherwise (pre-transfer) poor households out of poverty in 1983, that is offset by increased numbers of the poor. Compared to what existed before these programs, more of the U.S. population have fallen below the poverty line, so that there is no net reduction of persons in 'poverty' (Stiglitz, 1988, p. 361).

This comparison gives plausible support to the idea that if welfare payments were not available or were attractive only to persons in unavoidably desperate circumstances, most of those now on welfare would be employed. If so, the net benefit to recipients is about half the cost to taxpayers. On the basis of present information, this efficiency figure would represent a plausible lower limit. We have few reliable studies and not much in the way of data on displaced earnings. Many of the additional persons who, pre-transfer, have fallen below the poverty line could have done so for reasons other than the inducements of the benefits. At the upper limit, the net benefits to the recipients of the various transfer programs in welfare might conceivably be as high as 80 percent of the cost to taxpayers. For discussion purposes, we use 65 percent, half way between 50 and 80, as the ratio of benefits to costs.

The final example we will consider is Medicare. As a prelude to discussion of the relation of taxpayer costs to recipient benefits, consider for a moment what the program is and is not. It is not true insurance and it is not aid to people suffering exceptional hardship. Instead it is a major subsidy combined with a 'level-pay' plan, like level-pay plans for household fuel or electricity. It is a major subsidy because taxpayers other than the covered elderly population pay about two-thirds of its cost. Like almost all medical third-party coverage, for many recipients it lacks the key feature of insurance, that of protecting them from a disastrous financial loss that could render them destitute, because its hospital coverage is cut off after ninety days of hospitalization. (There is no corresponding limit on doctor bills, however.) It differs from normal insurance also in that it has tiny deductibles, where larger ones would benefit all concerned by keeping down administrative costs and reducing waste. Because it does not cover long hospital stays, someone with a chronic or otherwise protracted illness must turn to the Medicaid program after becoming destitute. Because elderly persons in poverty for whatever reason receive coverage from Medicaid, the Medicare program mainly benefits those elderly persons who are comparatively well off.

Because they have accumulated savings over their lifetimes, most of these persons are better off than is the typical taxpayer. Most of them will pass some wealth on to their children and grandchildren, both as gifts and as bequests. To these elderly persons the only advantage of the Medicare subsidy is that as a group they receive money from their children and grandchildren so that they can give more back. But this recycling of family money has costs. It has administrative costs, and it encourages wasteful spending on medical care that would not occur if control of the money never left each family's hands.

Most illnesses fall within the 60 days that receive full Medicare coverage after the small deductible. For these short-term patients an admission to hospital obliges them to pay only the deductible, and extra days oblige them to pay nothing (other than a co-payment for physician fees). The covered cost is paid by taxpayers in general. A number of studies have reliably measured the effect of these near-zero prices on people's choices about medical services. Compared to no third-party coverage, coverage of 80 to 100 percent of costs results in roughly a 50 percent increase in the amount of medical care demanded. That is, if without Medicare its present beneficiaries would have spent $80 billion on medical care, with Medicare they spend $120 billion. Suppose that the program pays 90 percent of this amount, $108 billion, whereas the patients pay 10 percent, or $12 billion. Suppose also that the administrative cost is 10 percent of the amount covered, raising the program cost from $108 to about $119 billion (Pauly, 1986). When a downward-sloping demand curve is nearly a straight line, the value to recipients of such extra medical care is about half what it costs. That is, when the amount of medical care rises by $40 billion, due to coverage by the program, the extra value to recipients is only $20 billion, raising their benefit from $80 to $100 billion. The other $20 billion of the added $40 billion of medical care, plus the administrative cost, is waste.

The net transfer to Medicare patients of $108 billion represents a benefit to them of 90 percent of the $100 billion of value to them of the total medical care that they receive under the program, or $90 billion. The cost to all taxpayers, including the elderly, is $119 billion. Hence the ratio of the benefit to the cost is 90/119, or about 76 cents on the dollar. This ratio does not depend on what share of the cost is borne by taxpayers in general and what share is borne by the elderly through their premiums. If the proportionate effect of the insurance on the amount of medical care elderly patients receive remains unchanged over time, then this ratio is constant and applies equally to each share of the cost.

Table 1.3 sums up all of the foregoing examples. This table spans most of the activities that governments engage in, and covers a substantial fraction of government budgets. The largest single omission is social security. Also omitted are higher education, highways, police and courts, various regulatory activities, and others. I do not have estimates for these omitted items.

The numbers in the table, taken together, seem to convey the impression that government returns about 50 cents in value for each dollar it spends or that it obliges consumers to spend. If this overall figure for government waste is correct, the potential gain in living standards from fixing the problem would be quite large. Almost every government in Western Europe spends more than half its nation's GNP. The corresponding figure for federal, state, and local governments combined in the U.S. is one-third of GNP, whereas for Japan the figure is lower.

Table 1.3 Estimates of efficiency of government activities, U.S. and other developed countries

A. Government Services	Ratio
Clean Water, U.S.	.16
Defense, U.S.	.50*
Various Services**	.67*
B. Income Transfers	
Agriculture, U.S.	.2 to .5
Agriculture, European Union and Japan	.11
Textiles and Apparel	.16
Welfare, U.S.	.65
Medicare, U.S.	.76

* Ratio of efficient cost to actual cost. All others are ratios of benefit to actual cost.

** Airlines, garbage collection, electricity production, public housing, elementary and secondary schools, and other services that are also privately provided, in Australia, Canada, Switzerland, the U.S., and W. Germany.

Sources: See footnotes 5-11 and references in pp. 6-10 above.

The percentage shares of government understate its drain on private living standards for various reasons, providing for a margin of error in our estimates. In the case of welfare expenditures, our estimate took account of an indirect effect of the program, namely that the program induces some persons to depend on welfare payments rather than finish school or accept jobs. There are indirect effects that explain the low efficiency of agricultural programs also. Other programs that have such indirect effects are disaster aid and federal Old Age and Survivor Insurance (OASI). The knowledge that federal disaster aid will be available if needed induces some comparatively high-income persons to build (and rebuild) expensive vacation homes and condominiums on beaches that have a high risk of hurricane damage. Similarly, disaster aid gives an incentive to build (and rebuild) in flood-prone areas that would otherwise be left vacant as parkland or farmland.

Also similar is the probable effect of OASI on national saving. While some prudent householders will save for old age just as much as they would have if there were no OASI system, and some would not save in any case but would depend on their children for support in old age, many allow the expectation of OASI benefits to substitute for some of the saving they would otherwise do. To that extent, the system forces young people to transfer income to retired people, and reduces the country's wealth and future growth of living standards. These and other induced inefficiencies would further reduce our estimate of the value of government expenditures, if we took them into account. Nevertheless, the figure of 50 percent waste will serve as an overall average for illustration.[11]

1.5 INTERPRETING GOVERNMENT WASTE

To interpret the effect on household well-being of a 50 percent waste rate for all government, consider the case of Western Europe. Suppose that national income per household is $40,000, and that of this amount government takes and spends $20,000. Suppose that about $10,000 of the government spending per household is transfer payments, and that of this, $5,000 is net gain. Then the residual command over goods and services (at factor cost) per household—the value of what the average household consumes now—is $25,000. The avoidable waste of 50 percent waste by government applies both to the transfer payments and to the other government activities, so that $10,000 of the total government share is wasted. If this waste were eliminated, the household's effective income would rise to $35,000—a 40 percent increase.

For the United States, national income per typical household is approaching $60,000, of which government at all levels takes and spends $20,000. With the same adjustment for transfer payments, the residual command per household over goods and services at factor cost is $45,000. Again, $10,000 of the government share is wasted, and if that waste were instead returned to the household, its command over goods and services would rise to $55,000, a 22 percent increase.

These estimates of waste in and by government refer to the ongoing inefficiency of government purchases of goods and services and of transfers from taxpayers and consumers to members of organized interest groups. In addition, we have seen that the larger and more intrusive the government is in economic activity, the slower is the country's growth in standards of living. For the more intrusive European countries, the effect on growth would appear, based on the experience of socialist countries and of heavily interventionist third-world countries, to be at least about two percent per year. For the United States it would appear to be somewhat less, but probably more than one percent per year and perhaps as much as two percent. (If we were to use the Asian 'tigers' as a benchmark, we would estimate the developed country governments' drag on growth to be even higher, in the neighborhood of four percent per year.) These rates are compound rates, of course.

A differential in the growth rate of Country A over Country B as large as two percent per year would imply that after about 35 years Country A's standard of living would be twice that of Country B, and its superiority would double again in the next 35 years. From the perspective of someone choosing a constitution, this advantage of allowing the private sector to do its best would surely be even more impressive than that indicated by the ongoing waste in government activity.

It is still more impressive to consider the two kinds of effects together. They imply a massive advantage to having a constitution that leads the economy, in all its aspects, to realize its full potential.

1.6 WHAT CAN BE DONE?

Given this large potential for improvement, it is fair to ask, what does this tell us? The leader of a new government, having noted that all governments prevent their people from enjoying the highest attainable levels of well-being, might in particular ask a group of expert advisers why this happens. Let us appoint ourselves to this hypothetical advisory group. Drawing upon our historical perspective, we would first explain that governments have always had this defect, even though government was usually better than the alternative. We would then note that although the fundamental reasons remain unchanged, the particulars are especially well understood in the case of modern governments that are based on citizen sovereignty.

The leader might persist by asking, if citizens are aware of these levels of waste, why don't concerned voters do something about it? A short answer is that unless they solve this problem at the stage of drafting and ratifying a constitution, under existing types of constitutions they cannot solve it at all. Individual concerns and efforts can be effective only through organized interest groups and political parties. This feature of modern forms of citizen sovereignty, and the resulting inefficiencies, trace back to some basic facts of government and of citizen interests that are now well understood.

To encourage rising production and a growing power base, governments have almost always provided a degree personal security, legal rights and their enforcement, roads and basic utilities, and other public goods. The only practical way to finance these items is through taxation, in cash or in kind. The power to tax and to maintain legal rights and security also implies some degree of power to regulate in other ways, such as by creating monopolies and prohibiting some private transactions. Once the mechanism of taxation exists, moreover, it need not be limited to allocating the burden of these minimal functions of government in whatever way the sovereign power finds expedient. It can also be used to finance questionable construction projects and other expenditures that benefit only influential persons and groups. These additional government projects began nearly six millennia ago with elaborate tombs and temples, and continue now with a dazzling variety of extravagances. The same point applies to the use of regulatory power, which can easily degenerate from socially productive applications to ones that benefit influential interests at the expense of all others, sometimes to the indirect detriment of the sovereign.[12]

In modern countries, as in the past, it is in each citizen's interest to get as much benefit from government services, paid for mostly by other persons, as possible. It is also in each citizen's interest to pay as little as possible of the cost, unless there are specific rewards connected with one's payment, or penalties for non-payment. Each citizen faces an incentive, in other words, to 'free ride' on the contributions of other citizens. This is the well-known free-rider problem (Olson, 1965; Mueller, 1989, pp. 34-5, 308-10).

For most citizens the free-rider problem implies that it is unproductive to try to overcome the free-rider problem's consequences, or to gain from them. Suppose I want to get together with all other citizens who wish to have most government spending, regulation, and taxes eliminated. In a large country we would need a huge number of citizens to work together to promote this objective, at substantial cost to each in time and money, particularly for those who take the lead. Unfortunately, the free rider problem itself stands in our way. Thus the underlying cost and benefit problems facing individual voters explain why, even if a large majority of voters agree on the problem of waste, as isolated individuals they can do nothing about it.

Successful interest groups need something similar to a small-town atmosphere to encourage voluntary participation, or must put together an organization that provides services to its members (and may also control sanctions for non-cooperation). Agriculturists have national farm organizations that provide member services, and they find it easy to encourage their members to vote for whichever political candidate will support programs that benefit farmers. Two groups whose methods of overcoming free-rider problems and obtaining effective influence are well documented are doctors and lawyers (Kessel, 1958; Rubin and Bailey, 1994).[13] Interest groups that, for various reasons, can overcome the free-rider problem can succeed in using government to benefit themselves at non-members' expense.

As just noted, many voters cannot overcome the free-rider problem and pay heavily for this failure. Nevertheless, given each such voter's situation, it does not pay to try to overcome it. Moreover, it does not pay to invest much effort of any kind in public affairs.

Consider the lack of incentive to be conscientious about one's vote. A typical ballot has a long list of candidates for various offices, plus some local bond issues, and, in some jurisdictions, ballot initiatives or referenda. A conscientious voter, who wishes to vote on the 'right' side of every ballot item, studies every candidate in minute detail before voting, weighing the pros and cons of each candidate in terms of background, qualifications, and proposals for the future. This voter also studies each other issue on the ballot with similar care. All that takes a great deal of time and effort, and in the end it almost certainly has no effect on the outcome. Of course, a person might do all that as a hobby interest. Failing that, one does not notice a great deal of social pressure to do it, nor a convenient opportunity to do it at low cost. It is much simpler to decide how to vote almost as casually or superficially as one decides which team to root for in an organized sport. Casual behavior of this kind is known as 'rational ignorance' (Mueller, 1989, pp. 205-206; Downs, 1957, pp. 238-74). An alternative description calls it voting 'expressively' or 'romantically' (Boudreaux, 1996).[14] One invests time and effort in gaining knowledge about something, if it is not a hobby interest, only if one will receive something in return for this effort. In elections, as a rule there is no benefit from a voter's conscientious behavior.

In fact, this logic applies equally, except as a matter of degree, to the act of voting itself. Political scientists wonder why, in the United States, voter turnout is so low compared to most other countries. By contrast, economists wonder why more than a few people turn out to vote, regardless of the country or jurisdiction. If the number of voters is more than a few hundred, the chance that a person's vote will change the outcome is negligible. It takes time and trouble to vote, and when a person's vote has no other consequence than the time and trouble it takes to do it, an economist wonders why anyone does (Mueller, 1989, pp. 205-206; Downs, 1957, pp. 238-74). In most elections, nevertheless, large numbers of them do. We must at least examine the issue of public-spirited and altruistic behavior to determine in what ways, if at all, it may affect our analysis and results. This we do in the appendix to Chapter 2.

Evidently the free-rider problem, rational ignorance, non-participation, and the methods of successful group action are all interrelated (Aranson, 1989-90). Furthermore, their interaction leads almost inevitably to those kinds of special interest benefits that waste resources or that promote resource waste in private production and trade (Dougan and Snyder, 1996). Together they create a trap from which citizens cannot escape under systems of government now prevailing.

This trap is simply reinforced, and not relieved, by the existence of political parties. Political parties are themselves interest groups whose active participants obtain benefits at the expense of other citizens, including those who consider themselves 'members' of these parties. To prosper in this enterprise, political parties provide extravagant services and benefits to well-organized interest groups at the expense of other consumers and taxpayers. In addition it is part of a political party's business to help organize and promote interest groups that can not independently overcome their free-rider problems (Wagner, 1966).[15]

In countries with two-party systems, even though at least one and sometimes both leading political parties promise to eliminate waste and to 'reduce' government spending, they never deliver on these promises. In countries with multiple parties grouped in two or three main coalitions, hardly any of the parties bother to make such promises. Successful political parties are part of the problem, not part of the solution. These rise to power only through elaborate organization, fund raising, propaganda, and so on. To hold these organizations together they must reward their leaders, organization workers, and constituencies with the fruits of power, which they cannot do by shrinking government.

1.7 OUTLINE OF CHAPTERS TO FOLLOW

The leader of our hypothetical new country, having heard all this explained, would want to know, does the work of constitutional scholars help us find solutions to these problems? We would have to reply that there is a large literature that analyzes these problems, but none that satisfactorily solves them.[16] There is an inconclusive literature on mechanisms other than simple balloting for collective choice, notably the demand-revealing processes, which we will explain and exploit in Chapters 2 and 3. Our further reply, then, would be that we have to use the available ideas to develop a constitutional plan on our own.

Therefore we must use our ingenuity to find a way to turn self-interest into constructive channels without relying upon self-denying, public-spirited behavior, either by voters or officials. Chapter 2 reviews what is possible to this end. Chapter 3 presents a draft constitution that uses the ideas set out in Chapter 2, and explains its features in detail. Chapter 4 summarizes the advantages of this draft constitution and explains the obstacles to its adoption. Chapters 5, 6, and 7, and the appendix to Chapter 6, present technical analysis of the central mechanisms used in the draft constitution.

Appendix: Are Governments Really Inefficient?

Despite the strong evidence for government inefficiency presented in this chapter, and despite the analysis that helps explain it, not everyone believes it. A contrary view, from Wittman (1989, 1995), claims that democracies are efficient.[17] He uses purely speculative arguments based on the widely cited insight of Coase (1960) that when all persons and firms have well-defined property rights and when costs of negotiations and contract enforcement are low enough, every opportunity for mutually advantageous agreement will be exploited. Asserting without benefit of evidence that the pertinent rights exist and that the costs are indeed low, Wittman concludes that democracies are as efficient as private markets. In a much earlier short comment, Ordeshook (1971) said that inefficiency in government would imply an opportunity for a political party to win by proposing a program to make everyone better off. That is in fact a technical possibility. Consequently, he said, political parties would in fact propose efficient programs, so that government must be efficient.[18]

The missing element in these chains of reasoning is any consideration of the enforceability of property rights and of agreements. When government uses its taxing powers, its police powers, and other vaguely defined powers that it can use without paying offsetting compensation, the victims have no recourse except through the political process. As a rule they can gain some advantage from this recourse only through organized interest groups. Such recourse, as a practical matter, requires reaching agreements with other interest groups, moderated or brokered by and among politicians. Agreements achieved in this political process can have effect only as long as they remain self-enforcing, however, through opportunities to retaliate. Political figures seldom bother to discuss potential agreements that lack this feature. Therefore, most potential agreements that would serve the mutual advantage of many citizens never reach the discussion stage. That is, this arena amounts to virtual anarchy when compared to private and business agreements subject to contract law and tort law, especially as they existed in the United States prior to the Second World War.

The issue is of course a question of fact as much as one of logical analysis, and Wittman's case flies in the face both of many relevant facts and of a well-developed line of analysis now taught to economics undergraduates. There is no need to bore the reader with a further catalogue of factual and analytical information that contradicts him, readily available in Mueller's works and in other sources,[19] nor with a full catalogue of Wittman's reckless and preposterous assertions.

One should not confuse the Wittman's Panglossian position with a more subtle view that in a democratic society each household optimizes in terms of its own self-interest, so that each actual outcome is inevitable, and there is no way to get more efficient outcomes. That is the message in articles by Becker (1983, 1985) on pressure groups, in which he describes the problems of democracy that I have described in this chapter and outlines a formal model to show how they combine to produce political equilibrium.[20] While noting that unexpected fundamental changes sometimes occur in unlikely places, one must concede the true but trite proposition, already noted, that 'that which is inevitable is ideal'. In effect I concede this in Chapter 4, when applying a cold dose of realism to the prospects for my own proposals in most countries, and especially in those with established governments. Wittman's view, by contrast, rather than accepting the inevitability of inefficiency in democratic outcomes, is so rosy as to deny the existence of democratic inefficiency.

2 Ways to Overcome the Public Goods Problem

Envy is the basis of democracy.[1]

2.1 INTRODUCTION

Although the overall picture presented in Chapter 1 is discouraging, the leader of a new country need not be intimidated. Experience with government and with the performance of privately organized activity under the protection of settled law and stable government provides several proven devices for channeling self interest to constructive ends. The analysis of untried mechanisms designed to mimic these devices suggests that there are additional ways to get this effect. Scholarly research on these mechanisms suggests that dramatic improvement is technically possible and that it is worthwhile to think seriously about practical rules and procedures designed to achieve better results. What the present study shows is that it can be done.

Although it takes note of and draws freely upon the constructive ideas of others on the constitutional problem when addressing this task, this book does not attempt to provide a comprehensive and critical review of all such ideas. Mueller (1996) has recently provided an excellent review, together with his own conclusions about the best constitutional plan. He favors several of the same concepts that we use here, but does not use them to their full potential. As a result, he stops short of an adequate solution to the problem of organized interest groups, rational ignorance, and the consequent misuse of government's taxing and spending authority. His review and plan nevertheless provide many valuable insights and perspectives.[2]

The challenge is to piece these things together into a workable constitution that is an acceptable social contract in the fullest sense. We would hope that it could be accepted almost unanimously at the time of ratification. If so, it would be a virtual social contract as that term is usually understood. In addition, we would hope that everything the government does after the constitution is in force would also, item by item, have the character of a virtual social contract.

These statements about our hopes must be qualified by two uncertainties, one about the assumptions underlying the design of such a constitution and one about its acceptability to a people in search of a constitutional plan. First, scholars working on theories of free riding, interest groups, rational ignorance, and mechanisms have almost invariably assumed consumers and voters whose preferences reflect only their own material self interest. For several reasons, one being that our work can be linked readily to previous scholarly work in this way, we reason here almost exclusively in the same terms. Although such theories are less narrowly restricted by this assumption than it seems, there is the possibility that on some points this analytical device might mislead us. Second, even though in fact a plan might work perfectly, people choosing a plan would not know that, especially if the plan is new and untried. They might also find it repugnant, especially inasmuch as it would almost surely face heavy opposition by potential leaders who see their own future and ideals best served by a more traditional plan. After reading on through this chapter and Chapter 3, the reader will surely understand this point.

We do not need to be apologetic, as a matter of fact, about basing the central parts of our analysis and constitutional plan exclusively on narrow material self-interest. There are two reasons for this lack of apology. First, the assumption is much more nearly true than most educated opinion-formers in developed countries can bring themselves to admit. Being steeped in the euphemisms of every-day discourse and in religious-based ethical precepts, we find it painful to accept the truth of the matter. Second, every device that works out well in a nation of materially self-interested (though generally law-abiding) citizens also works out equally well if many or most of them are genuinely altruistic, public spirited, beautiful people.

Consider the degree of truth of the self-interest assumption. Most phenomena in modern politics can easily be interpreted using the crassest concept of rationality, namely that one need only follow the money trail. Farm organizations lobby for higher prices for farm products, not lower prices. Labor unions almost always seek higher pay and benefits for their members, not lower pay, unless their members jobs are at stake (and sometimes even then). Medical doctors seek those forms of regulation of medical practice and education that raise doctors' incomes, not the opposite. Faculties at universities demand pay 'parity' with pay at those other universities that have higher salary levels, not with pay at those having lower salary levels than their own. One can multiply these examples. There is ample evidence from around the world that most people attach a dominant priority to their own material well-being.

This concern is apparent not only in those countries that have a degree of citizen sovereignty, but also in countries ruled by tyrants. Ancient Roman emperors provided Roman citizens with free grain, a practice emulated in one form or another by many modern dictators. Presumably they did this because they thought that it would reduce discontent with the regime, and so would contribute to the regime's stability.

These examples illustrate most people's keen concern for their own economic well-being, manifested in some of the details of political and economic affairs. It is manifested more broadly in times of extreme economic stress. Any long, painful period of poor economic performance has meant serious trouble for every government, from the Sixth Dynasty of the Old Kingdom of Egypt[3] to the Soviet Empire of the late 20th century.

Our second point about the use of the assumption of self interest is that a plan worked out on that basis will also work well for many reasonable departures from the assumption. Our inquiry will focus almost exclusively on constitutional rules and procedures that will improve general well-being and will promote sound economic growth. These objectives in no way restrict the citizen's interests to purely material interests such as food, a home, an automobile, vacation travel, and so on—those things conventionally measured in the nation's net national product and real national income or expenditure. Well-being may also include such interests as charitable causes, clean air and water, sustainable use of exhaustible resources, protection of endangered species, one policy or another on the legality of abortion, and so on. Whatever their combination of interests, a safe, more basic assumption is that citizens of a new country have well-ordered preferences. Having well-ordered preferences means that one will choose consistently, avoiding self-contradiction and avoiding impulsive and other behavior one will regret later, when deciding how much real income one will spend or sacrifice to satisfy each such personal objective.

Obliging altruistic and public spirited persons to weigh the costs of their well-intentioned ideas, through a procedure that mimics ordinary markets, in no way interferes with their unselfish preferences except when they wish to compel other persons to bear substantial costs of these preferences. Of course, if someone's devotion to charitable, conservationist, and other public spirited projects depends entirely on putting the costs on someone else's budget, we may fairly ask, is this altruism or public-spiritedness, or is it something else? This point is central to our approach. We can leave these other forms of motives and behavior in the background, being irrelevant to the question of design. This perspective enables us to bring the methods of economic analysis to bear on the constitutional problem facing the national leader of a new country, using the paradigm of rational behavior. On some minor points it may mislead us, but this perspective provides a powerful simplification of the analysis of what could otherwise be an overwhelming problem.

We can not totally disregard an undoubtedly real phenomenon, however, that of the herd instinct, under which people conform to what is fashionable at the moment among their peers. Perhaps this instinct can be subsumed entirely within the framework of the economic analysis of rational behavior in a broader sense than that of material self interest. For example, such manifestations as engaging in volunteer work, contributing to charity, and so on, could serve a rational interest in the interpersonal contact and social acceptance that such activities provide. An example of an apparent departure from rationality, in the narrower sense of material self-interest, is the difficulty we have in explaining why many citizens vote when they have no material incentive to do so. This apparent puzzle to economists has been noted by several authors.[4] We discuss this and related matters further in the appendix to this chapter.

If prudent people recognize self interest as the major force in human affairs, they will wisely see to it that their constitution provides incentives that direct all efforts toward personal advancement into constructive channels. They will recognize that in the private sector the provision of a framework of law and order, security of person and property, and enforcement of contracts are often enough for this purpose. Among other steps, however, they will pay close attention to the incentives they provide to all persons in official positions in government, and to the rules under which officials and the sovereign electorate decide the major issues of national policy.

The incentive structure facing officials has never been well thought through except on a piecemeal basis. In consequence, few if any past or modern governments can be said to have been models of efficiency. As noted earlier, it appears that when government originally arose among ancient peoples, it was usually an outgrowth of raiding and pillaging. The main accomplishment of governments was to transform those activities into a stable source of income for the monarch and for military commanders, government officials, and their retinues. On the one hand, this transformation permitted rapid population growth and the growth of trade and wealth. On the other hand, some of the monarch's decisions and the pursuit of personal advancement by others interfered with these constructive results and curtailed or reduced wealth. These features have been characteristic of governments ever since, regardless of who is sovereign.

Before launching into an explanation of the potential for dramatic improvement through a superior constitution drafted by wise leaders and approved by prudent voters, however, I must first say a few words about what cannot be done. A country rent by ethnic, racial, and religious hostilities, where each group's predominant elements actively pursue vindictive and destructive policies against other groups will have to solve these problems first, before this study can be of any help. A country with a military elite that has no respect for constitutional order, but whose officers are willing to support coup after coup, should of course find a way to get that problem under control, but I do not know what that way is. Some amount of social tension due to diversity of cultural backgrounds, interests, and beliefs can be accommodated within a sound constitutional framework, provided there is a broad consensus supporting that framework. Hence I emphasize that the potential audience for the present work is a country with wise leaders and prudent voters, willing and able to take a fresh look at an unorthodox approach to government that offers the best possible prospects for themselves and their descendants.

Another problem that this study does not pretend to solve but only to moderate is the resentment almost everyone feels toward high status, privilege, and wealth held by others. The evidence from ancient graves indicates that differences in rank and social status were commonplace even before civilization arose. Differences in wealth and status have subsequently characterized all civilized nations, ancient and modern. (Those modern civilized states that call themselves socialist have not changed any of these attributes, they have merely changed the details, though at times their leaders may have pretended otherwise.) Differences in wealth and status are intrinsic to highly organized societies with complex economies having individual specialization. No government or constitution can undo them, and prudent people accommodate them as constructively as possible.

The reason that it is important to do that is that inequality, besides being inevitable, can also be an instrument of progress that is beneficial to almost everyone. It provides the incentives for innovation, successful economic leadership, and effective productive effort. In the United States I think that most people realize that, as do those people elsewhere whose perspective is not unduly distorted by the sentiments of class warfare.

Prudent persons will recognize that the resentment of wealth among many of their fellow citizens is also endemic and ineradicable. They will therefore find ways to divert it into comparatively harmless channels. No doubt they will decide that they must concede a certain amount to this motive in the constitution itself, but their government must avoid repeated tinkering with tax schedules and other forms of continual harassment of persons of wealth and status. The trite reason that they must do so, by the definition of prudence, is that that which is inevitable is ideal. The more telling reason is that active resentment of this fact of life, if allowed to have political force, harms everyone's interests. Therefore a prudent people will include provisions in their constitution that keep this corrosive passion out of politics.

Let us now sum up the uncertainties about the limitations of our approach. The discussion of recent examples of new countries and of the inefficiencies of government poses a massive problem that we may or may not be able to solve. What we work out in this book is a theoretical skeleton, based almost entirely on standard, stylized assumptions of economic behavior. We solve a tractable problem, hoping that our solution can be applied directly. If not, it sets the stage for solving the more difficult problem with analysis that uses more accurate assumptions.

In sum, scholars who have studied the problems of interest groups, rational ignorance, and free riding outlined in Chapter 1 have found it convenient to highlight them using standard, simplified assumptions about economic behavior. Then, as a purely technical question, one can ask, using these same standard assumptions, does there in principle exist a way to overcome these problems, when there are considerable variations in consumer tastes? The purpose of this book is to answer that technical question, while taking note of some aspects of tastes that come closer to approximating real human societies than do the assumptions usually employed in scholarly work along these lines. It also attempts to cover the full array of functions and activities of government, in a sense that other work of this kind does not.

Trying to design an efficient constitution that would be workable in an actual country may turn out to be a more demanding and uncertain task. If so, the right research strategy is to check first whether the more limited task of this book is achievable, because if it were not, there would be no point in attempting the more difficult one. Therefore we ask, if there were a people who were predominantly self-interested, and who were intelligent enough to understand all the problems set out in this chapter, is there a constitutional plan that they could use to fix these problems and achieve a fully efficient economy? Such a plan would be novel and complicated, so they would have to be willing and able to study and understand why it would serve them well, because on first reading it might seem to be both ineffective and hopelessly complex.

If we find that such a plan exists, this study will have accomplished its task. The question of how to adapt the plan to an actual opportunity to apply it is one of many elaborations and extensions that need further study. Our discussion in this chapter of a hypothetical far-sighted, public-spirited national leader should therefore be viewed in an allegorical sense, as perhaps should the book as a whole. Some further concessions to realism will perhaps be necessary in the future elaboration of these concepts. It is too soon to tell what these concessions, if any, should be.

That said, we return to the problem of our hypothetical new country. Having learned the reasons for poor performance by existing governments, the leader would ask, is there any concept or central principle, not yet used, that would eliminate the problems? The answer is that a simple principle, if it can be implemented, would succeed remarkably well: tax no citizen to provide benefits that go exclusively to others—tax each citizen household only in proportion to the benefits it receives from government programs, item by item, and compensate fully all those who are harmed. A corresponding rule applies to regulations. If such proportionality were achieved perfectly, citizens who are affected by a government program or regulation would vote unanimously in favor of an outcome that provides a net benefit to all of them, and they would unanimously oppose an unsound, overly costly program or regulation. A tax structure with this proportionality conforms to the benefit principle of taxation, and is also called a Lindahl tax (Lindahl, 1958; Wicksell, 1958; Musgrave, 1959, Ch. 4).

A Lindahl tax structure, if it could be implemented, would have ideal properties. A system that used it would submit the voter to the same budget discipline one must apply to ordinary private budget decisions such as whether to buy a household durable, how much to spend on food and housing, and so on. As in the case of such ordinary personal spending decisions, it would confront each voter with a comparison of a pro-rata share of the cost of a government program with that voter's valuation of the program. A voter could not obtain a government benefit in the guise of a free gift, paid for by other taxpayers, except insofar as, by mutual consent, comparatively affluent voters agreed to tax themselves to assist persons in poverty or other desperate circumstances.

Lindahl and Wicksell seemed to think that one could rely on the public spiritedness or gentlemanly ethics of voters or legislators to induce them to volunteer the truth about their valuations, or their constituents' valuations, of government budget items under consideration. Unfortunately there is no incentive for a voter to be truthful in this matter, except in the rare event that the voter's true valuation is precisely enough to change the government decision in the voter's favor. Although public spiritedness may induce many people to vote, at slight cost to themselves, asking them to decide their own taxes in the Lindahl-Wicksell manner is another matter. If the authorities asked citizens to declare their benefits from government spending, all concerned would know that there would be no way to check their honesty except when a program directly and measurably affects their tangible financial interests. Some would declare their benefits honestly, perhaps, just as some are scrupulously honest when preparing their income tax returns, even if there is almost no chance that the tax authority will audit their returns. Most people in almost every country, however, would view it as entirely proper and reasonable to take advantage of the system: they would claim that almost every government program harmed them and would demand compensation for this 'harm'.

There are ways to induce a self-interested voter to declare a true valuation of a public good, however, provided that the government decides the voter's tax share for the good without this information. The problem is that there is no way to combine these two steps so as to assess the strictly correct amount of a Lindahl tax based on self-declarations by voters motivated by self interest. (For an elaboration of this negative proposition, see Chapter 7.) Therefore we must look for another device to approximate Lindahl taxes and to assess them, separately from the voter's declaration. We must also attend to other aspects of a government's functions.

We now proceed to review the known devices, mechanisms, and procedures that can provide the pieces for this purpose. After listing them and describing them, we will discuss how they fit together.

2.2 CONSTITUTIONAL VS. CONTRACTUAL REDISTRIBUTION TO DESTITUTE FAMILIES AND OTHERS

A problem in most modern governments is that the distribution of tax burdens is a constant source of tension and political competition so that it is constantly subject to tinkering and occasional unpredictable change. For taxpayers who rely mainly on wage or salary income, this lack of predictability is mostly only a minor nuisance. A more serious effect for such taxpayers, however, is that it adds to their uncertainties when planning for retirement. For taxpayers who invest in businesses, moreover, this uncertainty can seriously disrupt business planning. Such disruption can only reduce economic efficiency, and although its effect on income distribution as between employees and owners can not be clearly demonstrated, the best guess based on trends in observed income distributions is that it harms everyone. A step that would protect everyone's interests would be to set tight constraints on what kinds of taxes the government may use.

A similar line of thought applies to what kinds of benefits the government can provide. In recent centuries prior to the modern explosion of government activity, governments provided security from domestic and external threats to established order, they provided a legal structure, courts, roads, and they often provided some aid to the poor. All these items except the last can in principle be financed by those citizens who benefit from them, more or less in proportion to their benefits. Cash and other assistance to destitute persons is of a different kind, if their poverty is chronic and can not be averted by using ordinary private insurance.

Aid to chronically destitute persons has long been a difficult and controversial subject. From one perspective, it would be unconscionable to stand aside and allow people to starve. From another, almost any type of legally mandated or predictable aid creates perverse incentives, which can lead to costly side effects. For example, Malthus pointed out two centuries ago that the English poor laws, which supported poor families, encouraged irresponsible marriage and childbearing, and reduced labor mobility. He further argued that proposed aid based on family size would further encourage large families, population growth, and increased misery among the poor (Malthus, 1798, pp. 83-96, 134-35). His advice was apparently not well received. Similarly, victims of floods and other catastrophes invite our sympathy. Systematic disaster aid, however, encourages people to build in flood plains, on beaches threatened by hurricanes, and so on.

A prudent people will address these problems directly at the time of writing a constitution and will define and limit these kinds of aid. They will write clear constitutional rules for all such aid, whose financing includes taxation of those voters who oppose all or part of such aid, in such a way as to leave virtually no discretion to the processes of year-to-year policy making. By contrast, they will allow all forms of aid that can command (almost) unanimous consent, so that they do not victimize any identifiable taxpaying group of voters.

How much income a nation should redistribute from its comparatively affluent citizens to destitute persons has generally been controversial, as we have already noted. People disagree about how generous they should be to destitute persons and families and about how much weight they should give to side effects on incentives to procreate, to work for pay, and to modify life styles. It is unwise to allow these disagreements to poison the atmosphere with uncertainty and squabbling over government policy in such a way as to interfere with the nation's ongoing business. The wise thing is to specify in the constitution the criteria for aid to the destitute and an unambiguous rule for the allocation of taxes to pay for this aid.[5]

It is unlikely to be fruitful to speculate about how a new country's people, with their statesmanlike leader, might work through a political process to arrive at this result. Almost all new-country constitution-writing efforts proceed in chaotic circumstances, or amid the interplay of powerful interests. The legitimacy of a new constitution is confirmed only by the people's subsequent acquiescence to the outcome. Suppose, however, that the constitution writers do a manifestly good job of weighing opposing views and the facts supporting these views when they choose the structure of coercive redistribution for their draft constitution. Then even those citizens who dislike this structure most strongly may prudently accept it as a reasonable price to pay in exchange for a rule that the structure will be amendable only by virtually unanimous consent. If so, even this most contentious item will be settled at the time of ratification by a virtual social contract.

With this kind of constitutional rule on transfers, recurrent budget decisions could involve other transfers to poor persons, or to others in special circumstances, only when citizens of all levels of wealth and of all distinct demographic groups reached general (almost unanimous) agreement to tax themselves for this non-mandated purpose. By 'almost unanimous' we have in mind a decision procedure that implements the closest attainable approximation to a Lindahl tax. The aim of our procedure will be to rule out from serious consideration every proposal for a government policy that does not come near to commanding unanimous consent, apart from what is clearly defined and entrenched in the constitution itself. If we succeed in designing such a procedure, all households can plan their efforts, saving, and contracts of all kinds without fear of unpleasant surprises from arbitrary policy innovations. New forms of aid that meet this strict criterion we may refer to as contractual redistribution to distinguish it from the coercive redistribution entrenched in the constitution. Contractual redistribution is the same as 'Pareto-optimal redistribution' (Hochman and Rodgers, 1969).

The constitutional restriction on and clear specification of redistribution from wealthy to poor persons is a necessary step to two far more significant instrumental goals, which are the object of almost everything we specify in what follows. These larger goals are, first, the protection of private property, and second, the protection, enforcement, and encouragement of private contracts of all kinds not expressly prohibited in the constitution. The role of these goals as instruments of economic progress is widely understood, and we shall not belabor the point here.[6] They are so central that, besides specifying them in the powers of government and its limitations, almost everything in the constitution plays a role in achieving them.

Property rights and contracts would not be protected if the government could engage in indiscriminate takings and redistribution of wealth, as it can in all existing countries. They are not protected by mere constitutional prohibitions. Everything in the ideas that follow plays a role in achieving this protection, and in so doing promotes and protects the productive potential of the entire economy. It is also important that these ideas contribute to efficiency in government activities, as we anticipated in Chapter 1. We develop these ideas with both aims in mind.

2.3 ELICITING TRUE BIDS BY A SECOND-PRICE AUCTION

Chapter 1 discussed the advantages of Lindahl taxes and the seemingly impossible problem of designing a voting mechanism that would lead to the assessment of such taxes. The problem has two distinct parts, however, and it can largely be solved by separating them. One part is finding a mechanism that will induce voters to reveal truthfully their valuations of potential public policy outcomes such as decisions to produce certain public goods. The other part is the assessment of taxes (or tax refunds) that correspond, as accurately as necessary for responsible government, to these valuations. We will take up these two parts in the stated order.

There are two mechanisms, as a matter of fact, that can induce voters to reveal their true valuations of policy outcomes, provided that these voters know that neither is used to play a role, direct or indirect, in tax assessment. One, the demand-revealing process, which is a refinement of the second-price auction specifically designed for this problem, we will discuss now. Developed in separate papers by Vickrey, Clarke, and Groves, this mechanism is variously known as the demand-revealing process, the Clarke tax, the Groves mechanism, the pivotal mechanism, and the VCG mechanism.[7] Section 2.4 presents the other, the Thompson insurance mechanism.

To show the merits of a second-price auction, we contrast it with the conventional auction that one sees in estate sales and bankruptcy sales. At the start of a conventional auction each bidder interested in the item for sale either bids very low or waits for others to bid first, so as not to take the risk of paying more than necessary with a winning bid. A losing bidder's true valuation reveals itself, if at all, only when that bidder drops out. The winning bidder generally has a higher valuation than the price. Some potential bidders may let others carry the action and so may reveal nothing. All of this masking of true valuations is a natural consequence of the rule that the price paid is the winning bid. Although the process is both entertaining and time consuming it does not help solve our problem.

In a second-price auction, by contrast, the person with the highest bid wins, but pays only the second-highest bid. This small difference has large consequences. There is no need for the auctioneer's chant or for bidding in sequence. Everyone can submit a written bid, or all can simultaneously wave their bids, written in large letters, over their heads. Once the bids are noted and ranked, the process if finished. If I bid under this system, I have no incentive to hold back or understate my true valuation. I would regret either an undervaluation or an overvaluation if it makes any difference. I would not wish to state a bid less than my maximum, because that could turn a winning bid, with the chance to buy at the second-highest bid, into a losing bid. A bid lower than my true valuation could never enable me to 'get it for less'. Similarly, bidding to high either makes no difference or harms me. If someone else bids still higher my error has made no difference to me. If I would be the high bidder without bidding too high, bidding higher makes no difference. If bidding too high makes a difference, therefore, it must be that I win from someone whose bid is higher than my true willingness to pay. I would regret that. I bid only once and it serves my best interests to tell the truth.

In an auction conducted in this way, the only two bids that affect the outcome are the highest and second-highest bid. The highest bidder changes the outcome by bidding highest, taking the item from the second-highest bidder. The second-highest bid sets the price, which measures the value of the item to that bidder and so measures the social cost of delivering the item to the highest bidder. From a group standpoint, it is the cost or sacrifice required for the item to go to the highest bidder rather than to that other bidder who, among the other interested persons, values it highest.

Suppose that we apply this concept to a different example, namely to a proposal to buy new equipment for a local fire department. The equipment would enable the fire department to get to fires more quickly and put them out faster. Each local voter would be willing to pay some amount to have this improvement. If the sum of these amounts from individual voters is at least as much as the cost of the equipment, it is worth buying, so we need a way to find out the amounts.

Suppose that the rule is that the taxes to finance the new equipment will be predetermined somehow, prior to the process of approving or disapproving the purchase, and will not depend in any way upon each household's declared willingness to pay. These taxes exactly add up to the cost of the equipment. Each household is asked to state either what it is willing to pay in addition to the tax, or by how much the tax exceeds what it is willing to pay, as the case may be. Viewing the latter amounts as negative excess amounts, we can see that if the sum of all the excess amounts is positive then the sum of what all households are willing to pay for the equipment exceeds its cost.

In this problem the social cost of going ahead with the purchase of the equipment is simply the cost of the equipment. The relevant valuation or total bid is the sum of what voters are willing to pay to have it. Suppose that without my vote, the sum of other households' excess amounts is negative, but that my positive excess might put it over the top. To determine whether the purchase is worthwhile, the cost to set against what I bid in excess of my tax is the shortfall of the sum of what other voters are willing to pay for the equipment below its cost, that is, it is the negative sum of their declared excesses. If I am willing to pay at least enough in excess of my tax to raise that sum to zero, then the total amount all voters are willing to pay equals or exceeds the cost of the equipment. In effect, I am bidding against the seller of the equipment, after subtracting from the seller's price the amounts other bidders would be willing to pay. If I bid high enough, I win and I pay this *net* 'second price', the amount that is left for me to pay after this subtraction.

The rule then is that I pay only my tax plus that net excess of others' taxes over their willingness to pay, when the net excess is less than or equal to what I am willing to pay rather than have the proposal fail. In this case, just as in the case of the second-price auction, it is in my interest to state truthfully what I am willing to pay.

A household whose tax exceeds its willingness to pay might similarly have to pay a small supplementary tax if the vote fails to approve the equipment purchase. When this household is asked to state how much its willingness to pay exceeds, or falls short of, its tax share of the cost, the household will report a shortfall, a negative excess willingness to pay.

Suppose further that the sum of the other excess amounts is positive, and that this household's shortfall makes the grand sum negative. Its negative vote defeats the proposal, and in this case its supplementary tax is the sum of the other excess amounts. If neither supposition is true, so that a household's vote has no effect on the outcome, it pays no supplementary tax. Again, as in the case of the simple second-price auction, an inaccuracy in the household's statement of its willingness to pay can only harm the household, if it makes a difference to the outcome. It is in every household's interest to tell the truth about its willingness to pay for the equipment.

Figure 2.1 illustrates this notion of applying a second-price auction to the purchase of fire department equipment. Voters A, B, C, . . ., H favor the purchase and voters I, J, K, . . ., P oppose it, taking account of the proposed tax increase that will finance the equipment if approved. The height of a cell with a voter's label, such as the large cell A, shows how much extra (in addition to the proposed tax) taxpayer A would be willing to pay to secure passage of the proposal. The height T_1 of the entire vertical bar for those who favor the proposal is the sum of all the extra amounts they are willing to pay to secure its passage. Similarly, the height T_2 of the right-hand vertical bar is the sum of the amounts by which voters I through P consider their tax shares to exceed their willingness to pay for the equipment. Each cell in the right-hand bar is the amount the indicated voter would be willing to pay, if necessary, to secure defeat of the proposal.

If the amounts are as shown in Figure 2.1, voters A, B and C are the only 'pivotal' or swing voters. If a voter from among D, E, . . ., H were indifferent, and therefore unwilling to pay anything either to support or to oppose the proposal, the outcome would be unchanged because the remaining votes would still be enough to put the proposal over the top. Also, the proposal would of course still receive approval if a voter dropped out from among I, J, . . ., P. However, if any one of A, B, or C were absent, the proposal would fail.

All voters other than voter A, those in favor as well as those opposed, have as a net total willingness to pay the negative sum $T_3 - T_2$ for the equipment, that is, they are willing to pay $T_2 - T_3$ for its defeat. This amount is the 'second price' p_A that voter A must pay, as a supplementary tax, to obtain passage under the VCG mechanism. This second price is the amount needed from A to equalize the two totals T_1 and T_2, that is, to produce a tie vote. Voters B and C pay smaller supplementary taxes.

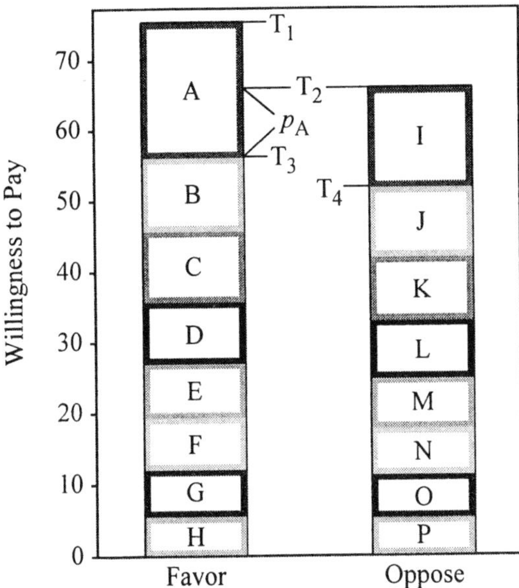

Figure 2.1 Applying a second-price auction to the purchase of fire department equipment

As noted, if voter A were absent, the proposal would fail. In this event, voter I would be the only pivotal voter and would pay a supplementary tax of $T_3 - T_4$. Every other voter among J, K, . . ., P whose willingness to pay exceeded the amount $T_3 - T_4$ would also be pivotal (if voter A were absent) and would pay a supplementary tax smaller than $T_3 - T_4$.

These supplementary taxes are necessary only if the government fails to assess accurate Lindahl taxes. In the case of the fire department equipment, Lindahl taxes would leave a small surplus of benefit above every voter's tax assessment, so that all would favor the purchase. There would be no pivotal voter and no supplementary tax. The closer the government could approximate Lindahl taxes, the smaller the totals in Figure 2.1 would be, and the fewer voters there would be who would oppose the project. Therefore whenever the government achieved a good enough approximation to Lindahl taxes, it would reduce the VCG mechanism to a mere formality, with no pivotal voter and no supplementary tax.

If the issue to be decided is a continuous one, such as how large a budget like the national defense budget should be, there is a procedure for deciding the budget size that is logically equivalent to the foregoing procedure. Here the counterpart to the case just considered is that I state the excess or shortfall of my willingness to pay, relative to my tax share, for each possible increment to the defense budget. Because there are many such possible increments I report this information as a schedule. Then these schedules are summed to find that budget size at which the schedule values sum to zero—the size such that voters are exactly willing to pay for the final small increment to the budget. For each small increment whose inclusion or exclusion from the budget is reversed by my schedule of net excess willingness to pay (positive or negative, as the case may be), I pay a supplementary tax of the absolute value of the sum of other voters' net amounts. For each such increment this procedure is the same as the procedure for the yes-or-no vote on whether to buy new equipment for the fire department.

Figure 2.2 shows Voter A's valuation curve, tax included, for spending on defense. Voter A's assigned tax share for each billion pesos added to the defense budget is T_A. At a level y_1 of defense spending, Voter A would be willing to pay V_A to increase the defense budget from y_1 to $y_1 + 1$ billion pesos. This is $V_A - T_A$ more than A's tax share. For a budget that seems too small to Voter A, such as y_1, Voter A is willing to pay extra to get an increase. At budgets closer to what seems to be the right size to Voter A, Voter A is willing to pay less to induce an increase. Therefore the valuation schedule is downward sloping, as shown. It intersects T_A at a budget size of y_A. If the government assessed Lindahl taxes perfectly, every voter's valuation schedule and would intersect his or her tax share at the same budget size, so that voters would choose that size unanimously. If Voter A's tax share is not a perfect Lindahl tax but is relatively low, then, as in Figure 2.2, y_A will be higher than the quantity preferred by most other voters.

Now suppose that at the budget level y_1 some voters favor an increase in y whereas other voters oppose it. For each voter i who favors an increase, the net willingness to pay, $V_{i1} - T_i$, is positive, whereas for each voter j who opposes it the net willingness to pay, $V_{j1} - T_j$, is negative. Suppose that when we sum all these amounts algebraically for both groups the total is positive, which is the same as saying that the sum of the positive values exceeds the sum of all $T_j - V_{j1}$ for those voters j who oppose the increase. If it is also true that $V_{A1} - T_A$ exceeds the difference between the two sums, then Voter A is a pivotal voter for changing the budget from y_1 to $y_1 + 1$, just as in Figure 2.1. The supplementary tax on Voter A for this addition is p_A, the portion of A's valuation that would be

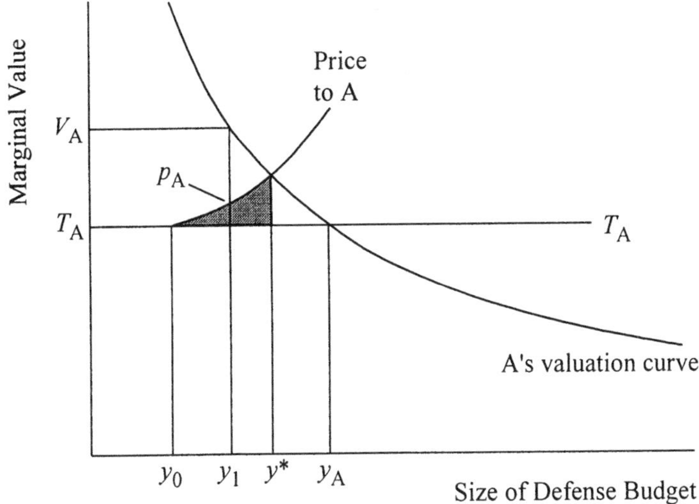

Figure 2.2 Determining the defense budget

needed to produce a tie vote, as in Figure 2.1. Thus the price of the budget increase to Voter A is less than A would have been willing to pay.

If all voters' valuation schedules are downward sloping, then as we move to the right in Figure 2.2 toward y_A, the net amounts those who favor an increase would be willing to pay for a still greater budget go down, while the amounts those who oppose it would be willing to pay to prevent it go up. That is, the price to A of increasing the budget increases as y increases. Hence we show the price to A as a rising schedule, starting at y_0, the outcome if A does not vote. For each increase of the budget above y_0, A pays T_A plus a supplementary tax equal to the excess of this schedule's price over T_A. When faced with this price schedule, A prefers the budget amount y^* and pays a total supplementary tax of the shaded area in Figure 2.2 between the price schedule and T_A up to y^*, by repeated application of the procedure of Figure 2.1.

At y^* it works out that the sum of all voters' willingnesses to pay for the last billion pesos of defense spending is just a billion pesos. The apparent gain that Voter A would enjoy from having the budget expanded beyond y^* would be offset by a larger loss to other voters, a fact reflected by Voter A's rising supplementary tax schedule. The effect of the supplementary tax schedules for all voters is to produce unanimous agreement that y^* is the right budget size.

The amount of the supplementary tax I might pay after the vote depends only on the amounts other voters declare they are willing to pay and on the total cost of the proposed expenditure. Whether I pay this given amount or pay nothing at all is the only thing that depends on the amount of my own willingness to pay. Except for this feature of the supplementary tax, all taxes must remain unaffected by each voter's stated willingness to pay for a public good or government program. Otherwise voters will have an incentive to misrepresent their valuations. In cases where my vote has no effect on the current outcome, such as whether to buy the fire department's new equipment, if I can lower one of my future taxes by claiming that I place no value on the equipment, I have an incentive to misrepresent in this way. Even if my vote were likely to affect the outcome I would reduce my stated willingness to pay in order to balance the future tax consequence against the expected benefit of bidding higher.

We shall see later that in countries larger than a small town, each voter's actual or expected supplementary tax becomes so small as to be almost inconsequential. One's intuitive reaction to this information is to suppose that in that case everyone will have an inclination, with good reason, to exaggerate their willingness to pay to get the result they want. It is tempting to suppose this, but it is wrong.

If the issue is the size of the defense budget, and the smallest coin is a 'pic', almost everyone pays a supplementary tax of a fraction of a pic. Even a massive overstatement of one's desire for a larger defense budget would increase this tax only by a few pics. Why not do it? There are two reasons not to do it. One is that any credible overstatement would increase the defense budget of several billion pesos by only a few thousand pesos. For that small an increase, the voter's true willingness to pay is only a fraction of a pic. For so small an increase, it is not worth it. The second reason is that the constitutional rules we have in mind prevent the voter from expressing a willingness to pay figure so impossible that it would bankrupt the voter if it had an appreciable effect on the budget.

In order to have a workable voting procedure that has constitutional restrictions on willingness to pay, we suppose that voting is computerized. That is, each voting booth would contain a computer terminal (possibly with an option to vote in the voter's own home via the Internet) and the voter would respond to voting instructions that appear on the screen. If the voter offers an unconstitutional vote, the screen would explain the voter's options for changes in the vote that would bring it into compliance. This procedure is of non-trivial significance for the use of the VCG mechanism, because of the role it plays in the overall structure in Chapter 3.

If the issue is a vote on whether to buy fire equipment, the potential supplementary tax in a larger community is whatever the voter declares as willingness to pay, but the probability that a vote will be decisive becomes negligible. The reason this circumstance should not tempt a voter to exaggerate is that if the vote is not decisive, then exaggeration has no effect. The only time it can possibly affect the outcome is when the vote is decisive, in which case one is liable for one's declared willingness to pay. Telling the truth is therefore the only strategy that makes sense. We discuss this issue further in the appendix to this chapter and in Chapter 4.

There are various technical nuances to the VCG mechanism just outlined that mainly interest specialists. We will mention them now and discuss them later. First, if the mechanism generates more than a negligible total of supplementary taxes, providing additional revenue besides the tax financing of the expenditure, this surplus should be disposed of in a manner that preserves each voter's incentive to be truthful. Second, if the voter's personal income and valuation of a public good are interrelated, the supplementary tax or its manner of disposal may need to be modified to take this interrelation into account. Otherwise there could be a perverse incentive to misrepresent the valuation. It is not possible to achieve precisely accurate, mutually compatible adjustments of these kinds in every case. However, perfect accuracy can be achieved for at least one of the adjustments, combined with negligible error in the other. See Chapter 6.

With these modifications the mechanism is technically sound and can be put to good use in a sound constitutional framework. It has limitations, however, and we do not have to rely upon it exclusively for decisions about government policy. As we have already noted, we have other mechanisms and procedures that can be combined with this mechanism for best effect.

2.4 THE THOMPSON INSURANCE MECHANISM

Under the insurance mechanism proposed by Thompson (1966), a central authority quotes odds and sets corresponding fair premiums for insurance against the success or failure of each proposed project. Each voting household then insures against those outcomes that would harm its financial or material welfare. The central authority declares a proposal approved if the insurance profit from approval of the proposal is greater than the profit from disapproval.

A voter harmed by the outcome receives from the insurance full compensation for this harm, less the insurance premium. Those voters who favor the outcome pay the fair insurance premium (for their insurance against the opposite outcome) to protect the benefit of the outcome, thus financing the payment of partial compensation to those harmed. When the insurance mechanism works in tandem with another procedure that assesses approximate Lindahl taxes, moreover, the amounts of insurance that voters would purchase would be small and the insurance mechanism would partly correct the errors of this other procedure.

The information needed to set fair insurance premiums would come from the decision process in a legislature, as discussed in Section 2.5. The excess of benefit over cost of a proposal that passes a legislature, together with statistical sampling theory, imply the required posterior odds that the proposal will pass a referendum. Voters would therefore have a sound basis for accepting the premiums as fair.

For all issues with strictly financial consequences for all voters, each voter can be expected to choose full coverage when insurance against unfavorable outcomes is available for a fair premium.[8] Thus this procedure would provide true information about costs and benefits of such government projects as streets, sewers, and other utilities. If voters perceive foreign threats purely as threats to their material welfare, then the insured amounts for alternative national defense programs would also provide true and complete voter valuations of the costs and benefits of these programs.

Under the most plausible assumption about the effects of intangible issues on a household's marginal utility of wealth, however, households would not buy insurance, or would buy less than full coverage, against intangible harms such as the enactment of a law the household regards as immoral or grossly offensive.[9] One should turn, therefore, to the VCG mechanism to weigh intangibles. Although in a large society voters have little incentive to participate carefully and accurately in the VCG mechanism by itself, linking it with the Thompson mechanism on all issues involving both tangible and intangible effects would provide the appropriate incentive.

Chapter 5 discusses the advantages and disadvantages of the Thompson insurance mechanism at length, together with details of its incentive effects. For the moment we note simply that another feature in its favor is that it provides every voter with an incentive to participate and to calculate carefully the personal gains and harms from proposed legislation. That is, it overcomes the problem of rational ignorance, discussed in Chapter 1. Whereas under present-day governments the consequences of each voter's vote are so imperceptible that the voter has almost no incentive to vote carefully (or to vote at all), under the Thompson mechanism, a vote reduces the voter's risk. Hence, regardless of whether the voter's vote will affect the outcome, the voter has the same incentive to vote carefully as to buy insurance against fire, theft, and automobile accidents. That feature would tend to get people's attention and would make voting a serious calculation of self-interest.

2.5 REPRESENTATIVE LEGISLATURES

Our previous discussion of the free-rider problem in relation to interest groups and political parties makes it abundantly clear that there is little room for electoral politics under a prudent social contract. If the constitution rules out a role for conventional electoral politics in policy-making, evidently it must provide an alternative.

To expedite our inquiry we take as compelling the case for having legislatures, instead of requiring voters to formulate and decide all legislative issues by an initiative mechanism, or by voting in a public assembly. Although households are the ultimate authority on their own values and preferences, we assume without serious question that the costs of gathering and interpreting information make it impractical to decide every detail of government by such purely democratic procedures. Most households will prefer to delegate part of this work to selected representatives.

One might be tempted to propose government by selected experts, but that is a snare and a delusion. However selected, these experts would have the power to promote their own interests, and the interests of those who helped select them, at everyone else's expense, just as lawyers who go into politics now do. The very process of defining 'experts' would inexorably involve special interest pressures and would result in legislation channeling the process itself to suit the interests of those selected. An even clearer example of policy control by experts is the control of almost all aspects of medical practice by the American Medical Association and by its local medical societies (Kessel, 1958). A representative legislature aiming for a valid social contract in each of its decisions would prudently hear and digest information provided by experts it selects. Speakers, judges, election officials, and other persons in specialized jobs would also be experts that the legislature selects. The legislature itself must be free of perverse incentives.

The one social invention that even comes close to freeing a legislature from perverse incentives is selection by lot, together with sequestration or other devices to protect those selected from bribery and extortion. Ancient Athens selected Council members and ad hoc legislators by lot from among those qualified citizens who volunteered to serve. The Council had limited legislative functions in the Fourth Century BCE, subject usually to the Assembly's approval, whereas the Assembly could not change laws passed by the legislators (Hansen, 1991, pp. 33-34, 246-65). Most present-day countries select jurors by lot and try to protect them from every type of improper influence.

The idea of random selection of legislators has found advocates from time to time, but to the best of my knowledge no one has proposed or discussed it as part of a constitutional framework to eliminate the effects of special interest groups.[10] For our present purposes, this idea is critical to the aim of approximating Lindahl taxes and to the further aim of eliminating the perverse effects of free riding and of interest-group politics.

To further these overall aims we must assure that the legislature truly and in due proportion represents all of the citizens' legitimate interests. One way to assure it would be to have a legislature, chosen by random selection, that is large enough to have a near certainty of including members of every economic, ethnic, regional, and other interest. In a large and diverse nation similar to the United States, that could require a legislature too large to be workable. The size requirement can be reduced if there is a proper way to identify the members of every significantly distinct economic, ethnic, regional, and other interest group and to give each such group proportional representation. The way to do that in a framework of selection by lot is to use stratified random sampling. Every identified group would have a representation quota of a uniform percentage of its members, and each qualified citizen would have the same chance of being selected as every other citizen.

The qualification to serve should be as inclusive as a prudent people can tolerate. One assumes that there must be a minimum age and that convicted felons would be excluded. Carefully defined incapacity, such as terminal illness and insanity, certified by due process, would no doubt also constitute proper grounds for exclusion. That said, every legitimate economic and policy interest would receive duly proportioned representation, with the aim of assuring that there would be no such thing as a 'special' interest.

The use of random or stratified random selection is a necessary but not a sufficient condition for the elimination of the perverse effects of special interests. Every element of constitutionally coordinated procedure must contribute and must fit together with every other element to serve that end. It is also wise to design the constitution, if possible, to limit honest mistakes and rash, impulsive acts that the people will later regret. In ancient Athens the people in assembly were at best mediocre managers of foreign policy and wartime alliances, in consequence of which they lost the Peloponnesian Wars in the Fifth Century BCE and lost their freedom to Macedon in the Fourth Century. One can think of modern examples as well. There is, of course, no way to achieve perfection in this respect, but it is important to recognize these mistakes as a problem to be dealt with.

To address information problems and other challenges to the integrity of policy-making processes one can use courtroom-like procedures to protect legislators from improper pressures. Legislators and their families, when necessary, would be sequestered. Rules such as present courtroom rules governing expert witnesses, relevance of evidence, and so on, would apply to legislative hearings and deliberations. A legislature would select a speaker from among qualified persons with judicial experience who would have both an incentive and a duty to preside in the most constructive way possible over legislative proceedings.

Given these features and procedures, one task that a legislature can perform eminently well is to estimate the Lindahl taxes appropriate for each demographic subgroup represented there, for financing each proposed government expenditure. To give a basis for estimating these taxes, each member of a subgroup in the legislature would have to declare a benefit or harm expected from each legislative proposal. If the stratification plan for a legislature is well designed, each subgroup's members in the population would have similar interests and valuations so that a legislator's declaration would be representative of the subgroup from which the legislator was drawn. To focus the legislator's mind we would use the VCG mechanism in the legislature and in addition would provide strong rewards for accuracy as revealed in subsequent information obtained from voters, described in Section 2.6. Then the information from declarations of harm ('votes') in the legislature would give valuations to be used for assessing taxes on the population subgroups the legislators represent.

2.6 DELEGATION OF POLICY ANALYSIS BY THE SOVEREIGN PEOPLE

A legislature, however selected, has a strong incentive to favor special interests, especially including those of its own members, to the extent that it has final authority on issues to be decided. A straightforward way to deny it this final authority is to require that every significant legislative proposal be ratified in a referendum in which every affected citizen participates.[11]

As noted in Section 2.4, legislative proceedings would provide proper odds for setting fair insurance premiums for Thompson insurance coverage of referendum outcomes. Thus the Thompson insurance mechanism would be the primary method of voting in referenda on proposals having financial consequences for most voters. The VCG mechanism would be coupled with this insurance wherever necessary, for voters to declare harms uninsured because of intangible, non-financial effects of proposed legislation or for other reasons. But the point to be emphasized here is that the effectiveness of coupling a legislature truly representative of voters with a referendum procedure, in order to eliminate special interest effects, depends on procedures that encourage informed, accurate voter participation. The Thompson mechanism would play a key role in achieving this result.

Under a system of almost universal use of referenda, the role of a legislature would be to serve, in effect, as a committee of the people that would sift through evidence, select efficient options, and reduce the number of proposed plans to a workable number. Legislative proceedings would reveal which proposals could command almost unanimous agreement among voters, which would unavoidably be divisive, and which would have little or no chance of acceptance. Then a clear set of rules would determine which proposals were appropriate for presentation to the voters. Voters would have the final say about which categories of spending to approve, how much to spend on each, which criminal laws and penalties to enact, and so on. That, it seems to me, would be an entirely different world from the one we have become accustomed to, in which elected politicians and their appointees and hired officials decide everything the government does. In place of that we propose voter sovereignty in the fullest sense.

2.7 COMPETITION IN THE LEGISLATIVE AND EXECUTIVE FUNCTIONS

A major reason why government agencies and officials use their positions to benefit friends, family, supporters, and organized interest groups is that they usually have a high degree of monopoly control over whatever it is that they do. Legislators and other elected officials must face elections after a term in office, of course, but during that term each has monopoly power over a specified domain of policy. We have already seen why elections as presently conducted are a seriously flawed mechanism for limiting the mistakes and abuses of government.

In the private sector monopolies are rare except when they have government protection against competition. Large businesses may appear to have the trappings of power, but without government protection or support there is no business so large that it cannot fail when its competitors offers its customers a better deal. In the past two decades we have seen several large airline companies fail outright or get into serious financial trouble, as have automobile companies, steel companies, major retailers, and others. Having competition that can lure away a company's customers tends to focus the minds of executives and forces them to hard choices about the use of resources and about ways to serve their customers better. One seldom sees similar behavior in government.

A lesson to be learned from this comparison is that the quality and efficiency of government could be improved by introducing competition into as many of its functions as possible. Legislators and officials of existing governments naturally prefer the tradition of monopoly in government functions and do not willingly change the rules to allow more competition. Past drafters of constitutions, moreover, have generally expected to play leadership roles after their governments are established and so usually have the same perspective as do officials of ongoing governments. The ideas we now consider have scarcely ever received even passing mention in either the scholarly literature or in political debates about constitutional provisions.

Inasmuch as a legislature's proposals would almost all be subject to ratification by referendum, there is no reason to limit the field to a single legislature or to require that the two houses of a legislature agree. It is both practical and desirable to have at least two stratified random samples of the population, each of which would make proposals independently of the other for inclusion on a referendum ballot. The rewards offered for the acceptability to the electorate of proposed expenditures and for the accuracy of proposed Lindahl taxes would be paid to that legislature that performed best in these respects. The rewards should be large and attractive, based on the social value of sound proposals. That is, they would offer legitimate opportunities for great wealth, at least comparable to what successful innovators and managers can achieve in the private sector.

Coupled with the opportunity for wealth would be an obligation to deliver the proposed program in detail, as approved by referendum. It is technically possible to specify promised results and to monitor them independently and reliably, for government goods and services just as for private goods and services. A legislature with an approved program can therefore be held to it as a legally binding contract, with financial penalties for nonperformance. The remarks at the beginning of this chapter concerning a social contract are serious, not merely rhetorical. Each law and each budget item of the government would be not only a social contract but also a contract in law. The enforcement of such contracts would be in the hands of a non-governing official legislature and the courts.

Although one must have official legislatures to provide estimates of Lindahl taxes and the appropriate insurance premiums for the Thompson mechanism, there is no reason to exclude additional competition from purely private 'legislatures'. These would compete for the same incentive payments as those offered to official legislatures, subject to their paying the added costs placing their proposals on the ballot and evaluating them.

With this type of competition and incentive structure in force there would be no need to use the present separation of powers whereby the U.S. Constitution purportedly protects us from abuses of government. A legislature whose major budget proposals received voter approval could recruit a management team from the private sector to administer its program and could replace this team at will just as stockholders can in a private corporation. That is, one could copy this feature from parliamentary governments, although it would not be wise to permit legislators to take executive positions. In fact, the incentives to achieve contract-quality performance in government functions would point the winning legislature toward hiring the best executives available from the private sector. Although on balance we will prefer to prohibit legislators from withdrawing from a legislature to serve as executives, it is not clear that such a prohibition would be necessary.

2.8 THE JUDICIARY AND COMPETITION

By and large, most features of present-day judiciaries could well be retained. Jury selection, rules of evidence, strict control of the proceedings by the judge, and other related practices designed to assure an effective search for the truth and an impartial judgment are hard to fault. Although the framers of a constitution for a new country would wish to review practices in several countries to determine the best rules and procedures, that review is generally beyond the scope of the present inquiry.

We must discuss two major faults with most judicial systems, however. One of these faults is the existence of a judicial cartel that in principle determines a single court that has jurisdiction for each case. The other fault is that when there are several courts at which a case could be brought, the initiative in choosing among them lies entirely with one side. Wherever the system offers more than one possible venue for a case, under Anglo-American law, the plaintiff or prosecutor who can convince a court to accept jurisdiction can choose that court, regardless of the defendant's preference. This system results in many avoidable abuses. Experience suggests that it would be better to give both parties a veto of the choice. Whenever the system offers only one venue for a case, furthermore, that is too few.

Experience both with the medieval British legal system and, more recently, with private arbitrators indicates that competition among alternative judiciaries can bring major benefits.[12] Hence one must have at least three venues available to try each case. That would assure competition in the supply of judicial services. Although judicial appointments should be the responsibility of a legislature, moreover, judicial tenure should be determined by judges' success under the market test. That is, judges who fail to attract cases should be retired and replaced. Judges must earn their way through court fees and so compete successfully against other judges for cases. When both parties to a dispute or indictment have an equal role in choosing a venue, this competition will force judges to earn reputations for impartiality and for predictable interpretation of the law, just as baseball umpires must perform ably and impartially to retain the support of baseball club owners. As in the case of legislatures, moreover, there is no reason to prevent private arbitrators from competing with official courts for the settlement of civil disputes. Courts of appeals should be subject to similar rules.

Although private arbitrators can compete for many judicial functions, there must also be government courts with the power to compel compliance with court (or arbitrator) decisions and to compel participation by recalcitrant defendants. To prevent obstruction and to expedite agreement there must be some recourse if the two parties do not reach timely agreement on a venue. The plaintiff or prosecutor could therefore appear before a magistrate, who could compel the defendant to attend and who could preside over a procedure to assign a case to a court by a combination of random selection and veto by the parties, if necessary.

In a system with competing official courts, there necessarily must be a final court of appeal, to preserve a settled consistent order in the law. In England this final court evolved to a selected subset of members of the House of Lords, the 'Law Lords', who also participate in the legislative role of the whole House of Lords (Carter, 1944; Jackson, 1972). The United States chose not to follow the British example in this matter.

One can make a case for making this task a legislative function, especially because our constitutional design creates a judicious, deliberative, representative legislature. For our legislatures the appeals function would blend well with the role of creating new statute law. Similarly, it should be a legislative function to determine which disputes are actionable and who has standing to sue. If a new country's legislature can do better than the U.S. Supreme Court, it should. The ultimate interpretation of the law is too important to leave to tenured judges.

For the same reasons, the practice in the British legal tradition of allowing judges to make law gives too much scope for harm by irresponsible judges, whose decisions have too often been arbitrary and capricious. In the United States in the past century judges have felt free to amend the Constitution with reckless disregard for the long-term consequences and have been subject to interest-group pressure by mere repetition of lawsuits. If the legislative function is conducted efficiently and prudently, then a legislature uniformly responsive to all citizen interests is by far the best place to legislate. That is, with a sound legislative procedure the only law should be statute law, to the greatest extent possible. Although it is inevitable that gaps in the law will sometimes be filled temporarily by judicial ingenuity, the appeals process ending at a legislature should deal with this problem reliably when significant issues are involved.

Although I cannot pretend to represent the views of those who defend common law, we should deal with one of the arguments that appears to favor it. Representative governments have been subject to changing fashions and to temporary surges of public passion on one issue or another. The Federalist writers of the U.S. Constitution clearly worried about this phenomenon and built all the safeguards against it into the Constitution that they could think of. Clearly they counted on the judiciary to stand as a conservative bulwark against temporary public fashions. Continuation of common law as they understood it came naturally in these circumstances, and they showed not the slightest sign of wanting to curtail it. Apparently their hopes proved justified for the first hundred years after ratification. Since then judges have been creatures of fashion just as much as anyone else, and have sometimes led the way in setting new trends and in responding to organized pressure groups. Although in the next chapter we try to construct an optimal incentive structure for judges, that cannot by itself justify encouraging judges to make law. That role we pass upward to the legislature.

In that connection, a compelling reason for having an official legislature handle final appeals is that the proposed style of legislature would represent all interests in the law precisely and proportionately. Persons with each kind of interest in a legal rule would be members of the legislature in the same proportions as in the population and with the same financial interest (prior to receiving incentive compensation for their work as legislators.) This proportionality is what the opposing sides usually lack in a case to be decided (Bailey and Rubin, 1994). Sending appeals to a legislature also would alert legislatures to gaps or other deficiencies in the law that would require correction by legislation. Having the final state of legal interpretation controlled by a legislature would therefore move the law toward efficiency both through interpretation and through new statutes. The question of whether this role would be too burdensome for a legislature we defer until we have developed our other ideas and can see how they fit together.

A corollary to our proposition that the only law should be statute law is that no legislature should be empowered to delegate its legislative role to any person, regulatory commission, or the like. Only the voters can approve legislation, which implies that no rulings or decisions by zoning boards or other regulatory bodies may have the force of law. Social contracts may have loose ends to be resolved later only, at most, to the extent that private contracts may do so.

2.9 A MINIMUM OF MONOPOLY

Having noted that it is wise to maximize the amount of competition for the performance of government functions, we must take note of those functions where a monopoly is unavoidable. One of them we have discussed, namely the function of the highest court of appeals. Also, we noted that there would be a need for magistrates to compel attendance at preliminary proceedings prior to assigning a case to a court and to assign cases by random selection and veto if the parties do not reach timely agreement on a venue. The magistrate would have no authority for the final disposition of cases, and little discretion, and so could be entrusted with a monopoly within an assigned district. In the nature of the function, competition would be of little value because the plaintiff or prosecutor has the initiative in taking the case to the magistrate.

Also, in the nature of their offices, there can be only one Chief of State for ceremonial functions and only one Commander in Chief of the Armed Forces. There also must be an Election Commission to manage elections, set insurance premiums under the Thompson mechanism, enforce rules concerning items to appear on the ballot, and so on. This Commission would have limited discretion under strict rules and procedures but would nevertheless have monopoly power, just as baseball umpires have monopoly power during the course of a game. A few subordinate functions must at times also have little or no competition.

In the case of the military services, a prudent nation that faces foreign threats to its interests maintains a cadre of career soldiers who can provide a prompt response to a foreign threat and can provide other specialized functions during mobilization of reserves and wartime recruitment. During hostilities, competitive urges among different services and different commanders can be costly if not properly coordinated and harnessed to national objectives. Hence at these times the Commander in Chief must direct the armed services as a unified monopoly.

Nevertheless, properly managed competition in the development of weapons and tactics, in leadership, and in unit performance pays big dividends. Some of this competition can be provided by reservists, control of whom in peacetime can be separate from that of the active military services. Some can be provided by parallel services. For example, in the U.S. armed services, the Navy, the Marines, and the Army all have air forces, which can be permitted and encouraged to compete in all aspects of weapons development and tactics with those parts of the Air Force that directly support ground troops. Similarly, the Marines and the Army have overlapping skills and potential missions, in which a nation's leadership can foster constructive competition.

Furthermore, much of weapons development, logistics, maintenance, and other support functions can be provided by private firms competing for the business, with the uniformed military services acting in the role of customers, under the supervision of the governing legislature and its executive officials. Similar remarks apply to the intelligence functions of both the military services and domestic police organizations. Apart from an official intelligence organization, however, almost all police functions can be provided by private firms under contract, including competitors in the intelligence function.

Of course, in some instances (such as Costa Rica) a nation can function without armed services. If so, the nation will be safer not only from external threats but also from internal threats as well. In that case, we wish them well and hope that the rest of us can learn from their example.

2.10 CONCLUSION: PUTTING IT ALL TOGETHER

We have interlocking proposals here with interlocking effects, tending to promote outcomes more efficient than those that governments now permit. These include:

1. stratified random selection of official legislators;
2. a demand-revealing process in each official legislature;
3. estimated Lindahl taxes;
4. potentially generous compensation for legislators based on all relevant outcomes, combined with competition among legislatures;
5. protection from bribery and extortion;
6. referenda with combined demand-revealing mechanisms;
7. monitoring and enforcement of the performance of approved programs.

One can also construct sound incentives for Speakers and for the Election Commission.

These provisions leave almost no opportunity for rent-seekers to influence outcomes. I do not deny that sometimes a skillful salesperson can sell refrigerators to Eskimos, but present political systems do that kind of selling routinely. The question is, can we bring government closer to the efficiency of the marketplace, while recognizing that the marketplace is neither perfect nor all-wise? It is from this perspective that I argue the case for a constitution using the listed elements.

When we put these features together in a constitution, the result will have tightly woven armor to keep improper influences out of legislation and to prevent direct or indirect waste. Consider, for example, why corn farmers and sugar beet growers under such a constitution would not even attempt to lobby for any form of government subsidy or import protection for domestically produced sugar. If a program such as that now in place in the U.S. were to cost each household $5 per year in higher food prices, the set of Lindahl tax and transfers for the program would pay each rational, self-interested household an average of $5. Summing that up, however, legislators would find that the total potential gain to domestic producers, the basis for their estimated Lindahl taxes, would be no more than half the total offsetting compensation required by households.[13] A sound budget-balancing constraint would imply that sugar producers would have to pay full compensation, in which case they would prefer to do without the program. When the taxes must approximate Lindahl taxes, no interest group will try to get a program involving an economically unsound subsidy, price regulation, or the like.

Perhaps a better way to describe the resistance of this system to 'special interest' legislation is to point out that *every* interest is equally represented, in the sense that a dollar of value to one population subgroup has the same weight as a dollar of value to every other population subgroup. Because each citizen is a member of exactly one such subgroup, it is also true that a dollar of value to each citizen has exactly the same weight as has a dollar of value to every other citizen. The draft constitution will apply dollar democracy not just to the private sector, but to the entire economy. Because this constitution will also provide for competition for all parts of the government except for the Chief of State, the Commander in Chief, the Electoral Commission and magistrates, and will tightly circumscribes the authority of these officials, no interest group can take advantage of other citizens.

Because persons within interest groups disagree, the taxes and transfers would satisfy the Lindahl criterion only approximately and could not match individual differences in detail. Some issues that are highly divisive in present-day societies would also be divisive under the constitution proposed here. But they would be less so: advocates of legislation on every sort of issue would be obliged to put their money where their mouths are. Such a requirement can have a calming effect. All of the more obvious regional, occupational, and other such common interests would be accurately matched in the tax structure. Those persons who have the largest identifiable interests in a given program or project would pay for it; those who had no interest would pay nothing; and those tangibly harmed would be compensated. If this feature of the proposal is accurately implemented, the possibility of improper influence on legislation could arise only in cases of fraud and conspiracy, against which each citizen would have recourse in court in the same way as for fraud and conspiracy in the private sector (as we typically have now in developed countries). That narrows down the problem immensely.

The proposals interact in other ways as well. For example, the information generated by the use of the VCG mechanism in the legislature makes it possible to use the Thompson mechanism in referenda. In the reverse direction, the information generated by referenda plays a large role in the incentive system of compensation of legislators. We shall elaborate on these points as we go along.

Such compensation answers the concern that a representative sample of voters could not understand the technical issues in a government budget. Indeed, present-day juries deal with complex technical issues in civil lawsuits, involving sophisticated scientific, statistical, and engineering issues. No one supposes that juries are perfect or all-wise, but we have not found a better way to handle such disputes, other than alternative arrangements agreed to by the parties. We certainly have not found a better way to handle legislation. Present legislators have little incentive to understand either the technical or the efficiency aspects of what they do. If a country pays its legislators for well-monitored results, it can expect to get better results than if it pays them and reelects them with little systematic attention to the results.

These mechanisms are complicated to explain and justify, so one can ask, are they worth the trouble? In responding to this question, one must first recall that all that the voter needs to understand is what to do. That is not so complicated. For Thompson insurance, one decides how much insurance to buy against an unfavorable referendum outcome. For the VCG mechanism, one declares how much uninsured harm one would suffer from an unfavorable outcome, on the understanding that payment will be required only if one's vote changes the outcome in the direction one favors, and the payment will be at most the amount one declares. The actual amount owed will be the amount that would have produced a tie vote. (A slightly longer explanation, along the same lines, is necessary for a referendum that picks an optimal budget size as a continuous variable, rather than choosing among a specified set of increments.) The complicated part is explaining the VCG mechanism and its truth-inducing incentive, which is something one need do only at the stages of designing and adopting a constitution.

That said, we now recount the reasons why these mechanisms are worth the trouble. Broadly, the reason is the enormous waste in government, and induced by government, that Chapter 1 documents. In narrower technical terms, we have three main reasons to expect these mechanisms to eliminate most of the waste. First, using them in a referendum in the way proposed gives voters an incentive to participate and to inform themselves. This incentive comes from the Thompson mechanism and it spills over into the modified VCG mechanism that goes in tandem with it. Second, each legislature is a sample of the population so that even if the members were mechanically perfect and reliable, there would be sampling error. Correcting this sampling error requires all the information provided by the referendum. Third, legislators need the proper incentive to do their work so as to promote efficient outcomes. The referendum information, used in the right way, can provide them with strong incentives of the right sort.

In Chapter 3 we combine all these ideas in a draft constitution.

Appendix: Notes on Altruism, Ideology, and Anarchy

The saddest life is that of a political aspirant under democracy. His failure is ignominious and his success is disgraceful.[14]

A2.1 ALTRUISM AND PUBLIC-SPIRITEDNESS

In Chapter 1 we noted that gifts to charity, the act of voting, and the herd instinct fall outside the scope of an analysis that assumes only narrow, material-self-interested behavior, which I shall refer to as materialistic behavior. This entire work proceeds on the working premise that the narrow analysis that is traditional in economics is accurate enough for the purpose of constitutional design. The most direct challenge to this premise comes from Margolis (1982a, 1982b), who has argued that altruism invalidates the VCG mechanism. We argue in this appendix that it is in fact accurate enough for two reasons: (a) most of the non-materialistic behavior at issue has no effect on the analysis nor on the most effective constitutional design; and (b) where such behavior causes problems, the problems have no better solution than the proposed design.

To clarify these claims, we need to spell out the non-materialistic kinds of behavior that we can observe or that are suggested in the public choice literature. Consider first a married couple's donations of income and of leisure time that fall outside their own material self-interest:

1. Their children's food, clothing, upbringing, education, and possibly an eventual bequest to them.
2. Attendance at church, tithing, and volunteer work; and similar voluntary activity in clubs and charities.
3. Gifts to the United Way through employer-sponsored fund raising.
4. Voting, after study of candidates and issues.
5. Participation in political or lobbying organizations, in public protests, etc.

The first item on this list usually receives a substantial fraction of a couple's leisure time and income, on the order of one-third of the combined value of both, whereas the others usually receive five percent or less.[15] Economists have therefore traditionally disregarded charities and political participation and have viewed the household utility function as an attribute of the entire nuclear family. That is, the welfare or specific consumption of each child was a variable parallel to the variables representing the parents' consumption in the traditional utility function.

It turns out, however, that this traditional approach won't do. When we look at long-term wealth accumulation, including the effects of taxation and government deficits, this approach has preposterous implications, because the children marry and their welfare then links the in-laws to each other, and then through an endless chain to everyone else (Bernheim, 1987; Bernheim and Bagwell, 1988). Recent work on this issue and on altruism in general has taken a different tack. Although a household's gifts and bequests to children (and to others) may in part depend on the household's concern for the welfare of the recipients, it is mainly controlled by the household's satisfaction with the size of the gift. In technical terms, a household's utility is entirely or partly a function of the size of the gift and only partly, if at all, a function of the perceived need, welfare, or the list of goods consumed by the recipient. Compared to the traditional way, this alternative way to characterize utility has notably distinct and different implications.[16]

A2.2 PUBLIC GOODS

We also take account of public goods. For the present purpose we define a public good as a good in a government budget that wins approval in a referendum under the rules of Chapter 3. The motives for voter support can affect the analysis, but need not affect the definition of the good.

Of those goods and services that have been provided by modern governments, the following three kinds would very likely be continued by an efficient government using estimated Lindahl taxes:

1. Those that increase household and business incomes, property values, and security: local public streets, police, courts, and national defense.
2. Altruistic transfers: welfare programs, rescues.
3. Programs mixing the above two features: environmental programs, school tuition vouchers for poor families, support for basic science.

Households would support Group 1 primarily, if not exclusively, for the material benefits its programs provide. Although the constitution mandates a minimal safety-net program, households paying estimated Lindahl taxes might support Group 2, over and above the constitutionally mandated transfers, for compassionate or public-spirited reasons. Households would typically have both directly self-interested and public-spirited motives for supporting group 3 programs. Programs in group 1 are likely to be comparative necessities, for which household willingness to pay would rise roughly in proportion to household income and wealth. Programs in group 2, and the public-spirited component of their willingness to pay for programs in group 3, could be comparative luxuries, so that willingness to pay could rise more than proportionately to household income and wealth, although that is not certain. Even if not, there would be few public goods for which household willingness to pay would fail to rise with income. Accurate Lindahl taxes would reduce but might not eliminate the sensitivity to income of the willingness to pay in excess of the household tax assessment, for successful programs. Consequently, as our analysis in Chapter 5 shows, there would typically be some uninsurable benefits of successful programs, so that the VCG mechanism would have a role in most referenda.

A2.3 ALTRUISM, PUBLIC GOODS, AND WILLINGNESS TO PAY

To illustrate the issues of most interest here, consider the 'Smith' utility function $U = U(x, y, z)$, which the Smiths maximize subject to the budget constraint $x + y = I(z)$, where we measure all variables in units of the numeraire, and where

x = a private good that the adult Smiths consume
y = a donation by the Smiths
z = a public good
$I(z)$ = Smith real income, which increases with material benefits from z.

Each of the three kinds of programs of Section 2.3 would be included in z in Section 2.2, where for more detailed applications we would have to regard x, y, and z as vectors of goods and activities. In their private decisions, the Smiths choose x and y but have no effect on z, whose budget is so large that a Smith contribution to it would have a negligible effect. (Their votes, however, may change z.) The private maximization decision yields $U_x = U_y$. For simplicity, assume that y has no tax consequences such as tax deductibility for the Smith family, and that the economy as a whole satisfies all efficiency conditions except perhaps for its choice of the amount of z.

A referendum asks the Smiths to declare their willingness to pay schedule $w(z)$ for a range of values of z, taking into account the Smith share $T(z)$ of the tax financing of z. The direct material benefit to the Smiths of a change of z is an increase of $I(z)$, which the Smiths would allocate between x and y (if they do not reduce y due to what specialists refer to as crowding out), so that we write $x(z)$ and $y(z)$ for their values consequent upon the referendum outcome. The first derivatives of x, y, I, T, and w are x', y', I', T', and w', respectively. We disregard income effects, so that w' is a well-defined amount such that if the Smiths paid that amount in addition to T' when the government increases z by one unit, U would remain unchanged. Hence, noting that $I' = x' + y'$, we have

$$dU = (I' - y' - T')\, U_x dz + y'\, U_y dz + U_z dz - w'\, U_x dz = 0 \tag{2.1}$$

Because the Smiths maintain $U_x = U_y$, equation (2.1) simplifies to

$$w' = (I' - T') + U_z/U_x. \tag{2.2}$$

In equation (2.2), the term $(I' - T')$ is the net material benefit to the Smiths because of the increase in z, whereas U_z/U_x is the altruistic benefit to the Smiths, in units of the numeraire per unit of z. We add them 'vertically' at each quantity of z to obtain the household's virtual demand function for z, in a manner analogous to the addition of these virtual demand functions for all households to obtain a social demand function. The effect of changes in z on y cancels out of (2.2) and is therefore immaterial, because of the side condition $U_x = U_y$.[17]

This demonstration disproves the claim by Margolis that one cannot simply add the material benefit and the altruistic benefit to obtain the Smiths' willingness to pay taxes in support of z. Adding them is precisely the correct solution, so that w' has the same role in this problem as it has in a purely materialistic model. Contrary to Margolis's claim, the presence of altruism both in the variable y and in U_z has no effect on the proper use of demand-revealing processes. The Election Commission does not need to know the Smiths' motives. It asks their willingness to pay taxes (in addition to buying insurance) to increase the size of z, and uses their answer in the same way regardless of how much of this willingness comes from each motive.

A2.4 THE HERD INSTINCT

Despite the reassuring results of the analysis of motives, incentives, and willingness to pay, we must revisit the question of how this analysis can be affected by the human tendency to respond to peer-group pressure, referred to earlier as the herd instinct.

In primordial times, those early animals that were genetically disposed to protect personal or group territory for food and reproduction crowded out those competing animals that lacked this disposition, and perpetuated their genetic disposition. In the higher mammals, group territories and gregarious life styles, though not universal, have characterized most species. When humans came along, they conspicuously inherited these traits. Our possessiveness toward hunting and living space can be said to provide the primitive basis for the analysis throughout this book, and for most economic analysis. Our continued symbolic use of group hunting, group fighting and pillaging, and other tribal life styles, especially in our political life, introduce complicating factors that economists and philosophers would much prefer to ignore. Albeit reluctantly, we must now examine more carefully these primitive impediments to civilization.

As noted in Chapter 1, overtly vicious tribal behavior, such as one observes in Northern Ireland, the Balkans, Cyprus, the Middle East, and so on are more than we can handle. This study does not pretend to solve all the world's problems. In the more civilized parts of the world, such behavior is usually more muted and at times may even be subtle. The phenomenon of interest is the peer group and the pressures it brings on its members. In Europe, southern Asia, much of Latin America, and parts of the rural U.S., most people identify themselves strongly with the village, county, or province of their ancestors, with their particular religious and ethnic tradition, and with their craft and social class. In metropolitan areas, especially in the U.S., peer groups center mainly on industry and occupation. In all cases they are a major social and political force. Those that are well organized are particularly effective in politics, although the poorly organized ones may also have an occasional major impact if unity of the members' views translates into a significant bloc of votes.

The most pertinent aspect of peer-group identities for our inquiry is the effect they have on information flows in a world that has always been characterized by rational ignorance. Wherever raiding and warfare were endemic in the ancient world, group loyalty and group defense were essential to survival for the tribe and therefore for most of its members. When surprised by a nearby person or animal, one could not dither like Hamlet in answering the question, 'friend or foe?', and there was usually no practical alternative to conforming to one's tribe's customs and beliefs. The processing of information was largely a group activity, and did not allow an individual family much scope for deliberation. In a modern civilized country things are somewhat better, in that one can in part choose one's peer group or groups, and the penalties for nonconformity are mild compared to what they once were.

We need not distract ourselves with the influence of peer-group pressures on life styles. Economists have developed straightforward ways to characterize this influence by elaboration of standard utility and production analysis (Stigler and Becker, 1977).[18] The problem lies with individual acceptance of peer group beliefs about economic and political facts. In well-organized groups the important beliefs are those that support the groups' political agendas. In more amorphous groups there will also be some similarity of views about what favors or harms the group's interests.

Moreover, because of the ancient tribal provenance of modern peer-group behavior, almost every peer group has one or more other peer groups that it regards as repugnant and hostile. Such inimical groups will naturally include those that oppose a group's perceived interests, and may include others for historical reasons. These points apply whether a group is well organized or is comparatively amorphous, although an active and effective group is more likely to stir up direct opposition.

A peer group's point of view gives a member a ready means of dealing with cognitive dissonance amid the confusing mass of information the modern world provides. The member can simply accept the group's selective perception, relying on the group to process information. A well-organized peer group, almost by definition, has an elite leadership whom the members trust to set the group's current styles in information and other matters. When less well-organized, a peer group may or may not have a formal selection mechanism for its leadership group, but whether selection is formal and rigid or informal and fluid the leaders are persons who stand out as seeming to have exceptional qualities, appropriate to that group, of excellence, trustworthiness, and self-assurance. Often they are the modern equivalent of ancient shamans or prophets, although in some cases they are more like warlords.

As a further aid to simplified information processing, each member can easily see the selective perception at work in another peer group perceived as an enemy. The member can reject all information that that group disseminates, or that that group would find congenial (and that therefore, one assumes, that group must have fabricated), as self-serving and untrustworthy. Group loyalty requires wholesale use of such selective perception.

Not only because of the pressures of self-identification with a peer group but also because of the economy involved, a peer group member chooses a few information sources felt to be trustworthy. This behavior has the immediate benefit of wonderfully simplifying the acquisition and processing of information. To be sure, this simplification can have costly consequences, but even in the exceptional cases where the consequences are disastrous, they are long-term and difficult to anticipate. Policy initiatives have consequences in the economic and political realm, involving complex interactions, that are hard to predict even in the short term and are even harder to predict in the long term.

Those persons having the necessary stigmata and circumstances to rise to peer-group leadership positions seldom have an incentive in these circumstances to sort out life's complexities and make accurate predictions of the consequences of a group-supported policy. Whatever advantages they obtain from leadership can be protected and furthered equally well by supporting superficially attractive but shortsighted policies. Harm to the group arising from indirect, longer-term effects of those policies that the group actively or tacitly supports can be blamed on adversary groups and on other aspects of the external world. That is, peer-group leaders can behave like politicians and appeal to group loyalty to maintain their positions. While they are at it, they can clothe self-serving policies and practices in the language of good intentions and in selectively reported facts, in each case suitable to the ambiance of their peer group.

There is no need to bore the reader with a list of examples, especially because most aspects of the foregoing are true of every peer group. We must dwell for a moment, however, on the special case of the profession of journalism. In the United States it is an almost perfect example of *laissez faire* capitalism, an attribute that its members prefer not to emphasize. Journalists are almost totally unregulated, and in practice can mislead without limit (apart from egregious fraud) without penalty. Their success depends only on their ability to entertain and, secondarily, their reputations for reliability, which, given the values of the peer groups to which they play, gives them ample scope for selective and misleading reporting. Members of major news organizations are naturally under peer-group pressure to protect their own interests. They form tacit alliances with other interest groups to obtain information whose publication can serve the interests of both.

Among other things, it is good for the news business (especially for the major metropolitan newspapers and for network television newscasters) to have big, incompetent, wasteful government. It provides rewarding opportunities to get attention and creates large-scale employment opportunities for news gatherers. Conversely, reducing government intervention harms the interests of the major news organizations. In 1981, for example, when the Reagan administration successfully deregulated gasoline prices and allocation, about 1000 news reporter jobs disappeared, of which more than 100 were on the 'energy beat' (Brookes, 1993).

Those of us who pay attention will have noticed that the major news media have for decades been constantly campaigning for more government regulation, and for reversal of those instances of deregulation that have occurred. The press also campaigns for big government in numerous other ways, such as by its support for welfare, Medicare, and other transfer expenditures, routinely misrepresenting the costs, generosity, and longer-term implications of these expenditures.[19] Thus in most developed countries a self-serving press is a strong interest group that magnifies the effects of interest-group politics and of peer-group misuse of voters' altruism, public spiritedness, and rational ignorance.

This discussion of peer groups is important to our quest for an improved constitution both because of its relationship to the analysis of altruism and because of the effect it has on our main argument. What it implies is that 'altruism and public-spiritedness' in the forms discussed in this appendix are commonplace phenomena that invite and receive abuse by those in leadership positions. It therefore implies that 'altruism and public-spiritedness', more properly referred to as the herd instinct, is typically an obstacle to good government rather than something that promotes it.

Finally and most importantly, this discussion implies that the maximum use of honest competition and of clearly specified, generous rewards for performance, as set out in the proposed constitution, are the best we can hope for in the quest for better government. This constitution effectively abolishes the function of professional politicians. Its use of approximate Lindahl taxes almost completely neutralizes interest groups by obliging them to pay for what they get, except in cases of massively effective fraud. It provides for an assured, even-handed information flow that can undercut selective reporting by peer-group leaders and create such intolerable cognitive dissonance that selective perception fails, and can lead people to modify their peer-group memberships. Journalists would have to pay estimated Lindahl taxes as an offset to any job-creating or salary-raising effects of their campaigns for bigger government. For journalists as for all other persons, approximate Lindahl taxes would eliminate the major economic rewards of misrepresentation in political affairs. Thus most of the day-to-day harm from the herd instinct would be sharply curtailed or eliminated.

Lest we be carried away by too much enthusiasm, however, we must note that the herd instinct and the evils it permits would still be a problem. Consider two examples where it could be.

First, a good example is the issue in several countries of whether abortion shall be prohibited and subject to severe penalties. Suppose that a country with the constitution proposed in Chapter 3 has left this issue unsettled in its bill of rights, so that it is left as an issue for ordinary legislation. In many countries it would be a divisive issue that cuts across almost all identifiable demographic groups. Although there would likely be some predictability of predominant views in various demographic groups, so that the assessment of approximate Lindahl taxes and transfers could be partly accurate, many or even most demographic groups would have members on both sides of the issue. Most of the willingness to pay involved would furthermore be uninsurable, so that voters could feel free to be irresponsible in stating it. There would in fact be a large temptation to form conspiracies, on both sides, to overstate willingness to pay to change the outcome. This kind of issue is red meat for journalists. The performance of a country with our proposed constitution could be almost as arbitrary and capricious on this issue as the corresponding past performance of the United States' system of government has been. That is a pity, and if the reader can think of a constitutional order that would arrive at sound policy on such issues more reliably than that proposed here, please publish it.

A second problem case is entry into war. Consider, for example, the circumstances and steps leading to the adoption of the Gulf of Tonkin resolution in 1964, which was in effect a declaration of war by the United States against North Vietnam. President Johnson, who had already decided that U.S. entry into the war was inevitable, used the alleged attacks, almost certainly nonexistent, by North Vietnamese warships against U.S. warships to whip up irresistible political pressures for U.S. entry. (The U.S. initiation of the Spanish-American War had a similar provenance.) Nothing in our proposed constitution can prevent similar occurrences, and nothing in it guarantees that the country will win a war that it gets into. Once again, that is a pity, and if the reader can think of a constitutional order that would arrive at sound policy on such issues more reliably than that proposed here, please publish it.

3 The Draft Constitution and its Rationale

My apple trees will never get across
And eat the cones under his pines, I tell him.
He only says, "Good fences make good neighbors."[1]

This chapter presents a draft constitution that incorporates the features described in Chapter 2, discussing its parts clause by clause. It presents the document piecemeal in order to explain the reasons for and consequences of each provision, along with its precise language. The discussion passes more quickly over some of those provisions that remain unspecified. Then the entire document appears in one piece as an appendix.

> **PREAMBLE**
> We the people of [*the nation of Cumulanis*] adopt this constitution as a solemn contract, binding ourselves and our successors in perpetuity. Although in some circumstances it compels some of us to accept the will of others, we accept that minimum amount of such compulsion that, when applied consistently and without favor in all circumstances, serves our best interests and those of our successors. It is our aim to harmonize each public decision with our interests under this constitution so that we support each such decision, as nearly as possible, unanimously.

The constitution is, as nearly as possible, a social contract. The preamble says that, and says why the people would want it. This language is meant to reinforce the contract language that appears throughout the entire document, in order to facilitate its accurate interpretation.

> **Article I: Popular Sovereignty**
> Section 1. The government, a provider of services under contract with the people, implements and enforces such legislation as the people approve. The people delegate specified authority to its executive and judicial officers. Subject to the provisions of this constitution, officers and legislative programs shall compete for the people's approval.

This section puts the government in its place. It is also a short summary of the way it will work.

> **<u>Article II: Legislatures, Legislative Programs, and their Execution</u>**
> Section 1. (a) There shall be at least two official legislatures and there may be private ones as provided in Subsection 10(d), each drafting a separate legislative program to be presented to the people in such a manner that they may approve one or another in its entirety or may approve a composite of parts of more than one program. Two official legislatures (not including a third that may be approved under Subsection 10(d)) are referred to herein as the primary official legislatures.

This subsection provides a brief summary of certain key features of Article II. These points are (1) that legislatures, both official and private, compete with each other and (2) that they may merely propose legislation that will take effect only if a referendum approves it, in whole or in part.

> (b) Except as modified by Article V, Section 8, 'by law' means by a statute enacted under the procedures prescribed in Article II, Sections 8, 9, and 10.

The expression 'created by law' or 'provided by law' recurs in several Articles. To avoid a possible error of subsequent interpretation, this section specifies that the only law is statute law adopted by legislative referendum as provided in the constitution. The modification notes that the interpretation of laws, once enacted, is not generally a subject for ratification by referendum (although an interpretation could be reversed by further legislation).

> Section 2. (a) Each official legislature shall consist of citizens eligible to vote, selected by lot. The number selected shall be no fewer than [...] and no greater than [...]. The selection procedure shall be a stratified random drawing in which each population subgroup, classified by gender, age group, region, employment status, income, and income source by industry and occupation, if any, including career government servants, shall be [*proportionately*] represented. [*The subgroups shall be mutually exclusive and exhaustive, so that each citizen shall be a member of exactly one*

> *subgroup*.] The selection shall be supervised by an Election Commission of [*five*] members selected by the official legislatures in joint session in the fourth year of their term of office from among the successful arbitrators and judges, to take office [*three*] months prior to the commencement of the term of office of the incoming official legislatures. The term of an Election Commission shall be four years. No currently serving government official except a sitting judge shall be eligible to become an Election Commissioner. In particular, no Speaker may be selected, and no Election Commissioner may serve consecutive terms.

A fully representative legislature could be so large as to be unwieldy in a large, diverse country. In such a country a federal structure would very likely be necessary for the efficient conduct of business. A smaller country whose population is relatively homogeneous would not find that necessary, although even in that case the subgroup definitions could not be overly fine-grained. For example, a country with two regions, ten occupations, four income groups, two genders, and three age groups would have 480 subgroups minus empty categories, so that the size of the legislature would have to exceed 500 if few categories are non-empty and if each category is to have at least three representatives.

A small country with a homogeneous population might indulge in the luxury of a proportionately stratified legislature. A proportionately stratified random sample would assure proportionality of representation of all identifiable demographic groups, so that each eligible citizen has the same probability as every other eligible citizen of being selected to serve in the legislature. To the extent practicable, every economic and social interest group identifiable by objective criteria would have representatives.

A larger country would have to have representation in proportion to wealth, however. This step would sharply reduce the required representation without a corresponding sacrifice of accuracy. In such a country, legislative size could also be limited by having one demographic characteristic sampled independently of others, so that a legislator could represent both male and female voters on one dimension but only female voters on another. This procedure would complicate the estimation of the probability of passage of a measure in a referendum, but would greatly reduce the cost of organizing and supporting legislatures.

The Election Commission has duties, specified in subsequent sections, that affect the fortunes of legislators. Therefore the outgoing official legislators select the Election Commission that will supervise elections affecting the incoming legislators. Because commissioners may not succeed themselves, this procedure largely eliminates the possibility of favoritism by commissioners toward the legislators who selected them. A small risk of such favoritism remains because the continuation of the budget in force when legislators select the incoming Election Commission will compete with budgets proposed by the incoming legislatures. This competition has rigid rules, however, and the financial incentives for the Election Commission, specified in Subsection 10(f) below, should effectively deter favoritism.

> (b) A new demographic subgroup other than those specified in Subsection (a) may be created by law by subdividing an existing subgroup, provided that it has first been established in official legislative proceedings (1) that membership and nonmembership of such a group can be independently verified by nonmembers of the original demographic subgroup and (2) that creation of the new subgroup will reduce the within-group variability of declared harms on some significant public policy referenda.

A demographic subgroup may 'secede' from the larger subgroup of which it is a member if it is identifiable, as specified, and if its separation receives approval by the normal legislative procedure, including referendum. It is in the interest of legislators to propose such separation when it would improve the accuracy of Lindahl tax assessments, which in turn would increase legislators' incentive payments. A demographic subgroup would typically want to secede if its members often favored smaller government expenditures than those favored by other members of the larger pre-existing subgroup, because successful separation would lower the new subgroup's estimated Lindahl taxes.

By improving the accuracy of Lindahl taxes, separation would also tend to improve the efficiency of election outcomes, so that those who gain from the separation would be able to compensate those who lose. There are at least two reasons why outcomes would become more efficient. First, errors in Lindahl taxes give the overtaxed voters an incentive to campaign against the most efficient outcome, among other ways by using misleading information, but in any case in costly ways. The costs of such campaigning, and its effect on the outcome, reduce efficiency. Second, adjustments for income effects in the estimates of uninsured harms are necessary only when there are errors in the Lindahl taxes. These adjustments will generally involve approximations, and may themselves have errors, leading to inefficiencies in referendum outcomes. Knowing these effects, voters outside the subgroup being subdivided would have a positive interest in valid subdivision.

Basing the definition of a new subgroup, and all subgroup membership, on objective criteria will reduce the problem of self-selection arising from the incentive to free ride. If an identifiable subgroup generally prefers smaller government than do most other subgroups, it will pay comparatively low estimated Lindahl taxes. Citizens who in fact belong to other subgroups would prefer to join such a low-tax subgroup if they could, if the taxes entirely support national budget items. (By contrast, if the low-tax subgroup had its own low-budget local government, and if the national government's taxes were not a factor, then each citizen would prefer to join a local or regional subgroup with that citizen's preferences, as part of a comparatively homogeneous jurisdiction.[2]) Objective criteria that give the citizen no scope for changing to a new subgroup avoid this problem.

There is also no problem if a personal characteristic that the citizen can influence involves no perverse incentive. If a change of status, such as moving to a higher income group, consistently carries with it a change in the demand for government services, such as police and fire protection, then the expectation of estimated higher Lindahl taxes would be as neutral as would the expectation of buying a more expensive automobile. Here the incentive effect of Lindahl taxes is sound: it is efficient to have rising tax shares with income, because the higher-income person has more influence on the outcome. This higher influence applies if and only if the person will impose a higher cost on the community (apart from individual differences), so that it represents a true social cost.

A problem would arise if some regional subgroups of citizens have distinctive preferences, such as a preference for small government and for corresponding low national taxes, that could affect decisions by other citizens to move to such a region rather than to another. The proposed draft language permits the government to base each citizen family's taxes in part on where they have lived previously as well as on where they live now, although such a procedure could lead to multiplication of subgroups or to complex accounting. These problems do not arise, however, for a small country with a comparatively homogeneous citizenry.

> (c) Persons selected by lot shall be compelled to serve in an official legislature, except for [*(a)*] those excused for overriding reasons[*and (b) those, each of whom finds an alternate from the person's own demographic subgroup as a voluntarily replacement*].

Such overriding reasons are restricted to (1) terminal illness with a prognosis of less than [*two years*] of survival or permanently incapacitating ill health confirmed by a panel of doctors selected by the Election Commission, (2) indictment for a felony, in which case the person shall be temporarily excused until the case is concluded, including appeals, and if not convicted the person shall then be available as an alternate for a vacancy during the legislative term, (3) election to high office under Article IV, or (4) [*other.*]

Section 3. The official legislatures shall be selected every four years. If a legislator becomes ineligible to serve as a result of death, permanently incapacitating ill health, election to high office, or conviction for a felony, the Election Commission shall select an alternate if one is already available or if not conduct a special drawing to select a new legislator, in either case from the same population subgroup as that of the ineligible legislator.

Section 4. An official legislature shall have no authority to exclude a member for any reason, other than those prescribed by Section 3. Such exclusion shall not take effect until certified by the Election Commission. In the fourth year of each legislative term each primary official legislature shall propose a law defining felonious conduct in connection with legislative business, such as bribery, extortion, and obstruction, and such a law shall come into force at the beginning of the next legislative term, if it meets the requirements for legislation prescribed in this Article. Each such legislative proposal shall include provisions restricting subsequent employment of legislators by employers who do business with or otherwise tangibly benefit from government programs.

The proposal to have truly representative legislatures, drawn by lot from all persons eligible to vote, is likely to be viewed as one of the most surprising features of this document. It is natural to ask, why not limit eligibility at least to high school graduates, and why not exclude mentally disabled persons, or flighty, irresponsible persons, and so on? The answer in part is that eligibility can be limited by excluding mentally ill persons from voting, subject to procedural rules governed by the Bill of Rights in Article III, Section 2. All other adults, who are legally able to decide for themselves how to allocate their personal budgets in their own interest, also have a stake in the allocation of funds from their budgets to pay for government projects. The proposed system will ask them to express their own willingness to pay for such projects, in their own interest, where they have clear financial incentives to study their answers carefully.

A superficially plausible reason for suggesting that only those most qualified should serve is the notion that most legislators selected by lot would be unable to understand the complex issues that must be dealt with by legislation. In fact, this claim is not only partly true, but it is also true for existing legislatures. Legislators selected by *present* methods also are unable to understand many complex issues, and at present have no particular incentive to try to understand them. Often they see proposed laws of several hundred pages for the first time only a few hours, or even a few minutes, before they vote on them. In the case of trial juries, we have ordinary persons, some without high school educations, digesting and making decisions on technically complex issues. If someone suggests using juries of 'experts' instead, we must ask that person, 'Who will select the experts, and how will we specify their qualifications?' In our proposed legislature, expertise would come into the process through testimony, and would receive the weight it deserves from those legislators whose sub-group interests were most affected by the proposals at issue.

When a truly representative legislature of citizens thinks through its *own* interest in the costs and benefits of government programs, in so doing it will provide a good estimate of what is in the best interest of all citizens. Under the compensation rules in later sections, legislators will have strong incentives to do this job well. *Every* legislator would in fact be moved by these incentives to study the relevant facts carefully even on issues that, apart from these incentives, would be of only small importance to the legislator's family. Whenever such a legislature makes an error, the other official legislature or a shrewdly led private legislature would put forward alternative proposals that voters would approve. The continuation of the previous budget also appears on the ballot, as provided in Subsection 10(a). The referendum on competing proposals would be the citizens' protection against legislative mistakes.

Furthermore, if we accept a procedure to screen out persons who are 'unqualified,' we put power in some officials' hands to promote their own interests at the expense of everyone else. That is, the selection process could and would be abused. In addition, an elite 'better qualified' legislature would tend to favor proposals that benefit people like themselves, at the expense of the 'unqualified' voters whom the process excludes. Even if the set of rewards and penalties for legislators proposed in Section 11 and elsewhere would limit this problem, unless every citizen group has representatives there would be no way for legislators to know how excluded citizens would vote in a referendum.

That said, note that we have a suggested rule and an alternative. The suggested rule is strict compulsory service. The alternative is to allow each selected legislator to find a voluntary replacement. Here we face a difficult and delicate question about using compulsion in a system designed to emulate free markets.

The argument for using compulsory service is that it is the only way to obtain a representative sample. In each demographic subgroup there will be some persons more willing to serve than are others. Those most willing to serve are by definition unrepresentative. One suspects that in some cases those more willing to serve would be among the most competent, but that in other cases they would tend to be less competent and more inclined to make unnecessary trouble than would a strictly representative group of persons. As to representativeness, consider the following example. Suppose that random selection chooses the second of two wealthy corporate executives who according to official information are equally wealthy. The first is in fact on the brink of bankruptcy whereas the wealth of the one selected is likely to double in the next three years due to favorable business opportunities. The second would be highly reluctant to serve and if permitted to do so would recruit the first as a replacement. In general, allowing voluntary alternates would result in a legislature consisting only of persons who want the job and who therefore have various qualities that differ from those of a representative person.

There are two obvious arguments against this form of compulsory service. The first is that representative persons must be paid more to gain their acquiescence in serving, and perhaps to motivate them to do a good job. Everyday experience supports the general principle that people who self-select into their occupations usually are those best able to perform well in those occupations. The second is that our proposed bill of rights, in Article III, Section 2 prohibits all forms of involuntary servitude (other than the present legislative proposal), and the reader will no doubt perceive a jarring contradiction here. If involuntary servitude is categorically unacceptable everywhere else, and is contrary to the basic principles of this constitution, why use it at the very core of government?

There are many other difficult cases that highlight this dilemma about what the constitution should say about the reluctance of some voters to serve. Consider the cases of mothers with small children and members of certain religious groups, who might object vehemently. Our basic concern is that everyone should be accurately represented. To get that result, we must provide for ample compensation. Persons selected by lot will receive adequate compensation at least equal to their opportunity cost of serving, plus incentive pay based on their contribution as legislators to the well-being of all voters. As just noted, a country needs the help of every kind of citizen to write sound legislation. The groups who find such service difficult or positively objectionable would be reminded that they are needed to help write legislation that responds to their special concerns. I would think that this feature of the system would appeal especially to those groups who would resent and oppose the kinds of government we have now. For those who feel that serving would hamper their careers, the main answer is that their compensation as legislators would allow them to retire wealthy if they do a good job. These arguments apply whether or not service is to be compulsory.

Whatever the rule about compulsory service, a legislature may not exclude a member on frivolous or malicious grounds, but must have a reason provable in court. It must be possible to prevent obstruction, however, and legislators must not accept implicit bribes through subsequent employment. Hence we need the safeguards provided by Section 4.

> Section 5. Each official legislator shall receive a salary while serving equal to [*1.2*] times the full value of his or her personal services as measured by prior earnings, together with a reasonable expectation of current increase. Under this section, members of the official legislator's immediate family shall be considered to be official legislators. In addition, each legislator may receive incentive pay and may pay incentive taxes as prescribed in other sections of this article. For the income from property, including intellectual property, that an official legislator would otherwise receive, said legislator shall exchange such property for a portfolio of equal value, proportionately representing all property in the same industry or industries as that of the original property. Apart from these specified sources, no official legislator may receive royalties, honoraria, gifts of more than nominal value, or any other income while serving, except as otherwise provided in this constitution.

Legislators and their families can expect to receive more than the opportunity cost of serving. There is a risk of negative incentive pay, which is at least compensated by the expectation of positive incentive pay. If experience shows that the risk is so high that many legislators are genuinely reluctant to serve, a pay increase can be proposed and put in a budget referendum, as authorized in Article III Section 4(c) and in Section 10 of Article II. In order for our principle of proportional representation to work well, a legislator whose family receives income from property must represent the interests of all holders of property involved in the industry or industries with which the legislators' families' original property is associated. The legislator should not represent the interests of a particular firm or of an identifiable piece of property.

Restrictions on outside income are similar to those we now place on judges, and for a similar reason. The system must not only avoid actual bribery, but the appearance of bribery, as we have just noted.

Section 6. (a) Each official legislature shall select a presiding officer to be called 'Speaker' from among the successful appellate judges. The Speaker shall have the same authority that a judge has in a civil trial, to limit evidence and arguments presented on the grounds of relevance and reliability, to preserve order, and to determine specific rules of order pursuant to those prescribed by law. Upon receiving the Speaker's recommendation at the beginning of a session, the legislature shall determine its structure of committees, their membership, and the scope of their authority pursuant to the legislature's business. Each official legislature shall keep a journal of its proceedings and votes, which shall be published in a timely way prior to each referendum.

(b) An Election Commissioner's and a Speaker's income from property and other sources shall be subject to the same rules and restrictions as those prescribed for legislators in Section 5.

Section 7. [*The identities of legislators shall be kept secret until four years after they have served.*] Under exceptional conditions as may be prescribed by the Election Commission all official legislators, together with their families, shall be sequestered from all contact with persons other than government officials and witnesses for a period to be prescribed by the Election Commission. Their access to news, other information, and messages from outside the legislature may when necessary be controlled by the Speaker in such a manner as to protect the integrity of the official legislative process. There shall be no communication between the legislatures nor between their Speakers except as otherwise specifically provided herein. The proceedings of each legislature shall be kept secret to the extent deemed prudent by the legislature until the subsequent referendum

> ballot is set, whereupon subsection 10(e) applies. This provision shall not prohibit the Election Commission from arranging the presentation of evidence to official legislatures simultaneously, if these legislatures consent thereto, or from permitting relevant questions from legislators to experts and interested citizens who testify, in such a manner as to conform to the restrictions on communication. During periods of sequestration the Speakers and the members of the Election Commission, with their families, shall also separate themselves from all contact with persons other than government officials and witnesses.

These sections state particulars of the objective of having deliberative, reliable, truth-seeking legislative proceedings that follow the example of present-day court proceedings at their best. The legislatures or their committees would hold hearings, gather relevant information, and prepare to reach well-informed evaluations of self-interest, for themselves and for the population subgroups they represent. Such preparation is a necessary step toward informed decisions by the electorate, and should generally be a good antidote to such false and misleading claims as might be advertised during the referendum process.

The rule of prudence specified for giving out information about a legislature's proceedings follows the practice of private sector firms, who give advance notice of a new product they intend to offer, while cloaking in secrecy such details as might help their competitors at their expense. The main safeguard to the public is that we have competing legislatures that closely resemble large private sector firms competing for the public's favor. Penalties for nonperformance, specified in later sections, also discourage misleading claims as they do for private firms under traditional contract law. Inasmuch as the issues involved are often larger than the family car, however, we have additional safeguards for the integrity of the process.

The suggested secrecy rule may not be tenable, although elaborate procedures could be used for this purpose, similar to those of the witness protection program in the U.S. It would have to include a gag rule for the press, and perhaps protection for relatives to prevent intimidation or bribery through them. The need for great care to protect legislators arises from their role in determining everyone's taxes. The generous compensation for accuracy of tax assessments, provided in later sections, is a strong defense against bribery, but there is still a risk of some form of bribery or intimidation.

The prospect of sequestration would no doubt be objectionable to most legislators, although the generous incentive payments to be provided for in Section 11 should overcome most objections. Perhaps the most practical procedure would be to set up a town for each legislature with complete facilities similar to those now provided on some military bases for military families. A new country contemplating this constitution would want to think through carefully the advantages and disadvantages of alternative procedures in the context of that country's geography and other particular circumstances.

> Section 8. Each primary official legislator may initiate budget proposals and other legislative proposals and the Speaker may lay before the official legislature such proposals as have been presented to the Speaker by citizens. Speakers, Election Commissioners, and a third official legislature may propose legislation to create a new demographic subgroup as authorized under Subsection 2(c), but they may not propose or suggest other legislation, directly or indirectly.

Each primary official legislator has incentives, spelled out below in Section 11, to respond to and develop good ideas for legislation quickly, rather than see the ideas proposed successfully as ballot initiatives by private legislatures.

The restriction on speakers and election commissioners is necessary to preserve their neutrality on sets of issues that appear on ballots, and on the arguments pro and con. They play an essential role in developing the relevant information on merits and disadvantages for each proposal accurately, and in moving legislation to the ballot. They must carry out these tasks in a strictly impartial and diligent way, to maintain the integrity of the process.

> Section 9. (a) Each official legislator shall be instructed to vote within the legislature in such a manner as to maximize his or her family's best interests, taking both financial and intangible considerations into account, based on the family's incomes and interests prior to serving and on the modifications of property income prescribed by Section 5. The legislator shall also be instructed that truthful voting in this stage will maximize the legislator's prospects for generous incentive pay. The manner of voting is that each legislator shall state, in response to a proposal, how much money it is worth to that legislator's family to pass or to

> defeat the proposal, as the case may be. When an official legislature votes on several related issues, such that the votes on one issue may depend on the outcome of another issue, all such issues shall be considered together in a single procedure. All feasible outcomes shall be enumerated and each legislator shall state how much money it is worth to that legislator's family to obtain each outcome relative to each less preferred outcome. Each legislator shall also state by how much this money amount would change if the family's income were initially higher by a stated amount. If these amounts are inconsistent with a technically rational, self-consistent set of preferences, the legislator shall be required to bring them into conformity with same. Subject to adjustment procedures set out in part (a) of the Technical Annex, the amounts voted shall be summed and the proposal or package with the highest money amount voted in its favor is adopted as a formal proposal of the legislature. If the legislator's vote changes the outcome, compared to what it would have been had all others voted the same while this legislator did not vote, the legislator will pay an incentive tax equal to the minimum amount required from that legislator to produce a tie vote between the actual outcome and the alternative in a pairwise vote between the two. Alternative outcomes that are outvoted by a sufficiently narrow margin, as determined by criteria supplied by the Election Commission, shall also be presented by the legislature for possible inclusion in the referendum, in conformity with Subsection (b).

This subsection spells out the use of the VCG mechanism in legislative proceedings. This use of the mechanism results in those legislative proposals most likely to succeed in a referendum. Equally importantly, it also provides information needed for the assessment of approximate Lindahl taxes to each population subgroup and for the application of the Thompson insurance mechanism in the subsequent referendum. The legislative votes of dollar amounts for and against each reveal which voter subgroups are willing to pay large amounts and which are willing to pay very little to support or oppose a given proposal. This information would estimate the appropriate Lindahl taxes upon or transfers to each population subgroup. The closeness and direction of the vote would indicate whether the proposal has about an even chance of adoption, is almost certain to succeed, or is almost certain to fail.

(b) An advisory committee of statisticians appointed by the Election Commission shall determine the probability that a referendum as prescribed in Section 10 will approve each portion of a legislative proposal and each alternative portion. Those portions that face no competing proposals and that are found to have a probability of approval higher than [*95*] percent may be grouped together for a single up or down vote. Those portions with lower probabilities of approval and acceptable proposals facing competing alternatives shall appear as separate proposals on the referendum ballot. A noncompetitive proposal is acceptable for the ballot if the advisory committee of statisticians finds that the probability of acceptance exceeds [*ten*] percent. A group of competing proposals is acceptable as a group if the probability that a proposal from the group will pass exceeds [*ten*] percent and each competing proposal is acceptable if the probability of acceptance exceeds [*one*] percent. A budget proposal is defined to include every legislative proposal pursuant to the authority of Article III, Sections 3 and 4 and such other legislative proposals as are identified as budget proposals under Article II, Subsection 9(c). Budget proposals under Article III Section 4 shall include alternative funding levels for each kind of expenditure as separate proposals or as a continuous scale of options, over a range chosen on the basis of this probabilistic rule. Alternative budgets for inspection, auditing, and application of measures of performance of government programs shall be provided for as a set of separate budget proposals. When the official legislatures have decided their proposed legislative programs, the Speakers shall advise the Commission on the appropriate subject grouping of items on the ballot. Every legislative proposal must conform to the grouping selected by the Commission and within each proposal group it must state what it proposes (possibly including 'no action') for each subject and program in that group. However, a legislature may decline to propose legislation in an entire proposal group.

(c) Each legislative proposal pursuant to the authority of Article III, Sections 5, 6, 7, 8, or 9 shall be accompanied by a thorough, accurate analysis of its budget consequences. If said proposal requires a budget for its implementation, the legislature shall include it as a combined legislative and budget proposal as part of the overall proposal for the budget referendum ballot. Each such proposal, if included on the ballot, shall be subject to the rules of Subsection (b) on proposal groups.

These subsections control the agenda for referenda. There is no practical way to avoid giving some degree of agenda-setting power to a central authority such as the Election Commission. Therefore the proposal of subsection (b) gives the Election Commission and its advisory committee of statisticians a clear set of rules for carrying out its mandate, with little scope for discretion. Moreover, this set of rules can best be sustained by providing the Election Commission with the right incentives. Section 10 provides these incentives.

Subsection (c) requires that legislation other than ordinary government budget expenditures shall be coupled with its budget implications in a budget referendum. This provision would have an unmistakable sobering effect in situations where voters develop an urge to pass a well-intentioned law without considering its implementation. This effect is equally desirable for a war against drug trafficking or a war against another country.

(d) Using the official legislators' votes as guidance, each Speaker shall propose a set of taxes and, if necessary, positive transfers for each population subgroup represented in the legislature and, where appropriate, for each type of property, with a view to achieving a unanimous referendum vote for or against each legislative proposal that will appear in the same referendum. These taxes and transfers shall be itemized by proposal and by whether the tax basis is the household or an item of property. Upon receiving this tax proposal from its Speaker, each official legislature shall adopt a proposed schedule of taxes and transfers for each proposal, including the corresponding part, if any, of the continuation budget. The taxes to finance each proposal must pay for its entire expected cost, year by year, and the budget proposals as a whole from each legislature must have exact balance, inclusive of debt service payments and payments to the financial reserve as prescribed in Subsection 12(e), based on estimation procedures prescribed by the Election Commission. The Election Commission, advised by its statistical advisory committee, shall determine these estimation procedures taking account of foreseeable demographic changes and other changes affecting the sizes and economic circumstances of the population subgroups represented in the official legislatures. For identical or substantially identical proposals, according to the data from the official legislatures, the Election Commission shall consolidate the tax schedules proposed by the legislatures for each such proposal into a single schedule having the maximum likelihood of attaining a minimum-harm outcome (nearly unanimous in value terms) and a balanced budget. This consolidation shall also apply to compensation to property owners for property and easements to be acquired by court order.

There is no way to assess Lindahl taxes using information from a referendum, consistent with truth-telling voting and with efficient outcomes. The Election Commission must depend on information provided by the legislatures themselves and on the equivalent of income and property tax filings by citizens to assess these taxes. Therefore it must merge the tax portions of the budget proposals from the official legislatures into a single proposed tax schedule, using sound statistical methods. This step does not preclude providing each official legislature with an incentive for accuracy in its tax proposals, as is done in Section 10.

(e) A full and fair account of the facts and arguments for and against each plan, except for omissions or summaries required by considerations of military secrecy as prescribed by law, shall be assembled by the Election Commission, subject to the rules of evidence applicable to official legislative proceedings. These facts and arguments shall be distributed at least [*one month*] in advance of the referendum to all citizens eligible to vote.

Every citizen eligible to vote will receive a full and fair account of the arguments for and against each proposal, developed under rules of evidence similar to those applicable to courtroom proceedings. These arguments would resemble *Consumer Reports* analyses of durables and other consumer goods and services. On issues that are less concrete, such as environmental protection, the evidence on benefits is skimpy to nonexistent except for instances of extreme pollution, and so one would have to expect controversy similar to but more muted than what we have now.

This point might seem implausible when we view it from the perspective of present-day politics, but one must remember the sobering effect of estimated Lindahl taxes. Under the proposed system, beneficiaries and other proponents of a change, such as a shift to stricter environmental rules, would face clearly specified tax assessments designed to cover its entire cost. When these taxes are set by legislative proceedings without reference to referendum data on voter valuations, and when they are accurate for most voters, few voters would have reason to try to sway others' sentiments with misleading claims.

The importance of ambiguity of evidence on issues like pollution would depend on how well the estimated Lindahl taxes were allocated in the relevant referenda. If the enthusiasm for pollution control was centered among scientists and other faculty members at universities, who would have their own subgroup representation in the official legislatures, they would be obliged to express their enthusiasm in dollar terms, that is, in estimated Lindahl taxes. If there were disagreements within many demographic subgroups about how far controls should go, however, a member of each such subgroup would have an estimated Lindahl tax assessment for this issue equal to the average willingness to pay for the whole subgroup. The voting mechanism provides partial compensation for errors in Lindahl tax assessments, but there could still be some financial steam behind the disagreements about how stringent the anti-pollution incentives should be.

Therefore active public controversy may sometimes accompany the decision process, particularly when there are significant errors in the proposed Lindahl taxes. Voters will of course decide for themselves what to believe. The important thing is to place relevant, reliable information in their hands.

> (f) Beginning in the year [*2000*] and every [*twelfth*] year thereafter the budget proposals of the official legislatures shall include provision for a census of the population, designed and conducted in such a manner as to facilitate accurate implementation of Section 2. In addition, each official legislature shall include in the [*first*] budget proposal of its legislative term the funding of an analysis of trends in voter residence and registration to vote, to provide an authoritative basis for revision of the census numbers. These revisions shall be used to implement Section 2 in the selection of the official legislatures for the subsequent legislative term.

A periodic census would provide benchmark data for the allocation of legislative subgroups by location and demographic characteristics. Because of the importance of achieving accurate representation, the allocation can and should be updated every four years using voter registration and other data on voter migration. The census proposals would usually win approval because they promote efficient outcomes, which the balance of voter interests supports.

> Section 10. (a) Subject to Subsection 9(b), each legislative proposal from the primary official legislatures shall be presented in a referendum to all eligible voters, together with other proposals proposed under Subsection (d). There shall be a biennial budget proposal for the functions of government, which shall include a two-year extension representing its continuation. Each budget proposal shall also offer as an alternative 'no action' budget a set of programs representing a minimum program for public safety prescribed by a previously enacted law. This minimum program shall include provision for compensation of legislators, Speakers, Election Commissioners, the Chief of State, the Commander in Chief of the Armed Forces, and the two Vice Chiefs, for the census specified in Subsection 9(f), and for payment of government accounts payable, debt service, and scheduled payments to financial reserves as prescribed in this constitution. Each item in the 'no action' budget shall also be included in each larger budget proposal on the same subject in the referendum, and every item in the 'no action' budget shall be included in a budget category. Each regular budget referendum shall include the continuation of the budget adopted two years earlier and the 'no action' budget proposal for each proposal group. For non-budget proposals, the alternative of no action shall appear on the ballot. All no-action and continuation proposals herein prescribed shall appear on the ballot whether or not they meet the statistical tests prescribed in Subsection 9(b). Legislatures may at any time propose supplementary budgets and budget reductions whose costs shall include election costs. If they meet the statistical tests of Subsection 9(b) a referendum shall be held. Voting shall be secret, except that the matching of identified ballots to voters must be known to the Election Commission to carry out its duties under this section, and must be kept under permanent seal. The Election Commission shall also keep under seal all referendum-generated information about voter willingness to pay (by population subgroups) that could otherwise influence tax proposals under Subsection 9(d). The Election Commission may, however, use this information to assist in determining whether to propose the creation

of a new demographic subgroup under the provisions of Section 8 and Subsection 2(a) and to investigate possible conspiracies by voters to falsify their declared harms.

This subsection provides that a referendum on a budget program will always include several options for that program. One option will be to close down the program except for any part of it necessary for public safety. A second option will be to keep the current program unchanged. Then it will include such other options as have an acceptable likelihood of approval. For each such proposal, the tax consequences for each voter's family will be clearly stated. Further, it is a secret ballot. A voter who feels that the program structure is seriously wrong has the opportunity to influence it in the desired direction, and to insure against an unfavorable outcome. Voting will therefore be a serious, responsible step with appreciable, known personal financial consequences.

Votes and the information they generate on subgroup willingness to pay must be kept under seal and not be allowed to influence future tax proposals. (The confidentiality requirement would be similar to that applicable in the U.S. to individual income tax and social security information.) Otherwise voters will have an incentive to misrepresent their valuations because of their future tax consequences. The exception to this rule in the case of subdivision of a population subgroup, provided for here and in Section 8, does not create an incentive to voters to misrepresent their valuations because the tax consequences in the referendum itself on this decision cancel the subsequent tax consequences after its approval.

(b) For those proposals that the Election Commission places on the ballot, voters shall express their preferences among the proposals in monetary terms. They shall express such preferences in two ways. First, the Election Commission shall offer them insurance against each less-preferred proposal at a fair premium, based on the probabilities determined by the advisory committee of statisticians. The voter is expected to purchase insurance against each proposal other than the voter's most preferred proposal. The voter will receive the face value of said insurance for a referendum outcome that differs from the outcome that the voter most prefers. Second, each voter may declare, pairwise between every pair of mutually exclusive proposals, an uninsured harm that the voter would suffer if the outcome went against the voter's pairwise preference. The voter who declares uninsured harm shall also declare what the uninsured harm would be if (a) the outcome were the voter's least preferred rather than most preferred and if (b) the voter's income were higher by the amount of the greatest harm otherwise declared. Each such declaration of uninsured harm may not exceed [*ten*] percent of the voter's income and the sum of all declared uninsured harms on a ballot may not exceed [*twenty*] percent of the voter's income. The Election Commission shall set lower maximum declarations whenever legislative proceedings reveal that such maxima are appropriate. If the various amounts that a voter declares on a single ballot or on successive ballots are inconsistent with a technically rational, self-consistent set of preferences, the voter shall be required to bring them into conformity with same or, failing that, part or all of the voter's ballot shall be disqualified. If more than one manner of partial disqualification would satisfy the test, the voter shall select which disqualification to accept. The Election Commission shall sum the insurance plus the uninsured harms, subject to adjustment procedures set out in part (b) of the Technical Annex, and declare the outcome that results in the least aggregate harm [*provided that in order to enter into force, a legislative proposal must be approved by a voter declaration of net aggregate harm, in case it fails, of at least three times overall aggregate harm from its adoption declared by those who oppose it*]. It shall pay the insurance face value to those voters who insured against this outcome. It shall assess an incentive tax on each voter whose uninsured harm was great enough to change the outcome, setting the incentive tax on that voter as the amount that would have produced a tie vote in the referendum. It shall pay members of each official legislature an incentive fee prescribed by law, based on the accuracy with which the income effects predicted by that legislature's valuations predict voter income effects, and also based on the accuracy with which the legislature predicts the variability of declared harms for each proposal group, within each population subgroup. Corresponding procedures set out in the Technical Annex, part (d) shall apply for a proposal presented as a continuous scale of options. However, if no official legislature associates intangible values with some pairs of potential referendum outcomes, under part (a) of the procedure in the Technical Annex, then for such pairs no declarations of uninsured losses shall be accepted in the referendum procedure and the outcome shall be determined solely by the amounts of insurance purchased, without adjustments for income effects.

This subsection specifies Thompson insurance and the VCG mechanism as the mechanisms the nation will use to decide its government budget and other legislation. It provides an incentive payment to each official legislature for the accuracy of that legislature's estimates of income effects on uninsured harms. Finally, it specifies that the VCG mechanism enters the process only when there is reason to expect declarations of uninsured harm.

The declared harms, whether insured or uninsured, are what citizens are willing and able to pay to avoid an outcome harmful to their interests. Insured harms are usually prospective financial losses, and the fair insurance premium is its probability-weighted expected value. The voter, in buying the insurance, does in fact pay the expected value of the harm from the unwanted outcome. An uninsured harm declaration states the amount the voter will pay, if necessary, to reverse a bad outcome. Thus these amounts are unambiguous measures of willingness-to-pay.

The proviso in italics provides additional protection for the status quo, if a nation should, at the time of writing or amending the constitution, decide it wants this protection. In my view the rules and procedures of this constitution already provide enough protection against hasty, ill-considered ordinary legislation, so that the proviso in italics is unnecessary. However, for constitutional amendments such protection definitely seems appropriate, and is embodied in the amendment procedure in Article VI. Some sympathetic critics would argue that the same principle should apply to legislation as to constitutional amendments.

To operate this voting mechanism, the system would need to be only a little more complicated than what we do in elections now, where almost complete vote tallies are available the next morning. The basic summation task for dollar amounts requires more digits per vote than does the simple 'yes-no' tally. To pay off insurance and bill voters for their premium payments and incentive taxes, the Election Commission must identify voters and keep track of three distinct dollar amounts per voter per issue. This workload compares with that for a large business file of purchase orders and accounts receivable, with due dates and possible interest charges. The computational load is well within the capacity of existing computers. In the interest of speed, it would be desirable to have a small computer terminal in each voting booth (or each home) connected to a main frame computer. For a small country one central computer with a large multiplex input-output device could handle a day's election. For a country the size of the United States it would perhaps be necessary to have two tiers of main frames to handle the load. A local main frame computer could accept and total a million votes a day without difficulty, and the national central computer could receive and process totals and other summary information from 200 local main-frame computers.

With this arrangement, the computer screen could inform the voter of obvious errors and misunderstandings in a set of declarations of insurable and uninsurable harm. If the declarations were inconsistent with rational preferences, the screen would so inform the voter and suggest alternative ways to fix the problem. If the voter broke the rule limiting declarations of uninsured harm, the screen would so inform the voter of the unacceptable financial implications of the declaration and of the limit allowed, and of its budgetary and personal financial implications. Problems of these kinds could therefore be cleared up immediately during the voting process.

Feedback of insurance payoffs would be simple. Feedback of supplementary incentive taxes in response to declarations of uninsured harms would require some computations. Their economic importance is inversely proportional to the square of the population size, however, and so would not require much computer time for either a large or a small country.

> (c) Attempts to organize voter groups to misrepresent their harms shall be a felony with penalties prescribed by law.

Chapters 4 and 5 include analyses of the disincentive for a citizen to participate in an organized coalition to change the vote on an issue, or to go along with a wave of ill-considered popular sentiment on an issue. It pays to cheat on such a coalition and to be a contrarian. Some contentious, emotionally charged issues could nevertheless be vulnerable to irresponsible election tactics, and this problem could be worsened if voter conspiracies to engage in strategic voting were tolerated. One should note that under existing U.S. constitutional law, such conspiracies, such as crossover voting to nominate an opposite-party candidate that the conspirators hope to defeat later, receive the protection of the Bill of Rights. The language of a bill of rights, including a clear and restrictive definition of conspiracy, must therefore be carefully drawn. It should point toward policing the most blatant conspiracies, leaving trivial violations to be constrained by rational incentives.

> (d) A citizen, corporation, or group of citizens may offer budget proposals and other proposed legislation by petition to the Election Commission. The person or group offering such proposals shall post sufficient bond to cover a pro-rata share of incremental evaluation

and election costs due to the proposals, as defined by Subsection (f), and shall be liable for these costs whether the proposals succeed or fail, except in the case of proposals for measures of success under Subsection (h). The Election Commission shall specify procedures and venues for confidential copyright registration of such proposals, in whole or in part, while they are in the preparatory stages, to be used for determining incentive pay under Subsection 11(b). If the volume and quality of citizen petitions is high enough, in the judgement of the Election Commission, to justify it, the Commission shall ask the Speakers to participate with the Commission in a vote, under the procedure specified for a legislature in Subsection 9(a), on the question of whether to propose legislation to create a third official legislature. If they so decide, they shall prepare proposed taxes to finance it and shall place the entire proposal on a referendum ballot. Their incentive pay contingent on this proposal shall be that provided in Subsection 10(f). If such legislation receives approval, the Election Commission shall present all private proposals to the third official legislature, whose exclusive business shall be to prepare such proposals for the ballot. A third official legislature, if approved by referendum, may be abolished in a subsequent referendum. If there is no third official legislature, the Election Commission shall present all private proposals to both official legislatures, where they shall be subject to the same legislative procedures as are all other proposals. The Election Commission shall allow those proposals to appear on the ballot that meet the criteria of Subsection 9(b).

This subsection provides private-sector competition for the official legislatures, and thus provides a hedge against failures of these legislatures, for any reason, to serve voter interests. The language of this subsection flows from the presumption that it will be possible to prevent conspiracies within, or between two legislatures, or if not, that private competition can be fostered by a third official legislature created to support it. Otherwise the two legislatures could defraud the public and suppress such competition by misrepresenting the taxes to be assessed for a competing private proposal, and misrepresent the arguments for and against it. Private groups that discover imaginative, sound new proposals for government programs will have an incentive to develop these proposals for profit, in a manner patterned after an ordinary profit-seeking start-up enterprise. They could equally well discover sound ways to downsize or cut costs for ongoing government programs, also for profit, just in case the legislatures need such help.

> (e) [Each proposal for legislation under the authority of Article III, Sections 5, 6, 7, or 8 shall appear on two successive referendum ballots, except as otherwise provided under Article III Section 8. The first time it appears the legislation may be briefly though accurately summarized, as may the arguments for and against its adoption. The question put to the voters in this first referendum shall be, 'Shall this proposal be considered for adoption in the forthcoming referendum of {date}?' The criterion for success shall be {25%} of the votes cast. If voters reject this proposition, the proposal shall not appear on a subsequent referendum ballot until and unless the first vote is reversed, and the legislature that originated the proposal shall receive a reduction in its incentive payments. This reduction shall consist of the costs of placing the proposal on the ballot plus {20} percent of the net total harms declared by voters in rejecting it.]

In contrast to routine budget matters, for which as a rule voters have adequate advance notice and preparation, changes of criminal law, laws of contracts, torts, and so on, and in support of the conduct of foreign affairs, may require specific notice and preparation. Moreover, many voters may consider requests for such legislation burdensome and frivolous, and so may wish to vote them down on first notice. Requiring the proposer to have a good case for such legislation and risk a financial penalty if it fails the first try provides a hurdle.

Whether such a hurdle is appropriate depends on the costs and time delays for voters to become well informed. The procedure resembles that of the British Parliament, which requires more than one vote on a bill, with a time delay between votes, before it becomes law.

This approach is more humane than that purportedly used in the remote ancient Greek region of Lokris, as described in a speech by Demosthenes. He stated that the Lokrians changed only one law in two hundred years, 'because they had the marvelous custom that any proposal for a change of law must be made with a noose around the neck, and if the proposal was defeated the noose was drawn tight.' (Hansen, 1991, p. 174).[3]

> (f) The Compensation of each Election Commissioner for serving shall equal [*two*] times the average salary paid to official legislators as determined under Section 5; plus incentive pay of [*.02*] percent,

> for each subject group, of the net monetary value of the superiority, measured by total declared harms, of the programs approved by referenda over 'no action', net of the harms to those who prefer 'no action' to the approved programs; less [*.003*] percent, for each subject group, of the net total monetary value of the inferiority of the programs approved by referenda relative to 'no action,' for each population subgroup that on balance supported 'no action'; plus [*0.67*] percent of the cost and performance payments and penalties prescribed in Subsection 12(c) for the legislature that appoints executive officers (except that the penalty for revenue errors shall be based on the difference between actual revenues and planned revenues, rather than presumptive adjusted figures); less [*.02*] percent of all costs, including private costs, of the conduct of and participation in referenda sanctioned by the Election Commission during its term. The method of reckoning these costs shall be prescribed by law prior to the Commission's term.

It would create a perverse incentive for Election Commissioners to exclude promising proposals from the ballot if their incentive pay were based on the same formula as that for legislators. With that formula the Election Commission could generate monopoly rents for itself by limiting the number of proposals.

The proposed plan of compensation provides the optimal incentive to the commissioners. The benefit to voters of a new proposal on the ballot is the excess of the expected gain from having it there, taking sampling variability into account, over the administrative cost of including it. The proposed incentive payment for the Election Commission is at a maximum when the aggregate expected benefit to voters is at a maximum, and when the tax assessments are close enough to Lindahl taxes that all population subgroups show net support for the chosen alternative (disregarding disagreements within subgroups.) In particular, a proposal's costs are certain but its benefits are less certain, because they depend both on the accuracy of the estimates of its merits and on its chances of approval in the referendum. The Election Commission stands to gain from adding a sequence of proposals to the ballot when the aggregate benefits of the approved proposals, as declared by voters, exceed the costs of all proposals, approved and disapproved. Hence the incentive formula gives the Election Commission no incentive to disqualify sound proposals, regardless of source, nor any incentive to overload the ballot with too many proposals.

[(g) The Election Commission shall maintain an Election Fund in two parts, Fund A and Fund B. Fund A shall receive the insurance premiums, pay the insurance claims, receive the supplementary taxes provided for by Subsection (b), receive the incremental cost payments for private proposals prescribed by Subsection (d), and pay the costs of administration of elections. At the end of each legislative term, the surplus or deficit in this fund shall be allocated to voters according to the following rule. For each voter the Election Commission shall calculate what the amount in Fund A would have been if this voter had not participated in the referenda of that term. The fund adjusted in this way shall be divided by the number of voters, less one, and the quotient, if positive, shall be paid to this voter or if negative charged to this voter. Where applicable, the payment or charge to the voter shall be adjusted as indicated in the Technical Annex, part (d). If this method of division leaves a residual surplus or deficit in the fund, the residual shall be carried forward into the next legislative term and placed in Fund B. If the surplus or deficit in Fund B exceeds, in absolute value, [one-half] the planned amount in the financial reserve prescribed in Subsection 12(e), the excess shall be transferred to said financial reserve.]

The appropriate form of this provision depends on the size of the country. Suppose that the Thompson insurance easily pays for all election costs and provides a significant refund per voter. In a small island country or city state, each voter's incentive to tell the truth could be affected appreciably by the expected refund if the refund would change appreciably in response to the amount of this voter's declared harm, whether insured or uninsured. Then the system should provide each voter with a refund that is independent of that voter's declared harm. Chapter 6 and its appendices present the procedures for determining refunds appropriate for this problem, and show the order of accuracy that they can attain.

In a country of much more than a thousand families, the effect of one's vote on one's refund is negligible so that the formula for the refund can be arbitrary and, in particular, can balance the budget precisely. As we illustrate in Chapter 4, both the VCG tax and the likely refund in a town of 900 families, though small, are enough that there is a risk of affecting incentives. In a country the size of the United States the VCG tax is an infinitesimal fraction of a penny, and although the refund due to Thompson insurance does not depend on country size, the effect of a single vote on this refund is similarly small. For all but the smallest countries or towns, therefore, subsection (g) can either be omitted or considerably simplified. If the writers of the constitution wished to be sure that incentives were unaffected in close votes, they would still retain the feature for yes-or-no votes that each family's refund would be a pro-rata share of what the amount in Fund A would have been if this family had not participated in the election. This rule prevents a big change in the family's refund when the family's vote is pivotal and the insurance mechanism therefore changes from a profit to a loss or the reverse.

> (h) Legislation approved by the voters shall be deemed in law to be a contract between the legislature that proposed it and the voters. Measures or indicators of the success or effectiveness of government proposals shall be prescribed by law and shall be binding on the government. These measures of success shall be enacted or renewed in a separate law in the fourth year of each legislative term under the supervision of the outgoing Election Commission, to take effect for first and subsequent budget legislation of the following term, except that the first continuation budget, if enacted in whole or in part, shall be subject to the previously enacted measures of success that applied to it when it was first enacted as a regular budget. These measures of success shall include a procedure for estimating revenues for each proposed tax schedule and for determining those errors of estimation that are unpredictable and those that are avoidable. This law shall also prescribe measures of success for the functions of inspection, auditing, and application of measures of performance. At any time the Election Commission may accept private proposals for revised measures of success to apply to a future budget, provided that a referendum on these measures is held at least [*two months*] before the referendum on the budget to which they would apply and provided that the citizens offering such a proposal have no proprietary interest, direct or indirect, in a pending budget proposal for the budget referendum.
>
> (i) Legislators shall be immune from lawsuits concerning their individual conduct in the course of legislative business. However, executive officers, the legislature that appoints them, and the legislature that performs inspection, auditing, and application of measures of performance shall not be immune from lawsuits arising from the outcomes of legislation once enacted. The criteria for standing and admissibility of suits shall be identical to those for suits against private parties as specified by the laws of torts and contracts,

taking due account of the penalties prescribed in Article III, Section 4, that form part of the legislative contract and that shall have the status of liquidated damages.

(j) Election Commissioners shall be immune from lawsuits concerning their conduct of elections, except (a) that a Commissioner who is impeached and removed from office may be sued for damages arising from the misconduct that is specified in the bill of impeachment, and (b) that even without impeachment Election Commissioners may be sued for fraud or false advertising, in connection with official descriptions of legislative proposals that they have approved. The criteria for standing and admissibility of suits of the second kind shall be identical to those for suits against private parties as specified by the laws of torts and contracts governing fraud and advertising.

(k) An Election Commissioner may be impeached and removed from office under the same procedures as those prescribed by Article IV, Section 5 for the Chief of State and for other high officials, except that the trial shall be held before the more successful of the official legislatures that had appointed the Commissioner. The grounds shall be those for removal of a legislator, and in addition may include the flagrant and malicious disregard for the law.

These two subsections place legislators in the same position as the owners of a large business firm with major commitments, and are the key to implementing Article I. Their incentive payments may enrich them, but they must deliver on their commitments. Because this combination of incentives is sound, it is important to specify them, to avoid misunderstanding. The concept of sovereign immunity is so nearly universal among existing governments that an opposite intention must be spelled out.

Section 11. (a) Incentive pay for legislators, official or private, shall be based on the value of their proposals and the accuracy with which they estimate voters' preferences. In the case of proposals by official legislatures, the declared harms used to calculate this incentive pay shall be adjusted by the difference between the legislature's proposed tax assessments and the actual tax assessments, where applicable. Subject to the modifications prescribed by Sections 10 and 12 and by Article III, Section 4, the aggregate incentive pay for a legislature for each of its proposals that is adopted will be [*0.1*] percent of the budget amount contained in the proposal plus [*30*] percent of the total declared insured and uninsured harm from non-adoption, net of the declared harm from adoption, relative to the next most valuable distinct and different alternative proposed by another legislature, less [*5*] percent of the net inferiority of those proposals, relative to distinct and different alternatives on the ballot, for each population subgroup that on net would have supported an alternative proposal in the group, under the legislature's proposed taxes and accurate taxes for the alternative. If, however, the only such alternative is 'no action', the incentive pay shall instead be [*0.1*] percent of the budget amount contained in the approved proposal plus [*3*] percent of the total declared insured and uninsured harm from non-adoption, net of the declared harm from adoption, less [*.5*] percent of the net inferiority of those proposals relative to 'no action', for each population subgroup that on net supported no action under the legislature's proposed taxes. In the case of legislation to subdivide a population subgroup, these incentive payments shall be calculated using the proposed new subgroups as if they were already approved.

(b) The incentive pay for those proposal groups on which official legislatures make identical or equivalent new proposals shall be divided equally between them. If a private legislative proposal receives voter approval, the incentive pay shall be divided between the private party and the official legislature(s) that deliberated on it. If the proposal on the ballot is identical or substantially and technically equivalent to the proposal submitted by the private petitioner, the petitioner shall receive [*two-thirds*] of the incentive pay provided for in Subsection 11(a), adjusted so that the private share is not reduced by the net total harms declared by those voters who oppose the proposal. If the legislative process revises the proposal, or if the final proposal on the ballot merges the private proposal with elements that originated in the legislature, the petitioner shall receive less than [*two-thirds*] of the incentive pay provided for in Subsection 11(a) after the foregoing adjustment, and instead shall receive a proportion to be determined prior to the referendum by the Election Commission after it determines original authorship of the components of the proposal from the legislative history of this and related proposals and from the documented history of the private proposal. When substantially equivalent proposals appear in both records, whichever source documented it first shall receive full credit for it. The petitioner's incentive pay shall be reduced by the same percentage share of costs, specified by

Subsection 10(d), as the petitioner's share of the adjusted incentive pay. The share of the incentive pay not paid to the private petitioner shall be paid to the official legislature(s) that deliberated on it, with the penalty for harms declared by some subgroups scaled down in this proportion. If a portion of a continuation budget wins in the referendum and if this portion was also proposed by a currently sitting primary official legislature, three-fourths of the resulting incentive pay shall be paid to the members of the legislature(s) of whose budget it is a continuation and one-fourth shall be paid to the primary official legislature that proposes to continue it. Subsequently this portion shall be deemed to be part of the budget proposal of this currently sitting primary official legislature. If a portion of a continuation budget wins in the referendum and if no currently sitting official legislature proposed it, the entire incentive pay for this portion shall be paid to the members of the legislature(s) of whose budget it is a continuation. If more than one legislature had originally shared the incentive pay of said budget portion, they shall divide their portion of the continuation incentive pay equally.

(c) The incentive pay to each official legislature shall be divided among its members as follows: [*One half*] shall be divided equally among them and [*one half*] shall be divided among them in proportion to their minimum individual incomes as determined under Section 5. Incentive pay for a sitting legislature shall be placed in escrow and paid to its members at the end of their term.

This section pays legislators, in addition to their opportunity costs of serving, (1) a small flat percentage of 'sales' plus (2) a bonus for the superiority of the legislature's winning proposals over the nearest losing competitor, minus (3) a penalty (for an official legislature) for errors of the legislature's estimates of subgroup Lindahl taxes including those for proposed new subgroups, plus or minus (4) the adjustments prescribed elsewhere in the document. The first three of these percentages must at least be generous enough to compensate for the unavoidable risks of penalties and lawsuits due to shortfalls of performance. Although Election Commissioners and Speakers receive incentive pay for the superiority of chosen legislation over 'no action', a major portion of a legislature's compensation depends on the superiority of its winning program over the nearest competing program. This feature, inappropriate for the Election Commission's compensation, matches the rewards to successful private businesses. The object is to induce legislatures to perform about as well as private businesses do.

For this reason the rules should keep to an efficient low level the risk of the theft of the intellectual property that is contained in sound proposals, so as to protect legislatures to a degree comparable to the degree that private businesses are protected. Subsection 10(d) protects private legislatures from having their ideas copied, and the incentive pay taken, by an official legislature. Subsection 11(b) protects official legislatures from having their proposals leaked and used by a private legislature.

The legislation to create a new subdivision of a population subgroup has its own estimated Lindahl taxes and transfers, so that a new subgroup that expects lower future taxes to result from the subdivision will pay the expected value of the gain, while the new subgroup that expects higher future taxes will receive compensation. Hence, there is no harmful incentive effect from permitting the Election Commission to use voting patterns in referenda to influence legislative proposals to subdivide a population subgroup, as provided in Section 8.

> (d) All official legislators shall be exempt from tax assessments under the budgets for which they have made proposals until the first regular budget enacted after they leave office.

The decision mechanism in the legislature and the incentive payments together give legislators an incentive to propose sound programs based on accurate information, provided that these legislators do not subsequently pay the taxes that their proposals help to determine. Such tax payments would distort their incentives. Consequently this tax exemption must be part of their compensation.

> (e) The compensation of the Speaker of an official legislature shall be [*two*] times the average pay, including incentive pay less penalties, of the members of that official legislature.

The Speaker's role is closely similar to that of the chair of the board of directors of a corporation, which implies that the Speaker's income should depend on the legislature's performance, including the rewards and penalties of fulfilling lawful contracts with the public, where applicable. This incentive structure is the principal protection against false advertising and other misrepresentation of the legislature's program, although it is reinforced by the Election Commission's role in supervising electoral claims. This safeguard, and the Speaker's prior reputation for judicial probity, provide a substitute for reputational capital that an official legislature has little opportunity to accumulate.

> Section 12. (a) That official or private sitting legislature whose budget proposals approved by referendum sum to the largest aggregate total shall appoint executive officers to carry out the approved budget programs and enforce the approved laws, except as provided otherwise under Subsection (b) and elsewhere herein. These executive officers shall serve at the pleasure of the legislature. Prior to a biennial budget referendum each legislature shall publish its proposed team of executive officers. In case two or more legislatures have received approval for identical budget totals, the choice of legislature for this role shall be determined by the toss of an honest coin supervised by the Election Commission.
>
> (b) An official legislature not responsible for executive functions shall be responsible for inspection, auditing, and application of measures of performance. If more than one official legislature is not responsible for executive functions, the one gaining the largest incentive pay under Section 11 of this Article shall be responsible for inspection, auditing, and application of measures of performance. If in this circumstance two or more official legislatures have gained the same incentive pay under Section 11, the choice of official legislature for inspection, auditing, and application of measures of performance shall be determined by the toss of an honest coin supervised by the Election Commission.

The winning legislature must be responsible for delivering on its program, and be subject to the rewards and penalties for the performance of the program, under the administration by executives it selects. The official legislature that is in second place wins the second-place prize, the opportunity to enforce performance on the winning legislature and thereby to earn incentive payments. These payments notwithstanding, the legislature in this role might perceive an incentive to be less than diligent because the roles might later be reversed, except that if it were to fail to apply the law properly it would expose itself to lawsuits.

> (c) The incentive pay of legislators in the legislature that appoints executive officers shall be reduced/increased by [*35*] percent of all cost overruns/underruns and shall be increased or reduced by

specified functions of the indicators of government performance under the legislation provided for in Subsection 10(h), as prescribed by law. The legislature responsible for inspection and audit shall calculate adjusted budget revenues, at the end of the budget period, by correcting the total for unpredictable changes in the numbers of citizens in the official population subgroups due to changes in status such as from employed to unemployed. This adjustment shall conform to the law on measures of performance. The Election Commission shall calculate the presumptive adjusted revenues and the presumptive planned revenues corresponding to the tax assessments that had been proposed by each official legislature for the budget just ending. The incentive pay of each official legislature shall be reduced by [*three*] percent of the absolute value of the discrepancy between presumptive adjusted budget revenues for that legislature and the presumptive planned budget revenues for the budget as enacted. For acquisitions of property and easements authorized by a referendum, the incentive pay of a legislature shall be reduced by [*five*] percent of the amount that the affected property owners have insured against financial harm (if any) arising from the success of this legislative proposal, except for noncompensable harms specified in Article III Section 5, after correcting the amount insured for the difference between actual compensation and the compensation the legislature had proposed for the property and easements. This reduction of incentive pay is additional to and separate from all other incentive pay adjustments herein prescribed. Cost overruns/underruns for a government program shall be assessed/allocated to voters in proportion to their taxes assessed for this program. For this purpose a 'program' means a budget proposal group or a portion of it that for each voter subgroup has a single tax assessment rate per taxpayer, and a single rate for each class of property. The pay of an executive officer shall be a fixed salary plus a fraction or multiple of the incentive pay received by a legislator under this subsection and Subsection 10(h).

(d) The incentive pay for the legislature responsible for inspection, auditing, and application of measures of performance shall include [*30*] percent of all improper or unauthorized costs recovered by this activity and shall be a function of the performance measures for this activity as prescribed by law.

These provisions are a central feature of the implementation of Article I, and provide specific rewards and penalties for the conformity of results to promises of the approved legislative program. The specified penalties, where applicable, provide legislators with a shield from lawsuits under Subsection 10(i) arising from errors in budgeting for which they are either penalized or exempt from penalty. The particulars of what constitutes a proper basis of a lawsuit will be prescribed by law in conformity with Subsection 10(i).

Subsection (c) exempts the responsible legislature from penalties for unpredictable changes in economic conditions, but provides it with a strong incentive to predict revenues as accurately as possible. The procedure for setting taxes prescribed by subsection 9(d) removes the traditional incentive to existing governments to overestimate revenues, but there is still a need for an incentive to estimate revenues accurately.

Executive officers' pay includes the equivalent of stock options, as well as salary, with precise terms to be negotiated at the time they are hired. Other miscellaneous provisions deal with appropriately scaled incentive pay for a legislature that does not control the government but contributes to its functioning.

> (e) The government shall plan to maintain a financial reserve of readily marketable assets equal to [*three*] percent of the approved biennial budget, for the purpose of paying unanticipated budget deficits other than those provided for in Subsection (c). These assets shall be located within the national boundaries and shall not include currency or financial claims issued by a foreign government nor shall it include the government's own bonds. Its balance of national currency shall not exceed [*0.2*] percent of the biennial budget. Whenever the financial reserve differs from [*three*] percent of the approved biennial budget by more than [*0.5*] percent but less than [*three*] percent, the next biennial budget proposal shall include a schedule of uniform payments to or from the financial reserve scaled to restore the reserve to the planned figure within [*four*] years. Whenever the difference is [*three*] percent or more, the next biennial budget proposal shall include a schedule of uniform payments to or from the financial reserve scaled to restore the reserve to the planned figure within [*six*] years. If the difference is a deficit and the reserve is exhausted, the government shall issue full faith and credit bonds with a maturity schedule to conform to the prescribed schedule of payments to the reserve. The incentive pay of each Election

> Commissioner shall be reduced by [*0.1*] percent of the absolute value of the discrepancy between adjusted budget revenues and the officially planned budget revenues that had been stated in the budget as enacted, for each biennial budget enacted under the Commissioner's supervision.

Although Section 9(d) requires a plan for exact budget balance for each legislative proposal, and although there are strong incentives for accuracy of these plans in other sections, there must be a provision for random errors in the estimates and errors due to unpredictable changes in economic conditions. Subsection 12(c) promptly allocates cost overruns and underruns to particular citizens, but other unexpected changes in outlays and revenues can be absorbed in a reserve fund and worked off over a period of years.

Adjustment of budget revenues as provided in Subsection 12(c) assures that no official will be penalized for unanticipated macroeconomic circumstances beyond the government's control. Legislatures and Election Commissioners may be penalized, however, for foreseeable errors of revenue estimation. The intent is to require responsible budgeting, producing budget balance over a period of years. The language of this subsection complements the incentives of Subsection 12(c).

> (f) Until the first budget referendum of the legislative term, the executive team from the end of the previous term shall continue in office in a caretaker role. In its proposals for the budget referendum each legislature shall specify the executive team it has selected. After the referendum the team chosen by the winning legislature shall take office until the next budget referendum unless an executive team is replaced by another team to serve the remainder of its term. No member of an official legislature may serve as an executive official or employee.

These provisions primarily copy practices of parliamentary government, except that a successful legislature will normally employ professional managers from the private sector and will not complicate its job by direct involvement in executive functions.

Article III: Powers of the Government and Limitations Thereto

Section 1. (a) All powers herein permitted to 'the government' refer to powers exercised in conformity with the procedures and restrictions specified in this constitution.

(b) The government may enact every law that receives unanimous consent or where a statement of indifference or voter absence may imply consent, provided (a) that the Election Commission conducts a diligent effort to locate every absent voter and to obtain an absentee ballot and (b) that a law that is inconsistent with Section 2 must have the freely given, voluntary written consent of each voter whose rights the law abridges.

A law that would otherwise violate the bill of rights or another part of the constitution will be valid if all voters know about it and no voter dissents. The main point of having this provision is that every right may be waived if the waiver is voluntary.

Section 2. [Bill of rights. Standard stuff, including strict prohibition of retroactive laws. Strict prohibition of involuntary servitude in any form, except that in the case of foreign invasion or an imminent threat of same, the government may use emergency powers to compel military service for up to a maximum of sixty days by citizens represented in official legislatures and qualified to vote, whose compensation shall be prescribed by law. Freedom of association and of political expression shall not include freedom to form coalitions or conspiracies by voters having the purpose of misrepresenting the harms to them of legislative proposals on the ballot.]

Retroactive provisions now arise most often when a tax law or a restriction on property comes under consideration in a national legislature, with full publicity, for an extended period before it is enacted. The rationale then is that many investors will arrange to avoid taxes or restrictions by redirecting their investments and other property during this period of consideration. Whatever the merits of that rationale, it does not apply to a system that assesses accurate Lindahl taxes for programs that affect property values. Backdating of laws breaches the contract entered into by the adoption of previous laws altered by the new ones without contributing to economic efficiency and growth, and is therefore prohibited.

The use of estimated Lindahl taxes, where young persons of military age are qualified to vote and to be represented in official legislatures, will largely eliminate any temptation to use conscription. It is nevertheless wise to say so while permitting its temporary emergency use if conscripts receive full compensation, as would approximately occur with estimated Lindahl taxes.

> Section 3. [Scope and terms of permitted forms of official income redistribution from rich to poor. Specified taxes for this purpose.] These provisions may not be modified, amplified, or compromised by ordinary legislation.

Chapter 2 has a full discussion of the reason for placing this section in the constitution.

> Section 4. (a) Pursuant to laws enacted by procedures specified in Article II, the government may acquire property by compulsory court order for public purposes such as highway and sewer construction, provided that previous owners are compensated by [*five*] percent in excess of fair market value of the property acquired and of the diminution of fair market value of adjacent or associated property of the same owners that the government does not acquire. The government may purchase goods and services at market prices to further the purposes of this section, Sections 5, 6, 8, 9, and Article II, Section 9 and Subsection 12(b). The government may obtain by compulsory purchase easements from property owners restricting the private use and enjoyment of their properties for furtherance of the general welfare as provided by law, provided that all owners required to provide such easements are compensated by [*five*] percent in excess of the reduction of fair market value of said properties that results from the purchase of all such easements for a given specific purpose, except as otherwise provided in Section 5.
>
> (b) The government may collect taxes in the manner prescribed in Article II, to finance the activities authorized herein. For this purpose it may require all citizens to file periodic reports of their incomes from all sources, to identify their property income by its industry and location, and to provide such other information as may be necessary to identify each citizen's membership in a population subgroup for the purposes of Article II, Subsection 2(a). The

government may not collect money as taxes or fees nor disburse it in any manner except as prescribed by law.

(c) In addition to the compensation provided for under Article II, the government may provide such additional compensation to officials as is prescribed by law.

(d) The government may issue full faith and credit bonds to finance budget deficits in conformity with Article II, Subsection 12(e).

(e) The government may coin money and issue currency up to a total not to exceed [___ *pesos*]. [*It may not change the quantity of currency in circulation, either by destruction, creation, or payment into or out of the financial reserve, by more than two percent of this amount in a year nor by more than three percent of this amount in a four-year period. Deviations of the amount in circulation shall be restored to the authorized amount according to its own schedule with the same trigger points and correction schedule as those prescribed for the national financial reserve in Article II, Subsection 12(e).*]

[*(f) The government may not operate, franchise, nor have a financial interest, direct or indirect, in a banking institution nor create nor authorize the creation of a Central Bank. The government may not buy, sell, nor have a financial interest in the currency or in other obligations of a foreign government or of foreign financial institutions.*]

(g) The government may not acquire goods and services nor lend, rent, or deliver to private hands goods and services it has acquired, except as prescribed by law.

(h) The government may issue patents and copyrights for limited periods to inventors, tradespersons, and authors to protect their discoveries, trademarks, writings, and other original works, except that, wherever monitoring and assessment of economic value is practicable, the government shall instead offer prizes or royalties for limited periods approximating the economic value of the discoveries, etc.

(i) [*To the extent possible, all activities of the government, including the design and production of military weapons, communications except only military communications within military operations, and transportation, shall be contracted out to private firms. The executive team, subject to independent inspection and audit as prescribed in Subsection 12(b) and elsewhere herein, shall supervise the fulfillment of these contracts. Streets and highways shall be private toll roads except where their value is greater without tolls, due to the costs of collecting tolls, as determined by law. Career government employees shall be limited to the following categories: (1) a secretariat for each official legislature and a secretariat for the Election Commission; (2) magistrates and judges provided for in Article V and such court officers as they may appoint; (3) military officers in the line of command, their operational staffs including intelligence, and combat personnel; and (4) officials and operatives responsible for such anti-terrorist and other police intelligence functions as are prescribed by law. Competition for the intelligence functions shall be provided by parallel, independent units within the government and by private firms. The roles of career military officers and reservists shall be competitive in the development of military tactics, proposals for weapons selection, and troop training, but shall come under unified command for military operations as prescribed by law. Logistics and other military support functions shall be performed by military reserve units and private firms as prescribed by law. Promotion of career employees in categories (1), (3), and (4) shall be decided by the legislature that selects executive officers, after receiving the advice of the Commander in Chief for category (3) and of the chief executive official for category (4).*]

A system of estimated Lindahl taxes must by definition compensate everyone whose property is expropriated for a public purpose or who is harmed by a law, including zoning restrictions, environmental legislation, and so on. Similarly, a citizen who benefits through ownership of shares in a business that benefits from a new highway will pay a tax assessment based on that benefit. Implementation requires a reporting system similar to an income tax system, in addition to the census.

Contracting everything possible out to the private sector avoids the monopoly power that would otherwise develop in a tenured bureaucracy. This procedure supports the aim of minimizing monopoly power in government agencies. Although some intelligence work is of such a sensitive character that it requires the employment of specialists bound to secrecy, even this function can have the benefit of private competition. These provisions are easily enforced because the procedures for legislation will lead legislators and voters to abide by them in their own self-interest.

They would know about the problem of inefficiencies of government operations and would vote accordingly.

The monetary and banking provisions suggested in Subsections (e) and (f), if adopted, would prevent the use of inflation to circumvent taxation, unrelated to benefits, to finance special projects favored by interest groups, reinforcing the balanced-budget requirement in Article II, Subsection 12(e), which prevents the use of deficits for such a purpose. The strict assignment of central banking functions to the private sector (possibly including foreign banks) implies that this function will also be performed according to the market test, and that access to it will be governed by competition. Inasmuch as a rational, well-informed electorate would choose such provisions in ordinary legislation, these provisions, like the preference for private-sector in the present Subsection (i), might be considered redundant. By the same token, as just noted, their enforcement would be easy. Whether they should be entrenched in the constitution is arguable and uncertain.

> Section 5. (a) Under the procedures of Article II, the government may enact and enforce laws that define ordinary crimes and misdemeanors, for the protection of public safety and for the implementation of specific laws authorized by this constitution. If laws enacted under this section harm owners of some properties or reduce the incomes of some citizens whose activities, previously legal, become unlawful, these effects shall be considered easements for the purposes of Subsection 4(a).
>
> (b) The government may prohibit and punish the counterfeiting of its coin, currency, bonds, and of private securities and other private objects of value, however, without compensating citizens for the loss of income they might have received from such activities. In conformity with international law, the government may prohibit and punish felonies committed on the high seas.

While conferring the police power on the government, this provision prohibits it from using this power to evade the requirement to compensate citizens for compulsory easements. Although the requirement to assess Lindahl taxes as accurately as possible might suffice for this purpose, this provision leaves no room for misunderstanding. As in the case with Section 4, legislators and voters will comply with it easily in their own self-interest.

Section 6. (a) Under the procedures of Article II, the government may enact and enforce laws defining those kinds of contracts and contract provisions that will be enforced in official courts and, clarifying for new and unanticipated circumstances, those kinds of contracts that this constitution prohibits under Section 7. The government may not thereby create new prohibitions other than those listed in Section 7, however. In the case of contracts that are neither prohibited nor expressly sanctioned by law, the parties to such contracts shall exhaust every remedy that the contracts themselves provide before seeking recourse in an official court. Subject to this provision, the official courts shall accept jurisdiction to interpret and enforce all contracts not specifically prohibited by law. The government may pay court fees and fees of private arbitrators arising from government business, including amicus curiae submissions.

(b) The government may enact and enforce laws governing bankruptcy. The government may prescribe by law uniform units of measure and definitions, measures or indicators of quality for private goods and services. Such units, definitions, etc., shall have no restrictive effect on goods and services offered for sale unless such restrictions are expressly provided for by easements in conformity with Subsection 4(a).

The courts shall not be permitted to pick and choose which contracts they wish to enforce. Although there is a place for standard weights and measures, the government may not use these to introduce back door regulation or to restrict free contracting.

Section 7. [List of prohibited private contracts.]

Contracts to commit murder would no doubt be prohibited in every civilized country. Contracts that harm third parties in other ways might also be prohibited, such as racial or religious covenants on real estate. A nation may also reach a consensus that it must prohibit certain private vices, and in some cases one might even make a persuasive case for doing so in terms of third-party effects. In any event, there will be such a list of prohibited contracts.

Section 8. (a) The government shall conduct foreign affairs as prescribed by law. No official or private person shall negotiate or conclude treaties with a foreign government, except as authorized by law. The government may negotiate treaties and propose their provisions as legislation. If approved in a referendum, a treaty or a part thereof may be revoked only in a manner provided for in the treaty itself or else under the procedure and requirements prescribed in Article VI, Section 1 for constitutional amendments. The government may enact and enforce laws governing immigration and naturalization. The government may enact and enforce laws delimiting the nation's territory and may acquire or cede territory in conformity with international law, except that a proposal to cede territory shall be subject to the procedures and requirements prescribed in Article VI, Section 1 for constitutional amendments.

(b) The government may establish and support armed forces.

(c) The government may declare war, following the legislative procedures prescribed in Article II. In the event of foreign invasion or an imminent threat to the armed forces, however, the Commander in Chief may order the armed forces to defend themselves and to defend the nation's territory, following emergency procedures prescribed by law. No private person or group or persons may make war or maintain troops, except that in the event of foreign invasion or an imminent threat to citizens' homes and property, they may form temporary militias in their own defense. This provision shall not restrict the right of citizens to organize private organizations of security guards or to supply police and military services to government as prescribed by law.

Authority to conduct foreign affairs may be implicit in Sec. 4 and in Article II, but Section 8 is nevertheless appropriate. Declarations of war ordinarily require due process, but it is prudent to have procedures for extreme emergencies. The suggested rules are an example, but it is difficult to analyze alternative possibilities from a standpoint of incentives and the balancing of risks. A new nation's leader or leaders will no doubt have their own ideas on this matter.

Section 9. [(a) The national government may delegate governmental powers to regional or local authorities, either created ad hoc from time to time or created on a permanent basis, as prescribed by law, provided that, in the referendum for the enabling legislation, the sum of the absolute values of declared harms both of voters who favor and of voters who oppose the legislation outside the participating regions or localities shall not exceed {10} percent of the net total declared harms from nonadoption in the participating regions or localities.]

[(b) The legislation creating a regional or local authority may establish that this authority shall conform to Article II, (except that the size of its official legislatures may be scaled as appropriate and will normally have more finely subdivided demographic subgroups than those in the national legislatures), and shall conform to Article III, Sections 1(b), 2, 4(a), 4(b), 4(f), 4(g), 4(i), 5(a), 7, and 10, and to such other articles and sections of this constitution as this legislation may provide. Once such regional or local authorities are established by such legislation, in the process of proposing, each official legislature shall employ an official legislature from each regional and local authority as a committee for determining the regional/local benefits and costs, and their allocations by demographic subgroups, of subsequent legislative proposals. The compensation of legislatures of a regional or local authority shall be governed by the same rules as those herein prescribed for national legislatures, except that the national legislatures shall be solely responsible for the executive functions, and their related incentives, for national legislation.]

[(c) If the property owners and residents of a locality agree unanimously thereto, the governance of the locality shall be determined by a lawful contract among them, without authorization by legislation, provided that this contract satisfies all holders of easements and conforms to all covenants that apply to any and all property in the locality, and provided also that the parties to the contract post public notice of its provisions at least 180 days prior to its coming into force, so that legislation relating to its effects on other property or persons may be proposed and enacted if appropriate.]

The most important point is that many regional problems can be said to have no effect on other regions only if the regional boundaries are picked to fit that particular problem. If such boundaries can be found, an efficient procedure would be to create an ad hoc regional government to deal with each such problem. Subordinate governments in a conventional federal system can meet efficiency criteria, and can implement accurate Lindahl taxes, only by rare accident unless the nation consists of several separate islands, or the equivalent. In the case of the U.S., Hawaii could have a permanent subordinate government, for example, without much concern about the effects of local laws on other jurisdictions.

Subsection (c) allows the creation of towns and local governments by proprietors, by condominium agreement, or by any other contract among the owners and residents. Such arrangements would especially flourish under this constitution, which prevents arbitrary restrictions on land use and on contracts. Examples in the United States where proprietary developments created towns on farm land are Reston, Virginia; Columbia, Maryland; and Disneyland, Florida. An example of an entire town operated as a condominium (having started as a proprietary development) is Arden, Delaware. Smaller examples of condominium by contract are of course abundant. Examples of voluntary neighborhood associations or contractual arrangements that provide some of the services of local government are especially numerous in St. Louis City and County, Missouri.[4] These have succeeded despite a legal climate that is in some ways hostile to such developments.

A nation as large as the United States, and perhaps even much smaller nations, would probably have to have permanent local governments simply because the national legislatures would otherwise be too unwieldy if the were large enough to have full sets of demographic subgroups. Procedures for legislative coordination in the review of proposed laws would then be necessary for all laws of national scope that had regional differences in their impact. Although I think that efficient coordination is possible and workable, it would be a major project to work out and analyze its procedures. We discuss the issues about workability and legislative workloads in Chapter 4.

> Section 10. No power or authority herein granted may be delegated to any person, commission, or other body except as expressly authorized in this constitution. Neither the executive authority nor the courts may impose rules, regulations, or other comparable restraints on private persons other than such rules, regulations, and restraints as are duly enacted in legislation. This constitution has the force of law and may not be compromised nor amended except as provided in Article VI, Section 2.

Regulatory bodies and administrative agencies have proven their ability to impose arbitrary and capricious restraints on individual freedom, so that almost every modern government has extensively substituted the rule of officials for the rule of law. Such procedures would be highly unlikely to pass the test of an estimated Lindahl tax, but a specific prohibition in the constitution nevertheless has the virtue of providing a clear basis for challenging questionable legislation that might otherwise come into force.

Article IV: Chief of State and Commander in Chief

Section 1. Each official legislature shall, at the beginning of its term, nominate a candidate for the ceremonial function of Chief of State, a candidate for Commander in Chief of the Armed Forces, a candidate for Vice Chief of State, and a candidate for Vice Commander in Chief of the Armed Forces. These candidates shall be four different citizens. Private legislative enterprises may also nominate such candidates under the provisions of Article II, Subsection 10(d). These candidates shall be presented to voters under the same procedures as those for legislation, Article II, Sections 8 through 11, inclusive. The winner of each of these contests shall serve for a term of four years and may serve successive terms, except that the Commander in Chief may serve at most [*three*] terms, except in a time of war or of extreme emergency coming under the provisions of Article III, Section 8. If the Chief of State or Commander in Chief ceases to serve due to death or disability, the Vice Chief shall serve as Chief for the remainder of the term. In that event candidates for Vice Chief shall be nominated and presented in a referendum, to be elected to serve the remainder of the unexpired term. If the office of Chief falls vacant when there is no Vice Chief, the official legislature that appoints executive officials (or if neither does, the official legislature that performs the inspection and audit functions) shall appoint an Acting Chief to serve until a referendum to fill the positions of Chief and Vice Chief, for the remainder of the unexpired term, can be held.

Section 2. Each candidate for the office of Chief of State, for Commander in Chief, or for Vice Chief of either office shall be a native-born citizen of [*Cumulanis*] and shall be at least [*35*] years old. A candidate for Commander in Chief or for Vice Commander in Chief of the Armed Forces shall have had at least [*four*] years of experience in the active military service of [*Cumulanis*].

Section 3. (a) The Chief of State or when necessary the Vice Chief of State shall receive foreign ambassadors and higher-ranking foreign dignitaries in conformity with the foreign policy authorized by law and they shall perform such other ceremonial duties as may be prescribed by law. Neither the Chief of State nor the Vice Chief of State shall be an executive official for functions prescribed under Article II, Subsections 12(a) and (b) nor shall either serve as an official legislator. Financing and support for the activities of the Chief of State shall be provided by budget legislation and by executive officials as prescribed by law.

(b) The Commander in Chief of the Armed Forces shall have sole command of military operations subject to the foreign policy and military strategy prescribed by law, or as determined in extreme emergency under Article III, Subsection 8(c). Neither the Commander in Chief nor the Vice Commander in Chief shall be an executive official for functions prescribed under Article II, Subsections 12(a) and (b) nor shall either serve as an official legislator.

Section 4. The pay of the Chief of State and of the Vice Chief of State shall be at least equal to that of each of the Speakers or of an Election Commissioner, whichever is higher, under Article II. The pay of the Commander in Chief and of the Vice Commander in Chief shall be at least equal to that of the highest-paid executive among those appointed by the governing legislature.

Section 5. The Chief of State, the Commander in Chief, or the Vice Chief of either office may be removed from office upon the same grounds and procedures as those for removing an official legislator, except that the impeachment of either of these high officials shall be the responsibility of the legislature that controls the executive functions, and that the trial of this official, for removal from office, shall be the held in the official legislature responsible for inspection and auditing. The procedures for these steps shall be the same as those for legislative proposals and final appeals.

These provisions are similar to those for modern parliamentary governments, and do not seem to need detailed discussion. Although it might be desirable to provide expressly for incentive pay for these high officials, we shall not attempt to spell that out here. Nothing in the document prevents its use, as prescribed by law.

Article V: The Judiciary.

Section 1. (a) Magistrates and official courts shall have the power to compel attendance by defendants at their proceedings. In addition, official courts shall have the power to bring to trial and to sentence criminal offenders, to enforce contracts, to issue writs and injunctions [*etc.*] as prescribed by law, and to collect fees to support their operations.

(b) The courts shall interpret the law as it meant when enacted and shall not amend or modify the law. The only law, in addition to this constitution, shall be statute law. The courts shall interpret the constitution in terms of the meaning it had at the time it was ratified and similarly for the interpretation of each constitutional amendment and of each law.

Chapter 2 spells out our choice of the rule of law in preference to the rule of judges. Therefore we exclude any use of common law or of judge-made constitutional law, which in this century in the United States has become increasingly capricious. This section amplifies on the canons of judicial ethics, which we presume to be otherwise well-defined.

Section 2. The courts shall be supported by their fees, which may include fees for amicus curiae submissions, and by such other compensation as may be prescribed by law.

Chapter 2 spells out the role of competition, provided for here. Courts facing competition from arbitrators and from other courts must be mindful of the possibility of reversal on appeal, whose adjudication at the highest level is a legislature reliably representing all interests in the law. Courts will therefore find it in their interest to pay attention to amicus submissions, and to charge them favorable fees, if any. Official amicus briefs, as permitted by Article II, Section 6, will in particular alert courts to broader interests in legal interpretation than those represented by the parties to a dispute.

Section 3. (a) The legislature that selects executive officers shall nominate judges and magistrates, using the procedures of Article II, Subsection 9(a), for proposing legislation, except that these nominations shall not be submitted to a referendum. Instead, such nominations shall be presented to the official legislature responsible for inspection, auditing, and application of measures of performance.

This legislature shall approve or disapprove each nominee using the procedures of Article II, Subsection 9(a). Judges in courts of first instance and magistrates shall normally be selected from among successful arbitrators. The legislature shall appoint judges to appellate courts from among successful judges, which here and throughout this document means those judges whose lower courts have consistently covered their costs.

(b) Judges whose courts fail to be supported by fees and other income as provided by law shall be retired under the procedures for judicial appointments. Whenever, because of delays in the resolution of cases, a sufficient number of parties with standing in active disputes petition that a successful private arbitrator be appointed an official judge, the appointing legislature shall approve such an appointment unless it finds that the delays are temporary.

These provisions spell out a major part of the working of competition and prescribe the procedure for judicial appointments. If a legislature should prove dilatory in nominating or approving judges, another legislature may propose incentive pay and measures of performance for this function, under Article III, Subsection 4(c). Such legislation is likely to be approved, possibly even before the occasion for it arises.

Chapter 2 discusses at length the advantages of competition among courts, under which they must support themselves by fees just as doctors, lawyers, and other professionals do. If voters see a large enough advantage to having excess capacity in the courts, they may choose by referendum to bear the cost of additional compensation for judges. Under this system some judges might specialize in giving expedited service at higher fees than other judges charge, so that parties preferring speedy justice could have it for an appropriate price.

(c) The legislature shall appoint one magistrate for each judicial district.

(d) Rules for determining which persons have standing to participate in civil or criminal cases before courts of law shall be prescribed by law.

These provisions are straightforward.

Section 4. For each civil or criminal case that arises, there shall be at least three official judges who may accept jurisdiction. If the parties

> to a case reach timely agreement on a judge, the agreed court shall receive jurisdiction. If they fail to reach timely agreement, the plaintiff or prosecutor shall ask the magistrate to select an odd number (three or more) judges by weighted random choice from a list consisting of (1) the judges proposed by the two sides and (2) as many as three additional judges that have settled more cases than have any of those proposed by the two sides. To obtain the weights for this choice, the magistrate shall sum those cases settled by each proposed judge in the past year in which the two sides agreed on a judge and use the fraction of this total settled by each such judge as the weight or probability for the random selection. (For these purposes the magistrate may restrict the calculation to cases of the particular class of which the case in question is a member.) From among the three or more judges thus selected, each side may veto judges until one remains.

This provision provides the other key element for competition as described in Chapter 2. Both parties have an equal say in the choice of a court to try their case. Among all those instances where they cannot agree, random selection will result in distributing their trials among the eligible venues in proportion to those cases these venues receive by mutual agreement of the parties. For example, if a very popular judge receives 20 percent of all those tort cases in which the two sides agree on the venue, this judge will also receive, by weighted random selection, about 20 percent of those tort cases in which the two sides cannot agree on a venue.

As is now the case with arbitrators, to succeed judges would have to earn reputations that stood them well with both sides of disputes and criminal cases. A judge with known bias would not be acceptable to the party that would be hurt by that bias. A judge who was careless or incompetent would often be ruled out by both parties to a case, just as incompetent or careless baseball umpires usually cannot make it in the major leagues. Having their decisions overturned would drive away business for future cases, providing ample incentive to interpret and uphold the law diligently.

> Section 5. In addition to the functions prescribed elsewhere in this constitution, magistrates may perform marriages, notarize documents, [*and perform other customary routine functions of magistrates*.]

Section 6. The provisions of Sections 3(a), 3(b), 3(d), and 4 apply also to appellate courts.

Section 7. (a) If a party should choose to appeal an appellate court decision, the venue for the final appeal shall ordinarily be the official legislature whose legislative proposals approved by the electorate have the greatest aggregate value, measured by their budget amounts plus the declared net aggregate value of votes of the electorate. However, an official legislator who is a defendant or a member of whose family is a defendant in a suit as provided in Article II, Subsection 10(i) or in a criminal trial may not participate in the review of said suit or trial. In such cases the same rules regarding venue as those in Article V, Section 8 shall apply. The procedure for handling appeals shall be the same as that for legislation, except that such appeals shall not be subject to referendum; the decision of the legislature is final.

(b) If new legislation approved subsequent to a decision under Subsection (a) expressly reverses that decision within [*three*] years after the decision is announced, the incentive pay prescribed in Article II attributable to that part of the new legislation shall be subtracted from the incentive pay of the legislature that made the decision.

As set out in Chapter 2, the arguments in favor of competition for courts of first instance apply equally to the appellate function except at the highest level of appeal. If a decision is bad law, however, it can of course be corrected by new legislation. If it is corrected promptly, the legislature that made the bad decision loses some incentive pay. Therefore the incentive to maintain efficient law in such decisions would be almost the same as the incentive to propose good law.

Section 8. (a) A person with standing may contest a law or other action by any part of the government on the grounds of its constitutionality, and courts at each level may accept the case and rule on this issue. If the official legislature whose legislative proposals approved by the electorate have the greatest aggregate value, measured by their budget amounts plus the declared net aggregate value of votes of the electorate, enacted the challenged law or was responsible for the challenged action, the official legislature ranking second by this criterion shall sit as the constitutional court for the case unless it is similarly foreclosed from this role. If all official legislatures have a significant share of the responsibility for a challenged law, the previous legislature that appointed executive officers and judges in the most recent past term shall be convened to sit as the constitutional court for the case. The decision procedure shall be the same as that for legislation, except that the decision of the constitutional court shall be final.

(b) A decision of the constitutional court may be reversed, under the procedures of Article VI Section 2, except that for the reversal to succeed the voter declarations of net aggregate harm, in case it fails, instead shall be at least [*0.5*] percent of one year's value of the nation's aggregate production of goods and services. In addition, if those subgroups of the population, defined by Article II Sec. 2, that oppose the reversal (that is, those in which the votes sum to aggregate declared harm) have an overall aggregate declared harm in excess of [*0.5*] percent of the nation's aggregate production of goods and services, the reversal is disapproved. If a referendum expressly reverses a decision under Subsection (a) within [*3*] years after the decision is announced, the incentive pay attributable to that reversal shall be subtracted from the incentive pay of the legislature that made the decision. The combined incentive pay of private petitioners, where relevant, and of official legislatures for a the reversal of a constitutional court decision, when the reversal is approved by a referendum, shall be [*30*] percent of the excess of the total harm from disapproval, net of declared harms due to approval, over [*0.5*] percent of one year's value of the nation's aggregate production of goods and services, less [*5*] percent of the net total monetary value of the harms declared by each population subgroup that on balance opposes the reversal, or shall be [*0.005*] percent of one year's value of the nation's aggregate production of goods and services, whichever is greater. This incentive pay shall be allocated among petitioners and legislatures with the same percentages and procedures as are prescribed in Article II, Subsection 11(b). If the constitutional court's decision is upheld, the election costs shall be allocated to petitioners and official legislatures with the same proportions and procedures as is incentive pay for reversal.

The canons of judicial ethics apply also to legislators when they perform a judicial function. Their decisions may be reversed, as in the case of a decision interpreting the law, under a stricter test based on that required for ratification of a constitutional amendment. In this case also, the incentive to interpret the constitution soundly will resemble the incentive to propose sound constitutional amendments.

Section 9. The compensation of an official legislature or constitutional court for deciding each appeal or constitutional issue shall be [*500*] times the court fees paid by all parties except the government in the court of first instance for the case at issue, plus such additional compensation as has been prescribed by law enacted prior to the first filing of said case.

Section 10. (a) Judges shall be immune from lawsuits concerning their conduct of court business, so long as this conduct conforms to the canons of judicial ethics and so long as they interpret the applicable law in good faith as provided in this constitution. A reversal of a judge's decision on appeal shall not constitute grounds for a lawsuit against this judge unless the opinion in the reversal states that the judge's decision showed flagrant or malicious disregard of the law or of the canons of judicial ethics.

(b) The grounds for removal of magistrates and successful judges shall include those for disqualification of an official legislator, and in addition may include repeated decisions by a judge or magistrate found by a higher court to be in flagrant or malicious disregard of the law. The procedure shall be the same as that prescribed in Article IV, Section 5 for the Chief of State and for other high officials, except for cases coming under Subsection 3(b).

These are routine matters. Some compensation is required, as it would impose an extra workload on a sitting legislature, and would be a major inconvenience to a former legislature recalled to judge a case. In the case of immunity from lawsuits of judges, their understood obligation is to preside impartially over court proceedings in conformity with judicial ethics. Reversal of a good-faith judicial decision by a higher court is a risk that a party can insure against privately, or against which the judge may offer a warranty. Therefore there is no reason to require a warranty by mandating judicial liability.

Article VI: Ratification

Section 1. This constitution shall come into force if it is ratified by a referendum in which at least [*80*] percent of citizens eligible to vote

> participate. Voting citizens shall declare the monetary value of the harm to them if ratification succeeds or fails. Ratification will depend on [*two*] criteria: (a) at least [*90*] percent of those voting shall have declared a harm if ratification fails, that is, shall have voted in favor of ratification; and (b) the aggregate amount of declared harm in case of failure shall be at least [*five*] times the aggregate amount of declared harm in case of ratification. No insurance against these harms shall be offered. The procedure shall otherwise conform to Article II, Subsection 10(b).

This procedure resembles that which applied to the ratification of the Constitution of the United States. It is logical to recommend that attempts to organize voter coalitions to misrepresent their harms in this vote should be a felony, but of course such a law would have to be put into force separately, prior to the referendum on this constitution itself.

> Section 2. This constitution may be amended by the procedures of Article II, including positive and negative tax assessments, except that in order to enter into force, an amendment must be approved by a voter declaration of net aggregate harm, in case it fails, of at least [*3*] percent of one year's value of the nation's aggregate production of goods and services. In addition, if those subgroups of the population, defined by Article II, Sec. 2, that oppose the amendment (that is, those in which the votes sum to aggregate declared harm) have an overall aggregate declared harm in excess of [*1*] percent of the nation's aggregate production of goods and services the amendment is disapproved. It must be proposed at least one year prior to the referendum to approve or disapprove it. When a constitutional amendment is under consideration, each official legislature considering it shall sequester itself at least until the completed proposal is published. A proposed amendment that is not adopted may not be considered again for at least [*ten*] years. The combined incentive pay of private petitioners, where relevant, and of official legislatures for a constitutional amendment approved by a referendum shall be [*30*] percent of the excess of the total harm from non-adoption, net of declared harms due to adoption, over [*3*] percent of one year's value of the nation's aggregate production of goods and services, less [*5*] percent of the net total monetary value of the harms declared by each population subgroup that on balance opposes the amendment, or shall be [*0.03*] percent of one year's value of the nation's aggregate

production of goods and services, whichever is greater. This incentive pay shall be allocated among petitioners and legislatures with the same percentages and procedures as are prescribed in Article II, Subsection 11(b). If the amendment is disapproved, the election costs shall be allocated with the same proportions and procedures as is incentive pay for approval.

This provision has a high hurdle for constitutional amendments, as does the U.S. constitution and as do many others. The requirement that the harm to some subgroups, if any, must have a relatively low aggregate value has the effect of requiring a specified accuracy of approximation to Lindahl taxes in the amendment proposal. The delay before a defeated amendment can be reconsidered is a barrier to subgroups that might attempt to improve their tax assessments by blocking ratification.

Section 3. (a) Upon ratification of this constitution, [*the existing proto-government*] shall serve in a caretaker capacity until the following provision creating an Interim Official Legislature can be implemented. [____] shall select [*two*] eminent jurists from [*Cumulanis*] and [*three*] from former members of [*the International Court of Justice*] to serve as the Interim Election Commission for [*two*] years, during the transition to the constitution's full implementation. As soon as it can be constituted, the Interim Election Commission shall choose a random sample of [*400*] citizens, from among those eligible to vote, to serve as the Interim Official Legislature. The Interim Official Legislature shall select a Speaker and shall function in the same manner as does an official legislature under Article II, except that there shall be no requirement for an Interim Legislator to exchange property as prescribed in Article II, Section 5.

(b) Using the procedure of Article II, Subsection 9(a), within six months of being constituted the Interim Official Legislature shall (1) propose a temporary 'no action' budget containing the minimum for public safety, represented by a continuation of previous year's military and police budgets for the predecessor government, plus interim family assistance as provided by Article III, Section 3, plus compensation of [__ *pesos*] each for the Election Commissioners, plus compensation for government officials and private Legislators as herein provided until the first regular budget, plus provision for an audit of the interim 'no action' budget, plus provision for an interim

Census, designed and conducted in such a manner as to facilitate accurate implementation of Article II, Section 2, plus provision for a budget surplus of [*one*] percent of the budget total to commence building the national financial reserve prescribed in Article II, Subsection 12(e), and shall include proposed payroll taxes and property taxes to finance it; (2) propose legislation defining costs of elections and measures of success for subsequent budgets; (3) select an Election Commission to begin serving a regular four-year term within one year of the date at which the Interim Official Legislature was chosen; (4) nominate candidates for Chief of State, Commander in Chief of the Armed Forces, Vice Chief of State, and Vice Commander in Chief of the Armed Forces and appoint acting officials to fill these four positions; (5) appoint [__] judges and interim magistrates to proceed under the provisions of Article V; (6) propose a law defining felonious conduct in connection with legislative business, such as bribery, extortion, and obstruction, including provisions governing subsequent employment of legislators by employers who do business with or otherwise tangibly benefit from government programs; (7) propose an interim set of demographic subgroups to be used by the first regular Election Commission; and (8) propose an interim executive team to administer the interim budget.

(c) As soon as practicable, the Interim Election Commission shall conduct a referendum for approval of the proposals of the Interim Official Legislature. The referendum shall follow the procedures prescribed in Article II, Subsections 10(a) and 10(b), except that no insurance shall be offered and all declared harms shall be uninsured. Private proposals for these referendum issues shall be included, as provided in Article II, Subsection 10(d), for the two private proposals on each issue that post the largest bond among those competing. Compensation for the Interim Official Legislature shall be that provided in Article II, Section 5, plus [*0.1*] percent of the budget amounts contained in those of the Interim Official Legislature's proposals that the voters approve, plus [*3*] percent of the net total harm, of non-adoption of these approved proposals, declared by voters. Compensation for successful private proposals shall be [*0.1*] percent of the budget amounts contained in those proposals plus [*3*] percent of the net total harm of non-adoption of these approved proposals, declared by voters. No other proposals for legislation shall be included in the referendum unless an imminent threat of war requires implementation of Article III, Section 8.

(d) Members of the Interim Official Legislature shall not be exempt from the taxes prescribed in Subsection (b).

(e) Judges and magistrates shall enforce all laws, rights, and obligations that were in force prior to the ratification of this constitution that do not conflict with it for [*four*] years, after which all such laws, rights, and obligations mandated by those laws, shall be null and void, unless superceded or reinstated sooner by legislation enacted under the full provisions of this constitution. Private rights and obligations arising from existing contracts and customs shall continue in force on the same basis as if this constitution had always been in force, except that previously legal contracts that this constitution prohibits and that were entered into before this constitution was presented for ratification shall be enforced for [*four*] years, after which all such contracts shall be null and void.

(f) Within [*three*] months of taking office, the Election Commission selected under Subsection (b)(3) shall select two official legislatures as provided under Article II. [*etc.*]

The transitional provisions suggested here provide a review of the problems that evidently must be solved if a constitution like this one is adopted. The first referendum on a 'no-action' budget has no insurance because at this stage there is no way to provide fair insurance premiums. Moreover, this budget is merely transitional and is almost certain to be approved. There is no reason to exempt the interim official legislature from this budget's taxes, inasmuch as they are small, temporary, and not part of the interlocking incentive system that will follow. The interim legislators are generously compensated. The other provisions of these subsections are routine and self-explanatory.

The following technical annex and its various procedures are needed only if (a) the legislative history reveals uninsured harms to be declared in a referendum; (b) Lindahl tax assessments have significant inaccuracies, so that the referendum will reveal significant numbers of votes on the losing side; and (c) the uninsured harms involve significant income effects that differ among voters affected.

Technical Annex

Procedure for Adjusting Legislative Votes and Voters' Uninsured Harms

This Technical Annex is part of and has the same legal force as the Constitution.

If the rate of change with respect to income (the 'income effect') of a legislator's willingness to pay to change an outcome is the same for all legislators in both official legislatures, there shall be no adjustments of the kind herein provided. The following procedure shall apply if this income effect differs among legislators.

(a) Legislative Decisions on Discrete Sets of Alternative Proposals. Within each legislature, the official monetary effects on each legislator's family of each issue to be decided, in terms of taxes, changes in property values, and changes in prices and wages shall be calculated in a manner determined by the legislature subject to the rules of evidence. Each legislator, when stating a willingness to pay for an outcome relative to an alternative, shall state whether it includes perceived monetary effects that disagree with the official monetary effects. If a legislator's willingness to pay is equal to the perceived monetary effects for the legislator's family, there is no intangible value involved; otherwise there is such a value. The legislator's willingness to pay to change each pairwise choice will be used as stated for all issues having no intangible value for that legislator.

Adjustments for income effects apply only to intangible (nonfinancial) values.

For sets of issues, some of which include intangible values for one or more legislators, that are to be considered together in a referendum, the declarations of willingness to pay shall be adjusted for income effects and the outcomes ranked using the Cardinal Ranking Procedure and related steps using the legislator's stated pairwise income effects. The Election Commission shall use the resulting ranking of outcomes and their estimated net aggregate gains to determine the probabilities of success of the possible outcomes in the pending referendum.

The procedures described here are explained in Chapter 6.

(b) Legislative Decisions on Continuous-Scale Issues. When a legislature considers a budget proposal or other legislative proposal whose outcome is to be chosen as a point on a continuous scale together with associated schedules of taxes and transfers, each legislator shall declare two valuation schedules showing, at each point on the scale, what the legislator's family would be willing to pay to increase the outcome by one unit. The first of the two valuation schedules shall show the portion of the valuation that represents the family's financial interest in the outcome and the second shows intangible valuation. The legislator shall also declare by what amount the intangible valuation schedule would differ in the event of a specified increase in the legislator's family income.

This information prescribed in paragraphs (a) and (b) permits appropriate estimates of and adjustments to voters' declared harms in referenda.

(c) Referenda with Discrete Sets of Outcomes. When the legislative process reveals intangible values associated with a pairwise choice between outcomes, if the Election Commission finds that income effects can affect the outcome, the declarations of uninsured harms by voters shall be adjusted for income effects and the outcome determined according to the Cardinal Ranking Procedure and related steps. The income effects shall be estimated by efficient statistical procedures from legislative votes and procedures from both official legislatures.

As noted, an explanation of the Cardinal Ranking Procedure appears in Chapter 6.

(d) Referenda with Continuous-Scale Outcomes. When a referendum offers a budget proposal or other legislative proposal whose outcome is to be chosen as a point on a continuous scale together with associated schedules of taxes and transfers, the Election Commission shall offer corresponding fair insurance whose premium varies continuously along this scale. If the legislative process reveals uninsurable intangible values, each voter shall declare two valuation schedules showing at each point on the scale what the voter would be willing to pay to increase/decrease the outcome by one unit. The first of the two valuation schedules shall show the portion of the valuation that the voter wishes to insure and the second shall show the uninsured part of the valuation. The voter shall also declare an income effect for the uninsured valuation schedule. The voter's insurance payout will be the absolute value of the integral of the insured curve from the outcome to the voter's most preferred outcome. The voter's incentive tax will be the integral for all other voters measuring the areas under their combined curves, plus the integral measuring the area under this voter's insured curve, from the value the outcome would have had, without this voter's uninsured valuation schedule, to the actual outcome. [*A further transfer to each voter will be determined by the applicable formulas in the appendices to Chapter 6.*]

This subsection describes the VCG tax and its refunds, with the latter designed to balance the budget and to maintain the incentive to declare harms truthfully. The income effects involved will be of negligible importance in an economy of thousands of citizens or more.

This completes the draft constitution and the rationale for its particulars. The appendix repeats the entire document without interruption.

Appendix: The Draft Constitution

PREAMBLE

We the people of [*the nation of Cumulanis*] adopt this constitution as a solemn contract, binding ourselves and our successors in perpetuity. Although in some circumstances it compels some of us to accept the will of others, we accept that minimum amount of such compulsion that, when applied consistently and without favor in all circumstances, serves our best interests and those of our successors. It is our aim to harmonize each public decision with our interests under this constitution so that we support each such decision, as nearly as possible, unanimously.

Article I: Popular Sovereignty

Section 1. The government, a provider of services under contract with the people, implements and enforces such legislation as the people approve. The people delegate specified authority to its executive and judicial officers. Subject to the provisions of this constitution, officers and legislative programs shall compete for the people's approval.

Article II: Legislatures, Legislative Programs, and their Execution

Section 1. (a) There shall be at least two official legislatures and there may be private ones as provided in Subsection 10(d), each drafting a separate legislative program to be presented to the people in such a manner that they may approve one or another in its entirety or may approve a composite of parts of more than one program. Two official legislatures (not including a third that may be approved under Subsection 10(d)) are referred to herein as the primary official legislatures.

(b) Except as modified by Article V, Section 8, 'by law' means by a statute enacted under the procedures prescribed in Article II, Sections 8, 9, and 10.

Section 2. (a) Each official legislature shall consist of citizens eligible to vote, selected by lot. The number selected shall be no fewer than [...] and no greater than [...]. The selection procedure shall be a stratified random drawing in which each population subgroup, classified by gender, age group, region, employment status, income, and income source by industry and occupation, if any, including career government servants, shall be [*proportionately*] represented. [*The subgroups shall be mutually exclusive and exhaustive, so that each citizen shall be a member of exactly one subgroup.*] The selection shall be supervised by an Election Commission of [*five*] members selected by the official legislatures in joint session in the fourth year of their term of office from among the successful arbitrators and judges, to take office [*three*] months prior to the commencement of the term of office of the incoming official legislatures. The term of an Election Commission shall be four years. No currently serving government official except a sitting judge shall be eligible to become an Election Commissioner. In particular, no Speaker may be selected, and no Election Commissioner may serve consecutive terms.

(b) A new demographic subgroup other than those specified in Subsection (a) may be created by law by subdividing an existing subgroup, provided that it has first been established in official legislative proceedings (1) that membership and nonmembership of such a group can be independently verified by nonmembers of the original demographic subgroup and (2) that creation of the new subgroup will reduce the within-group variability of declared harms on some significant public policy referenda.

(c) Persons selected by lot shall be compelled to serve in an official legislature, except for [*(a)*] those excused for overriding reasons[*and (b) those, each of whom finds an alternate from the person's own demographic subgroup as a voluntarily replacement*]. Such overriding reasons are restricted to (1) terminal illness with a prognosis of less than [*two years*] of survival or permanently incapacitating ill health confirmed by a panel of doctors selected by the Election Commission, (2) indictment for a felony, in which case the person shall be temporarily excused until the case is concluded, including appeals, and if not convicted the person shall then be available as an alternate for a vacancy during the legislative term, (3) election to high office under Article IV, or (4) [*other.*]

Section 3. The official legislatures shall be selected every four years. If a legislator becomes ineligible to serve as a result of death, permanently incapacitating ill health, election to high office, or conviction for a felony, the Election Commission shall select an alternate if one is already available or if not conduct a special drawing to select a new legislator, in either case from the same population subgroup as that of the ineligible legislator.

Section 4. An official legislature shall have no authority to exclude a member for any reason, other than those prescribed by Section 3. Such exclusion shall not take effect until certified by the Election Commission. In the fourth year of each legislative term each primary official legislature shall propose a law defining felonious conduct in connection with legislative business, such as bribery, extortion, and obstruction, and such a law shall come into force at the beginning of the next legislative term, if it meets the requirements for legislation prescribed in this Article. Each such legislative proposal shall include provisions restricting subsequent employment of legislators by employers who do business with or otherwise tangibly benefit from government programs.

Section 5. Each official legislator shall receive a salary while serving equal to [*1.2*] times the full value of his or her personal services as measured by prior earnings, together with a reasonable expectation of current increase. Under this section, members of the official legislator's immediate family shall be considered to be official legislators. In addition, each legislator may receive incentive pay and may pay incentive taxes as prescribed in other sections of this article. For the income from property, including intellectual property, that an official legislator would otherwise receive, said legislator shall exchange such property for a portfolio of equal value, proportionately representing all property in the same industry or industries as that of the original property. Apart from these specified sources, no official legislator may receive royalties, honoraria, gifts of more than nominal value, or any other income while serving, except as otherwise provided in this constitution.

Section 6. (a) Each official legislature shall select a presiding officer to be called 'Speaker' from among the successful appellate judges. The Speaker shall have the same authority that a judge has in a civil trial, to limit evidence and arguments presented on the grounds of relevance and reliability, to preserve order, and to determine specific rules of order pursuant to those prescribed by law. Upon receiving the Speaker's recommendation at the beginning of a session, the legislature shall determine its structure of committees, their membership, and the scope of their authority pursuant to the legislature's business. Each official legislature shall keep a journal of its proceedings and votes, which shall be published in a timely way prior to each referendum.

(b) An Election Commissioner's and a Speaker's income from property and other sources shall be subject to the same rules and restrictions as those prescribed for legislators in Section 5.

Section 7. [*The identities of legislators shall be kept secret until four years after they have served.*] Under exceptional conditions as may be prescribed by the Election Commission all official legislators, together with their families, shall be sequestered from all contact with persons other than government officials and witnesses for a period to be prescribed by the Election Commission. Their access to news, other information, and messages from outside the legislature may when necessary be controlled by the Speaker in such a manner as to protect the integrity of the official legislative process. There shall be no communication between the legislatures nor between their Speakers except as otherwise specifically provided herein. The proceedings of each legislature shall be kept secret to the extent deemed prudent by the legislature until the subsequent referendum ballot is set, whereupon subsection 10(e) applies. This provision shall not prohibit the Election Commission from arranging the presentation of evidence to official legislatures simultaneously, if these legislatures consent thereto, or from permitting relevant questions from legislators to experts and interested citizens who testify, in such a manner as to conform to the restrictions on communication. During periods of sequestration the Speakers and the members of the Election Commission, with their families, shall also separate themselves from all contact with persons other than government officials and witnesses.

Section 8. Each primary official legislator may initiate budget proposals and other legislative proposals and the Speaker may lay before the official legislature such proposals as have been presented to the Speaker by citizens. Speakers, Election Commissioners, and a third official legislature may propose legislation to create a new demographic subgroup as authorized under Subsection 2(c), but they may not propose or suggest other legislation, directly or indirectly.

Section 9. (a) Each official legislator shall be instructed to vote within the legislature in such a manner as to maximize his or her family's best interests, taking both financial and intangible considerations into account, based on the family's incomes and interests prior to serving and on the modifications of property income prescribed by Section 5. The legislator shall also be instructed that truthful voting in this stage will maximize the legislator's prospects for generous incentive pay. The manner of voting is that each legislator shall state, in response to a proposal, how much money it is worth to that legislator's family to pass or to defeat the proposal, as the case may be. When an official legislature votes on several related issues, such that the votes on one issue may depend on the outcome of another issue, all such issues shall be considered together in a single procedure. All feasible outcomes shall be enumerated and each legislator shall state how much money it is worth to that legislator's family to obtain each outcome relative to each less preferred outcome. Each legislator shall also state by how much this money amount would change if the family's income were initially higher by a stated amount. If these amounts are inconsistent with a technically rational, self-consistent set of preferences, the legislator shall be required to bring them into conformity with same. Subject to adjustment procedures set out in part (a) of the Technical Annex, the amounts voted shall be summed and the proposal or package with the highest money amount voted in its favor is adopted as a formal proposal of the legislature. If the legislator's vote changes the outcome, compared to what it would have been had all others voted the same while this legislator did not vote, the legislator will pay an incentive tax equal to the minimum amount required from that legislator to produce a tie vote between the actual outcome and the alternative in a pairwise vote between the two. Alternative outcomes that are outvoted by a sufficiently narrow margin, as determined by criteria supplied by the Election Commission, shall also be presented by the legislature for possible inclusion in the referendum, in conformity with Subsection (b).

(b) An advisory committee of statisticians appointed by the Election Commission shall determine the probability that a referendum as prescribed in Section 10 will approve each portion of a legislative proposal and each alternative portion. Those portions that face no competing proposals and that are found to have a probability of approval higher than [*95*] percent may be grouped together for a single up or down vote. Those portions with lower probabilities of approval and acceptable proposals facing competing alternatives shall appear as separate proposals on the referendum ballot. A noncompetitive proposal is acceptable for the ballot if the advisory committee of statisticians finds that the probability of acceptance exceeds [*ten*] percent. A group of competing proposals is acceptable as a group if the probability that a proposal from the group will pass exceeds [*ten*] percent and each competing proposal is acceptable if the probability of acceptance exceeds [*one*] percent. A budget proposal is defined to include every legislative proposal pursuant to the authority of Article III, Sections 3 and 4 and such other legislative proposals as are identified as budget proposals under Article II, Subsection 9(c). Budget proposals under Article III Section 4 shall include alternative funding levels for each kind of expenditure as separate proposals or as a continuous scale of options, over a range chosen on the basis of this probabilistic rule. Alternative budgets for inspection, auditing, and application of measures of performance of government programs shall be provided for as a set of separate budget proposals. When the official legislatures have decided their proposed legislative programs, the Speakers shall advise the Commission on the appropriate subject grouping of items on the ballot. Every legislative proposal must conform to the grouping selected by the Commission and within each proposal group it must state what it proposes (possibly including 'no action') for each subject and program in that group. However, a legislature may decline to propose legislation in an entire proposal group.

(c) Each legislative proposal pursuant to the authority of Article III, Sections 5, 6, 7, 8, or 9 shall be accompanied by a thorough, accurate analysis of its budget consequences. If said proposal requires a budget for its implementation, the legislature shall include it as a combined legislative and budget proposal as part of the overall proposal for the budget referendum ballot. Each such proposal, if included on the ballot, shall be subject to the rules of Subsection (b) on proposal groups.

(d) Using the official legislators' votes as guidance, each Speaker shall propose a set of taxes and, if necessary, positive transfers for each population subgroup represented in the legislature and, where appropriate, for each type of property, with a view to achieving a unanimous referendum vote for or against each legislative proposal that will appear in the same referendum. These taxes and transfers shall be itemized by proposal and by whether the tax basis is the household or an item of property. Upon receiving this tax proposal from its Speaker, each official legislature shall adopt a proposed schedule of taxes and transfers for each proposal, including the corresponding part, if any, of the continuation budget. The taxes to finance each proposal must pay for its entire expected cost, year by year, and the budget proposals as a whole from each legislature must have exact balance, inclusive of debt service payments and payments to the financial reserve as prescribed in Subsection 12(e), based on estimation procedures prescribed by the Election Commission. The Election Commission, advised by its statistical advisory committee, shall determine these estimation procedures taking account of foreseeable demographic changes and other changes affecting the sizes and economic circumstances of the population subgroups represented in the official legislatures. For identical or substantially identical proposals, according to the data from the official legislatures, the Election Commission shall consolidate the tax schedules proposed by the legislatures for each such proposal into a single schedule having the maximum likelihood of attaining a minimum-harm outcome (nearly unanimous in value terms) and a balanced budget. This consolidation shall also apply to compensation to property owners for property and easements to be acquired by court order.

(e) A full and fair account of the facts and arguments for and against each plan, except for omissions or summaries required by considerations of military secrecy as prescribed by law, shall be assembled by the Election Commission, subject to the rules of evidence applicable to official legislative proceedings. These facts and arguments shall be distributed at least [*one month*] in advance of the referendum to all citizens eligible to vote.

(f) Beginning in the year [*2000*] and every [*twelfth*] year thereafter the budget proposals of the official legislatures shall include provision for a census of the population, designed and conducted in such a manner as to facilitate accurate implementation of Section 2. In addition, each official legislature shall include in the [*first*] budget proposal of its legislative term the funding of an analysis of trends in voter residence and registration to vote, to provide an authoritative basis for revision of the census numbers. These revisions shall be used to implement Section 2 in the selection of the official legislatures for the subsequent legislative term.

Section 10. (a) Subject to Subsection 9(b), each legislative proposal from the primary official legislatures shall be presented in a referendum to all eligible voters, together with other proposals proposed under Subsection (d). There shall be a biennial budget proposal for the functions of government, which shall include a two-year extension representing its continuation. Each budget proposal shall also offer as an alternative 'no action' budget a set of programs representing a minimum program for public safety prescribed by a previously enacted law. This minimum program shall include provision for compensation of legislators, Speakers, Election Commissioners, the Chief of State, the Commander in Chief of the Armed Forces, and the two Vice Chiefs, for the census specified in Subsection 9(f), and for payment of government accounts payable, debt service, and scheduled payments to financial reserves as prescribed in this constitution. Each item in the 'no action' budget shall also be included in each larger budget proposal on the same subject in the referendum, and every item in the 'no action' budget shall be included in a budget category. Each regular budget referendum shall include the continuation of the budget adopted two years earlier and the 'no action' budget proposal for each proposal group. For non-budget proposals, the alternative of no action shall appear on the ballot. All no-action and continuation proposals herein prescribed shall appear on the ballot whether or not they meet the statistical tests prescribed in Subsection 9(b). Legislatures may at any time propose supplementary budgets and budget reductions whose costs shall include election costs. If they meet the statistical tests of Subsection 9(b) a referendum shall be held. Voting shall be secret, except that the matching of identified ballots to voters must be known to the Election Commission to carry out its duties under this section, and must be kept under permanent seal. The Election Commission shall also keep under seal all referendum-generated information about voter willingness to pay (by population subgroups) that could otherwise influence tax proposals under Subsection 9(d). The Election Commission may, however, use this information to assist in determining whether to propose the creation of a new demographic subgroup under the provisions of Section 8 and Subsection 2(a) and to investigate possible conspiracies by voters to falsify their declared harms.

(b) For those proposals that the Election Commission places on the ballot, voters shall express their preferences among the proposals in monetary terms. They shall express such preferences in two ways. First, the Election Commission shall offer them insurance against each less-preferred proposal at a fair premium, based on the probabilities determined by the advisory committee of statisticians. The voter is expected to purchase insurance against each proposal other than the voter's most preferred proposal. The voter will receive the face value of said insurance for a referendum outcome that differs from the outcome that the voter most prefers. Second, each voter may declare, pairwise between every pair of mutually exclusive proposals, an uninsured harm that the voter would suffer if the outcome went against the voter's pairwise preference. The voter who declares uninsured harm shall also declare what the uninsured harm would be if (a) the outcome were the voter's least preferred rather than most preferred and if (b) the voter's income were higher by the amount of the greatest harm otherwise declared. Each such declaration of uninsured harm may not exceed [*ten*] percent of the voter's income and the sum of all declared uninsured harms on a ballot may not exceed [*twenty*] percent of the voter's income. The Election Commission shall set lower maximum declarations whenever legislative proceedings reveal that such maxima are appropriate. If the various amounts that a voter declares on a single ballot or on successive ballots are inconsistent with a technically rational, self-consistent set of preferences, the voter shall be required to bring them into conformity with same or, failing that, part or all of the voter's ballot shall be disqualified. If more than one manner of partial disqualification would satisfy the test, the voter shall select which disqualification to accept. The Election Commission shall sum the insurance plus the uninsured harms, subject to adjustment procedures set out in part (b) of the Technical Annex, and declare the outcome that results in the least aggregate harm [*provided that in order to enter into force, a legislative proposal must be approved by a voter declaration of net aggregate harm, in case it fails, of at least three times overall aggregate harm from its adoption declared by those who oppose it*]. It shall pay the insurance face value to those voters who insured against this outcome. It shall assess an incentive tax on each voter whose uninsured harm was great enough to change the outcome, setting the incentive tax on that voter as the amount that would have produced a tie vote in the referendum. It shall pay members of each official legislature an incentive fee prescribed by law, based on the accuracy with which the income effects predicted by that legislature's valuations predict voter income effects, and also based on the accuracy with which the legislature predicts the variability of declared harms for each proposal group, within each population subgroup. Corresponding procedures set out in the Technical Annex, part (d) shall apply for a proposal presented as a continuous scale of options. However, if no official legislature associates intangible values with some pairs of potential referendum outcomes, under part (a) of the procedure in the Technical Annex, then for such pairs no declarations of uninsured losses shall be accepted in the referendum procedure and the outcome shall be determined solely by the amounts of insurance purchased, without adjustments for income effects.

(c) Attempts to organize voter groups to misrepresent their harms shall be a felony with penalties prescribed by law.

(d) A citizen, corporation, or group of citizens may offer budget proposals and other proposed legislation by petition to the Election Commission. The person or group offering such proposals shall post sufficient bond to cover a pro-rata share of incremental evaluation and election costs due to the proposals, as defined by Subsection (f), and shall be liable for these costs whether the proposals succeed or fail, except in the case of proposals for measures of success under Subsection (h). The Election Commission shall specify procedures and venues for confidential copyright registration of such proposals, in whole or in part, while they are in the preparatory stages, to be used for determining incentive pay under Subsection 11(b). If the volume and quality of citizen petitions is high enough, in the judgement of the Election Commission, to justify it, the Commission shall ask the Speakers to participate with the Commission in a vote, under the procedure specified for a legislature in Subsection 9(a), on the question of whether to propose legislation to create a third official legislature. If they so decide, they shall prepare proposed taxes to finance it and shall place the entire proposal on a referendum ballot. Their incentive pay contingent on this proposal shall be that provided in Subsection 10(f). If such legislation receives approval, the Election Commission shall present all private proposals to the third official legislature, whose exclusive business shall be to prepare such proposals for the ballot. A third official legislature, if approved by referendum, may be abolished in a subsequent referendum. If there is no third official legislature, the Election Commission shall present all private proposals to both official legislatures, where they shall be subject to the same legislative procedures as are all other proposals. The Election Commission shall allow those proposals to appear on the ballot that meet the criteria of Subsection 9(b).

(e) [Each proposal for legislation under the authority of Article III, Sections 5, 6, 7, or 8 shall appear on two successive referendum ballots, except as otherwise provided under Article III Section 8. The first time it appears the legislation may be briefly though accurately summarized, as may the arguments for and against its adoption. The question put to the voters in this first referendum shall be, 'Shall this proposal be considered for adoption in the forthcoming referendum of {date}?' The criterion for success shall be {25%} of the votes cast. If voters reject this proposition, the proposal shall not appear on a subsequent referendum ballot until and unless the first vote is reversed, and the legislature that originated the proposal shall receive a reduction in its incentive payments. This reduction shall consist of the costs of placing the proposal on the ballot plus {20} percent of the net total harms declared by voters in rejecting it.]

(f) The Compensation of each Election Commissioner for serving shall equal [*two*] times the average salary paid to official legislators as determined under Section 5; plus incentive pay of [*.02*] percent, for each subject group, of the net monetary value of the superiority, measured by total declared harms, of the programs approved by referenda over 'no action' net of the harms to those who prefer 'no action', to the approved programs; less [*.003*] percent, for each subject group, of the net total monetary value of the inferiority of the programs approved by referenda relative to 'no action,' for each population subgroup that on balance supported 'no action'; plus [*0.67*] percent of the cost and performance payments and penalties prescribed in Subsection 12(c) for the legislature that appoints executive officers (except that the penalty for revenue errors shall be based on the difference between actual revenues and planned revenues, rather than presumptive adjusted figures); less [*.02*] percent of all costs, including private costs, of the conduct of and participation in referenda sanctioned by the Election Commission during its term. The method of reckoning these costs shall be prescribed by law prior to the Commission's term.

[(g) The Election Commission shall maintain an Election Fund in two parts, Fund A and Fund B. Fund A shall receive the insurance premiums, pay the insurance claims, receive the supplementary taxes provided for by Subsection (b), receive the incremental cost payments for private proposals prescribed by Subsection (d), and pay the costs of administration of elections. At the end of each legislative term, the surplus or deficit in this fund shall be allocated to voters according to the following rule. For each voter the Election Commission shall calculate what the amount in Fund A would have been if this voter had not participated in the referenda of that term. The fund adjusted in this way shall be divided by the number of voters, less one, and the quotient, if positive, shall be paid to this voter or if negative charged to this voter. Where applicable, the payment or charge to the voter shall be adjusted as indicated in the Technical Annex, part (d). If this method of division leaves a residual surplus or deficit in the fund, the residual shall be carried forward into the next legislative term and placed in Fund B. If the surplus or deficit in Fund B exceeds, in absolute value, [one-half] the planned amount in the financial reserve prescribed in Subsection 12(e), the excess shall be transferred to said financial reserve.]

(h) Legislation approved by the voters shall be deemed in law to be a contract between the legislature that proposed it and the voters. Measures or indicators of the success or effectiveness of government proposals shall be prescribed by law and shall be binding on the government. These measures of success shall be enacted or renewed in a separate law in the fourth year of each legislative term under the supervision of the outgoing Election Commission, to take effect for first and subsequent budget legislation of the following term, except that the first continuation budget, if enacted in whole or in part, shall be subject to the previously enacted measures of success that applied to it when it was first enacted as a regular budget. These measures of success shall include a procedure for estimating revenues for each proposed tax schedule and for determining those errors of estimation that are unpredictable and those that are avoidable. This law shall also prescribe measures of success for the functions of inspection, auditing, and application of measures of performance. At any time the Election Commission may accept private proposals for revised measures of success to apply to a future budget, provided that a referendum on these measures is held at least [*two months*] before the referendum on the budget to which they would apply and provided that the citizens offering such a proposal have no proprietary interest, direct or indirect, in a pending budget proposal for the budget referendum.

(i) Legislators shall be immune from lawsuits concerning their individual conduct in the course of legislative business. However, executive officers, the legislature that appoints them, and the legislature that performs inspection, auditing, and application of measures of performance shall not be immune from lawsuits arising from the outcomes of legislation once enacted. The criteria for standing and admissibility of suits shall be identical to those for suits against private parties as specified by the laws of torts and contracts, taking due account of the penalties prescribed in Article III, Section 4, that form part of the legislative contract and that shall have the status of liquidated damages.

(j) Election Commissioners shall be immune from lawsuits concerning their conduct of elections, except (a) that a Commissioner who is impeached and removed from office may be sued for damages arising from the misconduct that is specified in the bill of impeachment, and (b) that even without impeachment Election Commissioners may be sued for fraud or false advertising, in connection with official descriptions of legislative proposals that they have approved. The criteria for standing and admissibility of suits of the second kind shall be identical to those for suits against private parties as specified by the laws of torts and contracts governing fraud and advertising.

(k) An Election Commissioner may be impeached and removed from office under the same procedures as those prescribed by Article IV, Section 5 for the Chief of State and for other high officials, except that the trial shall be held before the more successful of the official legislatures that had appointed the Commissioner. The grounds shall be those for removal of a legislator, and in addition may include the flagrant and malicious disregard for the law.

Section 11. (a) Incentive pay for legislators, official or private, shall be based on the value of their proposals and the accuracy with which they estimate voters' preferences. In the case of proposals by official legislatures, the declared harms used to calculate this incentive pay shall be adjusted by the difference between the legislature's proposed tax assessments and the actual tax assessments, where applicable. Subject to the modifications prescribed by Sections 10 and 12 and by Article III, Section 4, the aggregate incentive pay for a legislature for each of its proposals that is adopted will be [*0.1*] percent of the budget amount contained in the proposal plus [*30*] percent of the total declared insured and uninsured harm from non-adoption, net of the declared harm from adoption, relative to the next most valuable distinct and different alternative proposed by another legislature, less [*5*] percent of the net inferiority of those proposals, relative to distinct and different alternatives on the ballot, for each population subgroup that on net would have supported an alternative proposal in the group, under the legislature's proposed taxes and accurate taxes for the alternative. If, however, the only such alternative is 'no action', the incentive pay shall instead be [*0.1*] percent of the budget amount contained in the approved proposal plus [*3*] percent of the total declared insured and uninsured harm from non-adoption, net of the declared harm from adoption, less [*.5*] percent of the net inferiority of those proposals relative to 'no action', for each population subgroup that on net supported no action under the legislature's proposed taxes. In the case of legislation to subdivide a population subgroup, these incentive payments shall be calculated using the proposed new subgroups as if they were already approved.

(b) The incentive pay for those proposal groups on which official legislatures make identical or equivalent new proposals shall be divided equally between them. If a private legislative proposal receives voter approval, the incentive pay shall be divided between the private party and the official legislature(s) that deliberated on it. If the proposal on the ballot is identical or substantially and technically equivalent to the proposal submitted by the private petitioner, the petitioner shall receive [*two-thirds*] of the incentive pay provided for in Subsection 11(a), adjusted so that the private share is not reduced by the net total harms declared by those voters who oppose the proposal. If the legislative process revises the proposal, or if the final proposal on the ballot merges the private proposal with elements that originated in the legislature, the petitioner shall receive less than [*two-thirds*] of the incentive pay provided for in Subsection 11(a) after the foregoing adjustment, and instead shall receive a proportion to be determined prior to the referendum by the Election Commission after it determines original authorship of the components of the proposal from the legislative history of this and related proposals and from the documented history of the private proposal. When substantially equivalent proposals appear in both records, whichever source documented it first shall receive full credit for it. The petitioner's incentive pay shall be reduced by the same percentage share of costs, specified by Subsection 10(d), as the petitioner's share of the adjusted incentive pay. The share of the incentive pay not paid to the private petitioner shall be paid to the official legislature(s) that deliberated on it, with the penalty for harms declared by some subgroups scaled down in this proportion. If a portion of a continuation budget wins in the referendum and if this portion was also proposed by a currently sitting primary official legislature, three-fourths of the resulting incentive pay shall be paid to the members of the legislature(s) of whose budget it is a continuation and one-fourth shall be paid to the primary official legislature that proposes to continue it. Subsequently this portion shall be deemed to be part of the budget proposal of this currently sitting primary official legislature. If a portion of a continuation budget wins in the referendum and if no currently sitting official legislature proposed it, the entire incentive pay for this portion shall be paid to the members of the legislature(s) of whose budget it is a continuation. If more than one legislature had originally shared the incentive pay of said budget portion, they shall divide their portion of the continuation incentive pay equally.

(c) The incentive pay to each official legislature shall be divided among its members as follows: [*One half*] shall be divided equally among them and [*one half*] shall be divided among them in proportion to their minimum individual incomes as determined under Section 5. Incentive pay for a sitting legislature shall be placed in escrow and paid to its members at the end of their term.

(d) All official legislators shall be exempt from tax assessments under the budgets for which they have made proposals until the first regular budget enacted after they leave office.

(e) The compensation of the Speaker of an official legislature shall be [*two*] times the average pay, including incentive pay less penalties, of the members of that official legislature.

Section 12. (a) That official or private sitting legislature whose budget proposals approved by referendum sum to the largest aggregate total shall appoint executive officers to carry out the approved budget programs and enforce the approved laws, except as provided otherwise under Subsection (b) and elsewhere herein. These executive officers shall serve at the pleasure of the legislature. Prior to a biennial budget referendum each legislature shall publish its proposed team of executive officers. In case two or more legislatures have received approval for identical budget totals, the choice of legislature for this role shall be determined by the toss of an honest coin supervised by the Election Commission.

(b) An official legislature not responsible for executive functions shall be responsible for inspection, auditing, and application of measures of performance. If more than one official legislature is not responsible for executive functions, the one gaining the largest incentive pay under Section 11 of this Article shall be responsible for inspection, auditing, and application of measures of performance. If in this circumstance two or more official legislatures have gained the same incentive pay under Section 11, the choice of official legislature for inspection, auditing, and application of measures of performance shall be determined by the toss of an honest coin supervised by the Election Commission.

(c) The incentive pay of legislators in the legislature that appoints executive officers shall be reduced/increased by [*35*] percent of all cost overruns/underruns and shall be increased or reduced by specified functions of the indicators of government performance under the legislation provided for in Subsection 10(h), as prescribed by law. The legislature responsible for inspection and audit shall calculate adjusted budget revenues, at the end of the budget period, by correcting the total for unpredictable changes in the numbers of citizens in the official population subgroups due to changes in status such as from employed to unemployed. This adjustment shall conform to the law on measures of performance. The Election Commission shall calculate the presumptive adjusted revenues and the presumptive planned revenues corresponding to the tax assessments that had been proposed by each official legislature for the budget just ending. The incentive pay of each official legislature shall be reduced by [*three*] percent of the absolute value of the discrepancy between presumptive adjusted budget revenues for that legislature and the presumptive planned budget revenues for the budget as enacted. For acquisitions of property and easements authorized by a referendum, the incentive pay of a legislature shall be reduced by [*five*] percent of the amount that the affected property owners have insured against financial harm (if any) arising from the success of this legislative proposal, except for noncompensable harms specified in Article III Section 5, after correcting the amount insured for the difference between actual compensation and the compensation the legislature had proposed for the property and easements. This reduction of incentive pay is additional to and separate from all other incentive pay adjustments herein prescribed. Cost overruns/underruns for a government program shall be assessed/allocated to voters in proportion to their taxes assessed for this program. For this purpose a ‘program’ means a budget proposal group or a portion of it that for each voter subgroup has a single tax assessment rate per taxpayer, and a single rate for each class of property. The pay of an executive officer shall be a fixed salary plus a fraction or multiple of the incentive pay received by a legislator under this subsection and Subsection 10(h).

(d) The incentive pay for the legislature responsible for inspection, auditing, and application of measures of performance shall include [*30*] percent of all improper or unauthorized costs recovered by this activity and shall be a function of the performance measures for this activity as prescribed by law.

(e) The government shall plan to maintain a financial reserve of readily marketable assets equal to [*three*] percent of the approved biennial budget, for the purpose of paying unanticipated budget deficits other than those provided for in Subsection (c). These assets shall be located within the national boundaries and shall not include currency or financial claims issued by a foreign government nor shall it include the government's own bonds. Its balance of national currency shall not exceed [*0.2*] percent of the biennial budget. Whenever the financial reserve differs from [*three*] percent of the approved biennial budget by more than [*0.5*] percent but less than [*three*] percent, the next biennial budget proposal shall include a schedule of uniform payments to or from the financial reserve scaled to restore the reserve to the planned figure within [*four*] years. Whenever the difference is [*three*] percent or more, the next biennial budget proposal shall include a schedule of uniform payments to or from the financial reserve scaled to restore the reserve to the planned figure within [*six*] years. If the difference is a deficit and the reserve is exhausted, the government shall issue full faith and credit bonds with a maturity schedule to conform to the prescribed schedule of payments to the reserve. The incentive pay of each Election Commissioner shall be reduced by [*0.1*] percent of the absolute value of the discrepancy between adjusted budget revenues and the officially planned budget revenues that had been stated in the budget as enacted, for each biennial budget enacted under the Commissioner's supervision.

(f) Until the first budget referendum of the legislative term, the executive team from the end of the previous term shall continue in office in a caretaker role. In its proposals for the budget referendum each legislature shall specify the executive team it has selected. After the referendum the team chosen by the winning legislature shall take office until the next budget referendum unless an executive team is replaced by another team to serve the remainder of its term. No member of an official legislature may serve as an executive official or employee.

Article III: Powers of the Government and Limitations Thereto

Section 1. (a) All powers herein permitted to 'the government' refer to powers exercised in conformity with the procedures and restrictions specified in this constitution.

(b) The government may enact every law that receives unanimous consent or where a statement of indifference or voter absence may imply consent, provided (a) that the Election Commission conducts a diligent effort to locate every absent voter and to obtain an absentee ballot and (b) that a law that is inconsistent with Section 2 must have the freely given, voluntary written consent of each voter whose rights the law abridges.

Section 2. [Bill of rights. Standard stuff, including strict prohibition of retroactive laws. Strict prohibition of involuntary servitude in any form, except that in the case of foreign invasion or an imminent threat of same, the government may use emergency powers to compel military service for up to a maximum of sixty days by citizens represented in official legislatures and qualified to vote, whose compensation shall be prescribed by law. Freedom of association and of political expression shall not include freedom to form coalitions or conspiracies by voters having the purpose of misrepresenting the harms to them of legislative proposals on the ballot.]

Section 3. [Scope and terms of permitted forms of official income redistribution from rich to poor. Specified taxes for this purpose.] These provisions may not be modified, amplified, or compromised by ordinary legislation.

Section 4. (a) Pursuant to laws enacted by procedures specified in Article II, the government may acquire property by compulsory court order for public purposes such as highway and sewer construction, provided that previous owners are compensated by [*five*] percent in excess of fair market value of the property acquired and of the diminution of fair market value of adjacent or associated property of the same owners that the government does not acquire. The government may purchase goods and services at market prices to further the purposes of this section, Sections 5, 6, 8, 9, and Article II, Section 9 and Subsection 12(b). The government may obtain by compulsory purchase easements from property owners restricting the private use and enjoyment of their properties for furtherance of the general welfare as provided by law, provided that all owners required to provide such easements are compensated by [*five*] percent in excess of the reduction of fair market value of said properties that results from the purchase of all such easements for a given specific purpose, except as otherwise provided in Section 5.

(b) The government may collect taxes in the manner prescribed in Article II, to finance the activities authorized herein. For this purpose it may require all citizens to file periodic reports of their incomes from all sources, to identify their property income by its industry and location, and to provide such other information as may be necessary to identify each citizen's membership in a population subgroup for the purposes of Article II, Subsection 2(a). The government may not collect money as taxes or fees nor disburse it in any manner except as prescribed by law.

(c) In addition to the compensation provided for under Article II, the government may provide such additional compensation to officials as is prescribed by law.

(d) The government may issue full faith and credit bonds to finance budget deficits in conformity with Article II, Subsection 12(e).

(e) The government may coin money and issue currency up to a total not to exceed [___ *pesos*]. [*It may not change the quantity of currency in circulation, either by destruction, creation, or payment into or out of the financial reserve, by more than two percent of this amount in a year nor by more than three percent of this amount in a four-year period. Deviations of the amount in circulation shall be restored to the authorized amount according to its own schedule with the same trigger points and correction schedule as those prescribed for the national financial reserve in Article II, Subsection 12(e).*]

[*(f) The government may not operate, franchise, nor have a financial interest, direct or indirect, in a banking institution nor create nor authorize the creation of a Central Bank. The government may not buy, sell, nor have a financial interest in the currency or in other obligations of a foreign government or of foreign financial institutions.*]

(g) The government may not acquire goods and services nor lend, rent, or deliver to private hands goods and services it has acquired, except as prescribed by law.

(h) The government may issue patents and copyrights for limited periods to inventors, tradespersons, and authors to protect their discoveries, trademarks, writings, and other original works, except that, wherever monitoring and assessment of economic value is practicable, the government shall instead offer prizes or royalties for limited periods approximating the economic value of the discoveries, etc.

(i) [*To the extent possible, all activities of the government, including the design and production of military weapons, communications except only military communications within military operations, and transportation, shall be contracted out to private firms. The executive team, subject to independent inspection and audit as prescribed in Subsection 12(b) and elsewhere herein, shall supervise the fulfillment of these contracts. Streets and highways shall be private toll roads except where their value is greater without tolls, due to the costs of collecting tolls, as determined by law. Career government employees shall be limited to the following categories: (1) a secretariat for each official legislature and a secretariat for the Election Commission; (2) magistrates and judges provided for in Article V and such court officers as they may appoint; (3)*

military officers in the line of command, their operational staffs including intelligence, and combat personnel; and (4) officials and operatives responsible for such anti-terrorist and other police intelligence functions as are prescribed by law. Competition for the intelligence functions shall be provided by parallel, independent units within the government and by private firms. The roles of career military officers and reservists shall be competitive in the development of military tactics, proposals for weapons selection, and troop training, but shall come under unified command for military operations as prescribed by law. Logistics and other military support functions shall be performed by military reserve units and private firms as prescribed by law. Promotion of career employees in categories (1), (3), and (4) shall be decided by the legislature that selects executive officers, after receiving the advice of the Commander in Chief for category (3) and of the chief executive official for category (4).]

Section 5. (a) Under the procedures of Article II, the government may enact and enforce laws that define ordinary crimes and misdemeanors, for the protection of public safety and for the implementation of specific laws authorized by this constitution. If laws enacted under this section harm owners of some properties or reduce the incomes of some citizens whose activities, previously legal, become unlawful, these effects shall be considered easements for the purposes of Subsection 4(a).

(b) The government may prohibit and punish the counterfeiting of its coin, currency, bonds, and of private securities and other private objects of value, however, without compensating citizens for the loss of income they might have received from such activities. In conformity with international law, the government may prohibit and punish felonies committed on the high seas.

Section 6. (a) Under the procedures of Article II, the government may enact and enforce laws defining those kinds of contracts and contract provisions that will be enforced in official courts and, clarifying for new and unanticipated circumstances, those kinds of contracts that this constitution prohibits under Section 7. The government may not thereby create new prohibitions other than those listed in Section 7, however. In the case of contracts that are neither prohibited nor expressly sanctioned by law, the parties to such contracts shall exhaust every remedy that the contracts themselves provide before seeking recourse in an official court. Subject to this provision, the official courts shall accept jurisdiction to interpret and enforce all contracts not specifically prohibited by law. The government may pay court fees and fees of private arbitrators arising from government business, including amicus curiae submissions.

(b) The government may enact and enforce laws governing bankruptcy. The government may prescribe by law uniform units of measure and definitions, measures or indicators of quality for private goods and services. Such units, definitions, etc., shall have no restrictive effect on goods and services offered for sale unless such restrictions are expressly provided for by easements in conformity with Subsection 4(a).

Section 7. [List of prohibited private contracts.]

Section 8. (a) The government shall conduct foreign affairs as prescribed by law. No official or private person shall negotiate or conclude treaties with a foreign government, except as authorized by law. The government may negotiate treaties and propose their provisions as legislation. If approved in a referendum, a treaty or a part thereof may be revoked only in a manner provided for in the treaty itself or else under the procedure and requirements prescribed in Article VI, Section 1 for constitutional amendments. The government may enact and enforce laws governing immigration and naturalization. The government may enact and enforce laws delimiting the nation's territory and may acquire or cede territory in conformity with international law, except that a proposal to cede territory shall be subject to the procedures and requirements prescribed in Article VI, Section 1 for constitutional amendments.

(b) The government may establish and support armed forces.

(c) The government may declare war, following the legislative procedures prescribed in Article II. In the event of foreign invasion or an imminent threat to the armed forces, however, the Commander in Chief may order the armed forces to defend themselves and to defend the nation's territory, following emergency procedures prescribed by law. No private person or group or persons may make war or maintain troops, except that in the event of foreign invasion or an imminent threat to citizens' homes and property, they may form temporary militias in their own defense. This provision shall not restrict the right of citizens to organize private organizations of security guards or to supply police and military services to government as prescribed by law.

Section 9. [(a) The national government may delegate governmental powers to regional or local authorities, either created ad hoc from time to time or created on a permanent basis, as prescribed by law, provided that, in the referendum for the enabling legislation, the sum of the absolute values of declared harms both of voters who favor and of voters who oppose the legislation outside the participating regions or localities shall not exceed {10} percent of the net total declared harms from nonadoption in the participating regions or localities.]

[(b) The legislation creating a regional or local authority may establish that this authority shall conform to Article II, (except that the size of its official legislatures may be scaled as appropriate and will normally have more finely subdivided demographic subgroups than those in the national legislatures), and shall conform to Article III, Sections 1(b), 2, 4(a), 4(b), 4(f), 4(g), 4(i), 5(a), 7, and 10, and to such other articles and sections of this constitution as this legislation may provide. Once such regional or local authorities are established by such legislation, in the process of proposing, each official legislature shall employ an official legislature from each regional and local authority as a committee for determining the regional/local benefits and costs, and their allocations by demographic subgroups, of subsequent legislative proposals. The compensation of legislatures of a regional or local authority shall be governed by the same rules as those herein prescribed for national legislatures, except that the national legislatures shall be solely responsible for the executive functions, and their related incentives, for national legislation.]

[(c) If the property owners and residents of a locality agree unanimously thereto, the governance of the locality shall be determined by a lawful contract among them, without authorization by legislation, provided that this contract satisfies all holders of easements and conforms to all covenants that apply to any and all property in the locality, and provided also that the parties to the contract post public notice of its provisions at least 180 days prior to its coming into force, so that legislation relating to its effects on other property or persons may be proposed and enacted if appropriate.]

Section 10. No power or authority herein granted may be delegated to any person, commission, or other body except as expressly authorized in this constitution. Neither the executive authority nor the courts may impose rules, regulations, or other comparable restraints on private persons other than such rules, regulations, and restraints as are duly enacted in legislation. This constitution has the force of law and may not be compromised nor amended except as provided in Article VI, Section 2.

Article IV: Chief of State and Commander in Chief

Section 1. Each official legislature shall, at the beginning of its term, nominate a candidate for the ceremonial function of Chief of State, a candidate for Commander in Chief of the Armed Forces, a candidate for Vice Chief of State, and a candidate for Vice Commander in Chief of the Armed Forces. These candidates shall be four different citizens. Private legislative enterprises may also nominate such candidates under the provisions of Article II, Subsection 10(d). These candidates shall be presented to voters under the same procedures as those for legislation, Article II, Sections 8 through 11, inclusive. The winner of each of these contests shall serve for a term of four years and may serve successive terms, except that the Commander in Chief may serve at most [*three*] terms, except in a time of war or of extreme emergency coming under the provisions of Article III, Section 8. If the Chief of State or Commander in Chief ceases to serve due to death or disability, the Vice Chief shall serve as Chief for the remainder of the term. In that event candidates for Vice Chief shall be nominated and presented in a referendum, to be elected to serve the remainder of the unexpired term. If the office of Chief falls vacant when there is no Vice Chief, the official legislature that appoints executive officials (or if neither does, the official legislature that performs the inspection and audit functions) shall appoint an Acting Chief to serve until a referendum to fill the positions of Chief and Vice Chief, for the remainder of the unexpired term, can be held.

Section 2. Each candidate for the office of Chief of State, for Commander in Chief, or for Vice Chief of either office shall be a native-born citizen of [*Cumulanis*] and shall be at least [*35*] years old. A candidate for Commander in Chief or for Vice Commander in Chief of the Armed Forces shall have had at least [*four*] years of experience in the active military service of [*Cumulanis*].

Section 3. (a) The Chief of State or when necessary the Vice Chief of State shall receive foreign ambassadors and higher-ranking foreign dignitaries in conformity with the foreign policy authorized by law and they shall perform such other ceremonial duties as may be prescribed by law. Neither the Chief of State nor the Vice Chief of State shall be an executive official for functions prescribed under Article II, Subsections 12(a) and (b) nor shall either serve as an official legislator. Financing and support for the activities of the Chief of State shall be provided by budget legislation and by executive officials as prescribed by law.

(b) The Commander in Chief of the Armed Forces shall have sole command of military operations subject to the foreign policy and military strategy prescribed by law, or as determined in extreme emergency under Article III, Subsection 8(c). Neither the Commander in Chief nor the Vice Commander in Chief shall be an executive official for functions prescribed under Article II, Subsections 12(a) and (b) nor shall either serve as an official legislator.

Section 4. The pay of the Chief of State and of the Vice Chief of State shall be at least equal to that of each of the Speakers or of an Election Commissioner, whichever is higher, under Article II. The pay of the Commander in Chief and of the Vice Commander in Chief shall be at least equal to that of the highest-paid executive among those appointed by the governing legislature.

Section 5. The Chief of State, the Commander in Chief, or the Vice Chief of either office may be removed from office upon the same grounds and procedures as those for removing an official legislator, except that the impeachment of either of these high officials shall be the responsibility of the legislature that controls the executive functions, and that the trial of this official, for removal from office, shall be the held in the official legislature responsible for inspection and auditing. The procedures for these steps shall be the same as those for legislative proposals and final appeals.

Article V: The Judiciary.

Section 1. (a) Magistrates and official courts shall have the power to compel attendance by defendants at their proceedings. In addition, official courts shall have the power to bring to trial and to sentence criminal offenders, to enforce contracts, to issue writs and injunctions [*etc.*] as prescribed by law, and to collect fees to support their operations.

(b) The courts shall interpret the law as it meant when enacted and shall not amend or modify the law. The only law, in addition to this constitution, shall be statute law. The courts shall interpret the constitution in terms of the meaning it had at the time it was ratified and similarly for the interpretation of each constitutional amendment and of each law.

Section 2. The courts shall be supported by their fees, which may include fees for amicus curiae submissions, and by such other compensation as may be prescribed by law.

Section 3. (a) The legislature that selects executive officers shall nominate judges and magistrates, using the procedures of Article II, Subsection 9(a), for proposing legislation, except that these nominations shall not be submitted to a referendum. Instead, such nominations shall be presented to the official legislature responsible for inspection, auditing, and application of measures of performance. This legislature shall approve or disapprove each nominee using the procedures of Article II, Subsection 9(a). Judges in courts of first instance and magistrates shall normally be selected from among successful arbitrators. The legislature shall appoint judges to appellate courts from among successful judges, which here and throughout this document means those judges whose lower courts have consistently covered their costs.

(b) Judges whose courts fail to be supported by fees and other income as provided by law shall be retired under the procedures for judicial appointments. Whenever, because of delays in the resolution of cases, a sufficient number of parties with standing in active disputes petition that a successful private arbitrator be appointed an official judge, the appointing legislature shall approve such an appointment unless it finds that the delays are temporary.

(c) The legislature shall appoint one magistrate for each judicial district.

(d) Rules for determining which persons have standing to participate in civil or criminal cases before courts of law shall be prescribed by law.

Section 4. For each civil or criminal case that arises, there shall be at least three official judges who may accept jurisdiction. If the parties to a case reach timely agreement on a judge, the agreed court shall receive jurisdiction. If they fail to reach timely agreement, the plaintiff or prosecutor shall ask the magistrate to select an odd number (three or more) judges by weighted random choice from a list consisting of (1) the judges proposed by the two sides and (2) as many as three additional judges that have settled more cases than have any of those proposed by the two sides. To obtain the weights for this choice, the magistrate shall sum those cases settled by each proposed judge in the past year in which the two sides agreed on a judge and use the fraction of this total settled by each such judge as the weight or probability for the random selection. (For these purposes the magistrate may restrict the calculation to cases of the particular class of which the case in question is a member.) From among the three or more judges thus selected, each side may veto judges until one remains.

Section 5. In addition to the functions prescribed elsewhere in this constitution, magistrates may perform marriages, notarize documents, [*and perform other customary routine functions of magistrates.*]

Section 6. The provisions of Sections 3(a), 3(b), 3(d), and 4 apply also to appellate courts.

Section 7. (a) If a party should choose to appeal an appellate court decision, the venue for the final appeal shall ordinarily be the official legislature whose legislative proposals approved by the electorate have the greatest aggregate value, measured by their budget amounts plus the declared net aggregate value of votes of the electorate. However, an official legislator who is a defendant or a member of whose family is a defendant in a suit as provided in Article II, Subsection 10(i) or in a criminal trial may not participate in the review of said suit or trial. In such cases the same rules regarding venue as those in Article V, Section 8 shall apply. The procedure for handling appeals shall be the same as that for legislation, except that such appeals shall not be subject to referendum; the decision of the legislature is final.

(b) If new legislation approved subsequent to a decision under Subsection (a) expressly reverses that decision within [*three*] years after the decision is announced, the incentive pay prescribed in Article II attributable to that part of the new legislation shall be subtracted from the incentive pay of the legislature that made the decision.

Section 8. (a) A person with standing may contest a law or other action by any part of the government on the grounds of its constitutionality, and courts at each level may accept the case and rule on this issue. If the official legislature whose legislative proposals approved by the electorate have the greatest aggregate value, measured by their budget amounts plus the declared net aggregate value of votes of the electorate, enacted the challenged law or was responsible for the challenged action, the official legislature ranking second by this criterion shall sit as the constitutional court for the case unless it is similarly foreclosed from this role. If all official legislatures have a significant share of the responsibility for a challenged law, the previous legislature that appointed executive officers and judges in the most recent past term shall be convened to sit as the constitutional court for the case. The decision procedure shall be the same as that for legislation, except that the decision of the constitutional court shall be final.

(b) A decision of the constitutional court may be reversed, under the procedures of Article VI Section 2, except that for the reversal to succeed the voter declarations of net aggregate harm, in case it fails, instead shall be at least [*0.5*] percent of one year's value of the nation's aggregate production of goods and services. In addition, if those subgroups of the population, defined by Article II Sec. 2, that oppose the reversal (that is, those in which the votes sum to aggregate declared harm) have an overall aggregate declared harm in excess of [*0.5*] percent of the nation's aggregate production of goods and services, the reversal is disapproved. If a referendum expressly reverses a decision under Subsection (a) within [*3*] years after the decision is announced, the incentive pay attributable to that reversal shall be subtracted from the incentive pay of the legislature that made the decision. The combined incentive pay of private petitioners, where relevant, and of official legislatures for a the reversal of a constitutional court decision, when the reversal is approved by a referendum, shall be [*30*] percent of the excess of the total harm from disapproval, net of declared harms due to approval, over [*0.5*] percent of one year's value of the nation's aggregate production of goods and services, less [*5*] percent of the net total monetary value of the harms declared by each population subgroup that on balance opposes the reversal, or shall be [*0.005*] percent of one year's value of the nation's aggregate production of goods and services, whichever is greater. This incentive pay shall be allocated among petitioners and legislatures with the same percentages and procedures as are prescribed in Article II, Subsection 11(b). If the constitutional court's decision is upheld, the election costs shall be allocated to petitioners and official legislatures with the same proportions and procedures as is incentive pay for reversal.

Section 9. The compensation of an official legislature or constitutional court for deciding each appeal or constitutional issue shall be [*500*] times the court fees paid by all parties except the government in the court of first instance for the case at issue, plus such additional compensation as has been prescribed by law enacted prior to the first filing of said case.

Section 10. (a) Judges shall be immune from lawsuits concerning their conduct of court business, so long as this conduct conforms to the canons of judicial ethics and so long as they interpret the applicable law in good faith as provided in this constitution. A reversal of a judge's decision on appeal shall not constitute grounds for a lawsuit against this judge unless the opinion in the reversal states that the judge's decision showed flagrant or malicious disregard of the law or of the canons of judicial ethics.

(b) The grounds for removal of magistrates and successful judges shall include those for disqualification of an official legislator, and in addition may include repeated decisions by a judge or magistrate found by a higher court to be in flagrant or malicious disregard of the law. The procedure shall be the same as that prescribed in Article IV, Section 5 for the Chief of State and for other high officials, except for cases coming under Subsection 3(b).

Article VI: Ratification

Section 1. This constitution shall come into force if it is ratified by a referendum in which at least [*80*] percent of citizens eligible to vote participate. Voting citizens shall declare the monetary value of the harm to them if ratification succeeds or fails. Ratification will depend on [*two*] criteria: (a) at least [*90*] percent of those voting shall have declared a harm if ratification fails, that is, shall have voted in favor of ratification; and (b) the aggregate amount of declared harm in case of failure shall be at least [*five*] times the aggregate amount of declared harm in case of ratification. No insurance against these harms shall be offered. The procedure shall otherwise conform to Article II, Subsection 10(b).

Section 2. This constitution may be amended by the procedures of Article II, including positive and negative tax assessments, except that in order to enter into force, an amendment must be approved by a voter declaration of net aggregate harm, in case it fails, of at least [*3*] percent of one year's value of the nation's aggregate production of goods and services. In addition, if those subgroups of the population, defined by Article II, Sec. 2, that oppose the amendment (that is, those in which the votes sum to aggregate declared harm) have an overall aggregate declared harm in excess of [*1*] percent of the nation's aggregate production of goods and services the amendment is disapproved. It must be proposed at least one year prior to the referendum to approve or disapprove it. When a constitutional amendment is under consideration, each official legislature considering it shall sequester itself at least until the completed proposal is published. A proposed amendment that is not adopted may not be considered again for at least [*ten*] years. The combined incentive pay of private petitioners, where relevant, and of official legislatures for a constitutional amendment approved by a referendum shall be [*30*] percent of the excess of the total harm from non-adoption, net of declared harms due to adoption, over [*3*] percent of one year's value of the nation's aggregate production of goods and services, less [*5*] percent of the net total monetary value of the harms declared by each population subgroup that on balance opposes the amendment, or shall be [*0.03*] percent of one year's value of the nation's aggregate production of goods and services, whichever is greater. This incentive pay shall be allocated among petitioners and legislatures with the same percentages and procedures as are prescribed in Article II, Subsection 11(b). If the amendment is disapproved, the election costs shall be allocated with the same proportions and procedures as is incentive pay for approval.

Section 3. (a) Upon ratification of this constitution, [*the existing proto-government*] shall serve in a caretaker capacity until the following provision creating an Interim Official Legislature can be implemented. [____] shall select [*two*] eminent jurists from [*Cumulanis*] and [*three*] from former members of [*the International Court of Justice*] to serve as the Interim Election Commission for [*two*] years, during the transition to the constitution's full implementation. As soon as it can be constituted, the Interim Election Commission shall choose a random sample of [*400*] citizens, from among those eligible to vote, to serve as the Interim Official Legislature. The Interim Official Legislature shall select a Speaker and shall function in the same manner as does an official legislature under Article II, except that there shall be no requirement for an Interim Legislator to exchange property as prescribed in Article II, Section 5.

(b) Using the procedure of Article II, Subsection 9(a), within six months of being constituted the Interim Official Legislature shall (1) propose a temporary 'no action' budget containing the minimum for public safety, represented by a continuation of previous year's military and police budgets for the predecessor government, plus interim family assistance as provided by Article III, Section 3, plus compensation of [__ *pesos*] each for the Election Commissioners, plus compensation for government officials and private Legislators as herein provided until the first regular budget, plus provision for an audit of the interim 'no action' budget, plus provision for an interim Census, designed and conducted in such a manner as to facilitate accurate implementation of Article II, Section 2, plus provision for a budget surplus of [*one*] percent of the budget total to commence building the national financial reserve prescribed in Article II, Subsection 12(e), and shall include proposed payroll taxes and property taxes to finance it; (2) propose legislation defining costs of elections and measures of success for subsequent budgets; (3) select an Election Commission to begin serving a regular four-year term within one year of the date at which the Interim Official Legislature was chosen; (4) nominate candidates for Chief of State, Commander in Chief of the Armed Forces, Vice Chief of State, and Vice Commander in Chief of the Armed Forces and appoint acting officials to fill these four positions; (5) appoint [__] judges and interim magistrates to proceed under the provisions of Article V; (6) propose a law defining felonious conduct in connection with legislative business, such as bribery, extortion, and obstruction, including provisions governing subsequent employment of legislators by employers who do business with or otherwise tangibly benefit from government programs; (7) propose an interim set of demographic subgroups to be used by the first regular Election Commission; and (8) propose an interim executive team to administer the interim budget.

(c) As soon as practicable, the Interim Election Commission shall conduct a referendum for approval of the proposals of the Interim Official Legislature. The referendum shall follow the procedures prescribed in Article II, Subsections 10(a) and 10(b), except that no insurance shall be offered and all declared harms shall be uninsured. Private proposals for these referendum issues shall be included, as provided in Article II, Subsection 10(d), for the two private proposals on each issue that post the largest bond among those competing. Compensation for the Interim Official Legislature shall be that provided in Article II, Section 5, plus [*0.1*] percent of the budget amounts contained in those of the Interim Official Legislature's proposals that the voters approve, plus [*3*] percent of the net total harm, of non-adoption of these approved proposals, declared by voters. Compensation for successful private proposals shall be [*0.1*] percent of the budget amounts contained in those proposals plus [*3*] percent of the net total harm of non-adoption of these approved proposals, declared by voters. No other proposals for legislation shall be included in the referendum unless an imminent threat of war requires implementation of Article III, Section 8.

(d) Members of the Interim Official Legislature shall not be exempt from the taxes prescribed in Subsection (b).

(e) Judges and magistrates shall enforce all laws, rights, and obligations that were in force prior to the ratification of this constitution that do not conflict with it for [*four*] years, after which all such laws, rights, and obligations mandated by those laws, shall be null and void, unless superceded or reinstated sooner by legislation enacted under the full provisions of this constitution. Private rights and obligations arising from existing contracts and customs shall continue in force on the same basis as if this constitution had always been in force, except that previously legal contracts that this constitution prohibits and that were entered into before this constitution was presented for ratification shall be enforced for [*four*] years, after which all such contracts shall be null and void.

(f) Within [*three*] months of taking office, the Election Commission selected under Subsection (b)(3) shall select two official legislatures as provided under Article II. [*etc.*]

Technical Annex

Procedure for Adjusting Legislative Votes and Voters' Uninsured Harms

This Technical Annex is part of and has the same legal force as the Constitution.

If the rate of change with respect to income (the 'income effect') of a legislator's willingness to pay to change an outcome is the same for all legislators in both official legislatures, there shall be no adjustments of the kind herein provided. The following procedure shall apply if this income effect differs among legislators.

(a) Legislative Decisions on Discrete Sets of Alternative Proposals. Within each legislature, the official monetary effects on each legislator's family of each issue to be decided, in terms of taxes, changes in property values, and changes in prices and wages shall be calculated in a manner determined by the legislature subject to the rules of evidence. Each legislator, when stating a willingness to pay for an outcome relative to an alternative, shall state whether it includes perceived monetary effects that disagree with the official monetary effects. If a legislator's willingness to pay is equal to the perceived monetary effects for the legislator's family, there is no intangible value involved; otherwise there is such a value. The legislator's willingness to pay to change each pairwise choice will be used as stated for all issues having no intangible value for that legislator.

For sets of issues, some of which include intangible values for one or more legislators, that are to be considered together in a referendum, the declarations of willingness to pay shall be adjusted for income effects and the outcomes ranked using the Cardinal Ranking Procedure and related steps using the legislator's stated pairwise income effects. The Election Commission shall use the resulting ranking of outcomes and their estimated net aggregate gains to determine the probabilities of success of the possible outcomes in the pending referendum.

(b) Legislative Decisions on Continuous-Scale Issues. When a legislature considers a budget proposal or other legislative proposal whose outcome is to be chosen as a point on a continuous scale together with associated schedules of taxes and transfers, each legislator shall declare two valuation schedules showing, at each point on the scale, what the legislator's family would be willing to pay to increase the outcome by one unit. The first of the two valuation schedules shall show the portion of the valuation that represents the family's financial interest in the outcome and the second shows intangible valuation. The legislator shall also declare by what amount the intangible valuation schedule would differ in the event of a specified increase in the legislator's family income.

(c) Referenda with Discrete Sets of Outcomes. When the legislative process reveals intangible values associated with a pairwise choice between outcomes, if the Election Commission finds that income effects can affect the outcome, the declarations of uninsured harms by voters shall be adjusted for income effects and the outcome determined according to the Cardinal Ranking Procedure and related steps. The income effects shall be estimated by efficient statistical procedures from legislative votes and procedures from both official legislatures.

(d) Referenda with Continuous-Scale Outcomes. When a referendum offers a budget proposal or other legislative proposal whose outcome is to be chosen as a point on a continuous scale together with associated schedules of taxes and transfers, the Election Commission shall offer corresponding fair insurance whose premium varies continuously along this scale. If the legislative process reveals uninsurable intangible values, each voter shall declare two valuation schedules showing at each point on the scale what the voter would be willing to pay to increase/decrease the outcome by one unit. The first of the two valuation schedules shall show the portion of the valuation that the voter wishes to insure and the second shall show the uninsured part of the valuation. The voter shall also declare an income effect for the uninsured valuation schedule. The voter's insurance payout will be the absolute value of the integral of the insured curve from the outcome to the voter's most preferred outcome. The voter's incentive tax will be the integral for all other voters measuring the areas under their combined curves, plus the integral measuring the area under this voter's insured curve, from the value the outcome would have had, without this voter's uninsured valuation schedule, to the actual outcome. [*A further transfer to each voter will be determined by the applicable formulas in the appendices to Chapter 6.*]

4 Perspectives and Alternatives

The truth which makes men free is for the most part the truth which men prefer not to hear.[1]

4.1 INTRODUCTION

The reader may have at least a vague impression of utopian overtones in the discussion in Chapters 1 and 2, and perhaps even in the particulars of Chapter 3. I have been careful not to claim that we have here a plan for Utopia, however, and indeed have clearly and specifically avoided such a claim. In particular, Chapter 2 spells out some kinds of uncivilized conduct with which the proposed approach to government cannot deal. Furthermore, the draft constitution is loaded with provisions deemed necessary because of the postulate that the day-to-day behavior of the citizens of 'Cumulanis' will be considerably less than saintly.

In the marketplaces for ordinary private goods, even apart from endemic conspiracies and campaigns to justify cartels, monopoly franchises, and so on, it is not unusual to encounter misleading claims and breach of contract. It is easy to build up a persuasive case against the acceptability of free, competitive markets. Indeed, if I may take liberties with a well-known statement by Winston Churchill, I would put it in the following way. In this world of sin and woe, few pretend that free, competitive markets are perfect or all-wise. Indeed, one can truthfully say that free, competitive markets are the worst form of economic organization, except all those other forms that have been tried from time to time. Churchill's statement in fact referred to democracy as a form of government rather than to free, competitive markets.[2] He was right at the time he said it, because at that time no one knew of a way to design a genuine approximation to free, competitive markets for application to the structure and operation of a national government. Scholarly research since then has shown that there is a way. If a country chooses it, there will still be a world of sin and woe, but that country will have improved its fortunes.

An aura of utopian overtones surrounds the notion that somewhere, somehow there will be a nation of prudent citizens who would choose this document to provide the starting point and central structure for their constitution. Besides being civilized, these citizens would be able to resist seductive promises and proclamations of good intentions by would-be politicians and other charismatic, self-seeking persons. They would have the self-discipline to set aside their own wishful thinking, so that they could see far enough ahead, clearly enough to appreciate the long-term benefits of a market-simulating approach to government. They would adopt this approach and stay with it. A combination of statesmanlike leadership and public vigilance would exclude the influence of interest groups, hoping to promote their own interests, from the constitution-writing process. To expect all that as a probable or easily managed event would itself be a bad case of wishful thinking. There is no reason to expect it to happen anytime soon.[3]

4.2 CAN IT HAPPEN?

The reader, if so inclined, would search in vain for a program or even for the slightest hint here of an impending campaign or crusade to persuade the countries of the world, old or new, to adopt this constitution. Instead what you find here is an attempt to fill a major gap in constitutional concepts. During the half-century since the end of World War II, dozens of new countries have emerged from alien rule or have ended homegrown tyrannies, and have set about to establish new governments. If they asked for help on how to design the most advantageous constitution for themselves, all anyone has offered them was a warmed-over, revised version of an existing constitution.[4] An observer who was even vaguely familiar with the inefficiencies and abuses of government had to be dismayed but could not offer a better alternative. Now that fundamental thinking on alternative mechanisms has shown that there are other possibilities, however, the picture has changed. There is a better way, even if most people will find it hard to accept.

There are many reasons why a new approach to government like that suggested here is difficult to accept under any circumstances. Every established government protects a large array of entrenched interests, including its politicians and officials, who would powerfully oppose a plan that eliminates their privileges. Among the majority of a country's citizens who bear the cost of these entrenched interests, few will readily abandon a social system to which they have become accustomed when the only reason for doing so is the logic of a likely benefit. A new constitution is generally put in place only when a powerful minority, with the acquiescence of the majority, overthrows or expels an existing government for other reasons. This minority will then control the writing of a new constitution, and will usually plan to entrench their own leaders and favorite charities in the process. Other interested groups may also jostle for influence, and may obtain some, working toward and through a traditional governmental framework. That is the way that it has always been.

In fact, all governments trace their origins back to the tyrannies of ancient times, which substituted systematic taxation for banditry and plunder, to the advantage of the monarchs, their armies, families, and supporters. Governments evolved toward broader participation and their societies toward greater egalitarianism after their armies, due to the cheapening of weapons, evolved toward mass armies. As the late Chairman Mao aptly put it, 'Political power grows out of the barrel of a gun.' The preposterous notion that government anywhere is in fact a 'social contract' has no basis in historical fact. (Of those who would mention the adoption of the U.S. Constitution as such a contract, I would ask several questions. Were slaves in the South a party to the contract? Were propertyless citizens, who could not vote, parties to it? Were those who voted against its adoption, or who otherwise resisted it, parties to it?) One can find innumerable cases where a nation's people *acquiesced* in the rule of their government, but that situation has no resemblance to their participation in a contract.

Although loftier sentiments have confused the issue in modern times, current governments are direct descendants of the ancient tyrannies and have many of their attributes. Sovereign immunity, monopoly power for most functions and agencies of government, and the central role of organized interests are the most important examples. No matter how a new government structure, with or without a written constitution, has become established, its leaders have seen fit to retain these features. As we have already noted, one reason for that is that there was no credible alternative plan that lacked these features. An even more compelling reason, however, is that under the circumstances there was no way to give them up. It will be a rare event if a new national leadership should ever be in a position to give them up, and even if it has that chance it will be an improbable event if such a leadership should choose to do so.

This strong statement of realistic pessimism is intended to focus attention on the true purpose of this book. Rather than an attempt to start a political movement, it is an attempt to promote practical analysis of sound, constructive constitutional principles. Occasionally a leadership group in an actual or intended new country asks for help on such principles. Our question is, does scholarly analysis lead only to minor variations on the principle constitutional ideas now in force in various countries, or can we offer a significant improvement? If there is a way to improve substantially on existing models, then we should not let down those who ask for help. We should have suggestions that can be supported with a well-considered set of facts and analysis.

4.3 IS THERE A BETTER WAY?

Among those scholars who dislike current forms of government enough to propose radical changes, only one or two have proposed anything like what we propose here.[5] Although I shall not attempt to survey alternative views, it is appropriate to mention a few.

A point of view that we have totally ignored up to this point is the view that favors anarchy. An engaging example is Benson (1990, pp. 312-21). He points out that along much of the frontier areas of the U.S. in the 19th century people got along peaceably without organized government. Then he uses selected examples of government by hoodlums and of successful vigilante justice in support of the suggestion that all justice should be by private police or vigilantes. Even as presented, these examples scarcely make the case, however. In his vigilante examples, there was an organized government, and the vigilantes executed a few criminal officials, among other persons, and then allowed organized government to resume its functions. He did not establish that a city can successfully operate without an organized government, or that rural areas can do so either if they have enough wealth to have something worth stealing. (He also did not mention the costs and dangers of purely private means of protecting livestock herds against rustling.) As Benson points out, bandits in frontier areas did rob stagecoaches and trains, which was where most of the money was. His conclusion was that law enforcement can and should be left to voluntary private associations.

This strikes me as a mixture of wishful thinking and a counsel of despair. Benson's impression that existing governments abuse their powers and may particularly attract criminals and unprincipled people to the ranks of their officials is certainly credible. To propose abolishing government's monopoly of force, and its monopoly of anything else, is undoubtedly a move in the right direction, but overshoots the mark.

Our draft constitution does eliminate as much government monopoly as seems practicable, and expressly protects private law enforcement as part of the system. It provides only for such publicly supplied courts as can survive by their fees, unless voters almost unanimously vote to provide them with subsidies from the public budget. Within this framework, there can be as little or as much organized government as voters approve with their votes in units of willingness-to-pay. If perhaps there is a society here and there so civil and so isolated from the threat of invasion that it could prosper indefinitely without organized government, I wish it the best of everything. Our interest here centers on a middle ground of societies that are mostly civil and law-abiding, and not so torn by ethnic or class hatreds as to make them ungovernable. Such countries have enough lawlessness, enough disputes, and enough external threats that they can gain benefits, too great to brush aside, from sound government. Given that perspective, we want the best conceivable plan for government that one can devise, to have it ready in case the opportunity to use it should arise.

A related alternative that has a more carefully reasoned structure is the concept of government as a confederation of local and higher level governments developed by Foldvary (1994, esp. Chs 6, 7 and 15), where each level is like a profitable developer town, a condominium, or an association of property owners. Our proposed constitution expressly provides in Article III Subsection 9(c) for local governments of this kind, in addition to other provisions that implicitly encourage them. Foldvary argues, however, that government at every level could be arrived at by contract, working from the bottom up, relying on covenants placed in deed restrictions by private land developers to overcome free rider problems. He does not explain who establishes and enforces the contract law that governs these arrangements as they work their way from small localities and towns upward to the formation of higher levels of government. That is one difficulty with his concept, but there are others, which together place Foldvary's concept in the same category as Benson's advocacy of anarchy.

Foldvary supports his remarkable and provocative plan with two spurious claims, without which his whole argument for higher-than-local levels fails. First, he claims that free rider problems at higher levels can be solved, when there are public goods like national defense whose benefits are not excludable within the national territory, by finding other excludable goods and/or peer-group pressures to oblige holdouts to pay their shares of the costs (Foldvary, 1994, p. 209). Second, he claims (pp. 26-30, 200-201, and 211-12) that all differences in public services, at all levels of government, are capitalized into land values. Neither claim can survive close examination.

The first of his claims is simply wishful thinking. Without prior covenants in local deeds to create a property tax obligation for regional and national public goods, which it would not be in a developer-proprietor's interest to insert, the consequent free rider problems would correspond to the standard analysis of these problems. In almost every country, peer-group pressures within each small locality, favoring rivalry and mistrust toward other localities, would outweigh the claimed favorable pressures from other towns, and would aggravate rather than ameliorate the free-rider problem.

The second of his claims is a major technical error. Capitalization of the benefits of local or regional amenities and public goods occurs only to the extent that people, like capital, are perfectly and costlessly mobile.[6] In cases like Disneyland, Florida and Reston, Virginia, this assumption is a good enough approximation that one can properly say that it is 'true.' For whole counties or parishes it is a questionable approximation, and for a jurisdiction as large as a state in the United States, it is unquestionably false and misleading. But to see the point more clearly, consider the national level. To apply the mobility assumption to nations one would have to assume that all or several nations have absolutely unlimited immigration and emigration at zero cost. Then, when real wages and other real personal service incomes in a rich country like the U.S. were driven down to the same level as in Mexico or Bangladesh, the benefits of living in the U.S. would be fully capitalized into land values.

The differences between his viewpoint and mine may at first glance appear to be small but in fact are substantial. They appear to be small because the constitution proposed here, including its ratification procedures in Article VI, resembles a contract, and because it emphasizes the use of contracts, both private and public, throughout. The disagreements are large, however, for three reasons. First, the proposed constitution recognizes that the process does not begin in a vacuum, but in the presence of an already established order whose national defense, laws, and contracts will continue in force except as otherwise provided in the new constitution and new law. Second, many persons have considerable wealth in the form of their ability to earn and enjoy personal service incomes, reflecting benefits from state and national government that are not capitalized into land values. The mechanisms of this constitution give these benefits the same policy influence as that accorded to benefits to land and to other kinds of property, whereas Foldvary's approach fails to provide that. Third, although this constitution provides strong incentives for legislatures to fashion proposals that command unanimous consent, it has a means for resolving difficult issues where unanimity is impossible. A nation's people may agree almost unanimously at the start that having this means is in their mutual interest, and if so the constitution comes into force without meeting the full technical requirements of a contract. My philosophy on this matter is that the perfect is the enemy of the good.

For another alternative, what is the case for government by experts? We have already discussed this issue in connection with our concept of genuinely representative legislatures. The extreme version of this concept is the rule of an elite, such as the example of Plato's Republic, and also such as government by an aristocracy, which existed almost everywhere in the civilized world prior to the 19th century. In less than the most extreme form, it is what most countries now have, in the form of professional politicians and career public servants with monopoly powers. Each such elite serves its own interests, which incidentally also serves the interests of non-members of the elite better than not to have a government at all. But such government is almost always inefficient, arbitrary, and capricious. The notion that there is a better way to select experts than the means employed historically or currently to select them, to have the powers of legislation and regulation, has no evidence to support it.

On the contrary, both past and recent experience in the U.S. with expert testimony in lawsuits highlights the difficulty of selecting reliable 'experts' of a specialized area of interest.[7] If such experts, somehow selected, were given the power to legislate, this problem could only be aggravated, and at best would have problems similar to those we now have with expert legislators in the form of professional politicians. Most importantly, even with the best will in the world, these experts would not know how to anticipate and serve the interests of the voting public, who as sovereigns must necessarily have the last word. Whereas for ordinary goods and services like automobiles, houses, and laundry services, we may allow experts, actual and pretended, to design products for popular consumption, for legislation the mechanics of our decision process requires information that only a representative group of voters can provide. It also requires that the agenda for referenda be controlled by such a representative group. Experts, however selected, cannot be relied upon to do either job accurately and impartially.

The whole point of the present exercise is to show how a nation can do better than that. We can allow wealthy elites to have influence proportionate to their willingness to pay for it, but we cannot allow them to have a monopoly of policy control. We can hire experts, including judges, under contract, and pay them the market value for their expertise. Subject to market forces or market simulation, we allow experts to perform those executive and judicial functions that citizens willingly support. Our central idea is to regularize competition within and among elites, as well as similar orderly competition with others, so that all interests, so far as possible, are equally well served.

4.4 COULD IT BE SUBVERTED?

To evaluate the prospects of a country that adopts the proposed constitution, we must also go beyond the foregoing detailed discussions of incentives and the claims of Chapter 2. We must consider the question, if an organized interest group wants to subvert the clear purpose and structure of this constitution, short of a military coup could they do it? In other words, in practice would this constitution be self-enforcing?

In addressing this question, we must draw the distinction between minor, occasional failures and a major, decisive breakdown of the constitutional plan. Every government has occasional instances of corruption and other offenses by officials, just as fraud, embezzlement, self-dealing, and other such offenses occur in the private sector. There is no reason to expect such problems to be either more or less frequent under the proposed constitution, except to the extent that it successfully provides for better monitoring of official performance than do existing constitutions and laws. It is fair to claim, I think, that the opportunity our plan provides to a second-best official legislature to recoup some bonus payments that it fails to win in the referendum, through its role in supervising the auditing and inspectorate function, should provide an effective level of monitoring of official wrong-doing. If so, it will match or better the performance of the best now observed anywhere in this official function, taking due account of cultural differences from one country to another in such matters.

By contrast, a major failure would be a successful effort to induce the government to spend money wastefully to benefit an organized group of voters at the expense of other voters, followed by another similar successful effort, and so on, so that the intended structure set out in the constitution breaks down. We must assume that, however clear the language of the constitution may be on this point, if any crack in its armor leaves an attractive incentive to organized groups to attempt such an effort, they will attempt it.[8] Is there a crack in the armor such that they could succeed?

The protective barriers that the draft constitution constructs around official legislatures make it unlikely that an interest group would attempt to bribe legislators. There is no legal way to find their identities and to approach them. Moreover, to limit the agenda before the voters, the interest group would have to bribe all official legislatures. Then private legislatures would step in with sound counterproposals, if anything were appropriate besides the constitutionally mandated 'status quo' budget. To keep out sound alternative proposals and to control the official assessment of these proposals, the interest group would have to bribe the Election Commission also. It strains credulity to suppose that there is a profitable way to bribe so many people enough to overcome their legal incentives. Moreover, if someone did there would still be the remedy of lawsuits. Under the proposed constitution, this remedy would apply equally to public sector programs and to private-sector goods and services. Laws relating to false advertising and fraud would be the same for both sectors.

Instead, what if an interest group were to advance a private proposal, using the mechanism authorized by the constitution, and use emotional arguments, etc., to sell it? To make this approach work, the group would also have to win referendum approval of phony measures of success, to avoid prohibitive penalties on performance. This plan would have to run the gauntlet of authoritative review in official legislatures, and of the sound arguments pro and con that these legislatures would produce for the referendum. If someone succeeded, would a subsequent effort at similar deceit succeed equally well? How often do product misrepresentations succeed in the private sector? When they do succeed, how materially do they subvert welfare and reduce general efficiency, compared to any known alternative approach to resource allocation? Although one can surely find examples where private businesses have sold worthless or overpriced products, it is hard to find any that compare with the excesses and misrepresentations by existing governments.

Consider the following example of deceit by governments. We noted in Chapter 1 the absurdly generous system of welfare payments (including Medicaid) in the U.S., the costly Medicare program for the elderly, and the perverse incentive effects of the social security program. What we did not point out there is that the cumulative effect of these programs, if continued on their present basis with its future projections, imply impossibly high tax obligations for future generations of taxpayers. That is, this system of transfers is a pyramid game that will cheat young people who still have several decades to work before their retirement (Kotlikoff, 1992).[9] For more than a decade, the Trustees of the Social Security Administration have published estimates using straightforward accounting methods showing that future tax increases for social security alone are improbably high. Politicians of every political persuasion know that the combination of transfer programs is unsustainable in the long run. Under either political party's proposals, however, the game will continue until it breaks down or unless, prior to that, there is a substantial correction.

Rather than assert a bald claim that nothing that bad would happen under the proposed constitution, let's examine the particulars. Suppose that an organized group purporting to represent the elderly mounts a campaign to increase Medicare and social security benefits to elderly persons, perhaps working in concert with another group purporting to represent the poor, who would propose increased supplements for this or that dire need of the poor. The constitutional rule for the referendum requires that the legislative process shall generate, for voters' use, a full and fair account of the waste occasioned by these programs and of the eventual collapse of the pyramid game the increased benefits would create. Most voters in the U.S. do not now know about the present pyramid game, because no one has been willing to spend the required sums to inform them, and no politician has an incentive to tell them. If they knew, it is hard to believe that it would go on. Under the proposed constitution, the official legislatures would have the relevant facts, would report them, and would indicate that the proposals for increased benefits had no chance of passage. To prevent this full and fair account from reaching the voters the organized groups would have to bribe the legislatures and the Election Commission handsomely enough to offset any reduction in prospective bonus payments and compensate for the enormous risks involved. The bribes would be paid to suppress the relevant facts and to substitute the kinds of emotional arguments we now see in politics. That's a lot of money and a large number of persons to bribe.

Moreover, there is a large group who would be harmed, namely taxpaying people from twenty to about fifty years old, who would pay much of the cost of the benefits to the present elderly and then would receive sharply reduced benefits themselves upon their retirement. Under the rational legal structure encouraged by the constitution, they could set up a class-action suit and win. They would win in the initial court proceeding because the court would be impartial and all the facts would come out. With so much bribe money going to so many people, it would be easy to prove. Even if bribery could not be proved, malfeasance could. In the final appeal to an official legislature (perhaps necessarily a reconvened previous one), the offended groups would be fully represented, the harm to them would outweigh the benefits to the elderly and poor, because of the inefficiency of these programs.[10] Hence under the VCG mechanism the suit would have a high probability of winning at the top level. The risk of this outcome would prevent the acceptance of bribes and therefore would prevent the formation of the organized interest groups.

To judge the likelihood of all this we should bear in mind that existing governments have two features that governments under our proposed constitution would not have. First, it is taken for granted that their programs benefit organized groups at the expense of other citizens. This constitution expressly prohibits and prevents income transfers through such programs except for constitutionally specified redistribution to the poor. Second, they have many channels for legalized or tolerated bribery, such as campaign contributions, employment on favorable terms after leaving government service, vacation trips and other gifts, and so on. This constitution almost eliminates campaigns and provides for clear prohibitions of bribery by other means. Large-scale bribery would be both risky and unprofitable.

Rather than resort to bribery, however, a group might resort to conspiracy to falsify declarations of willingness to pay on an issue that would in any case appear in a referendum. Although we show in Chapter 5 that such conspiracies will fail in the case of items dominated by Thompson insurance, we need to address here the case of items that are wholly or largely uninsurable, in the sense that because of income effects households will not insure against unfavorable outcomes on these items. When we look closely, what we find is that although there is a risk in this case, it is not serious.

Besides providing for criminal sanctions against conspiracy to falsify declared harms in referenda, the constitution's internal checks largely eliminate the potential rewards from such conspiracies. Consider the following example. A large country of 100 million voting families, with median family incomes of $50,000, has a defense budget of $100 billion, which comes to $1000 per family. No family buys Thompson insurance against an unwanted defense budget outcome, so that the budget results exclusively from declarations of uninsured harm. Half the families are 'hawks', who want a budget of $200 billion, and half are 'doves', who want a budget of $50 billion. Hawks and doves are scattered among the population evenly, so that there is no way to identify them by demographic groups. At the equilibrium budget, a 'hawk' family's willingness to pay is $15 per billion of additional budget, of which the family's tax share would be $10, leaving a net excess willingness to pay of $5. A dove family's willingness to pay is $5 per billion of additional budget, as against the tax share of $10. In both cases the elasticity of each willingness to pay schedule, as a function of budget size, is about – 2. The VCG tax for each family at the equilibrium budget works out at $\$.25\text{x}10^{-7}$, a ridiculously small fraction of a cent each.

In this circumstance, Margolis (1982a) argues that, even without collusion, voters will naturally tend to overstate their willingness to pay to obtain budget changes.[11] If the hawks and doves all follow Margolis's advice to 'spend a penny' of VCG tax to move the budget in their respective preferred directions, their misrepresentations will cancel and the budget will remain the same. Suppose, however, that the hawks alone have a reckless tendency or a conspiracy to exaggerate in this way, whereas the doves all tell the truth. To raise a hawkish family's VCG taxes to one penny, they would multiply by a factor of 400 their $5 net excess willingness to pay for the first $1 billion of defense spending, raising it to $2,000, and reduce their elasticity of demand by a corresponding factor so as to have their net willingness to pay to fall to zero at $200 billion, as before (or to a figure just above that.) The conspiracy would succeed in raising the defense budget to $200 billion, exactly or approximately, if all hawks behaved alike, because at all lower budget figures their excess willingness to pay in the aggregate would swamp the negative willingness to pay of the doves.

The constitution would permit all this to happen only if it had no internal checks on the reasonableness of the declared schedules of willingness to pay. The hypothetical exaggeration would imply that each hawkish family would be willing to pay, if necessary, about $700,000 to get the desired defense budget. The problem with that is that the typical hawkish family doesn't have that much money, so that the declared willingness to pay is inconsistent with budget-constrained rational preferences. The constitution's requirement in that respect, in Article II, Subsection 10(b), requires the voter to state credible willingness to pay figures, whose implied effect shall not exceed a reasonable figure such as 10 percent of the voter's income. This restriction would allow the hawks to exaggerate their net excess willingness to pay only about 30-fold, from $5 per family to $150 per family. With that restriction, the effect of the conspiracy on the defense budget would be less than $1 billion, which is hardly worth risking criminal sanctions in the case of actual conspiracy. Far fewer than 100 percent of hawkish families would take this risk, as a rule, so that such conspiracies or quasi-conspiratorial behavior would have very little effect in practice.

We can therefore conclude that neither bribery nor conspiracy would be a significant threat to the basic plan of the constitution. We examined this issue from another perspective in the appendix to Chapter 2.

At the same time, these examples and arguments cannot be claimed to rule out any possibility of fads, fashions, and temporary surges of public passion. These occur in the private sector, and have in one way or another (except perhaps in ancient Lokris, as noted in Chapter 3) always been a hallmark of government of every kind. (This point ties into our discussion of common law in Chapters 2 and 3 and of the herd instinct in the appendix to Chapter 2.) We must nevertheless recognize that the features of present-day representative governments that we reviewed in Chapter 1, which invite irresponsible behavior by almost everyone, magnify and exacerbate this problem. By requiring or approximating unanimous consent on every public issue, expressed in budget-constrained dollar terms, this constitution provides the most reliable legal barrier against hasty and foolish policies that one can design, short of a method like that used in ancient Lokris. It would of course be helpful if there were also a natural public conservatism to back it up, and to the extent that a country has this attribute our constitutional design will protect this public against manipulation. Where a country lacks it, there is no institution that will protect it from its own foolishness.

4.5 IS IT OVERLY SPECIFIC?

A further question is, have we written too many details into this draft constitution? The draft constitution includes some particulars that may be gratuitous, such as the requirement to minimize bureaucracy and contract out everything possible to the private sector. The rational incentives provided by the legislative process should be enough to guarantee such outsourcing without a specific constitutional mandate. An opposing view is that the outsourcing provisions are so fundamental a part of the objective to avoid government waste, and that bureaucracies can so easily control the flow of information relating to their efficiency, that there needs to be a constitutional barrier to overgrowth of government employment. This barrier could still be overcome, but only with much greater difficulty. If the leaders of a new country were supremely confident that this language is gratuitous, they could of course omit it from their constitution.

Indeed one can think of many examples of good law and good practice that one might want to entrench in the constitution, and it is important to resist the temptation to overdo it. Things that can be safely left to be worked out later by the due process specified in the constitution should in general be left out, so that the constitutional decision focuses only on its essentials. Its likelihood of acceptance is low enough already, without excess baggage. Conceivably that could be true of the provision about outsourcing.

However, (unlike Mueller) we are not discussing a campaign for a constitutional convention in a country that is already a going concern (Mueller, 1996, Ch. 22). Every such country already has too many entrenched interests for such a convention to have an appreciable chance of success. The only hope for its adoption anywhere is in a new country of unusually prudent voters with unusually perspicacious leaders. I haven't noticed any such country lately, but we should be properly prepared for that eventuality by having a sound plan ready to offer them. For that eventuality, the provisions on outsourcing might be a good selling point rather than an impediment to adoption.

Apart from the language on outsourcing, the reader may be startled to notice that the constitution is silent about the administration of tax collection, and in particular avoids any mention of it in the list of career government employees. A new government could of course change this feature if its leaders thought that appropriate. I would argue, however, that there is no reason to do so.

The tax rules under this constitution require each household to report its demographic characteristics identifying its population subgroup memberships and its property. The household would then receive, with its information package for a referendum, its tax implications for each program group in the referendum. The Election Commission would contract with private firms to provide a computer system for translating the voting outcome into household Lindahl taxes, Thompson insurance net balance payable or receivable, and VCG taxes. The private firms would post bond and would be subject to inspection and audit to protect the confidentiality of household information. Private auditors could provide the service of verifying household 'tax returns.' In a country that has reputable auditing firms, their reputations would generally provide the main guarantee of the integrity of their work. In a country that does not have such firms, the Election Commission might use specially trained government employees in a temporary role until such private firms could establish reputations and assume this function. (When they did, it would be appropriate to allow such firms to hire the government employees being dismissed, provided that these had no role in the selection of the firm that wins the government contract.) Although this plan differs markedly from past practice (except for tax-farming in eighteenth Century France), I see no reason to believe that official tax collectors have an advantage that would outweigh the disadvantage of giving them a monopoly of their function.

Problems of abuse arise not from the use of private or public auditors and tax collectors but rather from a lack of clarity in a household's legal obligation. Where the legal obligation is clear it is comparatively easy to curb corruption and other abuses. The main difficulty arises in the assessment of property taxes, performed by the official legislatures and the Election Commission, because of possible ambiguities in the classification of items of property. A special set of tax courts might be an efficient part of the system to deal with tax assessment problems, as we now have in the U.S. Such courts would have the same ground rules for competition and tenure as the rest of the judiciary under Article V.

Therefore I conclude that the sound rule is to have tax collection and auditing contracted out to private firms just as is the case for almost everything else the government does under this constitution.

Many readers will understandably feel a sense of outrage at a proposal whose effect is to institutionalize the influence of wealthy persons in a country's policy. In modern countries with governments chosen by election, nearly everyone's sense of fairness suggests that every person's vote should count the same as everyone else's, among those eligible to vote. Many of those who hold this view almost to the point of religious devotion have noticed that the practice and the results of representative democracy in the modern world leaves something to be desired, and their reaction, without serious or credible analysis of free-rider problems, interest groups, and so on, is to suppose that it can be fixed.[12]

Those of us who doubt that there is a way to fix the egregious problems of existing governments, understanding the obstacles more or less well, have generally been resigned to the consequences. Without undue admiration for or devotion to the workings of what we call representative democracy, we have had to accept Churchill's observation that every known way of governing works out worse. The point of this book is that his statement no longer applies: there is a better way.

It is enough to state and support this claim without overly belaboring it. A country using the constitution proposed here could achieve the high levels of output and growth that we indicated in Chapter 1. How much economic welfare would sincere advocates of traditional democracy be willing for their countries to sacrifice for that supposed ideal? Over time, the material sacrifice would be enormous. Moreover, the sacrifice would be pointless. If we think of government purely and simply as a provider of services, why shouldn't its provision of services be handled under procedures that give the same kinds of results as do private markets?

To see this point, we should look at some examples of how the system would work, from the voter's point of view. In Section 4.6 we consider several cases covering a broad spectrum of issues, showing in general terms how the decision mechanism in the proposed constitution would resolve them. Then in Section 4.7 we examine the role of the voting family, and the incentives it faces, with referenda on a 'binary' (yes-or-no) decision and on the choice of a point within a continuous range.

4.6 THE PAYOFF IN MORE CONCRETE TERMS

Chapter 2 mentioned specific instances such as import controls for sugar that would vanish under the draft constitution proposed here, and others that would undergo drastic modification. By and large, however, our discussion has focused on ideas and principles, and can benefit now from further examples.

The following examples illustrate the operation of our proposed rules. On the general principle involved, consider first the following example. A group of wealthy persons, living in an expensive subdivision, desires the construction of a yacht harbor suitable for their yachts as well as for smaller craft. They would be willing to pay a substantial part of its cost of construction, but the project can be economic only if other users pay part of the cost. A proposal on a referendum ballot to build a multi-purpose facility, under the proposed constitution, would lead them to declare valuations and accept Lindahl taxes for this improvement that were more than proportionate to their wealth, while other potential users would have comparatively small tax shares and would declare low valuations reflecting their more modest prospective use of the harbor. The proposed plan would have a sound marginal-cost based set of user fees that would also bear heaviest on the owners of large yachts. The wealthy yacht owners would thus pay most of the cost, and would have a correspondingly high influence on the approved construction budget. That seems entirely reasonable to me. Everything the government does, except the constitutionally mandated set of taxes to finance public assistance to destitute persons, would have tax financing based on the benefit principle, which would imply high influence for wealthy persons only in the case of projects of particular interest to them.

Next, we should look at some larger-scale issues that might come up in a national legislature. First, consider a project to dam a river, in a country with many such opportunities, to provide irrigation, flood control, hydroelectricity, and recreation. Second, assuming that there is no other special procedure for this decision, consider a proposal to abolish a symbolic, powerless, monarchy and to retire members of the royal family to the status of ordinary citizens. Third, consider the choice between a military draft and an all-volunteer armed force.

In the first example, a multipurpose dam, assume that, besides its financial consequences, its only effects are direct amenities that compete with other recreational opportunities of easily measured market value. That is, it does not reduce the habitat of an endangered species, nor destroy any special scenic area or archaeological treasures. The land it uses can be appraised accurately at market prices. Its irrigation water will serve known farmlands whose additional output will not disturb relative prices, nor do the project's other goods and services, such as electricity. In short, assume that customers who do not receive these benefits nor supply resources to this project have no interest in whether it is built.

In this case the decision process in the legislature would reveal zero interest in the project outside the region that it serves. The assumption of no effect on relative prices of farm products and electricity implies that there would be no consumer interest in the project, except for those who expect recreational benefits and flood protection. The legislative decision process would reveal the farm demand schedule for the irrigation water, and the value that local households place on recreational and flood control benefits. The value of the local electricity would be measured by its market price. The estimated Lindahl taxes for the project, which in this case would be quite accurate, would fall on the following groups: (a) farmers, to collect their gain in land values, if any, after their prospective payments for water; (b) those property owners who have a rise in their property values due to flood protection; and (c) those property owners whose property values rise due to increased actual or imputed rents due to the recreational benefits.

Suppose that the legislative result indicates that the estimated Lindahl taxes thus identified, plus the revenues from the sale of electricity, water, and admissions to the recreational facilities, would pay for the dam at the appropriate rate of return to capital. When the issue is put to a referendum, if the indication is correct, some voters would buy Thompson insurance, and none other than gamblers and those who disagree with the odds given by the insurance premiums would declare values under the VCG part of the mechanism. If in fact the benefits to the affected households exceeded the costs, the referendum would approve the project, and not otherwise.

Apart from gamblers, persons who disputed the official odds, and random errors in the matching of taxes to beneficiaries, the winning side would receive unanimous support. The outcome might nevertheless be hard to predict, with odds not far from even, if the project had benefits approximately equal to costs.

The second example differs sharply from the first in that it involves direct utility of a symbolic activity about which people may feel strongly, and for which there is no market counterpart. To emphasize this point, assume that the royal family covers all its expenses from its own wealth, which will be unaffected by the decision. Further, assume that the royal family's tastes for and uses of economic goods will be unaffected by the outcome, and that the tourist trade, if any, will also be unaffected. That is, there is no economic consequence other than the gains and losses of direct utility, stemming from the monarchy itself, for the voters. Assume that for every voter the marginal utility of wealth is unaffected by the outcome. Then the only voters who would use Thompson insurance would be gamblers and those voters who disagree with the odds quoted for the insurance mechanism. All voters would use the VCG mechanism. Consequently the referendum would be similar to an ordinary vote, except that votes would be weighted by the strength of ordinary preferences and by voter wealth.

The third example, the choice between a military draft and an all-volunteer armed force, has elements of both the two previous cases. In practice the draft has involved underpaid involuntary servitude, often at considerable personal risk, for draft-eligible young men. In the United States their pay rates were apparently sometimes less than 60 percent of the pay that would have been necessary to recruit a volunteer force.[13] Proponents of this system generally mentioned, among their reasons, that an all-volunteer force would be prohibitively costly, which is to say that these proponents wanted to hold down their own taxes by requiring the draftees to bear much of the financial cost. Assuming that potential draftees had proportional representation, or representation proportional to wealth, in the legislature, the proposed mechanism would rule out this kind of financing. The procedure for assessing approximate Lindahl taxes would result in full compensation for young men of military age, and the legislative mechanism would reveal that an all-volunteer force would be less costly than a draft. If a major group of voters nevertheless so strongly favored the principle of a draft that they would be willing to pay its extra cost, the referendum mechanism could choose a draft. To the extent that voters' differences in hawkishness or dovishness were correlated with regional and other identified groups in the representation matrix, hawkish groups would pay higher taxes than the dovish ones to support the military forces.

These examples illustrate how a combination of mechanisms along the suggested lines can achieve efficient outcomes. They also illustrate how this approach can protect minority interests, or indeed majority interests, against abuse of the government's power to tax and regulate.

4.7 THE PERSPECTIVE OF THE VOTING FAMILY

Having discussed the philosophical aspect of applying market simulation to government decisions, now let us consider two examples of how a referendum works out from the perspective of representative families in a small town. First we will consider an up-or-down vote on a budget item and then a budget item that can be approved anywhere in a range.

Suppose that the firm currently supplying local police in the town of Freemonia, with 900 voting families, proposes an improvement in service using a new high-technology communication system. The Smith household's tax assessment would rise by a one-time payment of $200 if the local referendum approves the proposal. The official odds of success published by the local Election Commission are .8 for approval and .2 for disapproval. The improved atmosphere of security, together with a small annual reduction in the homeowner's insurance premium on the Smiths' home, would raise their home's property value by $210. The Smiths' feeling of improved security against non-property crimes is worth an additional $90 one-time payment to them, of which $45 is the discounted present value of expected savings of health care costs and of avoided lost earnings. Thus, their expected gross gain is $300, of which $255 is material gain, which compares favorably with the tax assessment of $200. They would buy Thompson insurance for the $55 net material gain they stand to lose if the proposal is disapproved, at a cash premium of $11. In addition they would declare that disapproval would involve $45 of uninsured harm to them.

The vote turns out to be surprisingly close. The 500 families in favor insure for $15,000 of material harm and declare $5,040 of uninsured harm from failure of the proposal. The 400 families opposed insure for $10,000 of material loss and, many of them being concerned about a perceived threat to their civil liberties, declare $10,000 of uninsured harm from its adoption. The total dollar vote in favor is thus $20,040, compared to

$20,000 opposed. A total of 29 voters, including one member of the Smith family, have declared $40 or more of uninsured gain from adoption of the proposal, and each of these owes some amount of VCG tax, which sums to a total VCG tax collection of $1,160. The total insurance premium collection is $11,000, the sum of $3,000 from those in favor and $8,000 from those opposed, so that after paying off the $10,000 insurance of those opposed and $800 of election cost, the Election Commission has a profit of $1,360.

The Smiths pay a VCG tax of $5. The Smiths have a perceived gain of $100 less their VCG tax of $5 and less their insurance premium of $11, for a net gain of $84. The constitutional provision for declared harms of these average sizes does not include the sophisticated adjustment for income effects of the technical annex, which would be negligible. It does require the procedure to conform to Article II, Subsection 10(g), refunding to each family a share of what the election profit would be without that family's vote, however. The outcome without the Smiths would have been a loss of over $4,150, of which the share to the Smiths is an assessment of $4.62. For opponents and other non-pivotal voters the refund of election profit is about $1,335/899, or $1.48 each. The combination of refunds and assessments adds to a total net payment by the Election Commission of $1,155, leaving $205 to be placed in the election fund.

The second example also concerns the town of Freemonia, together with a nearby group of riverfront properties over a five-mile stretch where the river is appreciably affected by pollution from the town and from the riverfront properties themselves. The town and riverfront area together have 1,000 voting families.

A private syndicate proposes a new sewer system serving the town and the affected group of riverfront properties, and also proposes industry restrictions (easements) governing industrial and commercial effluents into the river. The river in this area is suitable only for boating, although there are some carp in the river, considered to be inedible and of no interest to game fishermen. The proposal offers a range of pollution reductions from 50 percent to 90 percent, with project cost rising quadratically with the percent reduction. The townspeople benefit from savings in septic tank costs and from improved prospects for beneficial further development. The riverfront properties benefit from improved recreational values, with the possibility of upscale development. Using willingness-to-pay estimates from the local official legislatures, the Election Commission allocates the project cost function to households in the town and along the river. The estimated referendum outcome is a cleanup of 80 percent, with a 99 percent confidence range from 75.2 percent to 84.6 percent. The estimated probability of 'no action' is 0.1 percent.

The official election information bulletin from the Election Commission explains the costs and advantages of the river cleanup plan, with estimates of property value changes. It also explains the schedule of insurance premiums for purchasing insurance against the outcomes in the referendum range and explains how to report a family's schedule of insurance purchases. Neighboring families get together to exchange views on the estimates and, when any of them knows an insurance agent, they bring her to the group to answer questions about the insurance procedure.

The Jones family lives by the river and expects that the project will change the character of the neighborhood, with a sharp increase in property values. The family's allocated share of cost is \$2,400 + $\$2x^2$, where x is the percentage by which the project cleans up pollution. The Jones family expects their property to be worth \$10,000 + $\$300x$. In addition, because some unwanted neighbors, faced with the projected high tax assessments, will probably sell out and move if a high-cleanup project is approved, the Joneses have an added uninsurable $\$50x$ of willingness to pay for project approval when x is in the range from 80 to 85. The Jones's prospective financial gain from the project is – \$2,400 + $\$300x - \$2x^2$, and it works out that they would have a maximum net financial gain of \$8,850 for a cleanup percentage of 75 percent. At higher percentages, their cost share rises faster than their property value. As just noted, they have uninsured willingness to pay of \$50 per percentage point of additional cleanup, however, because (a) the Jones family plans to stay to enjoy improved recreation, which they value more highly than the expected market valuation, and (b) because higher cost increases their confidence that unwanted neighbors will move. (If the percentage of cleanup were to exceed about 85, the Jones family's uninsured willingness to pay for additional cleanup would drop from \$50 per point to smaller figures.)

The property value gain is insurable, so that they insure the \$8,850 against no action for a premium of \$8.85. Added cleanup would lower this gain, so that despite their desire for more cleanup the Jones family buys Thompson insurance against each higher outcome above 75 percent. For improvements in the referendum range, this reduction of financial gain ranges from about \$1 for cleanup percentages from 75.2 to 76 to \$170 for percentages near 84.6. The Jones family insures for these amounts by reporting its insurable loss schedule, namely $\$11,250 - 300x + 2x^2$. (The incremental loss is less than \$50 per percentage point throughout the range, so that the Jones family would prefer an outcome above the range.)

The estimated probabilities of outcomes being a normal probability density over the stated range, the sum of the insurance premiums for the entire range works out at $55 plus small change. The family also reports their uninsured positive willingness to pay of $50*x*, which, contrary to their insurance, votes to enlarge the project.

The project wins approval at 82 percent cleanup, so that its insurable loss schedule gives an insurance payable to the Jones family of $98. Suppose that the typical marginal valuation schedule in Freemonia, like that of the Jones family, drops at the rate of about $4 for each percentage point of cleanup (given by the coefficient of *x* in the first derivative of the Jones family's insurable loss schedule.) Calculating this information from the voters' reported marginal valuation schedules, the Election Commission calculates the Jones family's VCG tax as follows. At 82 percent cleanup these marginal valuations net of cost sum to zero, so that their sum without the uninsured declaration by the Jones family is – $50 per point, or an average of 5 cents per family by which cost exceeds willingness to pay. The typical family's valuation schedule drops by this amount over a range of .0125 percentage points, so that without the Jones declaration of uninsured valuation the aggregate marginal valuation net of cost would sum to zero at a cleanup percentage .0125 less than 82. The Jones VCG tax is then approximately the area of a triangle with a base of .0125 and a height of $50, that is the amount (1/2)(.0125)($50)=$.31.

The Election Commission has a small profit from the insurance transactions and the VCG taxes collected from residents of Freemonia and of the riverfront area. The election commission disposes of the election profit in the same way as it did in the case of the police communication system.

Viewing these cases from a philosophical perspective, the constitutional plan has certain satisfying aspects that should have great appeal to thoughtful people at whatever income level. First, on budget issues and others involving a continuous scale of possible outcomes, every vote makes at least a small, if only symbolic, difference. If I am willing to pay to have a larger budget for police, education, or anything else, my vote will make it larger. Second, if I feel especially strongly about, say, education, and am willing to double my vote to increase its budget, my impact on actual budget size is doubled. No one would have a legitimate reason to feel excluded from the decision process. Reportedly, in present-day 'democratic' countries, they often have that feeling now.

In short, all in all it is easier to provide a reasoned defense of the proposed constitution than to provide one for the rule of one-person-one-vote, given the way that this rule works out in practice.

4.8 SOME FURTHER NOTES ON INCENTIVES

The example of the high-tech police communication system for the town of Freemonia raises two issues that may need further clarification. One is the incentive effect of the residual profit that remains in the election fund after the Commission uses the constitutionally mandated procedure to refund its profit. The other is the possibility that the referendum has a negative profit. This outcome is most likely to occur if the balance of uninsured harms outweighs the insured harms, so as to require paying off more insured claims than the total premium revenue.

The net balance in the election fund, after refunds, creates an incentive problem unless it is transferred to the national election fund. In that case the effect of one family's vote on that family's refunds from all referenda becomes truly negligible if the national population numbers in the hundreds of thousands or higher. If the constitution does not provide for such a transfer, the incentive effect is hard to predict in a particular case, but nevertheless is inconsistent in strict logic with incentive compatibility.

If the Smith family were to increase its declared uninsured harm by one dollar, even though so doing would have no effect on the family's primary refund (which is strictly unaffected by the family's vote), it would affect the amount of final surplus or deficit in the election fund. The reason is that the declaration by the Smiths not only raises the winning balance in the referendum to \$20041 in favor, but also raises the corresponding amount facing each other pivotal family (\$20041 minus this family's declaration of uninsured harm) for determining its VCG tax. That is, the amount of uninsured harm that such a family would need to declare to produce a tie is reduced by one dollar. For each pivotal family other than the Smiths, therefore, the effect is to reduce their VCG tax by one dollar. If, as assumed, there are 28 such families other than the Smiths, this effect reduces the surplus in the fund by \$28. Further, there may be one or two families without whose vote (including insured harm) the outcome would go the other way by a margin of less than a dollar before the change in the Smith declaration. Such a family would be charged an assessment of about \$4.62 before the change, but would instead receive a refund of about \$1.48 after the dollar increase in the Smith declaration, because their vote no longer affects the outcome at all. If there were two such families, this effect would reduce the election fund surplus by a further \$12.20, for a total reduction of about \$40. Whether distributed in equal shares to all immediately or carried forward, the surplus affects the Smith financial position by 1/900 of the total. The effect of each dollar of Smith declaration on the eventual Smith financial position is $40/900 or $.0444, in effect increasing the Smith insurance premium and VCG tax by $100 times .0444, or $4.44. This effect is like a loading charge on their insurance, as well as an overcharge of the VCG tax. The Smiths would therefore have a corresponding incentive to reduce both their insured and uninsured declared harms.

These effects are the same for all families, whether pivotal or not, who favor the proposed police communication system. By contrast, an extra dollar of declared harm by a family who opposes the proposal would increase the VCG tax on pivotal families such as the Smiths, and would likewise have the reverse of the other above effects. Consequently such a family would have an incentive to overstate their insured and uninsured declared harms.

These effects on incentives apply whenever a household knows whether it will be on the winning or losing side, or when the household's perceived probability of success of the proposal is different from .5. If a household has a Bayesian perspective, it would use this perceived probability, weigh its two incentives, and tilt its declarations accordingly. The result would be a small bias toward preserving the status quo. If the writers of the constitution wish to avoid this bias, they should consolidate all local election funds into the national fund.

The issue of losses on Thompson insurance is easier to deal with. Suppose that the election funds are consolidates as just suggested, so that the overall system is incentive compatible. In that case, the Smith family and every other family will in all cases declare a true combined total of insured and uninsured harms.

If a family disbelieves the official odds of the outcome, it will wish to falsify its insured harm but will offset this effect by an opposite change in its declaration of uninsured harm. Suppose, in an extreme case, that everyone is almost certain that the proposal will win, so that everyone considers it a good speculation to 'insure against' the proposal's success. That includes the Smiths, who insure against it also. Like other supporters of the proposal, they will then declare an uninsured harm from the proposal's failure of the amount of this insurance plus their true total harm from its failure, which for the Smiths is $100. The grand totals of declarations pro and con are shifted by equal amounts, and the proposal wins by $40 as before. The Election Commission has a big loss, and covers it with a special assessment, on average wiping out the various households' profits on their speculation. The extent to which each household would push this strategy would be limited either by its risk aversion or by the constitutional limit on the household's uninsured harm, whichever was more restrictive. (If their sense of certainty of the outcome pushes many of them to add substantially more insurance when their constitutional limit is binding, so that the extra insurance is unhedged, this exposure makes it likely that the proposal against whose success they are insuring will fail. The effect on the referendum outcome will teach them not to do that again. Most of the insurance account profit from this failure will be paid out as refunds to other families who didn't overshoot.)

The foregoing extreme example illustrates one incentive effect that complicates the overall picture. Another incentive effect arises when a family perceives an appreciable probability that its vote will be pivotal. In this case this family will have an incentive to insure more of its expected harm from a decision it opposes, and to declare less uninsured harm. This effect works the opposite way from the preceding one, and is similarly inconsequential.

The incentive to insure financial losses and (usually) not intangible losses comes from the diminishing marginal utility of income or wealth, that is, from risk aversion. If an intangible loss has no effect on the household's marginal utility of income, the household will not buy insurance coverage for any part of the loss. However, if the household's risk aversion is similar to that for $U = \log(Y)$, where Y is income, a modest subsidy to the insurance would make such coverage attractive.

An appreciable probability of paying the VCG tax provides such a subsidy. It works this way because adding a certain sum of insurance against the failure of a proposal has the same effect on the referendum outcome as adding that sum to a declaration of uninsured harm.

For simplicity, consider this point for a family who accept the official odds of the referendum outcome. Suppose that, instead of a .8 chance of success of the police communication system in the Freemonia referendum, the chance is given as .5, and that the Smith family believes that its chance of having a pivotal vote is .1. Suppose also that if its vote is pivotal, the conditional expected value of the family's VCG tax is \$22, so that its unconditional expected value is \$2.20. Where otherwise the Smiths buy \$55 of insurance and declare \$45 of uninsured harm against the failure of the proposal, they would have the same expectation of putting the proposal over the top and at the same time would save the \$2.20 of expected VCG tax by buying \$100 of insurance against the proposal's failure. The added \$45 of insurance costs \$22.50. If the Smith family's income is \$50,000, in round numbers this income rises by \$50 if the proposal fails and rises by \$5 if it succeeds (taking account of the tangible benefits of success), if the household buys the full $100 of insurance. Supposing that the Smith utility function can be accurately represented by $U = \ln(Y)$, over this range the marginal utility of income drops from 1/50005 to 1/50050. In that case the added insurance valued at this final margin is intrinsically worth $22.50 (50005/50050) = $22.48, or 2 cents less than it costs. The expected avoidance of the VCG tax is worth $2.20, making the substitution of insurance for a declaration of uninsured harm an attractive proposition.

The system thus provides various incentives to voting families to allocate their declarations between insurance and uninsured harm, depending on circumstances. In every case, however, the sum of insured and uninsured harm that each family declares is the true amount that the family is willing to pay to obtain the outcome it prefers. Typically those household opinions that disagree with official odds would be distributed randomly, so that the first, extreme case would not arise. Rumors, press campaigns, and so on could occasionally create an extreme case, however. In other cases (and perhaps in this case) many households would expect a close vote and would insure precisely their full willingness to pay. Our main point is that these cases make no difference to referendum outcomes.

4.9 INCONSISTENCIES

There are various ways that one declaration by a voter could contradict another declaration, although the main way would be through apparently inconsistent indications of risk aversion, perhaps because of differing kinds and amounts of publicity about two risks. For example, a voter might declare a willingness to pay $700 per year for a program that reduces the voter's risk of death by .001 per year from heart disease, but a willingness to pay only $50 per year for a program that reduces the voter's risk of death by .001 per year from a traffic accident. If queried by the election computer about this, the voter might respond that one can avoid traffic accidents by being careful. Suppose that the computer points out that almost half the victims of fatal traffic accidents were hit by a drunk driver or an errant truck, that is, under circumstances beyond the victim's control, and that it also points out that life style changes can cut the risk of a heart attack by more than half. It could ask the voter, are these two cases as dissimilar as the voter's declaration would indicate? (This information might have already been provided to voters in the Election Commission's constitutionally mandated analysis of the advantages and disadvantages of the proposed programs.) The computer would give the voter some choices about ways to vote consistently, including an option to say that one's family history makes one especially frightened of heart disease, as an explanation for the apparent inconsistency. That is, the voter could, in the end, insist, if this declaration did not later flatly contradict another.

If the voter's declaration of harm from an unwanted outcome is incredibly high, the computer would point out the financial liability that this declaration could under some circumstances imply, beyond the voter's means as declared on the family's income and property tax returns. Even if the declaration could not bankrupt the voter, it might exceed the constitutionally set upper limit on declarations. In the case of an issue with a continuous set of possible outcomes, such as a budget, it would also point out to the voter the probable effect of the maximum permitted declaration on the outcome. It would ask the voter, is it worth that much? The voter would then decide what to do within the permitted limits.

These procedures would discourage careless or collusive responses. Although both kinds of responses could still occur, their effects would tend to be reduced to harmless proportions. The procedures would actively discourage collusive voting, because they would remind the voter of the incentive to defect from the collusive arrangement and to be truthful. They might also remind the voter that clusters of questionable votes could draw the attention of investigators looking into the possibility of unlawful collusion.

4.10 CONCLUSION

We have reviewed a number of possible arguments against our constitutional concept, and possible misunderstandings about it, and have found that on closer inspection it is robust against these arguments and misunderstandings. We elaborated on some of these points in the appendix to Chapter 2. Some of these arguments and misunderstandings, or the points of view that lead to them, have occupied whole books, and of course one could elaborate with book-length counter arguments. So long as our reasoning is clear and understandable, however, there is no need for that. We do elaborate further on technical issues in the remaining chapters and their appendices, to cover technical gaps whose solutions need to be gathered together in one place. On the broad philosophical issues involved in our proposal, we have completed our case.

5 The Thompson Insurance Mechanism

5.1 INTRODUCTION

Chapter 2 provided a description of the insurance procedure for voting financial gains and losses, first proposed by Thompson. Chapter 3 presented constitutional language for its implementation. Thompson presented it as a plan for two-option choices, such as a choice between two candidates for elective office, each having a distinct set of priorities for government policies and for taxation. The proposal received very little subsequent attention, despite its unique advantage of the incentive it provides for informed voting. One reason for the disinterest in the idea among public choice economists was the apparently insuperable handicap that there did not seem to be a satisfactory way for election authorities to calculate fair insurance premiums that the public would believe, in preference, say, to those offered by private bookmakers (Eysenbach, 1967, pp. 105-107). This chapter elaborates on the advantages and disadvantages of the insurance plan, and on ways of overcoming the disadvantages, more thoroughly than do the preceding chapters.

The method for obtaining these odds, as we have pointed out, is to use a representative legislature, where the best method of selection is a stratified random sample, which is to say proportional representation with selection by lot. The concept of a randomly selected legislature was discussed by Mueller, Tollison, and Willett (1972). Green and Laffont (1977) proposed using classical statistical methods to calculate the odds that a proposal by such a legislature would be the same as one that voters would approve in a referendum. All these authors viewed the legislature as a law-making body, however, whereas we follow Thompson in proposing a referendum using his procedure. The proposal here to use competing legislatures to generate information with which to fine-tune the mechanism and to optimize incentives, to the best of my knowledge, is novel.

5.2 PERSPECTIVES ON THOMPSON'S INSURANCE MECHANISM

In summary, here once again is the insurance mechanism. Consider a binary choice between the status quo and a government project, such as a street improvement to be financed by a specified tax package whose incidence every voter knows. Suppose that the effects of the project consist solely of increases and decreases in voter wealth, as conventionally measured. That is, there is no nonmonetary feature or consequence of the project that has direct utility for any voter. Each voter can state a monetary sum representing the net advantage of the project to that voter, where this sum depends only on the objective features of the project and its financing. The problem for mechanism design for such a choice is to provide an accurate incentive to the voter to inform the Election Commission of this sum truthfully. If the Election Commission receives the true sums for all voters and if the mechanism has a balanced budget, the Pareto-efficient outcome will be to carry out the project if it has a positive aggregate sum of voter responses, or stay with the status quo otherwise.

Thompson proposed that the Election Commission offer fair insurance to each voter against the voter's less preferred outcome. Suppose that the outcome chosen by the government is to go ahead with the project, and that it harms the voter. Then the voter receives full compensation for this harm from the insurance, less the fair insurance premium. Those who benefit from the project, by contrast, pay the fair insurance premium to protect that benefit. Thompson demonstrated that under the assumptions just stated, risk averse voters will buy full coverage for their risks, so that their purchases of insurance will tell the Election Commission their true valuations of the project. The government chooses whichever outcome requires the smaller aggregate compensation to the losers, which is the Pareto-efficient choice.

To justify serious consideration of this mechanism, one must clarify its advantages and disadvantages, and deal effectively with the latter. Consider first the disadvantages, most of which have been discussed by Thompson (1966, 1967), Eysenbach (1967), and Mueller (1979).

1. The central agent must offer insurance premiums that the voters perceive as fair.
2. Except in the case of a tie vote, the government has a budget surplus. Distributing the surplus may disturb incentive compatibility.

3. Those features of a project or issue that involve direct utility, such as physical risk, 'pain and suffering', and highly charged non-financial political issues, are not usually fully insurable, so the mechanism will fail to achieve an optimum for such issues.
4. For the government to succeed, it must have a monopoly on this kind of insurance.
5. If some voters prefer risk, they will bet on the success of (buy insurance against) the outcome that they prefer, thus giving misleading information to the government.
6. The central agenda setter could abuse the mechanism by obtaining referenda on a series of unsound proposals chosen to damage the interests of a minority. While defeating the proposals, minority voters could be driven to bankruptcy.

For the moment we defer discussion of the first disadvantage. The second disadvantage is clearly and elegantly explained by Thompson, who points out that the central agency (that is, the Election Commission) decides the issue against and pays off that side whose claims are less than total premiums.

We will later elaborate upon the third issue, the problem of non-monetary gains and losses, that is, of choices that directly affect utility without affecting wealth. Here we note simply that in many cases, such as an issue involving civil rights, or pollution at a distant location, it is likely that each voter's marginal utility of wealth will be the same, at every level of wealth, regardless of which way the choice goes. In that case, the Thompson proof of full coverage fails and, in fact, the voter would buy no insurance coverage for the direct utility effect of the decision, but only for its financial consequences. Formal proof of the uninsurability of direct gains and losses of utility for such things as 'pain and suffering' appears in the literature of law and economics.[1]

Our fourth concern on the above list is that the Election Commission must have a monopoly on the insurance activity in order to have all necessary information to arrive at an efficient outcome. Closely related to this concern is the fifth: some voters may be gamblers rather than being risk averse. Such voters would bet on ('insure against') the outcome they favor. This behavior could prevent Thompson insurance, operating alone, from achieving optimal outcomes of binary choices, and would also interfere with optimal outcomes for continuous variables.

A final source of concern is that if too many issues go to the voters by this mechanism by itself, some may be driven to the edge of bankruptcy by their purchases of insurance. This is our central concern, in fact, and we would not wish to pass it over too lightly. Unless there is a procedure or incentive structure to prevent abuse, a central agenda setter representing a dominant interest could harass a less influential set of voters by advancing a series of proposals particularly harmful to these voters. The cost to them of insuring against these proposals could cumulate without limit.

Clearly these disadvantages prevent using the Thompson insurance method by itself as a method of social choice. As we have already indicated, we must combine it with a great deal more. We have also indicated the nature of what we combine it with, both for continuous variables and for binary choices. We have indicated the nature of the trade-offs that lead us down the particular path we chose, and do not need to elaborate further on them here. We do need to elaborate further, however, on the resistance of the insurance mechanism to collusion.

A voter joining a coalition of similar voters who would agree to overstate their preference for a project would have to purchase unwanted extra insurance against its failure. Not only would this insurance be unwanted if the effect of the coalition on the outcome were trivial, but it would be especially unwanted if the effect were substantial. As the odds shifted in favor of the project, the desire to purchase insurance against the project's failure would weaken accordingly. The coalition's claim *per se* would make the purchase of the insurance too expensive, and so would increase the incentive for the coalition members to cheat. Consequently most members would secretly cheat, buying less insurance rather than more. Knowing all this, voters would generally not attempt to form coalitions in the first place.

5.3 TECHNICAL ANALYSIS

For the case of a binary choice, such as approving a project of given size versus the status quo, the statistical theory giving the odds that the choice by the population sample agrees with the choice by all voters, for a given vote in the legislature, appears in Green and Laffont. They discussed this approach to legislative implementation of the VCG mechanism. Assuming that the voters are as well informed as the legislators, moreover, by using Bayesian theory one can extend the statistical theory used by Green and Laffont to obtain a posteriori odds for the insurance offered by the Thompson referendum, or any combination of the two together.

Consider then the case of an issue that has direct utility to voters, apart from its financial effect. If there is no effect of the issue on the marginal utility of wealth, the utility function $U(x, y)$ for the private good x and the public good y would have the particular form

$$U(x, y) = u(x) + g(y),$$

where a decision about the public good may or may not involve a financial effect as well as a utility effect. In this case Calfee and Rubin show that the voter will insure only against the financial effect, and will buy no insurance against the loss of direct utility from an adverse outcome. Thompson's proof of full insurance coverage is valid for a utility function of the form

$$U(x, y) = u[x + g(y)],$$

for which the marginal utility of wealth, U_x, is $u_x[x_0 + g(y_0)] = u_x[x_1 + g(y_1)]$ whenever $x_0 + g(y_0) = x_1 + g(y_1)$. In an intermediate case between that proposed by Thompson and the above zero-coverage case, the voter would insure only part of the loss of utility, and the proof of the optimality of the mechanism would again fail.

The combination mechanism, however, does not have this difficulty. It survives every challenge, because what is not insured is entered into the VCG mechanism, and the combination determines the outcome.

We now provide formal analysis in support of two of our claims. First, we said that it is straightforward to derive the correct odds for fair insurance using the information provided by the sample of voters who serve as a legislature. Second, we said that voting households will fully insure tangible financial losses at a fair premium but will not in general do so for other kinds of losses involving intangible or moral issues. We take up these questions in order.

Consider the issue of whether to approve a single proposed project y_1. Suppose that the variety of views among voters, approximately normally distributed, is known in a rough way to voters themselves and to the Election Commission. That is, we think of the total voter population as a random sample of size N from a hypothetical population whose individual willingness to pay for the project has a normal distribution $\mathcal{N}$, with a known mean μ and variance σ^2. The willingness to pay among the voter population has unknown mean m whose known variance is σ^2/N. An official legislature is a sample of size N with observed mean $\mathfrak{m}$. Then, from Green and Laffont (1977, n. 3), the Bayesian posterior distribution of m is

$$\mathcal{N}\left(\frac{\mu + nN\mathit{m}}{1+nN}, \frac{\sigma^2}{1+nN}\right) = f(\mathit{m}).$$

Then the probability of acceptance of the project, for an up or down choice, is

$$p(y_1) = \int_0^{\infty} f(\mathit{m})d\mathit{m}.$$

Where σ^2 is unknown, one would use a similar formulation with the Student t distribution. If y_1 is a continuous variable, the above $f(\mathit{m})$ is the posterior distribution of the optimal m, given m. Then for each increment to the value of (amount spent upon) y_1, the appropriate odds for the insurance premium are given by

$$p(\Delta y_1) = \int_{y_1^0}^{y_1^1} f(\mathit{m})d\mathit{m}.$$

These results can be generalized in a straightforward way to other probability distributions than the normal distribution, and to other assumptions about what is known about the mean and variance of the voter population's willingness to pay.

We now turn to the second question, that of the extent of insurance coverage voters will buy for different kinds of issues. When an issue involves intangible values, our claim is that the Thompson mechanism lacks incentive compatibility in the sense that voters will not generally insure against the exact amount of perceived harm from the proposed plan or from its failure. Denote by $\underline{x}_0{}^i$ voter i's initial wealth, including discounted future income, by y_0 the status quo government program, and by y_1 an alternative program. Suppose that the taxes to finance the alternative program exactly equal voter i's financial gains from that program, where both may be either positive or negative, so that $\underline{x}_0{}^i$ remains unchanged. Because positive and negative cases are symmetrical, without loss of generality we assume that voter i favors the adoption of the alternative program. For simplicity, we disregard relative prices, in effect assuming that they remain unchanged. Denote by $V^i(\underline{x}_0{}^i; y_j)$ the voter's indirect utility function. Denote the first partial derivative of indirect utility with respect to $\underline{x}^i$ by $V_x{}^i$, and the second derivative by $V_{xx}{}^i$. Suppose also that voter i is risk-averse, so that $V_{xx}{}^i < 0$. Denote by $\Delta' t^i$ voter i's willingness to pay to have y_1 adopted; that is, $V(\underline{x}_0{}^i - \Delta' t^i; y_1) = V^i(\underline{x}_0{}^i; y_0)$. The amount of insurance that voter i buys under the Thompson mechanism is I^i, and the probability of adoption of adoption of y_1 is p, so that the insurance premium is $(1 - p)I$. If there were no income effect we would have $\Delta' t^i$ constant as $\underline{x}_0{}^i$ changes: For every value of $\underline{x}^i$,

$$V^i(\underline{x}^i - \Delta' t^i; y_1) \equiv V^i(\underline{x}^i; y_0),$$

so that

$$V_x{}^i(\underline{x}^i - \Delta' t^i; y_1) \equiv V_x{}^i(\underline{x}^i; y_0).$$

In that case, voter i, maximizing expected utility, would respond to the Thompson mechanism in a referendum by insuring $\Delta' t^i$ in full against the possibility that y_1 would be rejected.

$$\text{Max E}(V^i) = \text{Max } \{pV^i(\underline{x}_0{}^i - [1-p]I^i; y_1) + [1-p]V^i(\underline{x}_0{}^i + pI^i; y_0)\},$$

which implies

$$p(1-p)V_x{}^i(\underline{x}_0{}^i - [1-p]I^i; y_1) = p(1-p)V_x{}^i(\underline{x}_0{}^i + pI^i; y_0),$$

which is to say,

$$V_x{}^i(\underline{x}_0{}^i - [1-p]I^i; y_1) = V_x{}^i(\underline{x}_0{}^i + pI^i; y_0), \qquad (5.1)$$

which holds when $I^i = \Delta' t^i$. However, when there is a positive income effect, so that $\Delta' t^i$ increases with $\underline{x}^i$, we have instead

$$V_x{}^i(\underline{x}^i - \Delta' t^i; y_1) > V_x{}^i(\underline{x}^i; y_0),$$

so that condition (5.1) is met at some smaller amount of insurance $I^i < \Delta' t^i$.[2] In this case, the voter is willing to declare an uninsured harm when the referendum has the VCG mechanism in tandem with the Thompson mechanism, and will declare the correct amount $\Delta' t^i - I^i$. On an up or down vote for a program y_1, the VCG mechanism is incentive compatible (see Chapter 6).

6 Adjustments for Income Effects

6.1 INTRODUCTION

The VCG mechanism has received detailed attention and analysis in many scholarly papers, with almost all the published work devoted to the case of transferable utility. That is, most such work assumes a consumer utility function of the form

$$U = x + f(y),$$

where x is the quantity of a single private good, y is the quantity of a single public good, and $f(y)$ is a smoothly differentiable function. Analysts have used this case because it is tractable, not because it has a real application. If y can take a value anywhere within a range such as [0,1], we call y 'continuous', and the consumer's message to the central agent is a demand function for y. If the choice is simply whether to produce a predetermined amount of a public good, then y can have just one of two values, such as 0 or 1, and we call y 'binary'. Here the consumer's message is a willingness to pay a specified amount of x to obtain one outcome instead of the other, which we designate as w.t.p.

If y is continuous, we have $U_x = 1$ and $U_y = f'$, so that for a given value of y, the w.t.p. for an additional unit of the public good, $U_y / U_x = f'$, is independent of the amount of x the consumer has. Being constant, U_x is independent of y. If $f'' < 0$, that is, if f' is diminishing, the household's demand price for y declines as y increases. The vertical sum of such demand prices, to be compared with the cost of y, is independent of the distribution of x among households, and is unaffected by tax assessments. Thus, w.t.p. and the criterion for optimality depend only on y. If y is binary, the discrete aggregate sum of households' w.t.p. is a single number, not a function.

Figure 6.1 illustrates the binary case for transferable utility. Utility is linear in x and the lines are parallel for the two values of y. This household prefers $y = 1$, with a w.t.p. of $x_0 - x_1$. (If the household prefers $y = 0$, one can interchange the two lines and also interchange x_0 and x_1.) Because, for every consumer, this quantity is invariant as x changes, the aggregate sum either exceeds the difference in cost between $y = 0$ and $y = 1$ or it does not,

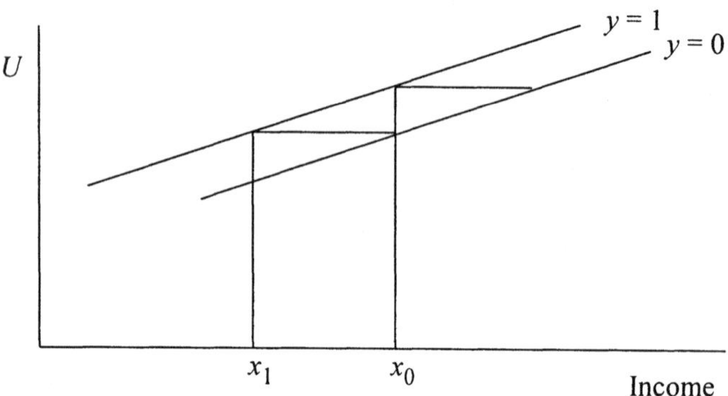

Figure 6.1 Utility as a function of income for a binary choice with transferable utility.

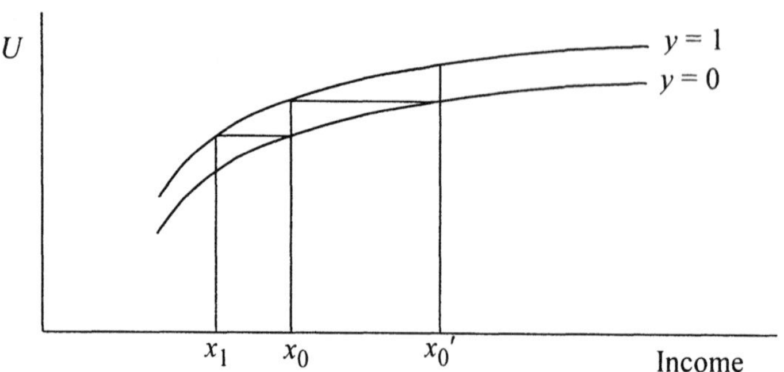

Figure 6.2 Utility as a function of income for a binary choice with non-separable and concave utility.

regardless of who pays the difference and regardless of whether a VCG tax must be assessed.

If y is continuous, then rescale y so that the value of y at which aggregate marginal w.t.p. equals marginal cost is 1. Then Figure 6.1 applies again. Each household's w.t.p. for this outcome instead of $y = 0$ remains the same if income changes. One way to characterize the constancy of each household's w.t.p. is to note that, for a change in y, the compensating variation equals the equivalent variation for every household, for every endowment x. When the marginal and total w.t.p. of all households are unaffected by changes in income, so are sums over all households, so that the equality of the marginal sum of w.t.p to marginal cost holds at all levels of endowments.

If a household's utility is non-separable and concave, by contrast, then the marginal utility of x is diminishing, and the w.t.p. for y is a function of both x and y. Figure 6.2 presents an example of this case. With an initial endowment of x_0, this household's w.t.p. for $y = 1$ instead of $y = 0$ is $x_0 - x_1$, whereas with an initial endowment of x_0', the corresponding amount is $x_0' - x_0 > x_0 - x_1$. In this example the marginal propensity to spend on y is increasing in x. Therefore, at an initial endowment of x_0, the household's compensating variation for a change of y from 0 to 1, namely $x_0 - x_1$, is less than the equivalent variation, $x_0' - x_0$. In this case the public good is a normal good, because as the household's income or wealth increases the household is willing to pay more for the good. That is, its income elasticity of demand is positive.

If the household's marginal valuation or marginal propensity to spend on y is negative, these inequalities are reversed. In that case the public good is an inferior good, which is unusual but not impossible. In either case we have nonzero income effects (a nonzero income elasticity of demand), and the household's purchase of Thompson insurance will not equal the household's w.t.p. to obtain its favored outcome. The balance of the household's w.t.p. can be revealed by proper application of one version or another of the VCG mechanism.

Nonzero income effects have technical effects on the operation of the VCG mechanism itself that one must consider with some care. There are four such effects of interest. First, each voter's reported w.t.p. affects the VCG taxes of other voters, which in turn affect the 'second price'—the effective price given by the mechanism—to this voter. This effect can create a perverse incentive for the voter, unless the mechanism is corrected to maintain the voter's incentive to tell the truth. Second, the collection of VCG taxes creates a budget surplus, which, if either refunded or used to reduce future taxes, contributes an additional item in both the foregoing effect and in the third. Third, inasmuch as the collection of VCG taxes reduces after-tax incomes, they change the w.t.p. values on which the VCG taxes depend. Therefore, whenever these income effects are non-negligible the Election Commission cannot simply add up w.t.p. schedules or values to determine an election outcome, but must solve a set of simultaneous equations. Fourth, for binary decisions an income effect distorts the household's w.t.p. in the sense that, for a proposal that the household opposes, it no longer represents the compensation that would make the household indifferent between the proposal and the alternative.

In most circumstances of practical interest, when the election outcome will be a value in a continuous range, such as the size of a budget, even the largest VCG tax anyone pays will be negligible for a community whose voters number in the thousands or millions. In the example concerning water pollution cleanup in and near the town of Freemonia, mentioned in Chapter 4, the Smith family was willing to pay for a substantially larger cleanup project than the one adopted, and paid a VCG tax of only 31 cents. If the community had one million families, for a substantially similar project of correspondingly larger cost but with similar w.t.p. by voting households, the corresponding VCG tax would be .006 cents. (See also the example of defense budget hawks and doves in Chapter 4.) In either case the income effects of this tax are so small that it is hard to see a practical reason to be concerned about such effects. This point is especially clear for the third of the income effects just mentioned—the effect on the voter's own w.t.p. of the tax itself. The first and second effects, the potentially perverse incentives due to income effects on other voters' w.t.p. and due to a refund, cannot be dismissed so readily, however. They scale down in about the same proportion as the tax itself, with increasing population size, so that the individually optimal misrepresentation of w.t.p. would remain about the same if there were no correction to this incentive.

In the following sections we will first discuss the technical issues that arise for decisions about budget size (and other continuous variables) and then discuss the technical issues for binary decisions. Section 6.2 discusses an incentive-compatible refund of VCG taxes. Section 6.3 discusses an adjustment to the VCG tax, to correct it for income effects on other voters, that maintains the incentive to tell the truth. Section 6.4 discusses the existence of a solution to the Election Commission's problem of simultaneous equations. Section 6.5 discusses decisions over multiple discrete options. The chapter is followed by a technical appendix that covers these topics more formally.

6.2 THE PRIMARY REFUND OF VCG TAXES FOR OUTCOMES IN A CONTINUOUS RANGE

We now present a way to achieve approximate budget balance for the VCG mechanism, for the case of a continuous public good y. In this case also the precise assessment of Lindahl taxes would achieve almost the same desired result: VCG tax assessments would be zero, and the budget would be balanced. There would nevertheless be income effects to disturb incentive compatibility, with which we deal in the next section. Moreover, the assumption of homogeneity within each recognized population subgroup strains credulity more in the case of continuous y than it does in the case of binary y. Homogeneity in the continuous case would mean that all members of a population subgroup, having equal tax shares of the cost of y, would favor exactly the same value for y. Here even the slightest variation among individuals would generate positive VCG tax revenues and a budget surplus to be disposed of.

A primary refund is a first step in the solution of the budget surplus problem, which can then be combined with a transfer designed for incentive compatibility (in a Bayesian sense). This first step is a refund to household i based only on what the VCG tax revenues would be if i did not participate. The VCG tax is always positive, and so generates a budget surplus because the approximate Lindahl taxes T of Chapter 2 finance public goods with a balanced budget. The standard view in the literature on this tax has been that the surplus must be destroyed or given to outsiders, to avoid distorting the sound incentives of the VCG tax (Tideman and Tullock, 1976). Collinge (1983) suggested advance auction of the surplus to a foreign country or to other wealthy underwriters who are indifferent about the amount of the home country's public good. This procedure would be satisfactory if there were outsiders willing to bid, because of some knowledge of likely election outcomes. Alternatively, in a federal system the national government could include local government budget surpluses in the national budget in exchange for an averaged transfer to each, diluting them so much that the incentive effects on voters under each local government would be negligible. Then for its own budget the national government would have to choose among the alternative improved transfers that we discuss in the next section.

Our first step is a formula for distributing the surplus from VCG taxes that has no effect on the incentive compatibility (or lack of it) of the VCG tax. Quite simply, for each voter the Election Commission calculates what the sum of VCG taxes would be if this voter had not participated. Denote this adjusted sum by S_{-i}. The refund to voter i is $S_{-i}(N-2)/(N-1)^2$. This refund for every voter results in an aggregate refund that is approximately equal to the sum of VCG taxes.

It is only a first step, however, because it is accurate only to a first approximation. The random remaining budget imbalance is vanishingly small, being of the order $O(1/N^2)$ when the number of voters N is large. Section A6.2 of the appendix to this chapter explains the technical properties of the primary refund, and, in particular, derives its degree of accuracy. We now turn to an additional transfer whose purpose is to correct the mechanism for the incentive effects of income effects, as consistently as possible with budget balance.

6.3 RECONCILING BUDGET BALANCE WITH BAYESIAN INCENTIVE COMPATIBILITY

The second transfer offsets income effects of VCG taxes and their variation in response to changes in a voter's reporting strategy so as to make the mechanism Bayesian incentive compatible (BIC). That is, the transfer creates an incentive effect that exactly cancels the perverse income effects on incentives, in terms of expected values. In the most general case of relatively unrestricted voter income effects, the objectives of budget balance and BIC cannot be perfectly reconciled. One or the other must be approximated, with an accuracy of approximation that depends on population size N.

Previous work using transferable utility has shown a way to achieve BIC with a precisely balanced budget. Our primary refund achieved the order of accuracy $O(1/N^2)$ without relying on transferable utility. The additional transfers proposed specifically in Section A6.3 in the appendix to this chapter can achieve precise BIC and precise budget balance in the presence of positive income effects if all voters have the same income effect on their marginal valuations. To a first approximation this restriction means that they have the same marginal propensity to spend on the public good. If their income effects are unequal, we can achieve BIC if we accept the primary refund's level of accuracy for budget balance. If, because of the feasibility constraint on a closed economy we opt for precise budget balance, the attainable approximation to BIC is $O(1/N^{3/2})$.

Section A6.3 presents the technical analysis of this transfer procedure for an economy that has one private good and one public good. Each consumer's message to the central agent provides a point on its valuation curve for y, the slope of the curve, and, where relevant, the income effect for the consumer's marginal valuation of the public good. Section A6.3 presents some properties of the mechanism for special cases, such as the case where all consumers have the same income effect. It then defines Bayesian expected values for the variables of the problem, where household messages are viewed as being drawn at random from a known probability distribution. It presents refund and transfer formulas that achieve BIC, both for the case of risk neutrality among consumers and for the case of equal risk aversion among them. As just noted, if consumers have equal income effects, the budget can be balanced precisely with a BIC mechanism.

6.4 THE EXISTENCE OF EQUILIBRIUM FOR CONTINUOUS PUBLIC GOODS

Our proposed use of population samples to determine a set of Lindahl taxes to finance public goods, to the extent that it succeeds, makes the mechanisms we have discussed almost redundant because, to that extent, the decisions will not only be unanimous, but no insurance or VCG tax money will change hands. In that case Foley's proof of the existence of Lindahl equilibrium applies without change (Foley, 1970). The use of a Thompson mechanism to choose discrete public projects or to determine their amounts might raise a new problem concerning the existence of equilibrium. The use of the VCG mechanism as modified in this chapter and in its appendices assuredly does raise a new problem, because one must establish the necessary continuity of the VCG tax with respect to the variables of the economy.

In Section A6.4 we address this issue for the most general economy whose technical properties we have yet considered, namely an economy with multiple private and public goods. In this economy, moreover, utility functions need not have continuous first and higher derivatives, although preferences are convex and utility is continuous and strictly monotonic. Using standard methods, but adding the necessary steps to establish the upper semi-continuity of the VCG tax and of the primary refunds r^i in prices and endowments of private goods, we clarify the definition of the tax and prove the existence of equilibrium. (It appears that this result could be extended readily to the case of an economy in which utility functions have continuous first and higher order derivatives, and the Thompson mechanism and the added transfers presented in Section A6.3 are used.) The proof uses Foley's (1970) line of proof and a mapping used by Debreu (1959), aided by an alternative line of proof used by Arrow and Hahn (1971).

This material is included for technical completeness, although the need for it is far less clear than in the cases of Sections A6.2 and A6.3. In a large economy the income effects of the VCG tax are negligible because the tax is typically a fraction of a penny per voter. In this case, Foley has already essentially proved the existence of equilibrium for an economic model as general as is typically used for this problem when considering only private goods.

6.5 MULTIPLE DISCRETE OPTIONS

In the case of binary decisions, the problems in the functioning of the pivotal mechanism due to income effects are more transparent. For binary decisions, such as the decision on police equipment for Freemonia mentioned in Chapter 4, a voter's potential liability for VCG tax is not a function of the size of the voting population but only of the voter's w.t.p. (The size of the electorate affects the probability having to pay, however, because the larger the electorate, the less likely it is that a household's vote will change the outcome.) In this case or equally if there are several options, in the absence of income effects one could rank several outcomes simply by the algebraic sum of w.t.p. to obtain or avoid each one, relative to the status quo. Then the outcome with the largest value relative to the status quo would win every pairwise comparison (or would tie with another winner, if more than one outcome has this same largest sum.)

Unfortunately, we invoke the VCG mechanism only when there are nonzero income effects, and unless we modify it, its performance can let us down in the case of binary decisions or decisions over multiple discrete options. The presence of income effects can make it hard to pick a winner, because the outcome with the largest sum of w.t.p.'s relative to the status quo not only need not win all pairwise contests, but might even lose unanimously to another outcome in a pairwise contest. Therefore we need a method of simultaneous ranking that will help us select the two best outcomes, which can then be ranked in a pairwise contest.

If neither of the resulting pair is the status quo, we also need a way to choose between them that does not depend on an arbitrary assumption placing either in that status.

Given that income effects can be appreciable for each voter, income effects cumulate in this kind of decision problem in such a way that the overall decision can easily be sensitive to how they are taken into account. In a constitutional structure like the one proposed here that attempts to avoid all redistributive effects, income effects affect the amount required to compensate those on the losing side of a decision.

No matter how we propose to deal with income effects, they complicate the unmodified mechanism. One problem of serious concern is the asymmetry of w.t.p. between those opposed to a proposal and those in favor. For those opposed w.t.p. is the equivalent variation, whereas for those in favor it is the compensating variation. A second, equally serious problem is that, when there are income effects and there are more than two possible public-goods outcomes, the binary decision mechanism is incompletely defined and, for almost every well-defined procedure for arriving at a decision, the mechanism is not incentive compatible.

If Lindahl taxes and transfers were perfectly predictable by population subgroup membership, and so revealed by the legislatures, every household that would otherwise be opposed to a proposal would receive at least enough compensation to make it indifferent to the change, if the proposal succeeds. With this compensation package, everyone would be in favor of or indifferent to the proposal, so that the first of the two problems would not apply. A problem arises, however, when there are differences of opinion within subgroups, so that the ideal of Lindahl compensation cannot be achieved. The constitutional rule for this case is that such compensation should be possible, so that households anticipating a long series of such decisions, in unpredictable order and of unknown content, would view the rule as offering the best attainable chance of a Pareto improvement for the whole collection of decisions. That is, from information supplied by the legislatures (and verified by voters), the Election Commission must estimate compensating variations for those households who oppose a change and use these in place of their stated w.t.p. in the criterion for a proposal's success against the status quo. For incentive compatibility, however, the w.t.p. must still set the upper limit on the household's VCG tax whenever the household's vote is pivotal.

If there is more than one binary proposal to consider in a referendum, and two potential winners both differ from the status quo, with income effects we are in the realm of the second problem, where the procedures for the Election Commission are even more demanding and complicated. Before explaining these, however, we must explain the problem further.

The outcome from applying the mechanism sequentially to pairwise decisions can depend on the order in which the proposed public goods packages are considered, even if households report their preferences truthfully. Furthermore, if a household is pivotal for a pairwise decision before the last stage of the process, it may be able to affect the final outcome favorably to itself by misreporting its preference for this decision. Similarly, if the household reports its w.t.p. to obtain or reject each of the outcomes in one simultaneous procedure, there can be cases where the household can manipulate the outcome to its advantage by misreporting part of this information.

Section A6.5 shows how the problem can be solved using our legislative procedures. First, it considers the case in which the population sample perfectly represents the preferences of every identifiable subgroup of the population, each subgroup being homogeneous. Section A6.5 has a formal proof that the Election Commission can use the sample information on w.t.p. to assess accurate Lindahl taxes for each outcome, such that the voter population will agree unanimously on the ranking of the outcomes. If this is accomplished, in the referendum all VCG taxes are zero, and there is no opportunity for strategic voting. Second, it considers the less demanding case in which the Lindahl taxes have errors, but are accurate enough that there remain only two candidate outcomes with a chance of success in a referendum.

The case of only two possible outcomes, that is, the strictly binary case, may be typical even without the use of Lindahl taxes. Most government decisions involve projects whose effects are predominantly wealth-creating. Emotionally charged cases involving non-financial values come up less frequently, and as a rule may be viewed disjointly. For example, it is hard to imagine that someone would vote strategically on the 17th amendment to the U.S. constitution, providing for the direct election of senators, in order to change, through income effects, the outcome of the 18th, prohibiting the manufacture of alcoholic beverages. This feature of such issues is helpful because for binary decisions the VCG pivotal mechanism is incentive compatible for all well-behaved utility functions even when the Election Commission adjusts w.t.p. to obtain a different quantity such as the compensating variation.

To see why it is incentive compatible, consider the amount $x_0 - x_1$ in Figure 6.2 that the household is willing to pay to have the outcome be $y = 1$ rather than $y = 0$. This amount is given and fixed for this decision, and is not affected by the VCG tax outcome in any way. If the household does in fact have to pay part of this amount because its vote is pivotal in a decision favoring $y = 1$, that does not change the balance of this amount that the household would be willing to pay if necessary to obtain the favorable outcome. Adjustments that the Election Commission's procedures may require in order to determine the winner and to determine who is pivotal have no effect on this incentive picture. For this reason there is no interaction among the income effects of different votes, and no problem of perverse incentives. Section A6.5 provides a formal proof of incentive compatibility for this case.

For emotionally charged, nonfinancial issues one does not expect homogeneity of preferences within every identifiable population subgroup. What one expects is substantially smaller variability of preferences within subgroups than between them. This is a major advantage of having a rule to approximate Lindahl taxes as closely as possible. If the approximation is reasonably good, it is plausible to assume that the ranking process, and the information from the legislature about variability of preferences, will result in a clear binary decision to be put to a referendum. That is, there will be enough information that the Election Commission can rule out all but at most two outcomes for a given referendum ballot as being so clearly ranked below the top that no general vote on them is needed (although 'no action' must appear in every case, by constitutional mandate).

Often the question would be 'yes' or 'no' on one issue, expressed in terms of w.t.p. Often, also, the outcome will be almost certain and no VCG tax will in fact be assessed.

In the multiple option case that does not end with a single alternative to the status quo on the ballot, the choice between two new proposals does not by itself raise the question of compensation of losers because neither proposal is the status quo. A procedure that attempted to assign status quo status to one proposal would prejudice the outcome. In particular, in cases of doubt the adjustment of w.t.p. from equivalent variation to compensating variation has the consequence, if both options are normal goods with the same income elasticity of demand, that the status quo is more likely to win. A neutral procedure that leaves no discretion to the Election Commission is therefore appropriate.

When the choice is not strictly binary, reports by members of population samples (that is, of official legislatures), of their pairwise w.t.p. to obtain one outcome over another, for every pairwise comparison, can be used to rank the projects by a 'cardinal ranking procedure' (CRP) that takes income effects into account. The procedure is neutral among options in the sense that it ranks them simultaneously and makes no assumption about a status quo or about a subsequent decision path.

We first explain the choice problem and the procedure when there are two households and two attractive proposals. Household 1 prefers proposal y_1, whereas Household 2 prefers y_2, when the taxes to pay for each have been chosen by a well-specified procedure to assure that both households prefer both proposals to the status quo. This tax package has been determined in advance of the referendum. In the referendum the households send w.t.p. messages comparing each option with the status quo and with the other. Suppose, for example, that these amounts are those shown in the following table.

Willingness to Pay to Move

Household 1			Household 2		
From	To Option		From	To Option	
Option	1	2	Option	1	2
0	80	70	0	60	80
1		– 45	1		40

We can see a choice problem immediately upon inspection of these numbers. If we add numbers in the first row for y_1, we have a combined w.t.p. of both households of 140 to obtain that option, compared with 150 for y_2. This comparison suggests that option 2 is better. By contrast, in the second row the combined w.t.p. to go from y_1 to y_2 (treating y_1 as the status quo) is – 5, which suggests that y_1 is better.

Supposing for simplicity that the w.t.p. figures are linear in wealth, we can calculate Household 1's $CV^1{}_{12} = EV^1{}_{21}$ (where the first subscript means 'for a change from y_1 to y_2' and the second means 'for a change from y_2 to y_1'). This is the amount one would have to add to initial after-tax wealth in combination with y_2 so that Household 1 would be indifferent between y_1 and y_2. Applying the logic of similar triangles, we have $CV^1{}_{12} = [-45/(45-80)]70 = 90$. The corresponding calculation for Household 2 yields $CV^2{}_{21} = 60$. Suppose that we use these to determine whether one household could compensate the other for its preferred change from one option to the other. If the status quo is y_1, Household 1 prefers no change whereas Household 2 would prefer to change to y_2. From the second row of the table we see that Household 2 is willing to pay only 40 to obtain this change, whereas Household 1 would have to be compensated 90 to secure its acquiescence to the change. By the Pareto test, y_1 is better. If we perform the same exercise starting with y_2 as the status quo, Household 1 is willing to pay 45 to change to y_1, whereas Household 2 would have to be compensated 60. Thus we find that, by the Pareto test, y_2 is better. This paradox and the previous one based on the w.t.p. figures of the first row indicate the need for a neutral, transparent formula that gives a plausible outcome.

For each household i the proposed formula uses a 'ranking variation' RV^i_j, ($j = 1, 2$) a number that is a compromise between CV^i_{12} and EV^i_{12}. We find a conjectural compensation package that would reduce the household's wealth with its preferred option and add to its wealth with its less preferred option, such that these wealth changes sum to zero and such that the household would be indifferent between the options. Reversing the signs of these wealth changes, we then sum them for each option over all households. The option with the highest sum becomes the winner. Because all the RV^i_j's sum to zero, the highest sum for an option $y_{j'}$ must be positive, which would imply a budget surplus if the government were to collect the positive $RV^i_{j'}$ as added taxes and pay out the negative $RV^i_{j'}$ as transfers. The option $y_{j'}$ with the largest (positive) sum could therefore have its $RV^i_{j'}$ adjusted favorably for every household (lower taxes, higher transfers) so as to balance the community budget and achieve unanimous agreement that this option is best. This description means that for all i, $RV^i_1 + RV^i_2 = 0$, that $-CV^i_{12} \lesseqgtr RV^i_1 - RV^i_2 \lesseqgtr EV^i_{12}$, and that we choose the winner $y_{j'}$ by finding $\text{Max}_j[RV^1_j + RV^2_j]$.

Denote by x^1_0 Household 1's wealth, which for notational simplicity we take to be the same for all outcomes. To calculate the ranking variations for Household 1, first note that $CV^1_{12} = 90$, whereas $EV^1_{12} = -45$. These numbers mean that giving back 45 to Household 1 would raise its utility $U^1(\cdot, y_1)$ by the same amount as giving this household 90 would raise $U^1(\cdot, y_2)$. That is, the marginal utility of wealth to Household 1 is twice as great when the public good package is y_1 as its marginal utility of wealth when the public good package is y_2. Therefore, to satisfy the requirement that $U^1(x^1_0 - RV^1_1, y_1) = U^1(x^1_0 - RV^1_2, y_2)$ at the same time that we have $RV^1_1 = -RV^1_2$, we must have

$$U^1(x^1_0, y_1) - U^1(x^1_0 - RV^1_1, y_1)$$

$$= 2[U^1(x^1_0 - RV^1_2, y_2) - U^1(x^1_0, y_2)]$$

$$= 2[U^1(x^1_0 - RV^1_1, y_1) - U^1(x^1_0 + EV^1_{12}, y_1)].$$

By our linearity assumption, it follows that

$$RV^1_1 = -2[RV^1_1 + EV^1_{12}] = -(2/3)EV^1_{12}.$$

With $EV^1_{12} = -45$, this gives $RV^1_1 = 30 = -RV^1_2$. The corresponding calculation for Household 2 gives the result $RV^2_1 = -10 = -RV^2_2$. Then for y_1, $RV^1{}_1 + RV^2{}_1 = 30 - 10 = 20$, whereas for y_2, we have $RV^1{}_2 + RV^2{}_2 = -20$, so that the mechanism chooses y_1.

If the Election Commission were to adjust the tax and transfer packages by the amounts of the $RV^i{}_j$, making both households indifferent between the two options, there would be a prospective budget surplus of 20 with option y_1 and a deficit of 20 with option y_2. The Election Commission could therefore balance the budget, as required by the constitution, by lowering the tax on Household 1 for option y_1 by 10 and increasing the transfer to Household 2 for this option by 10. For option y_2, it could reduce Household 1's transfer by 10 and increase Household 2's tax by 10. With these changes, both households would prefer y_1 to y_2, illustrating the general point just stated.

The Election Commission can have all these calculations done with simple computer software using only the w.t.p.'s as inputs, with no step leaving any discretion to the Commission. Moreover, it can calculate $RV^i{}_j$'s for multiple options at whichever stage of the legislative process it may need to do so, simply following the above rules. For multiple options, these rules are to choose a set of $RV^i{}_j$'s for each legislator such that

$$U^i(x^i{}_0 - RV^i{}_1, y_1) = U^i(x^i{}_0 - RV^i{}_j, y_j)$$

for all $j = 1, \ldots, h'$, if there are h' options to be ranked, and such that

$$\Sigma_j RV^i{}_j = 0.$$

Then the winner $y_{j'}$ of the CRP is that given by

$$\text{Max}_j [\Sigma_i RV^i{}_j].$$

Because the referendum outcomes determine the incentive payments that the proposed constitution provides to the official legislatures, it is always in their interest to give truthful w.t.p. information if the referendum itself will be incentive compatible. Therefore a procedure can be used in each official legislature that might prove to have perverse incentives in another context. In particular, there is no problem at all about using the cardinal ranking procedure in the simultaneous ranking of many legislative options.

For example, suppose that a proposal for legislation to protect wetlands had several alternative options concerning criteria for what is to be protected, with different amounts of land that would be preserved and protected from development. The legislative votes of w.t.p. would indicate a set of Lindahl taxes and transfers for the population subgroups so as to get a nearly unanimous agreement on the subset of options that have a chance of winning a referendum. This subset might contain three or four options that generate paradoxical comparisons with each other like the two-option case just considered. The Speaker could then use the CRP to rank the several options and to propose Lindahl taxes and transfers expected to produce a nearly unanimous referendum result in favor of the top-ranked option. If, after considering the proposals of all legislatures, the Election Commission's statistical committee determines that no other option has a one percent chance of acceptance, under Article II, Section 9(b) the referendum would contain only the one top-ranked option versus the status quo. If a second option has a greater chance of acceptance than one percent, there would be two options versus the status quo on the referendum ballot. In either case the Election Commission would use the CRP, in the event of a close vote, to determine the winning option. If the chance that the status quo will win is negligible, the referendum is still essentially a two-option contest, so that the proof in Section A6.5 of incentive compatibility is almost certain to be applicable.

An attractive feature of the CRP is that, although in the case of multiple options one can construct examples where strategic voting could advance a household's interests, these examples are convoluted, difficult to construct, and implausible. If the impression that these examples give is correct, then strategic voting would be advantageous so rarely and so unpredictably that it would be of negligible significance. In that case, even if a referendum would occasionally have multiple (though discrete) options, the CRP would in practice be a sound, reliable instrument for deciding the referendum outcome.

Note that to maintain incentive compatibility, the tax and transfer package decided prior to the referendum must remain unchanged. The notional taxes and transfers suggested by the votes, because of heterogeneity of household preferences within population subgroups, can be used to determine incentive payments to official legislatures, but not to determine individual taxes and transfers among the voters.

6.6 CONCLUSION

This summary statement of the more arcane aspects of demand-revealing mechanisms may explain more than one wishes to know, but is nevertheless regrettably necessary. The pure theory of the subject raises issues that are sometimes of great practical weight and sometimes not, and one can discern the difference only through careful study. The appendix to this chapter reviews the current state of the theory, while our largely informal discussion in this chapter gives the reader reasons why some of the theoretical issues are of practical importance and some are not. The constitution's Technical Appendix, which refers to adjustments to voter w.t.p. to improve the functioning of the referendum process, is necessary, as is the careful attention in previous chapters to the problems of the incentive to vote and of coordinated strategic voting, that is, of conspiracies. Whereas the theory to which the Technical Appendix refers is still incomplete, the appendix to this chapter shows that there has been enough progress that the remaining unsolved problems are of second-order importance.

Appendix: Formal Proofs

A6.1 FORMAL DEVELOPMENT OF THE VCG MECHANISM

The economy has k private goods x_j and h public goods $y_{j'}$. A vector of private and public goods is denoted by $(x; y) = (x_1, \ldots, x_k; y_1, \ldots, y_h)$. There are N consumers, $N \geq 6$, denoted by superscripts i. The economy has a vector of prices $p = (p_x; p_y)$, where each individual public good price p_{yj}, without superscript, is the marginal cost of y_j. A public good price $p_{yj}{}^i$ with a superscript represents a variable specific to an individual consumer, the *marginal value* of the good to that consumer. Prices for public goods of this latter type will be referred to as *Lindahl prices.*

We denote the inner product of two vectors such as p and z by $p{\cdot}z$, and the Cartesian product of sets X and Z by $X \times Z$. For a pair of vectors z, z^+ the inequality $z^+ > z$ means '$z^+{}_j > z_j \ \forall\, j$,' while $z^+ \geqq z$ means '$z^+{}_j \geqq z_j \ \forall\, j$,' and $z^+ \geq z$ means '$z^+ \geqq z$ but not $z^+ = z$.'

A6.1.A Consumption

Each consumer i chooses a point $(x^i; y)$ in a consumption set X^i, on which the consumer has a complete preference pre-ordering, represented here by the utility function $U^i(x^i; y)$. The consumer owns an initial endowment of private goods $\underline{x}^i$ above a bankruptcy level $\underline{\underline{x}}$ that is the same for all consumers. The vector of initial endowments is $\underline{x}$. Consumption points in X^i, and values of other variables that are consistent with such consumption points, are called *admissible*. For example, a tax that reduces a consumer i's endowment below $\underline{\underline{x}}$ is not admissible.

A.1. $\sum_i X^i$ has a lower bound.

The following hold $\forall$ i.

A.2. X^i is closed and convex, and has an interior in the private goods subspace. Moreover, $\forall(x^i; y) \in X^i$, if $(x^{+i}; y^+) \geq (x^i; y)$ then $(x^{+i}; y^+) \in X^i$.

A.3. (Non-Bankrupt Endowments.) If $(x^i; y) \in X^i$, then $\exists$ $(x^{+i}; y) \in X^i$ with $x^{+i} < \underline{x}^i$.

A.4. (Standard Bankruptcy.) $\exists$ $\underline{\underline{x}}^i = \underline{\underline{x}} > 0$ such that $\forall$ y with $(\underline{\underline{x}}^i, y) \in X^i$ we have $\forall$ $(x^i; y) \in X^i$, $x^i \geqq \underline{\underline{x}}^i$.

A.5. (Continuity of Preferences.) $\forall(x^i; y) \in X^i$ the utility function $U^i(x^i; y)$ is continuous.

A.6. (Convexity of Preferences.) $\forall$ $(x^i; y)$, $(x^{+i}; y^+) \in X^i$, if $U^i(x^i; y) > U^i(x^{+i}; y^+)$ then $\forall$ θ, $0 < \theta < 1$, $U^i[\theta(x^i; y) + (1 - \theta)(x^{+i}; y^+)] > U^i(x^{+i}; y^+)$.

A.7. (Monotonicity of Preferences.) $\forall$ $(x^i; y)$, $(x^{+i}; y^+) \in X^i$, if $(x^i; y) \geq (x^{+i}; y^+)$ then $U^i(x^i; y) > U^i(x^{+i}; y^+)$.

A.8 (Differentiability of Preferences.) U^i is everywhere differentiable, and all second and higher order derivatives exist.

A6.1.B Production

Production is denoted by a vector $(z; y)$ of private goods z and public goods y with inputs negative and outputs positive. The set of all technically possible production plans Z is the aggregate of the production possibility sets of individual firms and of activities conducted by the central agent (government). The separate production units in this aggregation remain implicit.

B.1. Z is a closed, convex cone.

B.2. $0 \in Z$.

B.3. (Necessity of private goods.) If $0 \neq (z; y) \in Z$, at least one $z_j < 0$.

B.4. (Possibility of producing public goods.) $\forall$ $j = 1, \ldots, h$, $\exists$ $(z; y) \in Z$ such that $y_j > 0$.

B.5. (No public good is indispensable as a production input.) If $(z; y) \in Z$ and we construct a vector y^+ by setting $y^+_j = y_j$ when $y_j \geq 0$ but $y^+_j = 0$ when $y_j < 0$, then $\exists$ $(z^+; y^+) \in Z$.

A6.1.C Allocations

C.1. A *consumption allocation* $(x, y) \in X$ is a set of N vectors of private goods $(x^1, \ldots, x^N)$, each $x^i \in \mathbb{R}^k$, and a vector of public goods $y \in \mathbb{R}^h$, such that $\forall\ i$ either $\exists\ (x^{+i}; y) \in X^i$ with $x^{+i} < x^i$, or $x^i = \underline{x}$. The set X is closed and convex.

C.2. An *allocation* w is a consumption allocation $(x, y) \in X$ and a production plan $(z, y^+) \in Z$, that is, $w \in W = X \times Z$. Since both X and Z are closed and convex, W is closed and convex.

C.3. A *feasible allocation* w' is an allocation $[(x, y), (z, y^+)] \in W$ such that $y = y^+$ and $(z, y^+) = [\sum_i (x^i - \underline{x}^i), y^+] \in Z$. The set of feasible allocations is $W' \subset W$. The set of consumption allocations that are components of feasible allocations is $X' \subset X$.

C.4. A *maximal allocation* $\mathcal{W}$ is a feasible allocation $[(x', y'), (z', y')] \in W'$ such that there is no other feasible allocation $[(x'^+, y'^+), (z'^+, y'^+)]$ with $x'^+ \geq x'$ and $y'^+ \geq y'$. The set of maximal allocations is $\mathcal{W} \subset W'$. The set of consumption allocations that are components of maximal allocations is $\mathcal{X} \subset X'$.

C.5. A *Pareto efficient allocation* $\mathcal{W}^*$ is a maximal allocation $[(x^*, y^*), (z^*, y^*)] \in \mathcal{W}$ such that there is no other maximal allocation $[(x', y'), (z', y')]$ with $U^i(x', y') > U^i(x^*, y^*), \forall\ i$. The set of Pareto efficient allocations is $\mathcal{W}^* \subset \mathcal{W}$. The set of consumption allocations that are components of Pareto efficient allocations is $\mathcal{X}^* \subset \mathcal{X}$.

C.6. A *public competitive equilibrium* is a Pareto efficient allocation, a vector of prices $p = (p_x; p_y)$, and a vector of taxes $T = (T^1, \ldots, T^N)$, with $p_y \cdot y = \sum_i T^i$ such that:

(a) $p \cdot (\sum_i [x^i - \underline{x}^i]; y) \geqq p \cdot (z'; y')\ \forall\ (z'; y') \in Z$;

(b) $p_x \cdot x^i = p_x \cdot \underline{x}^i - T^i$ and if $U^i(x^{+i}; y) > U^i(x^i; y)$ then $p_x \cdot x^{+i} > p_x \cdot x^i$;

(c) there is no vector of public goods and taxes $(y, T^{+1}, \ldots, T^{+N})$ with $p_y \cdot y = \sum_i T^{+i}$ such that $\forall\ i\ \exists\ x^{+i}$ with $(x^{+i}; y^+) \in X^i$, $U^i(x^{+i}; y^+) > U^i(x^i; y)$ and $p_x \cdot x^{+i} = p_x \cdot \underline{x}^i - T^{+i}$.

C.7. A *Lindahl equilibrium* is a public competitive equilibrium with $\partial T^i / \partial y_j = p_{yj}^{\ i}\ \forall\ i, j$.

Both a public competitive equilibrium and a Lindahl equilibrium involve profit maximization by producers, preference maximization under the after-tax budget constraint by consumers, and the impossibility of finding a new public sector with taxes to pay for it that leaves every consumer better off. In Lindahl equilibrium a consumer's tax per unit of each public good is less than or equal to that consumer's pertinent marginal rate of substitution. By contrast, in public competitive equilibrium the allocation of the tax, whose sum is the total cost of the public goods, can be arbitrary among consumers, subject to the stated assumption of an admissible allocation. Such taxes, not equal to Lindahl taxes, that finance public goods as in C.6, are *non-Lindahl taxes*.

The approach used here assumes a large economy with perfect competition. This framework is not strictly consistent with the use of the VCG tax, which becomes vanishingly small when the number of consumers becomes sufficiently large. However, I wish to establish that the presence of significant income effects does not interfere with the applicability of the VCG tax. For that purpose, it is a helpful simplification to treat the economy as having perfect competition even for finite values of N, where with small N the size of the VCG tax is restricted only by the non-bankruptcy requirement.

A6.1.D Tax Finance of Public Goods

Charges for public goods under the VCG mechanism traditionally have two parts, T and S, of which T provides the revenue to finance public goods while S is the VCG tax that provides incentives for truthful revelation of preferences and generates a budget imbalance. The allocation of T among consumers is predetermined.

We need a non-Lindahl tax formula for T that is consistent with feasible allocations. That is, it must not bankrupt anyone. Moreover, to simplify the statement of the requirement that every consumer have a positive budget, consider a refundable tax credit, a type of negative income tax that provides a non-zero safety net. Let

$$T^i = (T_1{}^i, \ldots, T_h{}^i)\cdot(y_1, \ldots, y_h) - p_x \cdot \eta, \tag{A6.1}$$

where $\eta > 0$ is a small fixed sector of private goods. (Clearly we must choose an $\eta < \sum_i [\underline{x}^i - \underline{\underline{x}}^i]$.) Then one of the public goods, say y_1, is the negative income tax $p_x \cdot N\eta$. Each $T_j{}^i$ is a scalar, a function of private goods prices, times the full price of y_j. For example, let

$$T_j{}^i = p_{yj} \frac{p_x \cdot (\underline{x}^i - \underline{\underline{x}}^i)}{p_x \cdot \sum_{i'} (\underline{x}^{i'} - \underline{\underline{x}}^{i'})} . \tag{A6.2}$$

One can readily verify that there are feasible allocations that can be attained while assessing these non-Lindahl taxes to finance positive quantities of public goods, and that each consumer's tax is a continuous function of p_x and y. It can also be shown that for this general type of tax formula that satisfies the non-bankruptcy requirement, a non-Lindahl public competitive equilibrium exists (Foley, 1967; Section A6.4 of this appendix).

The tax formulas (A6.1) and (A6.2) are parametric, in that the central agent, to assess the tax, knows the individual endowments $\underline{x}^i$. This departure from a general custom in the mechanism literature is necessary and appropriate for two reasons: (a) it is impossible to do without it, when there is a free-rider problem (Groves and Ledyard, 1977); and (b) governments do in fact impose taxes on income and property.

The tax formulas restrict the set of maximal allocations that can be attained:

C.8. A *maximal allocation authorized by public-goods financing taxes* (a maximal AFT allocation) is a maximal allocation $\mathcal{W}' = [(x, y), (z, y)]$ such that $p_x \cdot x^i = p_x \cdot \underline{x}^i - T^i$. The set of maximal AFT allocations is $\mathcal{W}' \subset \mathcal{W}$. The set of consumption allocations that are components of maximal AFT allocations is $\mathcal{X}' \subset \mathcal{X}$. The private goods component of a maximal AFT consumption allocation for consumer i is x'^i.

A6.1.E The VCG Tax

A central agent (the government) chooses the levels of spending on public goods that appear to be most efficient, y', based on messages sent by consumers. The *message from consumer i* is a vector of reported values of parameters that characterize the relative value of public goods in U^i. Restrictions such as A.5-A.8 limit the messages that may be reported. Each consumer's message is admissible iff it is consistent with a utility function that satisfies stated restrictions such as A.5-A.8.

A.9. The utility function $U^i(x^i, y)$ can be represented by a function $U(x^i, y; m^i)$, common to all i, where $m^i \in \mathbb{R}^b$, with b a finite positive integer, and where $U(\cdot, \cdot, \cdot)$ and b are known to all consumers and to the central agent. m^i is a b-vector of parameters of U, distinct for each consumer i, that fully characterizes i's utility.

M.1. Denote by m'^i the vector of not necessarily truthful values of the components of m^i reported by consumer i. Each consumer's strategy space is the set of all vectors m'^i that are consistent with utility functions that satisfy stated restrictions such as A.5 – A.8.[1] The *set of all admissible messages* from a consumer is $M \subset \mathbb{R}^b$. A *joint set of messages* is the matrix $m' = \{m'^1, \ldots, m'^N\} \in M^N \subset \mathbb{R}^{Nb}$.

M.2. A *mechanism* is a function $F\colon M^N \rightarrow X$. The *outcome* of the mechanism, $F(m')$, is an element of X, that is, a consumption allocation $(x, y) \in X$. A mechanism's *incentive structure* I_F induces consumers to map the true information m into the message m'. $I_F\colon M^N \rightarrow M^N$. A *successful, incentive-compatible mechanism* F^* maps a combined set of messages into a Pareto-efficient allocation, $F^*(m) = (x^*, y^*) \in \mathcal{X}^*$, with $I_{F^*}(m) = m$.

Here we focus attention exclusively on a specific variation and elaboration of the VCG mechanism. It is a game in which each consumer i selects a strategy consisting of a message, truthful or not, to send to the central agent. This version of the VCG mechanism uses a combination of taxes and transfers to implement $I_{F^*}(m)$, and it maps the set of true messages into a consumption allocation that is nearly if not exactly a Pareto-efficient consumption allocation (x^*, y^*).

C.9. A *maximal allocation authorized by all taxes and transfers* $\mathcal{W}''$ (a maximal AATT allocation) is a maximal allocation $[(x', y'), (z', y')]$ such that $p_x \cdot x' = p_x \cdot \underline{x} - \mathcal{T}$, where $\mathcal{T}$ is a vector in which $\mathcal{T}^i$ is the sum of all taxes on individual i, net of any refunds and other transfers. The set of maximal AATT allocations is $\mathcal{W}'' \subset \mathcal{W}$. The set of consumption allocations that are components of maximal AATT allocations is $\mathcal{X}'' \subset \mathcal{X}$. The private goods component of a maximal AATT consumption allocation for consumer i is x''^i.

Disregarding temporarily the problem of government budget imbalance, each consumer i faces the maximization problem,

$$\max_{x^i} U^i(x^i; y) \text{ subject to } p_x \cdot x^i \leq p_x \cdot \underline{x}^i - \mathcal{T}^i.$$

Corresponding to this maximization is the indirect utility function

$$V^i(p_x; \underline{x}^i; \mathcal{T}^i; y) = \max_{x^i} U^i(x^i; y) \text{ for } p_x \cdot x^i = p_x \cdot \underline{x}^i - \mathcal{T}^i(p_x; \underline{x}^i; y),$$

with the property that for each public good j, $V^i_j = U^i_j$. The consumer's marginal utility of the numeraire good, x_1, is $\lambda^i(p_x; \underline{x}^i; \mathcal{T}^i; y)$, and the marginal utility of $\mathcal{T}^i$, $\partial V^i / \partial \mathcal{T}^i$, is $-\lambda^i$.

The VCG mechanism requires that each consumer send a message to the central agent conveying valuation information sufficient to determine a vector y' that, together with the privately chosen aggregate x, meets some or all of the criteria for a Pareto-efficient allocation. For present purposes, assume a two-stage procedure in which the central agent has previously announced the individual tax rates T_j^i per unit of public good of equation (A6.2), having already identified the $\underline{x}^i$. Then the message from consumer i could be a vector of parameters that describe the ratio of the two functions $V^i(p_x; \underline{x}^i; T^i; y)$ and $\lambda^i(p_x; \underline{x}^i; T^i; y)$. Then, for each y_j, it is evident that $U^i_j/U^i_1 = V^i_j/\lambda^i$. It simplifies the task of the central agent if, at the time of the procedure, the vector p_x is known, which we now assume for our partial equilibrium analysis.

For each maximal AFT consumption allocation x'^+ that differs from the consumption allocation without a public sector, x'^0, consumer i has an *apparent total gain* $G^i(x'^+)$ from the production of public goods, which roughly approximates the maximum amount of the numeraire good that consumer i would pay for the existence of the public sector:

$$G^i(x'^+) = \int_{x'^0}^{x'^+} \left[\sum_j (p_{yj}{}^i - T_j{}^i)\right] dx', \tag{A6.3}$$

where the right-hand side is the integral along a path in X'.

For utility functions satisfying A.5-A.8, the integral (A6.3) is only an approximation to consumer's surplus, even if the messages are true, although components of the integrand measure precisely i's *marginal* consumer's surplus for the components of y, at each $x'^i \in X'^i$. This feature is appropriate because prior to the outcome neither the consumer nor the central agent knows which point in X' the mechanism will choose. Furthermore, efficiency requires that the true marginal valuation, not at $x'^i \in X'^i$ but at $x''^i \in X''^i$ be used, a requirement that we will attend to in due course.

The measure (A6.3) of i's consumer's surplus resulting from the choices y' of amounts of public goods is approximate for three reasons: because of the omission of the effects of the difference between X' and X'', because it is neither the compensating variation nor the equivalent variation, (but with true messages would be intermediate between the two), and because the strategically chosen messages may be false. (In the case of transferable utility, where $U^i(x^i, y) = A(x^i) + H^i(y)$, and where the mechanism elicits true schedules, equation (A6.3) precisely measures i's willingness to pay for public goods, and thus is i's consumer's surplus from the public sector.)

The aggregate value over all consumers of the apparent total gains from the production of public goods (A6.3), for each $(x, y) \in X'$, is

$$G(x, y) = \sum_i G^i(x^i, y), \tag{A6.4}$$

and the corresponding aggregate for all consumers except i we denote by

$$G_{-i}(x, y) = \sum_{i' \neq i} G^{i'}(x^{i'}, y). \tag{A6.5}$$

M.3. The central agent chooses the *apparent Pareto-efficient value* y' by finding $\text{Max}_y\, G(x, y)$, which by (A6.3) and (A6.4) is found where, $\forall\, j$,

$$\sum_i (p_{yj}{}^i - T_j{}^i) = 0. \tag{A6.6}$$

Further, denote by y''_{-i} the y where $\forall\, j$,

$$\sum_{i' \neq i} (p_{yj}{}^{i'} - T_j{}^{i'}) = 0. \tag{A6.7}$$

If the left-hand side of (A6.6) is negative for all $y_j > 0$, then $y' = 0$. Likewise, if the left-hand side of (A6.7) is negative for all $y_j > 0$, then $y''_{-i} = 0$. (These boundary cases present no problem, and henceforward will be disregarded.)

M.4. The *VCG tax for consumer i*, S^i, (the loss to others from accommodating the fact that consumer i is not indifferent among maximal AFT allocations) is[2]

$$S^i = G_{-i}(\cdot, y''_{-i}) - G_{-i}(\cdot, y'), \tag{A6.8}$$

which works out, using (A6.3), as

$$S^i = \sum_{i' \neq i} \int_{(\cdot,\, y')}^{(\cdot,\, y''_{-i})} \sum_j (p_{yj}{}^{i'} - T_j{}^{i'})\, dx\,. \tag{A6.9}$$

The two taxes (A6.2) and (A6.9) together imply that points on the opportunity cost curve of y_j to consumer i, under the VCG mechanism, are given by $p_{yj} - \sum_{i' \neq i} p_{yj}{}^{i'}$. The end points of each integral in (A6.9) are defined by the solutions to (A6.6) and (A6.7). Equation (A6.6), with true reporting, and with income effects taken into account, is the Bowen-Samuelson condition for optimal quantities $y_j{}^*$.

A sum over N consumers of the VCG tax is denoted S_N.

A6.1.F Definitions and Results for the Case of Separable Utility

As a preliminary step before considering the case where the demand for the public good has a positive income effect, consider the conventional case of separable utility. This step will provide a result that is easily obtained, and that generalizes easily to the more general case.

Taking account of the public-goods financing tax T^i and at first disregarding the VCG tax S^i, we have $p_x \cdot x^i = p_x \cdot \underline{x}^i - T^i$ and

$$U^i = U^i(x^i; y) = V^i(p_x; \underline{x}^i; T^i; y), \tag{A6.10}$$

from which it follows that

$$\left.\frac{dV^i}{dy_j}\right|_{\substack{\text{base}\\ \text{tax}\\ \text{paid}}} = V^i_{yj} - \lambda^i T_j{}^i .$$

The marginal consumer's surplus, or excess willingness to pay, above the basic tax T_j^i, is:

$$\frac{\dfrac{dV^i}{dy_j}}{\lambda^i} = \frac{V^i{}_{yj}}{\lambda^i} - T_j{}^i = p_{yj}{}^i - T_j{}^i.$$

The aggregate consumers' surplus from public goods at y^+ is

$$G(\cdot, y^+) = \textstyle\sum_i G^i(\cdot, y^+) = \sum_i \int_0^{y^+} \sum_j (p_{yj}{}^i - T_j{}^i)\, dy .$$

Recalling from (A6.2) that $\sum_i T_j^i = p_{yj}$, to maximize $G(\cdot, y^+)$, set

$$\frac{dG(\cdot, y^+)}{dy_j} = \left(\textstyle\sum_i p_{yj}{}^i\right) - p_{yj} = 0 , \ \forall j.$$

That is, for y', the value of y^+ that apparently satisfies this condition, we have, $\forall j$,

$$\textstyle\sum_i p_{yj}{}^i = p_{yj}, \tag{A6.11}$$

the Bowen-Samuelson result. Denote the true excess willingness to pay or net marginal valuation of public good j for consumer i by $v_j^i(x, y) \equiv p_{yj}{}^i - T_j^i$, so that (A6.11) can be written

$$\textstyle\sum_i v_j^i(x, y') = 0. \tag{A6.12a}$$

Similarly, let y''_{-i} be the value of y such that

$$\textstyle\sum_{i' \neq i} v_j^{i'}(x, y''_{-i}) = 0. \tag{A6.12b}$$

Then the VCG tax is

$$S^i = \textstyle\sum_{i' \neq i} [G^{i'}(\cdot, y''_{-i}) - G^{i'}(\cdot, y')]$$

$$= \sum_{i' \neq i} \int_{y'}^{y''_{-i}} \left[\sum_j v_j^{i'}(x, y) \right] dy. \tag{A6.13}$$

At the equilibrium of the mechanism, consumer i has the utility

$$V^i = V^i(p_x;\ \underline{x}^i;\ T^i + S^i;\ y) \tag{A6.14}$$

The standard assumption for the mechanism is that S^i has no income effect on $v_j^i(x, y)$. In that case, utility maximization by a consumer regarding what $m'^i = (m'^i_1 \dots m'^i_b)$ to report gives, for $g = 1, \dots, b$,

$$\underset{m'^i_g}{Max}\ V^i \Rightarrow \frac{dV^i}{dm'^i_g} = 0 \Rightarrow$$

$$\frac{\partial V^i}{\partial T^i}\frac{\partial T^i}{\partial m'^i_g} + \frac{\partial V^i}{\partial S^i}\frac{\partial S^i}{\partial m'^i_g} + \sum_j \left(\frac{\partial V^i}{\partial y'_j} \frac{\partial y'_j}{\partial m'^i_g} \right) = 0$$

$$-\lambda^i \left(\sum_j \left(T_j^i \frac{\partial y'_j}{\partial m'^i_g} \right) \right) - \lambda^i \frac{\partial S^i}{\partial m'^i_g} + \sum_j \left(V_{yj}^i \frac{\partial y'_j}{\partial m'^i_g} \right) = 0$$

$$\frac{\partial S^i}{\partial m'^i_g} = \sum_j \left(\frac{\partial y'_j}{\partial m'^i_g} (p_{yj}^i - T_j^i) \right) = \sum_j \left(\frac{\partial y'_j}{\partial m'^i_g} v_j^i \right) \tag{A6.15}$$

In words, this says that, for an optimized message, the rate at which a change in each reported parameter increases consumer i's VCG tax should equal the sum over public goods of the rates at which the change in that reported parameter increases the quantities of public goods, with each such quantity weighted by the net marginal value of that good to consumer i after the marginal tax that consumer i pays for the provision of that good.

Denote the marginal valuation schedule for public good j that consumer i chooses to report through message m'^i (truthful or not) by $v'^i_j(x, y; m'^i)$. Differentiating (A6.13) with respect to m'^i_g yields

$$\frac{\partial S^i}{\partial m'^i_g} = \sum_j \left(\frac{\partial y'_j}{\partial m'^i_g} \left[-\sum_{i' \neq i} v_j^{i'}(x, y') \right] \right)$$

$$= \sum_j \left(\frac{\partial y'_j}{\partial m'^i_g} v'^i_j(x, y';\ m'^i) \right), \tag{A6.16}$$

in view of (A6.12a). Combining (A6.15) and (A6.16) yields:

$$\sum_j\left(\frac{\partial y'_j}{\partial m'^{\,i}_g}\,v'^{\,i}_j(x,y';m'^i)\right)=\sum_j\left(\frac{\partial y'_j}{\partial m'^{\,i}_g}\,v_j^{\,i}(x,y')\right)$$

$$\sum_j\left(\frac{\partial y'_j}{\partial m'^{\,i}_g}\left[v'^{\,i}_j(x,y';m'^i)-v_j^{\,i}(x,y')\right]\right)=0. \qquad \text{(A6.17)}$$

The implications of this result for incentive compatibility are slightly obscure because of the summation over public goods j. It is clear that setting each $v'^{\,i}_j$ equal to the corresponding v_j^i is sufficient to satisfy (A6.17), but is this necessary? It appears that there might be other solutions in which positive and negative components of the sums in (A6.17) cancel. The actual implications are better, though not quite ideal. If for some g, $\partial y_j/\partial m'^{\,i}_g = 0$ for all j (that is, if a change in component g of consumer i's message has no impact on the quantities of any of the public goods), then (A6.16) implies that $\partial S^i/\partial m'^{\,i}_g = 0$, so that consumer i has no incentive to misrepresent m_g^i. This is not as satisfying as a positive incentive to tell the truth, but it is quite understandable that if a report of a parameter value affects nothing that concerns the reporter, there will be no positive incentive for the reporter to tell the truth. And a situation of no positive incentive to misrepresent is certainly an improvement upon a situation with a positive incentive to misrepresent. If $\partial y_j/\partial m'^{\,i}_g \neq 0$ for exactly one j, then setting $v'^{\,i}_j(x, y; m'^i) = v_j^i(x, y)$ for that j is necessary to satisfy the first-order condition for optimizing $m'^{\,i}_g$. Thus we assume:

M.5. For each public good j there is at least one message component g such that $m'^{\,i}_g$ affects y_j and no other public good quantity.

This implies that, $\forall\ j$, setting $v'^{\,i}_j(x, y; m'^i) = v'^{\,i}_j(x, y)$ is necessary to optimize the message m'^i. Incentive compatibility is thus assured. If there are other components of m'^i that affect more than one component of y, then from (A6.17), truthful reporting of $v'^{\,i}_j(x, y)$ insures that the optimality conditions for these components are also satisfied.

A6.2 THE PRIMARY REFUND OF VCG TAXES

A6.2.A Introduction

In the body of this chapter we saw that the problems of incentive compatibility and mechanism budget balance can be eliminated or reduced to harmless proportions in the case of decisions that are either binary or involve only a few possible outcomes. We found that these problems can become negligible when representative population samples serve as legislatures, which provide the information needed to assess Lindahl taxes, exactly or approximately. By this device the outcome has unanimous consent, or approaches it.

In this section of this appendix we address the problem of mechanism budget balance for the case of a continuous public good. In this case also the precise assessment of Lindahl taxes would achieve almost the same desired result: VCG tax assessments would be zero, and the budget would be balanced. There would nevertheless be income effects to disturb incentive compatibility, which we deal with in Section A6.3. Moreover, the assumption of homogeneity within each recognized population subgroup strains credulity more in the case of continuous good than it does in the case of discrete good. Homogeneity in the continuous case would mean that all members of a population subgroup, having equal tax shares of the cost of a good, would favor exactly the same quantity of the good. Here even the slightest variation among individuals would generate positive VCG tax revenues and a budget surplus to be disposed of.

This section presents a step in the solution of the budget surplus problem, which is then incorporated into a combined proposal for dealing with both incentive compatibility (in a Bayesian sense) and budget balance in Section A6.3. The step presented in this section is a refund to household i based only on what the VCG tax revenues would be if i did not participate. The VCG tax is always positive, and so generates a budget surplus because the approximate Lindahl taxes of Chapters 2 and 3 finance public goods with a balanced budget. The standard view in the literature on this tax has been that the surplus must be destroyed or given to outsiders to avoid distorting the sound incentives of the VCG tax (Tideman and Tullock, 1976, 1977). Collinge (1983) suggested advance auction of the surplus to a foreign country or to other wealthy underwriters who are indifferent about the amount of the home country's public good. This procedure would be satisfactory if there were outsiders willing to bid, because of some knowledge of likely election outcomes. We prefer here to develop a way to avoid depending on outsider knowledge and participation.

This section suggests a formula for distributing the VCG budget surplus that has no effect on the incentive compatibility (or lack of it) of the VCG tax. It is only a first step, however, because it is accurate only to a first approximation. The random remaining budget imbalance, though vanishingly small, being of the order $O(1/N^2)$ when the number of voters N is large, is inconsistent with Pareto efficiency if it is positive and must be destroyed, whereas it is infeasible if it is negative, in a simple economy with no capital transactions. Section A6.3 deals with this residual problem and with the issue of incentive compatibility in an economy with income effects, by developing a further transfer to combine with the refund.

Tideman and Tullock (1976, 1977) conjectured that the budget surplus of the VCG tax declines relative to the size of the economy at the rate O(1/N) as the economy grows large. Green, Kohlberg and Laffont (1976), and Rob (1982), proved variations of this conjecture in probabilistic terms for the case of a binary choice. Green, Kohlberg and Laffont (1976) also proved convergence on Pareto optimality in a large replicated economy, with a non-optimal distribution rule. This section further strengthens the merits of this concept.

A6.2.B The Refund

The proposed refund r^i to each consumer i, to distribute the budget surplus will be based on the total of VCG taxes if consumer i were to not participate in deciding the quantities of public goods. Inasmuch as this quantity depends only on information supplied by other consumers, the message from consumer i cannot affect it. Therefore, it cannot affect the incentive compatibility of the mechanism.

M.6. For an economy in which *consumer i is not present*, define S_{-i} as the *non-i sum of conjectural VCG taxes* over $N-1$ consumers $i' \neq i$ that would apply at y''_{-i}.

M.7. The *refund* r^i to each consumer i, to distribute the sum of the VCG taxes, S_N, is a predetermined fraction of S_{-i}.

M.8. The *budget imbalance B* is the excess of VCG taxes over refunds: $B = S_N - \sum r^i$.

M.9. The *non-i budget imbalance* B_{-i} is the budget imbalance that would apply at y''_{-i}, using S_{-i} less the sum of the corresponding refunds $r^{i'}_{-i}$ calculated as in M.7 for an economy of $N-1$ consumers that does not include consumer i.

As a first approximation, it would seem appropriate to use a refund of

$$r^i = \frac{S_{-i}}{N},$$

but a slightly more accurate refund is

$$r^i = \frac{S_{-i}}{N}\frac{N(N-2)}{N(N-2)+1} = \frac{S_{-i}(N-2)}{(N-1)^2}.$$

A yet more accurate refund is possible if the central agent knows certain characteristics, such as the general form (log linear, for example), of individual preferences in advance of the receipt of the messages. The next section gives an example. However, to preserve incentive compatibility the central agent may not use the messages to fine-tune the refunds. These refunds will have an unpredictable imprecision, so that the net budget surplus can be either positive or negative. As already noted, it converges to zero more rapidly than does the conventional VCG tax, when the size of the economy is increased by replication.

Under the general assumptions used in the preceding remarks, it is difficult to draw further specific conclusions. As motivation for the discussion that follows, consider the following points. First, if the mix and quantities of public goods, when varying over the range of interest, have no effect on the relative prices of private goods, then the set of private goods can be treated as a single composite good. This case is pertinent because the 'range of interest', namely the range from y' to y''_{-i}, becomes vanishingly small under replication. The clear benefit that follows in this case is that the central agent need not iterate the VCG mechanism to take account of interactions between the private and public sectors. It is similarly approximately true that the relative marginal-cost prices of public goods also remain constant over the relevant range. Therefore, the total size of the government budget could be determined by treating these goods as a composite good, so that the conclusions of the simplified model presented in the next subsection apply fully to this overall decision. (However, in determining the mix of public goods, one must use a more general mechanism that takes account of the cross-elasticities of demand among these goods.)

A6.2.C A Simplified Example

A6.2.C.1 Summary

The economy we now consider has a single private good x and a single public good y. The following additional assumptions, Groups A′ and B′, hold for this two-good economy:

A.9. (Neither x nor y is an inferior good.) $\partial(U^i_y/U^i_x)/\partial x \geq 0$ and $\partial(U^i_y/U^i_x)/\partial y \leq \phi < 0$, where $|\phi|$ is small.

A.10. (Limited passion for public goods.) $\forall\ (\underline{x}^i, y) \in X^i$,

$$\frac{\partial U^i(\underline{\underline{x}}^i,\ \underline{x}^i - \underline{\underline{x}}^i)}{\partial y} < \frac{\partial U^i(\underline{\underline{x}}^i,\ \underline{x}^i - \underline{\underline{x}}^i)}{\partial x}.$$

A.11. (Congestibility of the public good.) The public good is subject to congestion, such that what enters the utility function of each consumer is the per capita quantity of the public good, y/N.

B.6. Aggregate production has a constant cost function $Y \leq \sum_i (\underline{x}^i - x^i)$, which directly implies a production opportunity set. This set is represented by its upper boundary (the production possibility curve), which here is the linear function $\sum_i x^i + Y = \sum_i \underline{x}^i$.

B.7. Valued at its marginal cost, Y has a unit price: $p_Y = p_x = 1$.

Assumptions A.11 and B.6 together imply that when the economy is enlarged by R replications to a size RN, the optimal outlay on the public good rises in proportion to RN. (In the replicated economy there are R consumers with preferences and endowments identical to those of each of the consumers in the initial economy. This is the type of replication that is employed in Roberts, 1976). Examples would be street lights, fire protection, and police protection, whose optimal amounts could be proportional to the population. As will be evident, this case is analytically convenient. Also, it appears that our models can be generalized to other cases, such as that of a pure (noncongestible) public good, in a straightforward way, although this generalization would complicate some of our definitions and the analytical steps that use them.

It will be convenient for the technical analysis to measure the physical quantity of the public good as Y, where the per capita amount is $y = Y/RN$. Thus the optimal amount of the public good, y', measured relative to the total size of the economy, remains constant under replication. (Our results for the case of a congestible public good hold true *a fortiori* for the case without a congestion effect).

In this simplified problem the vector of parameters in the message from each consumer, m'^i, describes i's reported valuation curve for the public good, v'^i. The valuation curve appropriate to this problem, for each consumer, is the marginal rate of substitution between the private good and the public good evaluated at the $(x^i; y)$ combinations available to the consumer.

To further simplify notation, with a minor loss of generality, we assume that all endowments are equal.

A.12. $\forall^i$, $\underline{x}^i = \underline{x}$, a constant.

In an egalitarian society with equal tax shares, each consumer's T^i would equal y. For simplicity we use this tax throughout, in place of a general function for T^i:

C.10. $\forall^i$, the tax that finances the public good $T^i = y$, and total revenue from this tax is $T = \sum_i T^i = Y$. The tax 'price' to i is the unit price, $p_y = 1$.

The set of combinations of the public good and private good available to consumer i is thus $(\underline{x} - y; y)$, for all $y < \underline{x}$. The valuation curve is a 'production possibility demand curve'. (Bailey, 1954.)

If the public-good opportunity cost curve presented to the consumer, as derived under the VCG mechanism from the marginal valuation curves and tax shares of other consumers, were vertical, then for every y this single valuation curve would give the correct valuation for determining the outcome. In fact, this opportunity cost curve does approach the vertical as R becomes large. This feature explains the well-known finding that the individual VCG taxes vanish as R becomes large. Until R is large enough that the opportunity cost curve is nearly vertical, the consumer's marginal valuation of the public good cannot be described by a single, definitive curve, except by ignoring the income effect of the VCG tax on the consumer's valuation curve.

The optimal amount of y is that amount y' at which the sum of the marginal valuations equals N, the sum of the basic tax shares. Alternatively stated, y' is the amount at which the sum of the 'net valuations' is zero, where each net valuation is the marginal valuation minus the basic tax of 1 per unit of y.

An approximate measure of a single consumer's surplus resulting from the production of an amount y of the public good (disregarding the VCG tax component) is the area between the marginal valuation curve and the tax share 1 per unit of y. It is approximate both because of the omission of the VCG tax and because it is neither the compensating variation nor the equivalent variation, but is intermediate between the two. It is derived from the slopes of all the consumer indifference curves through points $(\underline{x} - y; y)$, for values of y between 0 and $\underline{x}$.

For the case of one private good and one public good, $G^i(x'^+)$ of equation (A6.3), the approximate measure of consumer i's surplus resulting from the provision of the amount y of the public good, reduces to

$$G^i(\underline{x} - y'; y') = \int_0^{y'} (p_y{}^i - T^i)\, dy,$$

and the VCG tax payable by consumer i (A6.9) reduces to

$$S^i = \sum_{i' \neq i} \int_{y'}^{y''_{-i}} (p_y{}^{i'} - T^{i'})\, dy.$$

The sum S_N of these individual VCG taxes equals the departure of the procedure from Pareto optimality in the absence of refunds, while the average ratio, for all consumers, of the VCG tax to initial endowment equals the size of this departure relative to the economy. As Tideman and Tullock (1976, 1977) suggested, this latter ratio vanishes at a rate $O(1/N)$ as N increases (or in the present notation, at the rate $1/RN$ as R increases). Our proof of this claim follows a different line from that used by Rob (1982), who had a different approach to replication.

In order to improve the tendency to Pareto optimality of the VCG mechanism, the tax refund here works out to be, as noted earlier,

$$r^i = \frac{S_{-i}(RN-2)}{(RN-1)^2}. \tag{A6.18}$$

It is shown below that the refunds in equation (A6.18) exactly balance S_N if the marginal valuation curves are linear with identical slopes for all consumers. It is also shown that when the slopes are unequal, the budget imbalance

$$B = \sum_i (S^i - r^i) \tag{A6.19}$$

vanishes at a rate $O(1/R^2)$ as R increases. The proposed tax refund (A6.18) is similar to one suggested by Laffont and Maskin (1979) in the context of a highly restrictive model.

It is evident that the VCG tax net of the refund (A6.18) is incentive compatible for each consumer i, for the same reasons that the VCG tax is, because the refund depends solely on the information supplied by consumers other than consumer i. The result here does not contradict the general proposition that there is no incentive-compatible mechanism that gives Pareto optimal outcomes for a broad class of economies, inasmuch as the refund is exact only in the special case where the marginal valuation curves are all linear with identical slopes.[3] In other cases, it refunds the tax imprecisely.

A6.2.C.2 Some General Results

Lemma 1. y' and y''_{-i} exist and are unique.

Proof. A.5-A.8 together imply that, over the relevant range of y, each reported marginal valuation curve $v'^i(\cdot, y; m'^i)$ is strictly monotonically decreasing, is differentiable, and is bounded. By M.3, if $\sum_i v'^i(\cdot, y; m'^i) < 0$ for all y, then $y' = 0$. By A.10, $\sum_i v'^i(\underline{\underline{x}}, \underline{x} - \underline{\underline{x}}; m'^i) \leq 0$. If $\sum_i v'^i(\underline{x}, 0; m'^i) > 0$ then the monotonically decreasing property of v'^i is sufficient to assure that there is a unique y' that satisfies (A6.6). The same reasoning proves existence and uniqueness of y''_{-i}. ■

This result makes use of A.10, the assumption of limited passion for public goods. To ensure existence and uniqueness in a model with multiple public and private goods, one would need to extend this assumption to that model.

Lemma 2. The VCG tax, with or without the refund, satisfies the non-bankruptcy constraint.

Proof. (A6.2) and A.10 imply that $y \leq (\underline{x} - \underline{\underline{x}})$, that is, that the basic tax bankrupts no one, so that the only question to consider is the possibility that the VCG tax could do so. The VCG tax is quadratic in the consumer's valuation $v'^i(\cdot, y; m'^i)$, so that bankruptcy is a threat for those consumers with the most extreme valuations, if for anyone. For a consumer i with a relatively high valuation $v'^i(\cdot, y; m'^i)$ at the outcome y', M.3 implies that $v'^i(\cdot, y') > 0$. However, by A.10 a consumer near bankruptcy would have $v'^i(\cdot, y') < 0$, a contradiction. For a consumer i with relatively low valuation, we have from monotonicity that $v'^i(\cdot, y') > -1$, and from M.3 that therefore for $j \neq i$, $\sum_j v'^j(\cdot, y') < 1$. Evaluating (A6.9) (for details, see Section A6.2), we find that

$$S^i = \tfrac{1}{2} \sum_{j \neq i} v'^j(\cdot, y')(y''_{-i} - y') < \tfrac{1}{2}(y''_{-i} - y').$$

Now at y''_{-i}, $x > \underline{\underline{x}}$, and at $y' < y''_{-i}$, from the fact that tax shares are proportional to endowments, we know that $x > \underline{\underline{x}} + y''_{-i} - y'$. Hence the final $x^i > \underline{\underline{x}} + y''_{-i} - y' - S^i > \underline{\underline{x}} + y''_{-i} - y' - \tfrac{1}{2}(y''_{-i} - y') > \underline{\underline{x}}$. ■

Note that this proof relies on the monotonicity assumption as well as the assumption that tax shares are proportional to endowments. These assumptions might be inappropriate for some public goods. By adding an assumption of limited passion for avoiding public goods we could establish the conclusion without these assumptions.

Lemma 3. The VCG tax is a continuous, continuously differentiable function of each component of consumer i's message, $\forall\, i$.

Proof. That the integral (A6.9) is a well-defined, bounded Riemann integral for every vector of messages m' is obvious. The $v'^i(\cdot, y; m'^i)$ are continuous, single-valued functions of y, by M.1 and A.5-A.8, which implies that (A6.9) is continuous and continuously differentiable in its lower and upper limits of integration. These limits are continuous and continuously differentiable in the components of m'^i, by M.1, the continuity of the $v'^i(\cdot, y; m'^i)$, the continuity of inverse functions of continuous functions, and by the definitions (A6.6) and (A6.7). Application of the function of a function rule completes the proof. ■

Lemma 4. If $v'^i(\cdot, y') = 0$, i's VCG tax is zero, and $y' = y''_{-i}$.

Proof. By the premise of the lemma, we have $v'^i(\cdot, y') = 0$, and inasmuch as $\sum_i v'^i(\cdot, y') = 0$ from M.3, we have $\sum_{j \neq i} v'^j(\cdot, y') = 0$. From this equality, together with the definition of y''_{-i}, plus M.3 and the uniqueness of the outcome, it follows that $y' = y''_{-i}$. Then the definition of the VCG tax, equation (A6.9), gives a zero tax, inasmuch as the v'^j, being continuously differentiable, are bounded. ■

A6.2.C.3 Definitions and Results for the Case of Separable Utility

The total cost relationship yN for the public good means that the good is congestible in proportion to N. This feature assures that y''_{-i} would be the optimal quantity of the public good if consumer i were not present.

For convenience, define the slope of consumer i's net marginal valuation of the public good,

$$a^i \equiv \frac{\partial v^i(x, y)}{\partial y}, \text{ evaluated at } y'. \tag{A6.20}$$

Rearranging (A6.12a), and using (A6.12b), we have

$$v^i(x,y') = -\sum_{i' \neq i} v^{i'}(x,y')$$
$$= \sum_{i' \neq i} \int_{y'}^{y''_{-i}} \frac{\partial v^{i'}(x,y)}{\partial y}\, dy$$
$$= (y''_{-i} - y') \sum_{i' \neq i} a^{i'} + \text{higher order terms.} \qquad \text{(A6.21)}$$

Under the assumed continuity conditions, the higher order terms of the Taylor's expansion (A6.21) vanish more rapidly than does the term shown when $R \to \infty$ and $y'' \to y'$, so that for present concerns they can be disregarded. Then (A6.21) rearranges to become

$$\frac{v^i(x,y')}{\sum_{i' \neq i} a^{i'}} \cong (y''_{-i} - y'). \qquad \text{(A6.22)}$$

Using (A6.21) and (A6.22) to evaluate the terms in the VCG tax formula (A6.13), for each consumer i' we have

$$G^{i'}(\,\cdot\,, y''_{-i}) - G^{i'}(\,\cdot\,, y') = \int_{y'}^{y''_{-i}} v^{i'}(x,y')\, dy$$
$$= \tfrac{1}{2}\, [v^{i'}(x,y') + v^{i'}(x,y''_{-i})](y''_{-i} - y')$$
$$+ \text{higher order terms.} \qquad \text{(A6.23)}$$

Then, disregarding the higher order terms, using (A6.12b) and (A6.22) and rearranging terms, we have the following expression for the VCG tax:

$$S^i \cong -\tfrac{1}{2}\, \frac{v^i(x,y''_{-i})^2}{\sum_{i' \neq i} a^{i'}} = -\tfrac{1}{2}\, \frac{(v^i)^2}{(\sum_{i'} a^{i'}) - a^i}. \qquad \text{(A6.24)}$$

(Recall that the $a^{i'}$ terms, being slopes of demand schedules, are negative.) Where there is no risk of ambiguity, we write v^i for $v^i(\cdot, y')$. Now when the economy is replicated R times, there are R consumers whose valuation curves are identical to the original one for consumer i, for every i.

Denote by ${}_RS^i$ the VCG tax for consumer i in an economy replicated R times. We have

$${}_RS^i = -\tfrac{1}{2}\, \frac{(v^i)^2}{R(\sum_{i'} a^{i'}) - a^i} = -\tfrac{1}{2}\, \frac{(v^i)^2/R}{(\sum_{i'} a^{i'}) - a^i/R}, \qquad \text{(A6.25)}$$

which vanishes at the rate $O(1/R)$. Total VCG tax revenue is

$$ {}_RS = R\sum_i {}_RS^i = -\tfrac{1}{2}\sum_i \frac{(v^i)^2}{(\sum_{i'} a^{i'}) - a^i/R}, \tag{A6.26}$$

which converges to a constant. Thus its ratio to total endowments converges to zero at the rate $O(1/R)$ as it does for each consumer.

Denote by ${}_RS_{-i}$ the total VCG tax revenue when one consumer of type i is deleted from the replicated economy. The tax ${}_RS^j_{-i}$ on a consumer of type j and the tax ${}_RS^i_{-i}$ on a remaining consumer of type i will be

$$\begin{aligned} {}_RS^j_{-i} &= -\tfrac{1}{2}\frac{v^j(x,y''_{-i})^2}{R(\sum_{i'} a^{i'}) - a^i - a^j} \\ {}_RS^i_{-i} &= -\tfrac{1}{2}\frac{v^i(x,y''_{-i})^2}{R(\sum_{i'} a^{i'}) - 2a^i} \end{aligned} \tag{A6.27}$$

and total revenue with i deleted is

$$ {}_RS_{-i} = R\left(\sum_j {}_RS^j_{-i}\right) - {}_RS^i_{-i}$$

$$ = -\tfrac{1}{2}R\left(\sum_j \frac{v^j(x,y''_{-i})^2}{R(\sum_{i'} a^{i'}) - a^i - a^j}\right) + \tfrac{1}{2}\frac{v^i(x,y''_{-i})^2}{R(\sum_{i'} a^{i'}) - 2a^i} \tag{A6.28}$$

The tax refund for consumer i, designed to reduce expected total revenue to zero without disturbing incentive compatibility, must be based on (A6.28), where of course each consumer's message and tax account is specific to that consumer, regardless of replication. The value of the expression (A6.28) is independent of information supplied by consumer i, so that a refund based on this expression can not disturb incentive compatibility.

To determine the refund that gives a zero expected budget surplus, it is helpful to start with the case in which a^i has the same value for all consumers (although the marginal valuations v^i differ among consumers): $a^i = a$ for all i. The marginal valuation curves $v^i(x, y)$ as functions of y are parallel to each other, all with the same constant slope. In this case, equations (A6.22) to (A6.27) are exact because the higher-order terms in (A6.21) are zero. Then we have

$$ {}_RS_{-i} = -\tfrac{1}{2}\frac{R\left(\sum_j v^j(x,y''_{-i})^2\right) - v^i(x,y''_{-i})^2}{a(RN-2)} \tag{A6.29a}$$

and

$$_RS = -\frac{1}{2}\,\frac{R\sum_j v^j(x,y')^2}{a(RN-1)} \tag{A6.29b}$$

The correct refund r^i to consumer i is

$$r_i = \frac{RN-2}{(RN-1)^2}\ {}_RS_{-i} \tag{A6.30}$$

for, substituting (A6.29a) into (A6.30), one finds that

$$R\sum_i r^i = {}_RS$$

for every R, including $R = 1$.

Inasmuch as the terms a^i are the slopes of the marginal valuation curves, they represent the sensitivity of the $v^i(x, y)$ to the amount of public good. For these slopes to be the same for all consumers means that all valuations decline at the same rate when y increases, e.g. both for those who are willing to pay for high government expenditure and those who prefer a low level of government spending. The proposition that a precisely accurate refund of this form is possible would also be true if the sensitivity measured by the a^i were uncorrelated with this preference characteristic of consumers.

When the a^i are unequal, as a general rule the sum of the refunds is only approximately $_RS$. Let

$$\bar{a} = \frac{1}{N}\sum_j a^j,$$

where our continuity and strict convexity assumptions assure that all a^i and $\bar{a}$ are finite and strictly negative. We have

$$_RS = -\tfrac{1}{2}\sum_i \frac{R(v^i)^2}{R(\sum_j a^j) - a^i} = -\tfrac{1}{2}\sum_i \frac{R(v^i)^2}{(RN-1)\bar{a} - (a^i - \bar{a})}. \tag{A6.31}$$

Now set $\alpha^i = \dfrac{a^i - \bar{a}}{(RN-1)\bar{a}}$. This expression converges to zero at the rate O($1/R$), so that for sufficiently large R, we have $-1 < \alpha^i < 1$. Then we can apply the algebra of a geometric progression to the expressions for $_RS$ and $_RS_{-i}$. For the first, we have and for the second,

$$_RS_{-i} = -\tfrac{1}{2}\left(\sum_j \frac{R(v^j)^2}{(RN-2)\,\bar{a}}\left[1+\frac{RN-1}{RN-2}(\alpha^i+\alpha^j)+\ldots\right]\right)$$

$$+\tfrac{1}{2}\,\frac{(v^i)^2}{(RN-2)\,\bar{a}}\left[1+\frac{2(RN-1)}{(RN-2)}\,\alpha^i+\ldots\right], \qquad \text{(A6.33)}$$

where we omit the higher order terms in α^i and α^j because they vanish $O(1/R^2)$ or faster.

Now when we use the refund formula (A6.30) and sum up the refunds in an R-replicated economy, ignoring terms higher than α^i, we obtain

$$R\sum_i \frac{RN-2}{(RN-1)^2}\,{}_RS_{-i}$$

$$= \frac{R(RN-2)}{(RN-1)^2}\sum_i\left[-\tfrac{1}{2}\sum_j\left(\frac{R(v^j)^2}{(RN-2)\,\bar{a}}\left[1+\frac{RN-1}{RN-2}(\alpha^i+\alpha^j)\right]\right)\right.$$

$$\left.+\tfrac{1}{2}\,\frac{(v^i)^2}{(RN-2)\,\bar{a}}\left(1+\frac{2(RN-1)}{RN-2}\,\alpha^i\right)\right]$$

$$= -\tfrac{1}{2}\,\frac{R}{RN-1}\sum_i\left[\sum_j\left(\frac{R(v^j)^2}{(RN-1)\,\bar{a}}\left[1+\frac{RN-1}{RN-2}(\alpha^i+\alpha^j)\right]\right)\right.$$

$$\left.-\frac{(v^i)^2}{(RN-1)\,\bar{a}}\left(1+\frac{2(RN-1)}{RN-2}\,\alpha^i\right)\right]$$

$$= -\tfrac{1}{2}\,\frac{R}{RN-1}\left[\frac{RN\sum_i(v^i)^2}{(RN-1)\,\bar{a}}+\frac{RN-1}{RN-2}\sum_i\sum_j\frac{R(v^j)^2}{(RN-1)\,\bar{a}}\,\alpha^i\right.$$

$$+\frac{RN-2+1}{RN-2}\,\frac{RN\sum_i(v^i)^2}{(RN-1)\,\bar{a}}\,\alpha^i-\frac{\sum_i(v^i)^2}{(RN-1)\,\bar{a}}$$

$$\left.-\frac{\sum_i(v^i)^2}{(RN-1)\,\bar{a}}\left(\frac{RN-2+RN}{RN-2}\,\alpha^i\right)\right]$$

$$= -\tfrac{1}{2}\frac{R}{RN-1}\left[\frac{\sum_i (v^i)^2}{\bar{a}} + \frac{RN-1}{RN-2}\left(\sum_i \alpha^i\right)\frac{\sum_j R(v^j)^2}{(RN-1)\,\bar{a}}\right.$$

$$\left. + \left(1+\frac{1}{RN-2}\right)\frac{RN\sum_i (v^i)^2}{(RN-1)\,\bar{a}}\alpha^i - \left(1+\frac{RN}{RN-2}\right)\frac{\sum_i (v^i)^2}{(RN-1)\,\bar{a}}\alpha^i\right]$$

$$= -\tfrac{1}{2}\frac{R}{RN-1}\frac{\sum_i (v^i)^2}{\bar{a}}\left(1+\alpha^i\right) = {}_R S \qquad \text{(A6.34)}$$

(The penultimate step makes use of the fact that $\sum_i \alpha^i = 0$.) Thus as the economy's size increases by replication, the size of difference between the surplus and the sum of the refunds converges to zero at the rate $O(1/R^2)$, as claimed.

A6.2.C.4 The case of positive income elasticities of demand for all goods

Suppose now that x and y are both normal goods, so that $U_{yx} > 0$, which implies a negative income effect of S^i on v^i. Suppose further that the VCG tax for this case continues to satisfy strictly the definition in equation (A6.8). Consumer i chooses to report m'^i, as before, so as to maximize utility. Then we have, for each message component g,

$$\max_{m'^i_g} U^i : \Rightarrow v^i(x - T^i - S^i, y')\frac{\partial y'}{\partial m'^i_g} = \frac{\partial S^i}{\partial m'^i_g}$$

For a replicated economy, differentiation of (A6.17) implies that

$$\frac{\partial S^i}{\partial m'^i_g} = v'^i\frac{\partial y'}{\partial m'^i_g} + (R-1)\left(\sum_{i'}\int_{y'}^{y''_{-i}}\frac{\partial v^{i'}(S^{i'}, y)}{\partial S^{i'}}\frac{\partial S^{i'}}{\partial m'^i_g}dy\right)$$
$$+ \sum_{i'\neq i}\int_{y'}^{y''_{-i}}\frac{\partial v^{i'}(S^{i'}, y)}{\partial S^{i'}}\frac{\partial S^{i'}}{\partial m'^i_g}dy.$$

Thus we have

$$v^i(S^i, y')\frac{\partial y'}{\partial m'^i_g} = v'^i\frac{\partial y'}{\partial m'^i_g} + (R-1)\left(\sum_{i'}\int_{y'}^{y''_{-i}}\frac{\partial v^{i'}(S^{i'}, y)}{\partial S^{i'}}\frac{\partial S^{i'}}{\partial m'^i_g}dy\right)$$
$$+ \sum_{i'\neq i}\int_{y'}^{y''_{-i}}\frac{\partial v^{i'}(S^{i'}, y)}{\partial S^{i'}}\frac{\partial S^{i'}}{\partial m'^i_g}dy,$$

which yields

$$[v^i(S^i_;\, y') - v'^i]\frac{\partial y'}{\partial m'^i_g} = (R-1)\left(\sum_{i'}\int_{y'}^{y''-i} \frac{\partial v^{i'}(S^{i'}, y)}{\partial S^{i'}}\, \frac{\partial S^{i'}}{\partial m'^i_g}\, dy\right)$$

$$+ \sum_{i'\neq i}\int_{y'}^{y''_{-i}} \frac{\partial v^{i'}(S^{i'}, y)}{\partial S^{i'}}\, \frac{\partial S^{i'}}{\partial m'^i_g}\, dy. \tag{A6.35}$$

In general, the expression on the right-hand side of (A6.35) is not zero, so that $v'^i \neq v^i$. Hence, in an economy of finite size we now have two sources of inefficiency for the mechanism. First, the revenue of the VCG tax itself, unless the formula proposed here refunds it precisely, is generally inconsistent with a strictly optimal outcome, and second, the mechanism no longer provides an incentive to reveal the private valuations v^i accurately. Moreover, if the mechanism designer tries to satisfy the Samuelson condition (A6.12a) precisely, despite the inefficiency problems, the mechanism must be complex. The central agent must either solve simultaneous equations to take account of income effects, or else iterate the messages, VCG taxes, and values of y'.

These problems, when the number N of participants is small enough that the problems could be significant, suggest that we consider alternative compromises. In particular, if a complex mechanism is not strategy proof, and can not be expected to achieve an efficient allocation, perhaps a simpler mechanism would do as well. (A rigorous statement, elaboration, and further refinement of the following ideas appear in the next section.)

In particular, an appealing alternative is to ask each consumer to report the parameters m^i that describe $v^i(x, y)$ on the assumption that the refund of the consumer's VCG tax, though given and fixed, will be precisely accurate, and then determine y' in a single pass as if there were no income effect. Each household's VCG tax will also be calculated from the reported schedules as given, as if there were no income effect. This approach has the incidental effect of restoring the incentive to report truthfully.

With the simplified mechanism, a consumer's message reporting a valuation schedule will not be changed, and must be sent in ignorance of the messages of other consumers. Hence, the messages sent by consumers cannot be interdependent, so that each consumer will view the messages due to come from other consumers as given and fixed. Consequently, the consumer's incentives are the same as they are for the mechanism in the absence of income effects. It follows that all the logic of Subsection A6.2.C.3 applies. Consumers will report true schedules, making whatever assumptions they think accurate about their prospective VCG taxes and refunds. One can then devise a set of transfers, using an elaboration of the refund proposed here, to balance the budget while maintaining efficient incentives.

These results also apply, trivially, to public good decision about a discrete choice, such as that of whether to build Project A or to stay with the status quo. For this type of choice, one can readily verify that, under replication as described here, for a project that is not strictly marginal the total VCG tax revenue drops to zero after a finite number of replications (as would the total refund, if used). In some boundary-case examples the refund is a poor approximation to the revenue in a small economy, so that it may be appropriate to have a supplementary rule about when to have the refund in connection with discrete choices.

These findings might be of interest for applications to clubs or 'town meetings' where the size of the electorate is small enough that the budget imbalance would be a matter of concern. I hasten to point out, however, that for local public goods, property-value maximization can be the principal means to attaining an efficient outcome (Cornes and Sandler, 1986). Where labor is imperfectly mobile, however, a VCG mechanism could supplement the property value rule to achieve full efficiency, and its post-refund budget imbalance, if any, could be allocated to absentee property owners).

The earlier results of Green, Kohlberg and Laffont (1976) and Rob (1982) deal only with the case of discrete choices, and seem weaker than the finding just stated on the disappearance of the VCG tax under replication. However, they reasoned in probabilistic terms, replicating by random sampling from the probability space of valuations, so their results and these are not strictly comparable.

A6.2.D Conclusion

Although the proposal here improves the performance of the VCG mechanism in a number of ways, it does nothing about the lack of incentive to vote in a large economy nor about the vulnerability of social aggregation mechanisms to coalitions. The lack of incentive to vote, a commonplace fact of life, is the subject of ongoing research by interested scholars. The problem of coalitions is common both to public choice mechanisms, especially when many consumers do not vote, and to the private sector. This section adds nothing to what has been said by others on these issues. That said, the improvement developed here puts the VCG mechanism even more clearly on a par with the performance of the private sector than it was before. One does not know how rapidly a pure exchange economy, or a production and exchange economy, converges to Pareto optimality as the economy grows large. What is clear is that each type of economy converges, as does an economy with a public good.

A6.3 NON-SEPARABLE UTILITY IN A VCG ECONOMY

A6.3.A Introduction and Summary

If one uses general (nonseparable) utility functions for all consumers, the income effects of the VCG tax present largely unsolved problems of incentive incompatibility, bankruptcy and cycles.

In this section I suggest a multi-part formula for refunding the budget surplus, which could be modified in various ways to obtain results with similar or distinctive properties. The first stage of the refund/transfer sequence to a consumer, as developed in Section A6.2, is independent of that consumer's message to the mechanism. An additional transfer, which has a Bayesian expected value of zero, can either balance the budget and make the entire mechanism approximately Bayesian incentive compatible, or it can approximate budget balance with precise Bayesian incentive compatibility, with the error of approximation in either case converging rapidly to zero as the size of the economy increases. The proposed transfers are in part an elaboration and extension of a proposed transfer formula by Conn (1983). This section presents their specific forms in the context of a series of model economies.

The usual presentation of the VCG mechanism suggests or implies that a necessary condition for incentive compatibility is that all utility functions be separable in public goods, a concept often presented in terms of *transferable* utility functions. These are generally developed for two-good economies and have the form $U = x + H(y)$, where x is the sole private good and numeraire, and y is the sole public good. This functional form has the advantage of tractability and pedagogical convenience, and seemingly has become almost an icon in contributions on this subject. What matters substantively, however, are two empirically significant features: All consumers have zero income effect (zero income elasticity of demand for the public good), and all are risk-neutral. In principle, these features limit the applicability of a mechanism that depends on them. The income effects of the VCG tax itself and of any simple pro-rata refunding of the budget surplus due to this tax both provide incentives to manipulate the mechanism. Manipulability due to refunds can be avoided if, as in section A6.2, the refund to a consumer is independent of the information provided by that consumer, or if it is expected in Bayesian terms to be independent. The problem from income effects of the tax itself is difficult, but our models show ways to reduce or eliminate this problem.

We have dealt with the issue of bankruptcy risk in previous sections by restraining our passion for the non-parametric framework. The possibility of cycles hinges on a supposed need for iteration, which is an artifact of a restriction on the message space. Our venture into non-zero income effects is aided by proofs elsewhere (Foley, 1967; Section A6.4 of this appendix) that, for this general type of problem, an equilibrium of the mechanism exists. We also draw on other work in this area.[4] Although this section does not address the case of binary choices or the case of choices over multiple discrete options, it extends and strengthens earlier findings relating to the case of a public good that is available in continuous amounts. Our results here improve the effectiveness of incentives while extending the analysis to non-separable preferences.

We proceed as follows. We continue with the simplifying assumptions of only one public good and one private good introduced in the previous section, and the associated assumptions in Groups A′ and B′. These assumptions apply to all the models presented in this section. At the end of Subsection A6.3.B we introduce certain special cases as steps toward more general results. We analyze some properties of these special cases in Subsection A6.3.C. In Subsection A6.3.D we present specific model economies that have positive income effects, including one with a restricted form of risk aversion. For example, in our first model we obtain precise results for the case of income effects that are uniform among all consumers, achieving an efficient outcome with a balanced budget. This case is a generalization of that studied by Bergstrom and Cornes (1983) and Conn (1983). Their models, unlike the one presented here, did not achieve an efficient outcome with a balanced budget.

The other two models, with less restrictive assumptions, are less precisely successful but extend and improve upon previous results.

A6.3.B The Budget-Balancing Transfer

A6.3.B.1 Definitions, Assumptions, and Notation

We now introduce a non-traditional part of the VCG mechanism, a budget-balancing transfer, t. The augmented mechanism combines the outcome, the VCG tax with a refund, and the budget-balancing transfer, all determined in one comprehensive procedure after receiving the messages m'^i.

For notational simplicity we now assume initially that $b = 2$, that is, that $\forall\ i$, two parameters suffice to characterize U^i.

M.10. The central agent specifies a hypothetical quantity y^0 to be used in all messages. Then the consumer reports a marginal valuation at y^0, $v'^{i0} = v'^i(\underline{x} - y^0, y^0; m'^i)$ and the reported slope of v'^i, $\partial v'^i(x, y; m'^i)/\partial y$, denoted as a'^i. That is, $m'^i = (v'^{i0}, a'^i)$ where all higher-order derivatives of U^i, including cross-partial derivatives, are zero. The true marginal valuation at y^0 is v^{i0}.

M.6′. For an economy in which *consumer i is not present*, the *conjectural VCG taxes* for this economy use, in (A6.13), the $v^{i'}$ unadjusted for income effects. S_{-i} is defined to be the *non-i sum of these conjectural VCG taxes* over $N - 1$ consumers $i' \neq i$ that would apply at y''_{-i}.

M.11. The *transfer* t^i to consumer i can be a function of B, of B_{-i}, or another function, designed for incentive compatibility and budget balance, if possible, or otherwise for the closest approximation possible.

M.12. The *income adjusted for non-financing taxes and transfers* for consumer i is $\underline{x}^i{}'_a = \underline{x}^i - S^i + r^i + t^i$.

The concepts set out in M.6′ and M.10 through M.12 are all functions of the joint set of messages m', or of their expected values in Bayesian terms when we come to that.

At the outcome of the mechanism, consumer i has the utility

$$U^i = U^i(\underline{x}^i{}'_a - y', y') = U^i(\underline{x} - y' - S^i + r^i + t^i, y'). \tag{A6.36}$$

These taxes and transfers are the adjustments of $\underline{x}$ specified in the definition of X'', so that

$$(\underline{x}^i{}'_a - y', y') \in X''^i. \tag{A6.37}$$

Thus when we test Pareto efficiency using (A6.6), we generally must use $v'^i(\underline{x}^i{}'_a - y', y; m'^i)$ in place of $v'^i(\underline{x} - y, y; m'^i) = v'^{i0} + a'^i(y - y^0)$.

A6.3.B.2 Preliminary Discussion

As noted earlier, the purpose of these steps is to achieve an optimal incentive structure I_{F*}. As part of this structure, the central agent and all consumers know A.5-A.8, other special restrictions when applicable, and the mechanism.

A balanced budget with the VCG tax and refund, with no other transfers, is possible if the central agent knows certain characteristics, such as the general form of the messages (log linear, for example), and the distribution of slopes in advance of receiving them. Without this knowledge, the refunds will produce a budget imbalance of unpredictable sign. This budget imbalance has a useful convergence property, which reduces the quantitative significance of the transfers (see Section A6.2). However, an unpredictable sign means possible infeasibility, and a failure to achieve strict Pareto efficiency. Our purpose is to overcome these problems.

A6.3.C Results for the Case of Equal Income Effects

We now use a strong restriction, a special case, to develop some preliminary results leading to our first model.

A.12. $\forall\, i,\, v^i_x = \underline{v}_x(y)$, a function identical for all consumers, known to the central agent and to consumers. There is no consumer i' who has such an extreme valuation of y that the proximity of bankruptcy distorts this common income effect.

This results immediately in:

Lemma 5. If the central agent exactly balances the budget, the apparent Pareto-efficient value Y' is unchanged when the messages are adjusted for taxes and transfers. That is, $\sum_i v'^i(\underline{x} - y', y') = \sum_i v'^i(\underline{x}^i{}_a - y', y') = 0$.

Proof. For each y', the common income effect applies equally to all taxes and transfers:

$$\underline{m}_x \equiv -\frac{\partial m^i}{\partial S^i} \equiv \frac{\partial m^i}{\partial r^i} \equiv \frac{\partial m^i}{\partial t^i} \equiv \frac{\partial m^i}{\partial x^i}. \tag{A6.38}$$

Therefore

$$\sum_i v'^i(\underline{x}^i{}_a - y', y') = \sum_i v'^i(\underline{x} - y', y') - \underline{m}_x(y')\sum_i (S^i - r^i - t^i)$$

By the premise of budget balance, $\sum_i (S^i - r^i - t^i) = 0$, so that

$$\sum_i v'^i(\underline{x}^i{}_a - y'\, y') = \sum_i v'^i(\underline{x} - y', y') = 0. \blacksquare$$

Through Lemma 5, the special case described by A.12 leads to other strong results.[5] Hence we have:

Lemma 6. If utility has the form $U^i(x^i, y) = A(y)x^i + H^i(y)$, where the function $A(y)$ is identical for all consumers, then Lemma 5 holds.

Proof. Immediate. Evaluating the derivatives, $v'^i_x(y) = A'(y)/A(y)$. ■

Lemma 7. If utility has the form $U^i(x^i, y) = A(y)x^i + H^i(y)$, where the function $A(y)$ is identical for all consumers, and if the refunds and transfers balance the central agent's budget, then $y' = y^*$, that is, the mechanism is Pareto-efficient.

Proof. Conn (1983) proves that there is a transfer that is incentive compatible, and its mechanism is successful, for an economy with the assumptions the same as ours and with the stated utility function. From Lemma 5 proof is immediate that $y' = y^*$. If, as assumed, $\sum_i t^i$ balances the budget for every economy, the outcome is efficient in all respects. ■

This result, though tantalizing, has the problem that we do not know of a transfer of the kind proposed by Conn that reliably balances the budget and is consistent with incentive compatibility. However, this result naturally sets the stage for an analysis of incentives, which follows.

A6.3.D The Incentive Implications of Budget-Balancing Transfers, with Income Effects

We now consider the strategy problem for the consumer, taking note of assumption M.1. In general, the combination of incentive compatibility and Pareto-efficiency can not always be achieved (Green and Laffont, 1979; Walker, 1980; Moulin, 1988; Hurwicz and Walker, 1990). To progress further, we must shift our focus to Bayesian incentive compatibility. Moreover, for the least restricted models we must consider degrees of approximation, lacking a way to achieve complete reconciliation of Bayesian incentive compatibility with efficiency. The presentation here will show the degree of approximation of each that on present knowledge we can combine with exact satisfaction of the other.

When we turn to the Bayesian approach, we assume that every consumer's knowledge of the utility functions of others is defined by a single probability distribution, the same for all, known also to the central agent prior to the arrival of the messages. This is the 'independence' assumption used by others. See d'Aspremont, Crémer, and Gérard-Varet (1990) and d'Aspremont and Gérard-Varet (1979).

A.13. The *comprehensive probability density of parameters* is a function $q\colon M^N \to \mathbb{R}_+$, such that

$$\int_{M^N} q(m)dm = 1.$$

In parallel to q, the *comprehensive probability density of messages* m' is a function $q'\colon M^N \to \mathbb{R}_+$, such that

$$\int_{M^N} q'(m')\,dm' = 1.$$

These functions, the latter being governed by the former and by incentives, are known to all consumers and to the central agent.

Similarly, we write $q(m_{-i})$ for the unconditional probability density of $m_{-i} = (m^1, \ldots, m^{i-1}, m^{i+1}, \ldots, m^N)$, that is, the corresponding function $q\colon M^{N-1} \to \mathbb{R}_+$, such that

$$\int_{M^{N-1}} q(m_{-i})dm_{-i} = 1,$$

and likewise, $\forall\ i$, the probability density of m^i is $q\colon M \to \mathbb{R}_+$. Each $q(m^i)$ is a joint density function on the components of m^i. For a variable $\phi(m)$, the *expected value of* ϕ is

$$\mathrm{E}(s) = \int_{M^N} \phi(m)q(m)\,dm,$$

or the corresponding integral on a more restricted domain, where appropriate. If a variable ϕ' is a function of m', we denote its *truth-conditional expected value* by

$$\mathrm{E}_M(\phi') = \int_{M^N} \phi'(m)q(m)\,dm,$$

that is, we evaluate its expected value for $m' = m$, and similarly for a function on a more restricted domain. The *unconditional expected value* of ϕ' we denote by

$$\mathrm{E}_{\underline{M}}(\phi') = \int_{\underline{M}^N} \phi'(m')q(m')\,dm',$$

and similarly for a function on a more restricted domain.

The expression $\partial\mathrm{E}_{M^{N-1}}(\phi')/\partial m'^i$ is the effect on $\mathrm{E}_{M^{N-1}}(\phi')$ of a deviation of m'^i from m^i, evaluated at m. Similarly, $\partial\mathrm{E}_{\underline{M}^{N-1}}(\phi')/\partial m'^i$ is the effect on $\mathrm{E}_{\underline{M}^{N-1}}(\phi')$ of a deviation of m'^i from m^i, evaluated at m'. Where first-order conditions are the principal concern, these derivatives are central to an investigation of Bayesian incentive compatibility.

A.14. $\forall\, i$, an *admissible* $q(m^i) \in Q$(where Q is the set of all admissible joint density functions), is a continuous density function and is therefore Riemann-integrable. Further, $\forall\, i$ and j, $q(m^i)$ is identical to and is independent of $q(m^j)$. Then $q(m) \in Q^N$, and $q(m_{-i}) = q(m)/q(m^i)$ is independent of $q(m^i)$. Each admissible $q(m^i)$ is *non-degenerate*: The dimensionality of the subset $M^+ \subset M$ on which $q(m^i) > 0$ is the same as the dimensionality of m^i. Finally, $q'(m') \in Q^N$ and $\forall\, i$, $q(m^i)$ satisfy all these criteria of admissibility.

M.13. A mechanism is *Bayesian Incentive Compatible* (*BIC*) iff for a given $q(m) \in Q^N$, and for all admissible $q'(m') \in Q^N$, $\mathrm{E}_{\underline{M}^{N-1}}(U^i|\, m'^i = m^i) = \mathrm{Max}\ \mathrm{E}_{\underline{M}^{N-1}}(U^i|\, m'^i \in M)$, $\forall\, i$, so that $I_F = I_{F^*}$.

We now specify the refund r^i with a general formula.

M.7′. The refund r^i to each consumer i is

$$r^i = S_{-i}\frac{\mathrm{E}_{\underline{M}}(S)}{\mathrm{E}_{\underline{M}}(\sum_j S_{-j})}. \tag{A6.39}$$

This formula implies that $\mathrm{E}_{\underline{M}}(\sum_i r^i) = \mathrm{E}_{\underline{M}}(S_N)$, that is, that $\mathrm{E}_{\underline{M}}(B) = 0$. Similarly, $\mathrm{E}_{\underline{M}^{N-1}}(B_{-i}) = 0$, $\forall\, i$.

In our first two model economies consumers have no risk aversion. Our third model loosens this restriction. For the moment our models maximize the expected value of the outcome.

A.16. Consumers are risk-neutral, that is,

$$\underset{m'^i}{Max}\, \mathrm{E}_{\underline{M}^{N-1}}(U^i) = \underset{m'^i}{Max}\, U^i\,[\mathrm{E}_{\underline{M}^{N-1}}(\underline{x} - y' - S^i + r^i + t^i,\, y')].$$

Statements about a variable $\phi'(m')$ that are true for every admissible m' are evidently true for $\mathrm{E}_{\underline{M}}(\phi')$. Furthermore, under A.14, statements about ϕ' that are true for almost every admissible m', in the sense of being true for all $m' \in M$ except for those in a set of Lesbegue measure zero in M, are also true for $\mathrm{E}_{\underline{M}}(\phi')$. Therefore we may usually deal with realized values, given m', and will need to take explicit account of expected values only as the context requires.

Combining the Samuelson condition (A6.14a) with maximization of utility enables one to derive the conditions for BIC. These conditions have the same general form for all components m'^i_g of m'. From (A6.36), with y^* replacing y', we have the first-order necessary condition

$$\operatorname*{Max}_{m'^i_g} u^i: \left(\frac{\partial (r^i + t^i - S^i - y^*)}{\partial m'^i_g} \right) u_x{}^i + \frac{\partial y^*}{\partial m'^i_g} u_y{}^i = 0,$$

which rearranges to the form

$$v^i(\cdot, y^*) \frac{\partial y^*}{\partial m'^i_g} = \frac{\partial S^i}{\partial m'^i_g} - \frac{\partial (r^i + t^i)}{\partial m'^i_g}. \tag{A6.40}$$

These definitions and concepts apply to all three of the following models.

A6.3.D.1 First Model: Equal Income Effects

Our first model is a special case that allows a precise BIC, efficient outcome. If A.12 holds, giving equal income effects for all consumers, so that M.10 is sufficient, the following form of transfer is of interest. Let

$$t^i = h^i B_{-i} + \ldots$$

By definition, the refund to consumer i is independent of the particular message m'^i. The transfer would also appear to be independent of m'^i. But B_{-i} is not identically zero, although it is independent of m'^i, and the weight h^i must be a function of m' to assure a balanced budget. Moreover, there is the possibility that all $B_{-i} = 0$ while $B \neq 0$. In that case (A6.40) cannot be satisfied, although this problem can arise only on a set of measure zero. To establish BIC, we must first define the function t^i precisely and deal with the special case just mentioned.

If at least one $B_{-j} \neq 0$, let

$$h^i = \frac{B_{-i} B}{\Sigma (B_{-j})^2}. \tag{A6.41}$$

Then let

$$t^i = h^i B_{-i} - \xi \cdot m'^i + \frac{1}{N-1} \xi \cdot \textstyle\sum_{j \neq i} m'^j, \tag{A6.42}$$

where ξ denotes the vector $\xi = \mathrm{E}_{\mathcal{M}^{N-1}}\left(\frac{\partial h^i B_{-i}}{\partial v'^{i0}}, \frac{\partial h^i B_{-i}}{\partial a'^i}\right)$, and where we again assume that this expected value has zero derivatives with respect to the components of m'^i. (The vectors are not necessarily identically zero because $\partial h^i/\partial m'^i_g$ can be correlated with B_{-i}.) If this assumption does not hold we add higher-order terms analogous to those in (A6.42) in order to satisfy (A6.40) while balancing the budget. Adding such terms (or the prospect of having to do so) implies a higher value of b than otherwise: Consumers' messages must include more parameters to define their utility.

Then we have

$$h^i B_{-i} = (B_{-i})^2 B / \left[\sum_j (B_{-j})^2\right]$$

and

$$\sum_i t^i = \sum_i h^i B_{-i} = B, \tag{A6.43}$$

so that this transfer precisely balances the budget. The coefficient h^i is continuous and has continuous derivatives in m', whenever $\sum_i (B_{-i})^2 > 0$. In the case $\sum_i (B_{-i})^2 = 0$, which occurs only on a set of measure zero, let $t^i = B/N$.

Theorem 1. Under M.6′, M.7-M.11, M.8′, A.1-A.12, A.14-A.16, and B.6-B.7, there is a mechanism that is BIC and efficient.

Proof. To satisfy the requirement (A6.42) for BIC we must have

$$\mathrm{E}_{\underline{M}^{N-1}}\left(\frac{\partial t^i}{\partial m'^i_g}\right) = \mathrm{E}_{\underline{M}^{N-1}}\left(S^{-i}\frac{\partial h^i}{\partial m'^i_g} + h^i\frac{\partial B^{-i}}{\partial m'^i_g}\right) - \xi_g$$

$$= \mathrm{E}_{\underline{M}^{N-1}}\left(S^{-i}\frac{\partial h^i}{\partial m'^i_g}\right) - \xi_g = 0,$$

where ξ_g is the component of ξ that corresponds to m'^i_g. This equation obviously holds whenever $\sum_i (B_{-i})^2 > 0$, because B_{-i} is independent of m'^i_g, and ξ_g, being an expectation, is constant except where otherwise noted. To the case where the B_{-i} are all zero, we apply the following consideration: Each B_{-i} is a multinomial function of $2N-2$ variables v'^{j0} and a'^j, each with a distinct combination of exponents and cross-products of these parameters. Hence these expressions are linearly independent, in the same sense that the sequence of terms 1, u, u^2, . . ., u^N in the variable u

are linearly independent. That is, the set $\{B_{-i}\}$ spans the space $\mathbb{R}^{2N}$. Once one assigns particular values to the parameters, the point (0, …, 0) is possible, but it can happen only for sets of parameters of Lesbegue measure zero in $\mathbb{R}^{2N}$: Such sets of parameters are a set of lower dimensionality than the domain or range of the mapping $M^N \rightarrow \mathbb{R}^{2N}$. Hence, since by A.15 all admissible $q'(m') \in Q^N$ are non-degenerate, the case $\sum_i (B_{-i})^2 = 0$ has probability zero, and cannot interfere with BIC.

Then $m' = m$, and by Lemma 5 the mechanism is efficient. ■

Corollary 1. (d'Aspremont and Gerard-Varet). If all utility functions are known to be separable so that $\forall\ i$, $v'^i_x = \underline{v}_x = 0$, under the premises of Theorem 1 other than A.12, there is a mechanism that is BIC and efficient.

Proof. Immediate, by Theorem 1.

Comment: This result, obtained originally by d'Aspremont and Gerard-Varet (1979), solves the efficiency problem of the VCG mechanism under the traditional separability (or transferability) assumption, at the cost of weakening incentive compatibility to BIC. Our result specifies transfer formulas that they proved possible, but did not specify.

A6.3.D.2 Second Model: Unequal Income Effects

We now consider a less restricted model, dropping A.12 to allow unequal income effects, within limits. These limits are implicit in the following assumption (Varian, 1992, p. 397):

A.17. The equilibrium y^*, at which (A6.6) is satisfied for schedules $v'^i(\underline{x}^i_a - y, y)$, is unique. When these schedules are continuously adjusted for income effects, as a parameter λ is varied, they are continuous and monotonically decreasing in $y(\lambda)$.

Although there is no reason to suppose that the mechanism would fail in case of multiple equilibria, we shall not attempt to deal with that problem here. Under A.17 without A.12, each consumer i has a distinct income elasticity of demand for the public good. In this case Lemma 5 does not hold. One must distinguish between y^* and y', where y' is no longer of interest. The other lemmas remain true.

We now revise the message space and the mechanism to deal with the problems raised by substituting A.17 for A.12, to allow different individual income effects.

M.10′. Each message m'^i includes the consumer's income effect: $m'^i = (v'^{i0}, a'^i, v'^i_x)$. The mechanism chooses the outcome value y^* at which

$$\sum_i v'^i(\underline{x}^i_a - y^*, y^*) = 0, \tag{A6.6'}$$

while assessing r^i without regard to the v'^i_x, that is, as stated in M.6-M.8. The first-stage VCG tax becomes

$$S^i = \sum_{j \neq i} \int_{y^*}^{y^{**}_{-i}} m'^j(\underline{x}^j_a - y, y)\, dy \tag{A6.9'}$$

holding $\underline{x}^j_a$ constant along the path of integration. In (A6.9′), y^{**}_{-i} has the same meaning as y''_{-i} in M.3, except that $\underline{x}^j_a$ replaces $\underline{x}$.

With this change in the mechanism, the central agent solves a set of simultaneous equations to determine y^* and each $\underline{x}^i_a$, with its components S^i, r^i, and t^i, so that they are mutually consistent. As already noted, there exists a solution.

Now from (A6.40), (A6.9′), and (A6.6′) we have

$$\frac{\partial S^i}{\partial m'^i_g} = -\frac{\partial y^*}{\partial m'^i_g} \sum_{j \neq i} m'^j(\cdot, y^*) + \sum_{j \neq i} \int_{y^*}^{y^{**}_{-i}} m'^j_x \frac{\partial \underline{x}^j_a}{\partial m'^i_g}\, dy$$

$$= \frac{\partial y^*}{\partial m'^i_g} m'^i(\cdot, y^*) + \sum_{j \neq i} \int_{y^*}^{y^{**}_{-i}} m'^j_x \frac{\partial \underline{x}^j_a}{\partial m'^i_g}\, dy,$$

which, when combined with (A6.40), gives

$$m^i(\cdot, y^*) \frac{\partial y^*}{\partial m'^i_g} =$$

$$m'^i(\cdot, y^*) \frac{\partial y^*}{\partial m'^i_g} + \sum_{j \neq i} \int_{y^*}^{y^{**}_{-i}} m'^j_x \frac{\partial \underline{x}^j_a}{\partial m'^i_g}\, dy - \frac{\partial (r^i + t^i)}{\partial m'^i_g}. \tag{A6.44}$$

One can readily verify that $\partial y^*/\partial m'^i_g \neq 0$, except for cases on a set of measure zero, such as $m'^i_g = a'^i$ with $y^* = y_0$ while A.12 holds. These cases do not affect the argument because when one of them holds there is no incentive to falsify a'^i, and all such cases have probability zero. Therefore, (A6.40) implies that if $v^i(x, y^*; m)\, \partial y^*/\partial m'^i_g = \partial S^i/\partial m'^i_g$, that is, if

$$\mathrm{E}_{\underline{M}^{N-1}}\left(\frac{\partial(r^i+t^i)}{\partial m'^i_g}\right)=\mathrm{E}_{\underline{M}^{N-1}}\left(\sum_{j\neq i}\int_{y^*}^{y^{**}_{-i}} m^j_x\,\frac{\partial \underline{x}^j_a}{\partial m'^i_g}\,dy\right)$$

$$=\mathrm{E}_{\underline{M}^{N-1}}\left(\sum_{j\neq i} m^j_x\,\frac{\partial \underline{x}^j_a}{\partial m'^i_g}\int_{y^*}^{y^{**}_{-i}} dy\right), \tag{A6.45}$$

then $m'^i_g = m^i_g$.

The last form obtains because the integrands in the first form of the right hand side of (A6.45) are constants with respect to the variable of integration y. Then because, by definition, $\partial r^i/\partial m'^i_g = 0$, one can write (A6.45) as

$$\mathrm{E}_{\underline{M}^{N-1}}\left(\frac{\partial t^i}{\partial m'^i_g}\right)=\mathrm{E}_{\underline{M}^{N-1}}\left(\sum_{j\neq i} m^j_x\,\frac{\partial \underline{x}^j_a}{\partial m'^i_g}\,[y^{**}_{-i}-y^*]\right), \tag{A6.45$'$}$$

A transfer t^i whose derivative $\partial t^i/\partial m'^i_g$ is the right-hand side of (A6.45′) and whose economy-wide sum balances the budget, approximately or exactly, would meet our present objective. A transfer that meets this criterion is

$$\begin{aligned} t^i = \sum_{j\neq i}\Big[& v'^j_x\,\underline{x}^j_a(y^{**}_{-i}-y^*) + v'^{i0}\,\mathrm{E}_{\underline{M}^{N-1}}\big(v'^j_x\,\underline{x}^j_a\,\frac{\partial y^*}{\partial v'^{i0}}\big) \\ & + a'^i\,\mathrm{E}_{\underline{M}^{N-1}}\big(v'^j_x\,\underline{x}^j_a\,\frac{\partial y^*}{\partial a'^i}\big) + v'^i_x\,\mathrm{E}_{\underline{M}^{N-1}}\big(v'^j_x\,\underline{x}^j_a\,\frac{\partial y^*}{\partial v'^i_x}\big)\Big] \\ & - \frac{1}{(N-1)}\,\mathrm{E}_{\underline{M}^{N-1}}\Big\{\sum_{j\neq i}\sum_{k\neq j} v'^k_x\big[\,\underline{x}^k_a(y^{**}_{-j}-y^*) \\ & + v'^{j0}\,\underline{x}^k_a\,\frac{\partial y^*}{\partial v'^{j0}} + a'^j\,\underline{x}^k_a\,\frac{\partial y^*}{\partial a'^j} + v'^j_x\,\underline{x}^k_a\,\frac{\partial y^*}{\partial v'^j_x}\big]\Big\} \end{aligned} \tag{A6.46}$$

in that its derivative satisfies (A6.45′), (provided that the expected values in this expression have zero derivatives with respect to all the components of m'^i), and in that, under A.15,

$$\mathrm{E}_{\underline{M}}\left(\sum t^i\right) = 0. \tag{A6.47}$$

If the expected values do not have zero derivatives with respect to all the components of m'^i, then we would add higher-order terms in m'^i_g with higher-order derivatives of $\mathrm{E}_{\underline{M}}(\cdot)$, in order to satisfy (A6.40) and (A6.47), until we reached that higher order of derivatives of $\mathrm{E}_{\underline{M}}(\cdot)$ that are all zero.

Inasmuch as the transfer (A6.46) satisfies (A6.40), by satisfying (A6.45′) $\forall\, q'(m')$, the strategy $m'^i \equiv m^i$ is dominant $\forall\, i$. In Section A6.2 I show that the budget imbalance B due to random error in the refund $\sum_i r^i$ vanishes at a rate $O(1/N^2)$ relative to the size of the economy, where the size of the economy increases by exact replication of the set of consumers. The outcome shift $(y^{**}_{-i} - y^*)$ due to consumer i is approximately inversely proportional to $-\sum_i a'^i$, so that it vanishes at a rate $O(1/N)$ as N approaches infinity. It is straightforward to show that $\partial y^*/\partial m'^i_g$ vanishes at this same rate. Inasmuch as the mean transfer $(1/N)\sum_i t^i$ measures the part of the budget imbalance due to $\sum_i t^i$ relative to the size of the economy, if each t^i had a constant expected standard deviation the standard deviation of this part of the budget imbalance would vanish at the rate $O(1/N^{1/2})$. Then, because the standard deviation of each t^i vanishes at the rate $O(1/N)$, the combination of these two effects of increasing N is that this transfer, relative to the size of the economy, vanishes at the rate $O(1/N^{3/2})$. Evidently, then, the random variation of the sum of transfers dominates the order of accuracy of approximation to budget balance of the entire mechanism. The inexactness of approximation represents the weaker part of M.11.

Thus we have proved:

Lemma 8. Under M.1-M.9, M.6′, M.7′, M.10′, A.1-A.10, A.14-A.17 and B.1-B.2, using the transfer (A6.46), the mechanism is BIC and is approximately Pareto efficient with an error that vanishes at the rate $O(1/N^{3/2})$.

Of course, rational consumers will expect $q'(m') \equiv q(m)$, so that we can substitute truth-conditional expectations for the expectations in (A6.45)-(A6.47).

This result is of interest primarily for application to a small sub-economy, such as a town in a federal system, or a legislature, where the budget imbalance can be shifted to the remainder of the entire national economy without risk of infeasibility. A similar idea, applied to the unrefunded budget surplus S_N, appears in Collinge (1983). Suppose now that we wish instead to require exact budget balance. This result we obtain by simply setting $t^i = B/N$. In this case, $\partial t^i/\partial m'^i_g = (1/N)\partial B/\partial m'^i_g$, which would contribute an additional deviation from BIC besides the absence of the right-hand term of (A6.45′). The term $\partial B/\partial m'^i_g$ vanishes at the same rate as B itself, where this rate is uniformly bounded for all m'^i_g, so that the deviation from BIC from this source vanishes at the rate $O(1/N^3)$. The deviation from BIC due to the absence of the right-hand term of (A6.23′) evidently vanishes at the rate $O(1/N^2)$, inasmuch as the constant term is independent of N, giving this term the dominant effect on the overall error. Thus we have:

Lemma 9. Under M.1-M.9, M.11, M.6′, M.7′, M.10′, A.1-A.10, A.14-A.17, and B.1-B.2, using the transfer $t^i = B/N$ the mechanism is Pareto efficient and is approximately BIC with an error that vanishes at the rate $O(1/N^2)$.

Together these results establish the following overall result:

Theorem 2. In an economy as described here, with income effects in consumer utility restricted only by A.17, and under the other premises of Lemmas 8 and 9, there exist VCG mechanisms each of which is either precisely BIC and approximately Pareto efficient or approximately BIC and precisely Pareto efficient for true messages. In either case, the error of approximation vanishes at a rate more rapid than $O(1/N)$.

A6.3.D.3 Third Model: Equal, Non-Zero Risk Aversion

Consider how the analysis leading to Lemmas 8 and 9 and Theorem 2 is changed if we replace A.15 with the following:

A.15′. Let β^i denote consumer i's index of risk aversion: $\beta^i = -U^i_{xx}/U^i_x > 0$. Then $\forall\ i$, let $\beta^i = \beta$, a constant, known to the central agent and to consumers.

If, as assumed, $\beta > 0$, then the transfer defined by (A6.46) requires adjustment to achieve BIC. Our problem now is to obtain

$$\max_{m'^i_g} E_{\underline{M}^{N-1}}(U^i) = \max_{m'^i_g} \int_{\underline{M}^{N-1}} U^i[\underline{x}^i_a(m'^i, m'_{-i}) - y^*; y^*]p'(m'_{-i})dm'_{-i},$$

which implies

$$\frac{\partial}{\partial m'^i_g}\int_{\underline{M}^{N-1}} U^i[\underline{x}^i_a(m'^i, m'_{-i}) - y^*; y^*]q'(m'_{-i})dm'_{-i} =$$
$$\int_{\underline{M}^{N-1}} \frac{\partial}{\partial m'^i_g} U^i[\underline{x}^i_a - y^*; y^*]q'(m'_{-i})\,dm'_{-i} = 0.$$

Taking the derivative under the integral sign, and drawing upon the steps already performed in obtaining (A6.40) and (A6.44), we have

$$\int_{\underline{M}^{N-1}} U^i_x[(m^i - m'^i)\frac{\partial y^*}{\partial m'^i_g} - (y^{**}_{-i} - y^*)\sum_{j\neq i} m^j_x \frac{\partial \underline{x}^j_a}{\partial m'^i_g} + \frac{\partial t^i}{\partial m'^i_g}]q'(m'_{-i})\,dm'_{-i}$$
$$= 0. \tag{A6.48}$$

Now denote by $\underline{t}^i$ the transfer defined by (A6.46). The derivative

$$\frac{\partial \underline{t}^i}{\partial m'^i_g} = (y^{**}_{-i} - y^*)\sum_{j\neq i} m'^j_x \frac{\partial \underline{x}^j_a}{\partial m'^i_g} - \frac{\partial y^*}{\partial m'^i_g}\sum_{j\neq i} m'^j_x \underline{x}^j_a$$
$$+ \mathrm{E}_{\underline{M}^{N-1}}\left(\frac{\partial y^*}{\partial m'^i_g}\sum_{j\neq i} m'^j_x \underline{x}^j_a\right) \tag{A6.49}$$

is consistent with strict incentive compatibility when and only when

$$\delta^i = \mathrm{E}_{\underline{M}^{N-1}}\left(\frac{\partial y^*}{\partial m'^i_g}\sum_{j\neq i} m'^j_x \underline{x}^j_a\right) - \frac{\partial y^*}{\partial m'^i_g}\sum_{j\neq i} m'^j_x \underline{x}^j_a = 0. \tag{A6.50}$$

The discrepancy δ^i is a random variable whose zero mean is required for BIC for risk-neutral consumers. As noted in the text, an incentive compatible mechanism is BIC, so that whenever $\delta^i = 0$ the variability of the other terms in is irrelevant to BIC, regardless of the degree of risk aversion. It follows that for given β the adjustment to (A6.46) required by A.15′ depends solely on the variability of δ^i.

In particular, the monetary adjustment to $\frac{\partial t^i}{\partial m'^i_g}$ to correct for risk is

$$-\mathrm{E}_{\underline{M}^{N-1}}[\delta^i U^i_x(\underline{x}^i_a - y^*, y^*)] / \mathrm{E}_{\underline{M}^{N-1}}[U^i_x],$$

which, as a textbook proposition (Nicholson, 1995, p. 265) is proportional to β:

$$-\mathrm{E}_{\underline{M}^{N-1}}[\delta^i U^i_x(\underline{x}^i_a - y^*, y^*)] / \mathrm{E}_{\underline{M}^{N-1}}[U^i_x] = \gamma_g \beta, \tag{A6.51}$$

where γ_g is a constant. Therefore, the transfer after adjustment for risk is

$$t^i = \underline{t}^i + \beta(m'^i \cdot \gamma) - \frac{\beta}{N-1} \mathrm{E}_{\underline{M}^{N-1}} \left[\sum_{j \neq i} (m'^j \cdot \gamma) \right], \tag{A6.42'}$$

where γ is the vector of the γ_g corresponding to the components of m'^i.

Then $\dfrac{\partial t^i}{\partial m'^i_g} = \dfrac{\partial \underline{t}^i}{\partial m'^i_g} + \gamma_g \beta$, so that when we evaluate (A6.48) at $m'^i = m^i$ using (A6.49) plus this correction, with (A6.50), and then simplify, we obtain

$$\int_{\underline{M}^{N-1}} U^i_x [\delta^i + \gamma_g \beta] p'(m'_{-i}) dm'_{-i} = 0, \tag{A6.52}$$

which by (A6.51) necessarily holds. Hence we have proved

Theorem 3. Under the premises of Lemmas 8 and 9, with A.15′ replacing A.15, there exist VCG mechanisms each of which is either precisely BIC and approximately Pareto efficient or approximately BIC and precisely Pareto efficient for true messages. In either case, the error of approximation vanishes at a rate more rapid than O(1/*N*).

Whether we can relax A.15′ to allow β^i to vary among consumers is an open question.

A6.3.D.4 Discussion of the three models

Although Green and Laffont (1979), Walker (1980), Moulin (1988), and Hurwicz and Walker (1990) proved that there is no mechanism that combines Pareto efficiency with incentive compatibility for all economies of finite size, their proof says nothing about BIC. Thus, our findings do not contradict the various impossibility theorems. The mechanism achieves partial success because, if the universally shared prior knowledge implies an opportunity for a consumer to manipulate *B* and thus to manipulate the combined set of refunds and transfers, then the agent can adapt the transfer $\underline{t}^i$ to nullify this opportunity, in terms of expected values. Choosing the correct refund formula (A6.39) is also necessary.

The overall approach used here to distribute the budget surplus is similar to but distinct from that proposed by Arrow (1979). Our transfer equation (A6.46) and the logic of its properties, together with those of the VCG tax (A6.9′) and the refund (A6.39), are closely related to Conn's

(1983) general condition for strict incentive compatibility and mechanism success. Conn followed the more traditional route, however, of seeking these outcomes in disregard of budget balance. See also Laffont and Maskin (1979).

A6.3.E Conclusion

Although the proposals here approximately optimize the performance of the VCG mechanism for an economy with one private good and one public good, they do nothing about the lack of incentive to vote in a large economy nor about the vulnerability of social aggregation mechanisms to coalitions. The lack of incentive to vote, a commonplace fact of life, is the subject of ongoing research by interested scholars. The problem of coalitions is common both to public choice mechanisms, especially when many consumers do not vote, and to the private sector.

Although I have not found a transfer formula that makes the VCG mechanism both BIC and precisely efficient for the present models or for more general ones, I do not know of a proof of the impossibility of such a formula. Our models provide a step forward in two respects. First, in a qualified way they extend results previously obtained only for separable utility functions to economies with fewer, more plausible restrictions. For the Bergstrom-Cornes-Conn economy, our model arguably gets stronger results. Second, whereas prior work established that the VCG mechanism converges on efficiency at the rate $O(1/N)$ as the economy grows large, the modified mechanism presented here converges on efficiency at the rate $O(1/N^{3/2})$. This result implies that the mechanism converges on efficiency faster than the incentive to participate declines, so that there are economies of intermediate size in which the incentive to participate is appreciable whereas the incentive to misrepresent preferences is negligible.

A6.4 GENERAL EQUILIBRIUM IN A VCG ECONOMY

A6.4.A Introduction and Summary

One of the major problems of the VCG mechanism is that the VCG tax has been undefined and its properties unknown except when utility functions are of a narrowly restricted form. This section addresses that problem in a general equilibrium framework. For an economy with multiple public goods whose quantities are continuous variables (that is, real numbers) and with quasi-concave and differentiable consumer utility functions, it offers a general definition of a set of VCG taxes and refunds with promising properties. We extend Foley's proof of the existence of a Pareto efficient allocation to prove the existence of a general equilibrium of this economy. This section complements Section A6.3, which addresses incentive compatibility and budget balance for the case of a two-good economy.

A signal contribution by Foley (1970) proved the existence, under standard general economic assumptions, of a Lindahl equilibrium goods allocation with its set of prices and taxes in an economy with multiple private and public goods. His method of proof showed that the technical restriction that the amount of each public good be the same for everyone does not contradict the assumptions required for the existence of an 'equilibrium' with Pareto-efficient prices and quantities. With an extended proof that used a social welfare function, Foley (1967) proved the existence of equilibrium, when taxes differ from Lindahl taxes, and proved that it is Pareto efficient. He did not consider the problem of finding a mechanism to implement either equilibrium, but the lack of a mechanism for determining Lindahl taxes or for implementing a Pareto-efficient equilibrium is immaterial to the existence issue. Here we modify Foley's income tax structure to include the incentive tax of the VCG mechanism. Using a modest extension of Foley's method and drawing upon his results, we prove here the existence of equilibrium under the same general assumptions (including no restrictions on income effects other than continuity), in an economy having this mechanism.

As is customary in general equilibrium analyses, in this section we do without assumption A.8, the differentiability of preferences.

A6.4.B Public Competitive Equilibrium

Foley (1970) proved the existence and Pareto efficiency of Lindahl equilibrium under Assumptions A.1-A.7, B.1-B.5, C.1 and C.2. With an extended proof that used a social welfare function, Foley (1967) proved the existence of public competitive equilibrium and proved that it is Pareto efficient. Relying on Foley's (1970) line of proof and on the mapping used by Debreu (1959) to prove the existence of equilibrium of a private goods economy, we prove the existence of public competitive equilibrium more directly, in a way that aids in proving its existence in the presence of a VCG mechanism.

Foley (1970) characterized a system with a production set and preference sets described by assumptions A.5-A.7 as having a distinct vector of public good quantities for each consumer, with the side constraint on production that these vectors must be equal. Using this construct, he established a virtual isomorphism between a strictly private goods economy and an economy with both private and public goods, when for each consumer the Lindahl prices for public goods equal their Lindahl taxes. (However, this isomorphism does not include a mechanism for assessing these taxes.) He proved

Lemma 10. (a) $\exists\ (p_x;\ p_y{}^i, \ldots, p_y{}^N) \geq 0$ that supports a Pareto efficient allocation and meets requirements (a) and (b) of a public competitive equilibrium as specified in C.6.
(b) There exists a Lindahl equilibrium.

For a public competitive equilibrium we need a non-Lindahl tax formula that is consistent with A.4. That is, in equilibrium it must not bankrupt anyone.

T.1. A tax vector T is *admissible* if $\forall\ i, p_x \cdot \underline{x}^i - T^i \geq p_x \cdot \underline{\underline{x}}^0$.

Moreover, let

$$T^i = (T_1{}^i, \ldots, T_h{}^i) \cdot (y_1, \ldots, y_h), \tag{A6.53}$$

and we use the following formula:

T.2. Consumer i's *tax share* per unit of public good j is the real number

$$T_j^i = p_{yj}\,[p_x \cdot (\underline{x}^i - \underline{\underline{x}}^0)/p_x \cdot \textstyle\sum_i (\underline{x}^i - \underline{\underline{x}}^0)]. \tag{A6.54}$$

This tax formula is equivalent to that used in Foley (1967). Its implementation requires that the taxing authority know each $\underline{x}^i$, and to that extent we depart from the customary assumption of a non-parametric central decision mechanism. Taking B.1 into account, one can quickly verify that with these taxes the public budget would balance. We now need

Lemma 11. There exist admissible taxes. That is, there are feasible allocations with positive quantities of public goods in an economy with non-Lindahl taxes.

Proof: Clearly, A.5 implies that an allocation with all $y_j = 0, j = 1, \ldots, h$, is feasible. A.6 implies that, for every vector of prices, $\exists\ \psi$ such that the consumption allocation $(\underline{x} - T;\ \psi, \ldots, \psi)$, for T determined by (A6.53) and (A6.54), is feasible and satisfies Lemma 11. Each distinct value of ψ

results in a distinct allocation, and we have a range of possible choices for ψ. ■

To proceed further we need additional notation and definitions. We freely use complete sets of Lindahl prices and normalize these prices using the rule $(p_x; p_y^1, \ldots, p_y^N; p_y)\cdot(1, \ldots, 1) = 1$. That is,

T.3. The set of all possible price vectors is the simplex $P =$

$$\{p = (p_x; p_y^1, \ldots, p_y^N; p_y) \mid (p_x; p_y^1, \ldots, p_y^N; p_y)\cdot(1, \ldots, 1) = 1\}.$$

We denote subspaces of P in self-evident ways, such as P_x and P_y^i. Further, it is helpful to have a unit of account. A good $x_{j'}$, chosen from among those consumed in positive, finite quantity, serves that purpose. Without loss of generality, let the good x_1 be the unit of account. Taxes T^i and other tax concepts, with their subcomponents, are denominated in this unit. Note, however, that because prices are normalized into the simplex P, we have $0 < p_{x1} < 1$. With slight loss of generality, we will require

T.4. p_{x1} is bounded away from zero.

We have

Lemma 12. $\forall$ i and $\forall$ y consumer i's demand correspondence ρ is upper semicontinuous (u.s.c.).

(Adapted essentially unchanged from Debreu [1959], p. 19.) For this correspondence the mapping is ρ: $P \times Z \times X \rightarrow X$ because the vectors y', through C.6, and $\underline{x}$ enter into the consumer's demand correspondence. Also relevant is

Lemma 13. The set of feasible allocations, W, is compact and convex.

(From Foley [1967] and Arrow and Hahn [1971].)

Then by trivial adaptation of the Debreu (1959) proof of existence of competitive equilibrium in a private goods economy, there is an alternative, direct proof of the Foley (1967) theorem,

Theorem 4. $\forall$ $\underline{x} = (\underline{x}^1, \ldots, \underline{x}^N) \in X$, a non-Lindahl public competitive equilibrium exists.

The proof of Theorem 4 that we use, which is more direct and pertinent than that employed by Foley (1967), goes along the following lines.

The consumer maximizes utility subject to given values of the vectors $(p_x; p_y^i)$ and to the consumer's given after-tax wealth $\underline{x}^i = \underline{x}^i - T^i$, choosing a vector (x^i, y^i). Each consumer i with utility function U^i faces the maximization problem

$$\max_{x^i,\, y^i} U^i(x^i; y^i) \text{ subject to } (p_x; p_y^i) \cdot (x^i, y^i) \leq \underline{x}^i. \tag{A6.55}$$

Then it is convenient to introduce the following definition.

C.12. For prices p and allocation w, the *consumer's budget surplus*, $\forall\ i$, is $s^i(p, x, T^i) = p_x \cdot \underline{x}^i - p_x \cdot x^i - T^i$. The vector of such budget surpluses is denoted by $s = (s^1, \ldots, s^N)$. The set of all non-negative budget surpluses $\forall\ i$ is a simplex $\mathcal{S}$.

Inasmuch as the after-tax wealth $\underline{x}^i$ and the budget surplus s^i are linear in allocations, it is evident that for each vector of Lindahl prices and for each y, they are continuous functions of $(\underline{x}^i, x^i, y^i)$, where y^i is here considered distinct from, and may be different from, y'. After-tax wealth and these budget surpluses are also continuous in y'. Note that we use y' in the tax formula (A6.54). Thus we reason as if consumers can purchase added units of public goods at prices p_y^i, whereas their taxes are determined by production of y', and so can be viewed by consumers as given. That is, consumers are price takers in the private sector and y'-takers in the public sector. In the maximization (A6.55) it is convenient to view them as if they were price-takers of the p_y^i for the y^i. At an equilibrium all $y^i = y'$, by C.11. Demand (x^i, y^i) is a function of p, y', and $\underline{x}^i$, that is, of p, y', and $\underline{x}$. Hence we have

C.13. The consumer's maximization (A6.55) establishes a *demand correspondence* ρ, which is a mapping ρ: $P \times Z \times X \to X$.

Following Debreu (1959), we henceforward limit attention to convex, compact subsets $\underline{X} \subset X$ and $\underline{Z} \subset Z$, such as a cube $\underline{W} \subset W$ that contains as a subset the set of all feasible allocations W'. Then the demand correspondence is a mapping from a convex, compact set into another convex, compact set, both of which are subsets of spaces of real numbers. Lemma 12 follows directly from Debreu's method of proof.

C.14. $\forall\, w \in W$ the *excess demands* for private goods are $d_x(w) = \sum_i (x^i - \underline{x}^i) - z$ and the excess demands for public goods are $d_y{}^i(w) = y^i - y'$, $i = 1, \ldots, N$.

These are linear functions over the set of allocations. Profit maximization by producers implies a supply correspondence σ, a mapping $\sigma\colon P \times X \to Z$. By standard reasoning parallel to that in Debreu's proof of Lemma 12, σ is u.s.c. Together, Lemma 12 and its counterpart for the supply correspondence imply that $[d_x(w), d_y(w)]$ is a correspondence that is u.s.c. In a private-goods economy, subtracting this correspondence from the demand correspondences gives excess demand. In the present economy, however, the supply correspondence maps into Z, which is part of the domain of the demand mapping ρ. The definition of excess demand must take that into account as well as the subtraction.

That is, for a given price vector $q \in Q$, to which there corresponds a public goods vector $y' \in Z$, consider the consumers' choices of a utility-maximizing consumption allocation $(x; y)$. Then the combination of y' and (x, y) is an allocation $w(p)$ that determines an excess demand $d[w(p)]$, giving a correspondence that maps $P \times X$ into D.

In this context, note that an allocation that has a positive excess demand is infeasible. That is, a feasible allocation has $(d_x; d_y) \leq 0$ so that a definition equivalent to C.3 is

C.15. A *feasible allocation* $w' \in W'$ is an allocation w with $[d_x(w); d_y(w)] \leq 0$. that is, $W' = W \cap \{w \mid [d_x(w); d_y(w)] \leq 0\}$.

C.16. The *set of excess demands* $D \in \mathbb{R}^{k+Nh}$ is the set

$$D = \{d = (d_x; d_y) \mid d = d(w) \text{ for } w \in W\}$$

and the *excess demand correspondence* $d = \rho \cdot \sigma - \sigma$ is the mapping $d\colon P \times X \to \mathbb{R}^{k+Nh}$.

Non-negative consumer budget surpluses and zero profits in production imply that $\forall\, w \in W$,

$$p_x \cdot d_x(w) + \textstyle\sum_i p_y{}^i \cdot y^i - p_y \cdot y' \leq 0. \tag{A6.56}$$

Then inasmuch as the set of possible excess demands D is the image of W under the linear mapping $d(w)$, D is convex.

Every relevant property of the demand correspondence C.13 remains unaffected by the modification to the consumer's maximization problem

(A6.55) to accommodate public goods. Although it now involves T^i and thereby involves y', which the consumer views as given, p determines y'. Therefore, inasmuch as the demand correspondence is a mapping from $P \times X$ into X, it is logically equivalent to the analogous mapping in an economy without public goods. Moreover, the excess-demand correspondence, a mapping from $P \times X$ into D in both types of economy, is u.s.c. and convex.

As in Debreu (1959), maximization of (A6.56) by varying p results in a correspondence Φ, a mapping $\Phi: D \to P$. This mapping is logically equivalent to that of the analogous correspondence for private goods alone, and is u.s.c. Hence, the combination of this mapping with the excess demand correspondence is a mapping $\Phi \cdot d$: $\mathrm{P} \times X \to P$ that is u.s.c. That is, for each given $\underline{x} \in X$, the u.s.c. correspondence $\Phi \cdot d$: $\mathrm{P} \times X \to P$ is a mapping $P \to P$, and by the Kakutani fixed-point theorem it has a fixed point p^*. ■

Corollary 1. For given consumer preferences and endowments and given production technology, the public competitive equilibrium (w^*, p^*, T^*) is a correspondence, $(w^*, p^*, T^*) = f^*(\underline{x})$: a mapping f^*: $X \to X \times P \times \mathbb{R}^N$ that is u.s.c.

Proof: The proof of Theorem 4 combines several correspondences to yield a mapping from $P \times X$ into P that is u.s.c., which implies that p^* is u.s.c. in $\underline{x}$. Each demand correspondence is u.s.c. in p and $\underline{x}$, so that w^* is also. Because T^* is a continuous function of w^* and p^*, it is also u.s.c. in p and $\underline{x}$. ■

A6.4.C Equilibrium with a VCG Tax.

At a Pareto-efficient allocation, the sum of consumer marginal rates of substitution of the unit of account for a public good at least equals the marginal cost of the good. Such a marginal rate of substitution for consumer i represents what consumer i is willing to pay to have one more unit of the public good produced. It will be convenient to refer to this quantity as consumer i's 'willingness to pay' (w.t.p.) for the good. The VCG tax was conceived as a method, under some circumstances incentive-compatible, for eliciting this information from consumers.

VCG taxes, added to arbitrary tax shares (A6.54) of the costs of public goods, present the consumer with a varying (normally rising) marginal cost of each public good. Facing this marginal cost, the mirror reflection of the sum of the valuation curves of other consumers net of their equation (A6.54) tax shares, each consumer is a discriminating monopsonist with no strategic reason to report false valuations. At the equilibrium, the marginal cost of a unit of public good is a marginal Lindahl tax, so that consumers unanimously prefer the optimum output to any other output. For a textbook description of the two-good economy case, see Varian (1992, p. 429).

A semantic problem arises from our assumption of a large economy in which consumers are price takers. Although it is anomalous to combine this assumption with a non-negligible VCG tax, the aim is to establish that the income effects of a VCG tax of every admissible size are consistent with public competitive equilibrium. For that purpose, it is a helpful simplification to treat the economy as having price-taking consumers while the size of the VCG tax is restricted only by the non-bankruptcy assumption.

Our problem is to determine whether the economy of our assumptions A.1-A.7 and B.1-B.5, with taxes (A6.54) and also with VCG taxes, necessarily has a public competitive equilibrium as defined by C.6. For that purpose, we will need a precise definition of VCG taxes and a workable definition of the mechanism that contains them, which we will provide after some necessary preliminaries.

Previous work on the VCG tax has been almost entirely preoccupied with the case of a two-good economy (with a private good x and a public good y) with transferable utility, where $\forall\ i$, $U^i(x^i; y) = x^i + H^i(y)$ and the pertinent marginal valuation for y is $U_y^i/U_x^i - T^i = U_y^i - T^i$. (It is also customary to use utility with continuous first and higher derivatives.) This marginal valuation is independent of x^i, so that it can be represented by a single curve that is unaffected by income effects arising from the VCG tax itself. The marginal cost to consumer i of a unit of the public good is therefore unaffected by such income effects, and is a single well-defined curve. In that case the optimal allocation $\mathcal{W}^*$ has that output of y such that $\sum_i (U_y{}^i - T^i) = 0$.

A necessary step in the computation of the VCG tax for consumer i is to find that allocation $\mathcal{W}^{**}_{-i}$ at which the sum $\sum_{i' \neq i} (U^{i'}{}_y - T^{i'})$ is zero. In the special case of transferable utility in a two-good economy this allocation is well-defined, as is the expression for consumer i's VCG tax:

$$S^i = \sum_{i' \neq i} \int_{y^*}^{y^{**}_{-i}} (U^{i'}_y - T^{i'})\, dy. \qquad \text{(A6.57)}$$

By contrast, there is no standard definition of a VCG tax for an economy with the general type of utility functions that we use here. One is faced with questions about whether and in what way to take income effects into account when defining the expression for the VCG tax. There are several possibilities, and the choice among them is not self-evident.

Rather than explore the possibilities in full here, we shall use the option that we used in Section A6.3. As a step toward proving the existence of equilibrium, we choose an arbitrary admissible trial vector J of VCG taxes and refunds and hold this vector constant so that the corresponding budget constraint is linear for each consumer. A positive transfer, $J^i > 0$, increases consumer i's budget, whereas $J^i < 0$ represents a net tax on consumer i. Denote by $\mathbb{F}$ the sum of all transfers-less-taxes: $\mathbb{F} = \sum_i (-T^i + J^i)$.

T.5. The *set of admissible taxes/transfers* $\mathbb{A}$ is bounded by endowments $p_x \cdot \underline{x}^i$ and the bankruptcy level $p_x \cdot \underline{\underline{x}}^0$: $\mathbb{A} = \{ \mathbb{F} \mid p_x \cdot \sum_i [\underline{x}^i - \underline{\underline{x}}^0] \geq \mathbb{F}^i \geq p_x \cdot [\underline{\underline{x}}^0 - \underline{x}^i], \forall\, i\}$.

Because $T \geqq 0$, every admissible $J \in \mathbb{A}$. That is, no consumer i can receive a transfer greater than the amount that would bankrupt everyone, so that $\forall\ i$, $p_x \cdot \sum_i [\underline{x}^i - \underline{\underline{x}}^0] \geq J^i$. Also, no consumer i can be taxed past bankruptcy, so that $\mathbb{F}^i \geq p_x \cdot [\underline{\underline{x}}^0 - \underline{x}^i]$. This step makes possible an unambiguous definition of $\mathcal{W}^{**}_{-i}$ and of the VCG tax formula that corresponds to (A6.57) for our present economy. Then the proof of existence of a fixed point equilibrium for this economy includes a fixed point for the VCG tax vector, so that at equilibrium the trial vector equals the final vector of values of the VCG tax formula.

The arbitrarily chosen admissible net transfer J^i to (from) each consumer i is momentarily given and fixed, so that its effect is to change $\underline{x}^i$, without changing the original value of $\underline{x}^i$ in (A6.54), shifting consumer i's budget constraint by this fixed amount. Taking this transfer into account, for a given vector of endowments and the tax formulas (A6.53) and (A6.54), by Theorem 4 there exists a non-Lindahl public competitive equilibrium (w^*, p^*, T^*).

Now consider an *i-abstaining economy* in which we modify each public-good's production price p_{yj} by subtracting consumer i's per unit tax contribution to that public good: $\forall j$, $p'_{yj} = p_{yj} - T_j^i$, and we then treat this economy as having no consumer i. Using the same arbitrarily chosen net transfers $J^{i'}$ as in the full economy, for all other consumers $i' \neq i$, Theorem 4 applies so that for this i-abstaining economy there is a public competitive equilibrium $(w^{**}_{-i}, p^{**}_{-i}, T^{**}_{-i})$.

T.6. The public competitive equilibrium $(w^{**}_{-i}, p^{**}_{-i}, T^{**}_{-i})$ is the equilibrium of the i-abstaining economy.

We now revise the definition of $\underline{\chi}^i$ and to fit the present context.

C.17. The *after-tax wealth* of each consumer i is $\underline{\chi}^i = p_x \cdot \underline{x}^i - T^i + J^i$. For utility maximization, each consumer i's *trial budget constraint* is $(p_x; p_y{}^i) \cdot (x^i; y^i) \leq \underline{\chi}^i$.

Given a price vector $(p_x;\ p_y{}^i)$, an adjusted endowment $\underline{x}^i + J^i$, and a vector y' of public goods, with the tax consequence T^i, consumer i maximizes $U^i(x^i;\ y^i)$. As before, $\underline{\chi}^i$ is a linear function of y'. The perspective of utility maximization in the standard stylized form is convenient for the proof of existence of equilibrium, although it does not properly characterize the consumer's choice problem when the VCG tax enters the budget constraint. We may defer the analysis of that choice problem until we need to reconcile it with our main result.

We may write $P_y = P_y{}^1 \times \ldots \times P_y{}^N$ and $X^i = X_x{}^i \times X_y{}^i$, so that the demand correspondence of Lemma 12 is the mapping $P_x \times P_y{}^i \times Z \times X^i \rightarrow X_x{}^i \times X_y{}^i$. Then if we choose a point $(p_x, y^i, y', \underline{x}^i + J^i)$ in the projection of this graph in $P_x \times X_y{}^i \times Z \times X^i$, the set of points in the graph of which this point is a projection provides us with a correspondence that maps $P_x \times X_y{}^i \times Z \times X^i \rightarrow X_x{}^i \times P_y{}^i$. In particular, we may choose a point $(p_x, y^i, y',\ \underline{x}^i)$ such that $y^i = y'$, so that the chosen point simplifies to $(p_x, y',\ \underline{x}^i + J^i)$. Restricting our attention to such points, we have the correspondence C^i that maps C^i: $P_x \times Z \times X^i \rightarrow X_x{}^i \times P_y{}^i$.

Lemma 14. The correspondence from $(p_x, y', \underline{x}^i + J^i)$ to $(x^i, p_y{}^i)$, $\forall\ i$, with the mapping C^i: $P_x \times Z \times X^i \rightarrow X_x{}^i \times P_y{}^i$, an inversion of the demand correspondence of Lemma 12, is u.s.c.

Proof: By Lemma 12 the demand correspondence obtained from the maximization (A6.55) is u.s.c. This property implies that the correspondence has a closed graph in $P_x \times P_y{}^i \times Z \times X^i \times X_x{}^i \times X_y{}^i$. Consequently the inverse correspondence, having the mapping C^i: $P_x \times Z \times X^i \rightarrow X_x{}^i \times P_y{}^i$, has the same closed graph, and is u.s.c. ■

Consider the vector $(p_x{}^*, y^*)$, a pair of component vectors of the public competitive equilibrium (w^*, p^*, T^*). For a given vector $(\underline{x} + J)$, for consumer i the correspondence C^i gives $C^i(p_x{}^*, y^*, \cdot) = (x^{i*},\ p_y{}^{i*})$, and $C^i(p_x{}^{**}{}_{-i}, y^{**}{}_{-i}, \cdot) = (x^{i**}{}_{-i}, p_y{}^{i**}{}_{-i})$. Similarly, for another vector (p_x', y') of interest, we have $C^i(p_x',\ y',\ \cdot) = (x'^i,\ p_y'^i)$. The sequence of points

$(p_x', y') = \theta(p_x{}^{**}{}_{-i}, y^{**}{}_{-i}) + (1-\theta)(p_x{}^*, y^*)$, with $0 \leq \theta \leq \theta^* \leq 1$, provides the path of integration for the following integral, in which we write $p_y{}^i(\theta)$ to represent a value of $p_y{}^i$ provided by the correspondence C^i at the indicated value of θ in this path. At each such point (p_x', y'), equation (A6.54) gives us $T_j'^i(\theta)$ from y_j'. The end of this path θ^* can be less than one because of the admissibility requirement.

T.7. The VCG tax S^i for consumer i is the following expression:

$$S^i = \sum_{i' \neq i} \int_0^{\theta^*} \sum_j \left(\frac{p_{yj}^{i'}(\theta)}{p_{x1}} - T_j^{i'}(\theta) \right) d\theta \,, \qquad \text{(A6.58)}$$

where $p_y{}^i(\theta)$ is a component vector of $C^i(p_x', y', \cdot) = (x'^i, p_y'^i)$, and $(p_x', y') = \theta(p_x{}^{**}{}_{-i}, y^{**}{}_{-i}) + (1-\theta)(p_x{}^*, y^*)$, with $0 \leq \theta \leq \theta^* \leq 1$.

The amount of consumer i's VCG tax (A6.58) is a measure of the willingness of consumers $i' \neq i$ to pay for increased output of public goods, mapped by prices along a line integral into an amount of value in the unit of account. It is similar to a Divisia index number that estimates a compensating/equivalent variation, but is not precisely either a compensating or equivalent variation.

We have not yet fully defined this tax, however, because the consumers' individual prices $p_{yj}{}^i$ of public goods represent an element of a correspondence that is not necessarily single-valued. At a utility-maximizing point on a budget constraint, if the derivatives of utility are continuous at this point, it is elementary that if the consumer i acts as a price taker then $U_{yj}{}^i/U_{x1}{}^i = p_{yj}{}^i/p_{x1}$, where the subscripts of the U^i indicate partial derivatives. Conversely, at an arbitrarily chosen point on a budget constraint, we can *define* $p_{yj}{}^i$ to be the product $p_{x1}U_{yj}{}^i/U_{x1}{}^i$. For the evaluation of each integral in (A6.58), we need a value of $p_{yj}{}^i$ at each point on the path of integration. Although this value was a Lindahl price in the development of Theorem 4, we no longer view the consumer as a price taker for this price, so we rename it to avoid confusion. Hence, to evaluate these integrals, we use

C.18. $\forall\, i$ and $\forall\, w'$, consumer i's *marginal valuation of public good* y_j is $p_{yj}{}^i = p_{x1}U_{yj}{}^i/U_{x1}{}^i$.

However, if a consumer's budget line touches or intersects a node in an indifference surface at a value y_j', at which the derivative $U_{yj}^{\ i}$ does not exist, we require a clear definition of the integrands of (A6.58).

To anticipate the general nature of the proper way to meet this requirement, consider the case of an economy with one private good and one public good. What a consumer is willing to pay to obtain more of a public good we would measure by the derivative from the right at that point, which by the convexity of preferences (quasi-concave utility) is less than or equal in absolute value to the derivative from the left. In the case of multiple public goods, we must find a counterpart to the 'derivative from the right' in the subderivative of U^i at a nodal point y_j'. After some further preliminaries, we shall deal with that problem using Lemma 15.

Along with the VCG tax, we also assume a refund r^i to each consumer. The refund has two parts, of which the first is of substantially the same form as S^i. The two parts together provide an aggregate refund of all VCG taxes collected in a manner that contributes to the aim of a weak version of incentive compatibility (see Section A6.3).

T.8. Denote by $S_{-i}^{\ i'}$ the VCG tax for consumer i' in the i-abstaining economy. Each consumer's *refund* is the sum of two parts: $r^i = r_1^{\ i} + r_2^{\ i}$. Part one is

$$r_1^{\ i} = f_1(N, \omega) \textstyle\sum_{i' \neq i} S_{-i}^{\ i'} \tag{A6.59a}$$

where $2/N \geq f_1(N, \omega) \approx 1/N$ is a function of N and of a fixed vector ω of other parameters of the economy. Part two is

$$r_2^{\ i} = f_2(w^* - w^{**}_{-i}, N, \omega) \textstyle\sum_{i'} (S^{i'} - r_1^{\ i'}) \tag{A6.59b}$$

where $f_2(\cdot, \cdot, \cdot)$ is a correspondence, u.s.c., mapping its arguments into $\mathbb{R}^1$.

The scalar J^i is a trial value for $(r^i - S^i)$, where r^i is itself a two-part quantity. The refund r^i is the sum of two numbers, the first independent of i's preferences and endowment and the second tailored either to (weak) incentive compatibility or to exact budget balance. The two aims of incentive compatibility and exact budget balance cannot be achieved simultaneously. However, I show in Section A6.3 that a form of incentive compatibility is compatible with a high order of approximation to the budget balance, or exact budget balance with a high order of approximation to incentive compatibility, using variations of either of the formulae of T.8. In the interest of brevity, (A6.59a) and (A6.59b) present a general form that encompasses these variations. The argument that follows applies equally to all the variations of interest, where we disregard errors of approximation.

T.9. Consumer i's *message* is a vector $m^i \in M$ of parameters of U^i consistent with A.3-A.5. The set of all admissible messages from a consumer is $M \in \mathbb{R}^b$. The message vector m^i has $b < \infty$ components, enough to specify U^i to within an affine transformation. The set of messages from N consumers is $m = (m^1, \ldots, m^N) \in M \times \ldots \times M = M^N$. The messages are *truthful*, in that the U^i's that they specify are the consumers' actual U^i's.

T.10. The *VCG mechanism* is a function F: $M^N \times X \rightarrow \mathcal{W} \times P \times \mathrm{A}$, a set of consumer messages m, a *rule*, an equilibrium (w', p', T'), and a set of VCG taxes and refunds (S', r'), where $F(m, \underline{x}) = (w', p', T', S', r')$ and where $r' - S' = J$. A *central agent* uses the messages, the rule, and the assumed prior knowledge of all $\underline{x}^i$, to implement the mechanism. The rule selects a single-valued equilibrium whenever the equilibrium correspondence is set-valued. The mechanism $F(m, \underline{x})$ is *successful* if $F(m, \underline{x}) = (w^*, p^*, T^*, S^*, r^*)$, a public competitive equilibrium.

Although the two-part refund balances the mechanism's budget, for each individual consumer i it will usually be true that $S^i \neq r^i$, so that the consumer's total tax bill can differ from T^i. This discrepancy displaces consumers' budgets and therefore affects their marginal valuations $p_{yj}{}^i$. This effect is our main concern in establishing the existence of equilibrium, because it implies a complicating difference between a VCG tax system and that used in proving Theorem 4. Moreover, the continuity properties of the VCG tax system are not equivalent to those of the simpler system of equations (A6.53) and (A6.54). Our concern now is to establish that, for each pair $(\mathcal{W}^*, \mathcal{W}^{**}{}_{-i})$, each integral in (A6.58) is well-defined and is u.s.c. in the vectors of variables p_x, y', and $\underline{x}^{i'} + J^{i'}$, with which the valuations $p_{yj}{}^{i'}$ in each integrand of (A6.58) have a correspondence. Also, the limits of integration of an integral in (A6.58) have a correspondence with $\underline{x}^{i'} + J^{i'}$.

The VCG mechanism requires each consumer i to provide a message $m^i \in M$ so that the central agent can evaluate $p_y{}^i = p_{x1} U_{yj}{}^i / U_{x1}{}^i$ on the feasible set of allocations, wherever these derivatives exist, and to specify the subderivative of U^i otherwise. That is, the central agent has the correspondence C^i with which to evaluate $p_y{}^i$. Now, given the definition of $p_y{}^i$, the component vector $p_y{}^i$ of the correspondence $C^i(p_x, y', \underline{x}^i + J^i)$ will have multiple values if consumer i's budget constraint touches a node of $U^i(x^i; y)$. The integral defining the VCG tax is nevertheless well-defined.

We turn now to the definition of the VCG tax (A6.58) and to the proof of its key properties. We note that the general assumptions about preferences A.1-A.7 do not rule out Giffen goods among the public goods, so that the trial budget hyperplane could intersect a continuum of nodes. This case would imply that the graph gr(C^i) of C^i, the correspondence of Lemma 14, has interior points, with a dimensionality that may be less than or equal to that of the hyperplane.

Consider now the set $\mathbb{C}^i$ of all well-behaved, almost-everywhere-continuous correspondences c^i: $P_x \times Z \times X^i \rightarrow X_x{}^i \times P_y{}^i$ whose graphs have no interior points. That is,

> $\mathbb{C}^i = \{c^i \mid \text{dom}(c^i) = \text{dom}(C^i);\ \text{gr}(c^i) \subseteq \text{gr}(C^i);\ \text{gr}(c^i)$ is closed; for each point in dom(C^i) at which int[gr(C^i)] $\neq \varnothing$, c^i is single-valued, continuous, and continuously differentiable; for each other point in dom(C^i), $c^i = C^i\}$.

Note that each region of gr(C^i) that has an interior is closed, because gr(C^i) is closed. A point in dom(C^i) that is a projection of a point that is in such a region, but is not in its interior, may be a discontinuity point of C^i. If so, $\exists\ c^i \in \mathbb{C}^i$ that have discontinuities at the same point. Evidently c^i is u.s.c.

Now $\forall\ c^{i'} \in \mathbb{C}^{i'}$ we define the integral

$$ {}_cL^i = \sum_{i' \neq i} \int_0^{\theta^*} \sum_j \left(\frac{{}_c p_{yj}^{i'}(\theta)}{p_{x1}} - t^{i'}_j(\theta) \right) d\theta \qquad \text{(A6.60)}$$

where ${}_c p_y{}^{i'}(\theta)$ is a component vector of $c^{i'}(p_x', y', \cdot) = (x'^{i'}, p_y{}'^{i'})$, where $(p_x', y') = \theta(p_x{}^{**}{}_{-i}, y^{**}{}_{-i}) + (1-\theta)(p_x{}^*, y^*)$, with $0 \leq \theta \leq \theta^* \leq 1$.

This step leads to the following result.

Lemma 15. The set $\mathbb{L}^i$ of all ${}_cL^i$, for $c^i \in \mathbb{C}^i$, has a greatest lower bound (g.l.b.) that is contained in $\mathbb{L}^i$, so that, for each pair of endpoints (p_x^*, y^*) and $(p_x^{**}{}_{-i}, y^{**}{}_{-i})$, $\min[{}_cL^i \in \mathbb{L}^i]$ exists.

Proof: The union $\cup c^i$ of all $c^i \in \mathbb{C}^i$ is dense. Moreover, because $\exists$ $c^i \in \mathbb{C}^i$ that have discontinuities at each discontinuity point of C^i, $\cup c^i = C^i$. Because $\mathrm{gr}(C^i)$ is closed, it follows that $\cup\, \mathrm{gr}(c^i)$ is closed, and so therefore is the set $\mathbb{L}^i$. Inasmuch as the g.l.b. of a closed set is in the set, this completes the proof. ■

Then let $L^i = \min[{}_cL^i \in \mathbb{L}^i]$, and let $L^{i'}$ be the integral in (A6.58), where now $p_{yj}^{i'}$ has the value ${}_cp_{yj}^{i'}$ used for ${}_cL^i$ in (A6.60). These steps provide the basis for the following results.

Lemma 16. The integrand of (A6.58) is bounded.

Proof: The marginal valuations $p_{yj}^{i'}$ in the integrand are elements of the simplex P, and so are bounded. Because p_{x1} is bounded away from zero, the ratio $p_{yj}^{i'}/p_{x1}$ is bounded. All individual endowments are finite, so that, by definition, all the T^i are bounded. Hence, the integrand is bounded. ■

Lemma 15 and Lemma 16 hold for every admissible trial vector J of VCG taxes and refunds. Then we have

Lemma 17. Given a vector of endowments $\underline{x}$ and an admissible trial vector J, $\forall\, i$ there is a pair of public competitive equilibria with component vectors $(p_x^{**}{}_{-i}, y^{**}{}_{-i}, \cdot)$ and $(p_x^*, y^*, \cdot)$, for which the integral (A6.58) is a well-defined, bounded Riemann integral.

Proof: By Corollary 1 and T.10, the upper and lower bounds of integration of (A6.56) exist and are single-valued. By Lemma 14, the integrand is u.s.c. in the variable of integration. By the construction of c^i and by Lemmas 15 and 16, the integrand of (A6.58) is a bounded, single-valued function almost everywhere. ■

Lemma 18. The VCG tax (A6.58) is u.s.c. and bounded in $(\underline{x} + J)$.

Proof: The prices $p_{yj}^{i'}$ in the integrand are continuous single-valued functions of p_x, $\underline{x}^{i'} + J^{i'}$, and y' almost everywhere. (Roberts and Varberg,

1973, p. 116-17), which implies that the integral in (A6.58) is continuous at its lower and upper limits. These limits, implicitly, are $(p_x^*, y^*, \cdot)$ and $(p_x^{**}{}_{-i'}, y^{**}{}_{-i'}, \cdot)$. By construction, $p_{yj}^{i'}$ is u.s.c. in p_x, $\underline{x}^{i'}$, $J^{i'}$, and y', which except for $\underline{x}^{i'}$ vary continuously over the range of integration. By Corollary 1, the equilibrium vectors $(p_x^*, y^*, \cdot)$ and $(p_x^{**}{}_{-i'}, y^{**}{}_{-i'}, \cdot)$ are u.s.c. in initial endowments, and hence in $\underline{x} + J$. Now inasmuch as the integrand of (A6.58) is u.s.c. in the variables of interest, as are the limits of integration, the value of the integral is u.s.c. as claimed. By Lemma 16 it is bounded. ■

It follows that the graph of the correspondence from $(\underline{x} + J)$ to S^i is compact.

Lemma 19. The refunds r^i are u.s.c. in $(\underline{x} + J)$.

Proof: Immediate, by definition, from (A6.59a) and (A6.59b), and from Lemma 18.

T.11. If there is a consumer i' such that, for $\theta^* = 1$, $\underline{x}^{i'} - T^{i'} - S^{i'} + r^{i'} < \underline{\underline{x}}^0$, find the maximum value $\theta^* < 1$ such that $\forall\, i$, $\exists\, (S^{i*}, r^{i*})$ such that $\underline{x}^i - T^{i*} - S^{i*} + r^{i*} \geq \underline{\underline{x}}^0$. Then θ^* is the upper bound of the integral (A6.58) $\forall\, i$, and the central agent chooses an admissible pair of vectors (S^*, r^*), that is, a pair such that $\forall\, i$, $(-T^{i*} - S^{i*} + r^{i*}) \in \mathbb{A}^i$.

Lemma 20: The set of VCG taxes/refunds is compact.

Proof: The correspondences considered in Lemmas 18 and 19, from $(\underline{x} + J)$ to S^i and to r^i, are u.s.c., which implies that the set of all $(r^i - S^i)$ is closed. By T.5 and T.11, $(r^1 - S^1, \ldots, r^N - S^N) \in \mathbb{A}$, which is compact. ■

Now consider an economy with a given technology Z, a given set of endowments $\underline{x}$, and with the tax equations (A6.53), (A6.54), and (A6.58). Choose an arbitrary value J, representing an N-vector of admissible terms $(r^i - S^i)$. By Theorem 4, there is a public competitive equilibrium. By Lemma 18, this equilibrium, with its particular values of p_x^* and y^*, implies an admissible pair of values S^i and r^i. These steps imply a mapping $\mathbb{A} \to \mathbb{A}$, a correspondence that is u.s.c., where $\mathbb{A}$ is compact and convex. Then, by the Kakutani fixed-point theorem, it has a fixed point.

By construction, this fixed point corresponds to a public competitive equilibrium. We have proved

Theorem 5. In an economy with messages T.9 and with a VCG mechanism T.10, a public competitive equilibrium exists and the mechanism is successful.

Discussion: This proof establishes that a public competitive equilibrium exists when the VCG tax augments the tax formulas (A6.53) and (A6.54). Of course, the integral (A6.58) can be set-valued. In a similar vein, the equilibrium of an economy that has only private goods may also be set-valued. Unlike a private goods economy, however, the present economy has a central agent who can have a rule for selection of an equilibrium.

The theorem does not establish that the VCG tax is incentive-compatible under the general conditions assumed here, so that T.9's truthfulness assumption might not hold, and therefore the VCG mechanism might not be successful. That it is successful except for the budget-balance problem if consumers provide the mechanism with their true functions, as be will the case when utility functions are separable, is now standard in the literature. See Green and Laffont [1977]. The revised mechanism used in Section A6.3 deals with income effects effectively for a simplified economy and, while not strictly successful, approximates success to a high order of approximation. It appears that the result can be generalized to an economy like that in this section, but this further result is not yet established.

A6.5 CHOICES OVER MULTIPLE DISCRETE OPTIONS

A6.5.A Introduction and Summary

In contrast to the public choice literature on majority voting, coalitions, and other related topics, the literature on demand-revealing processes has focused almost exclusively on theoretically ideal cases without regard to applicability. In particular, among other peculiarities of this literature, there has been little attention paid to the use of plausible restrictions on consumer preferences or to plausible use of information on consumer wealth and preferences. In the light of the pessimistic tone of many of the results on incentive compatibility, such restrictions and information deserve attention. This section provides examples of results obtainable from such an approach.

For the case of multiple public goods whose quantities are continuous variables (that is, elements of $\mathbb{R}^+$), I prove in Section A6.4 the existence of efficient equilibrium in a general equilibrium model with the VCG mechanism. The case considered departs from the conventional non-parametric premise by using a proportional wealth tax. This section generalizes this result to include the case in which the amount of a public good does not vary on a continuum, but offers only two or more discrete choices. The VCG pivotal mechanism is the variant of interest for such a good. The analysis here also corrects some misunderstandings about the pivotal mechanism and presents several results, of which some parallel those for the continuous case and some are distinct and different. For the most striking results, it abandons the non-parametric premise entirely, using the legislative structure set out in Chapters 2 and 3 to obtain information about consumer preferences. The basic existence result holds up, although under less general conditions, and in addition several detailed features emerge concerning efficiency and incentive compatibility. The analysis emphasizes those features of the VCG pivotal mechanism that depend on income effects, which have been excluded by assumption from most of the literature on this mechanism. Some of the desirable features of the mechanism hold whether or not there are income effects, whereas other desirable features depend on the absence of such effects.

In particular, for pairwise choices we find that the VCG pivotal mechanism is 'decisive,' meaning that, contrary to the claim of Green and Laffont (1977b), it always has an equilibrium and it is incentive compatible. (When consumers have positive income effects, however, it can fail to choose a Pareto-efficient outcome.) We then show that when we use a representative legislature, as proposed in Chapter 3, to assess approximate Lindahl taxes and transfers, the mechanism obtains Pareto-efficient outcomes in the ensuing referendum.

A6.5.B Definitions and Notation

A6.5.B.1 Production and Consumption

Throughout this section I assume that the options with respect to public goods are represented not by quantities of h public goods but rather by h' distinct alternatives, $y_1, y_2, \ldots, y_{h'}$, to the status quo, y^0. For simplicity I assume in this section that the economy has just one private good x, which is the numeraire, so that $p_x = 1$.

In the case of a public good whose level of output, if not zero, is predetermined, profit maximization and the equality of the good's price to a marginal rate of transformation are preserved, whereas this price need not necessarily equal the sum of individual marginal rates of substitution. Instead it must be compared with the sum of the discrete amounts of private wealth households are willing to give up (that is, with their willingness to pay), to have the public good produced. If a public good's predetermined size is optimal, however, it will of course also satisfy the marginal first- and second-order conditions for optimality. In that case (and in almost all other cases), such a project will be valued above its cost, in terms of the discrete amounts that households are willing to pay for it, so that it can make all households better off.

For notational simplicity, without loss of generality we scale each y_j so that either $y_j = 0$ or $y_j = 1$, for $j > 0$. Thus, for $j > 0$, we have $T_j^i = p_{yj} y_j = p_{yj}$, the last equality holding if $y_j = 1$.

A6.5.B.2 Taxes

Equations (A6.53) and (A6.54) express taxes in units of the private good. (It may be either a single good or a basket of goods.) Henceforward we will also express each consumer's remaining vector of private goods, after actual or potential taxes, in these units.

D.1. The *after-tax private wealth* of each consumer i is

$$\underline{\chi}^i = \underline{x}^i - T^i - S^i. \tag{A6.61}$$

To proceed further, we will use indirect utility functions. As a textbook proposition, one may derive directly, from constrained maximization of the utility function $U^i(x^i; y_j)$, an indirect utility function whose arguments depend on the constraints. For present purposes we view y_j as a constraint, so that it remains as an argument of indirect utility. The taxes that it entails reduce consumer i's wealth from $\underline{x}^i$ to $\underline{\chi}^i$, which determines i's budget constraint. Hence, we have $(\underline{\chi}^i; y_j)$ as arguments of the indirect utility function. Its continuity and differentiability in $\underline{\chi}^i$ follow from A.5 and A.8.

D.2. Denote the *indirect utility function for consumer i* by $V^i(\underline{\chi}^i; y_j)$.

A6.5.B.3 The Attributes of Public Goods

Those publicly provided goods that have no direct consumer utility but increase private wealth and consumption, such as roadways, environmentally benign hydroelectric projects with flood control, and so on can be ranked by their effect on private wealth alone. Similarly, there may be projects whose effect on utility is equivalent to this first type of project, and which may be described as perfect substitutes for private wealth. Both of these types create no difficulties for a demand-revealing process, and will be dealt with briefly. By contrast, most public projects have attributes that make them imperfect substitutes for wealth. These attributes, which we will refer to as 'intangible', enter directly into utility functions. Examples include national or regional improvements in air and water quality, new technology for police work that impinges on civil liberties, and decisions about intervention abroad to promote stability and democracy. These, though costly, may in some cases have little measurable positive effect on private wealth, and yet consumers may be willing to sacrifice some wealth to have their preferred public goods of this kind. These public goods, our principal concern, are the ones that present appreciable difficulties for demand revealing processes.

Our public goods are discrete projects or issues, as already noted. Some single goods, such as candidates for president, are mutually exclusive; they cannot appear together in a combined package of goods. After the status quo y^0 and incremental to it, the first several of the goods are individual goods, taken singly; next come all permissible pairs of these goods, then all permissible groups of three, and so on, until y_h represents the adoption of a maximum-sized permissible set of goods simultaneously accepted. Under this convention, we may refer to y_j as package y_j. Given this notation and the scaling of each y_j, we have:

D.3. Denote by $\mathcal{Y}$ the set of packages y_j of public goods, $j = 0, 1, \ldots, h$. Then $T^i = T_j^i$ and

$$\underline{\chi}^i = \underline{x}^i - T_j^i - S^i \qquad \text{(A6.62)}$$

Denote consumer i's *after-tax private wealth in the status quo* by $\underline{\chi}_0{}^i$. Denote consumer i's share of the *incremental cost u_j of y_j compared to the status quo* by $\Delta T_j^i = T_j^i - T_0{}^i$, where $\sum_i \Delta T_j^i = u_j$. The allocation $w_0 = (\underline{\chi}_0, y_0)$ represents the status quo, containing a package of public goods whose quantities are continuous variables. There is a *lower bound at bankruptcy* for $\underline{\chi}^i$; denote this lower bound by $\underline{\underline{\chi}}^i = \underline{\underline{x}}^i$.

Without loss of generality, we normalize V^i by setting $V^i(\underline{\underline{\chi}}^i; y_0) = 0$.

D.4. A consumer $i \in I \subset \{1, \ldots, N\}$ iff $V^i(\underline{x}_0{}^i - \Delta T_j{}^i; y_j) > V^i(\underline{x}_0{}^i; y_0)$ and is said *to favor public good* y_j. A consumer $i' \in I' \subset \{1, \ldots, N\}$ iff $V^{i'}(\underline{x}_0{}^{i'} - \Delta T_j{}^{i'}; y_j) < V^{i'}(\underline{x}_0{}^{i'}; y_0)$ and is said *to oppose public good* y_j.

D.5. Denote by $\underline{x}_j{}^i$ the value of $\underline{x}^i$ such that $V^i(\underline{x}_j{}^i; y_j) = V^i(\underline{x}_0{}^i; y_0)$, and by $\underline{x}_{0j}{}^i$ the value of $\underline{x}^i$ such that $V^i(\underline{x}_0{}^i - \Delta T_j{}^i; y_j) = V^i(\underline{x}_{0j}{}^i; y_0)$.

With modest loss of generality, we assume that, by comparison with the options under consideration before assessing package-related taxes, there is no fate worse than bankruptcy, and no option that makes bankruptcy worthwhile. Specifically,

D.6. $\forall\, j$ and $\forall\, i$, (a) $V^i(\underline{x}_0{}^i - T_j{}^i; y_j) > 0$, and (b) $V^i(\underline{\underline{x}}^i; y_j) \leq 0$.

Figure A6.1 shows the indirect utility function $V^i(\underline{x}^i; y_j)$, with wealth $\underline{x}^i$ on the horizontal axis and with an intangible public good y_j as a shift variable, for the case where its adoption makes the consumer better off. Utility level w_0 is the level that is produced by the status quo $(\underline{x}_0{}^i, y_0)$, and w_1 is the utility level produced by $(\underline{x}_0{}^i - \Delta T_j{}^i, y_1)$, that is, for when y_1, with its tax package, is adopted. For our main results we would not need to make an assumption about the slope of the upper curve relative to that of the lower curve. However, some proofs would have to be repeated with inequalities reversed if there is no restriction. Therefore we apply the restriction D.8 that every public good is a normal good (not an inferior good) in the interest of brevity, without loss of generality. The borderline case between the two types of good we will dispose of quickly in Subsection A6.5.B.6.

D.7. Consumer i's *willingness-to-pay* (w.t.p.$_j{}^i$), in addition to $\Delta T_j{}^i$, to have y_j adopted in preference to y_0 is the quantity $\underline{x}_0{}^i - \underline{x}_j{}^i - \Delta T_j{}^i$. The w.t.p.$_0{}^{i'}$ of consumer i' for y_j, that is, the negative of the amount i' is willing to pay to keep y_0 in preference to y_j with its $\Delta T_j{}^{i'}$, is the quantity $\underline{x}_{0j}{}^{i'} - \underline{x}_0{}^{i'}$.

D.8. Each w.t.p.$_j{}^i$ is strictly increasing in wealth $\underline{x}_0{}^i$, and each w.t.p.$_0{}^{i'}$ is strictly increasing in wealth $\underline{x}_0{}^{i'}$.

D.9. The *VCG mechanism choice* between a pair of packages (y_j, y_0), is denoted by $\chi(y_j, y_0, \underline{x}_0)$. Specifically, $\chi(y_j, y_0, \underline{x}_0) = y_j$ when

$$\textstyle\sum_i (\text{w.t.p.}_j{}^i) + \sum_{i'} (\text{w.t.p.}_0{}^{i'}) > 0 \qquad \text{(A6.63a)}$$

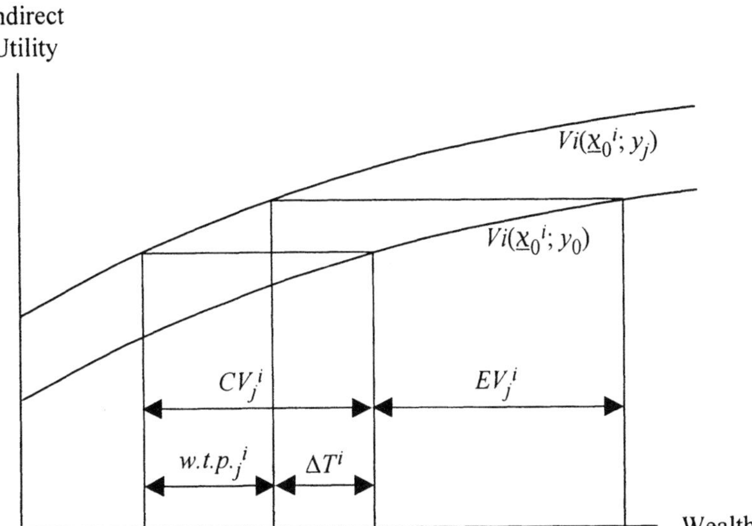

Figure 6A.1 Indirect utility as a function of wealth and public goods

whereas $\chi(y_j, y_0, \underline{x}_0) = y_0$ when

$$\textstyle\sum_i (\text{w.t.p.}_j{}^i) + \sum_{i'} (\text{w.t.p.}_0{}^{i'}) < 0 \qquad \text{(A6.63b)}$$

When the sum of these quantities is zero, (when there is a 'tie'), χ chooses between y_0 and y_j, by a random process. Information about the criterion values comes to the election mechanism from consumers as *messages*.

Note that the criterion described in (A6.63a) and (A6.63b) is simply $\sum_{i*}$ w.t.p.$_j{}^{i*}$, for $i* \in \{1, \ldots, N\}$. That is, to have $\chi = y_j$, those who favor the package must be willing to pay their own tax increments $\Delta T_j{}^i$ plus the sum of the x-equivalent of the direct loss of utility of those who oppose the package, given their tax increments $\Delta T_j{}^{i'}$.

D.10. $\forall\, i* \in \{1, \ldots, N\}$, if $V^{i*}(\underline{x}_j{}^{i*}; y_j) = V^i(\underline{x}_0{}^{i*}; y_0)$, then the amount $\underline{x}_j{}^{i*} - \underline{x}_0{}^{i*}$ is a *compensating variation* (CV$_j{}^{i*}$) for the substitution of y_j for y_0.

Note that CV_j^{i*} is defined independently of ΔT_j^{i*}. For each consumer $i \in \mathbb{I}$, $\text{w.t.p.}_j^{i} = -\text{CV}_j^{i} - \Delta T_j^{i}$.

D.11. $\forall\, i^* \in \{1, \ldots, N\}$, if $V^{i*}(\underline{x}_{0j}^{i*}; y_0) = V^{i}(\underline{x}_0^{i*} - \Delta T_j^{i*}; y_j)$, then the amount $\underline{x}_{0j}^{i*} - \underline{x}_0^{i*}$ is an *equivalent variation* (EV_j^{i*}) for the substitution of $(y_j, \Delta T_j^{i*})$ for y_0.

For each consumer $i' \in I'$, $\text{w.t.p.}_j^{i'} = \text{EV}_j^{i'}$, which, by D.11, is tax-inclusive.

Under the VCG mechanism, $\forall\, i^* \in \{1, \ldots, N\}$, consumer i^* pays the following added tax assessment.

D.12. The *VCG tax* S^i on consumer i^* is zero if consumer i^* opposes $\chi(y_j, y_0, \underline{x}_0)$. This tax is also zero if consumer i^* favors $\chi(y_j, y_0, \underline{x}_0)$, and if, when we arbitrarily set $\text{w.t.p.}_j^{i*} = 0$, $\chi(y_j, y_0, \underline{x}_0)$ would remain unchanged. If $\chi(y_j, y_0, \underline{x}_0)$ would be reversed when we set $\text{w.t.p.}_j^{i*} = 0$, however, the VCG tax on consumer i^* is the absolute value of the left-hand side of (A6.63a) when $\text{w.t.p.}_j^{i*} = 0$.

From this point forward we consider multiple packages j, j', so that our notation must include subscripts for the tax packages wherever there can be doubt about the meaning of the tax package.

D.13. A *compensated VCG mechanism* (*CVCG*), represented by the choice function $\chi_C(\mathcal{Y}, \Delta T, \underline{x}_0)$, includes a predetermined compensated tax package with each public goods decision, such that $\forall\, i^* \in \{1, \ldots, N\}$, the product $\Delta T_j^{i*} \cdot \text{CV}_j^{i*} < 0$, and such that $V^{i*}(\underline{x}_0^{i*} - \Delta T_C^{i*}; \chi_C) \geq V^{i*}(\underline{x}_0^{i*} - \Delta T_j^{i*}; y_j)$, $\forall\, y_j \in \mathcal{Y}$, where $\sum_j \Delta T_j^{i*} = u_j$. If for some j and $\forall\, i^*$, $V^{i*}(\underline{x}_0^{i*} - \Delta T_C^{i*}; \chi_C) = V^{i*}(\underline{x}_0^{i*} - \Delta T_j^{i*}; y_j)$, then χ_C chooses between χ_C and y_j by a random process.

The predetermined tax package comes from the legislative procedure of Chapter 3, where for D.13 to apply, the population subgroups must be homogeneous. With this rule, if the total of negative CV_j^{i*} exceeds in absolute value the total of positive CV_j^{i*} for a package y_j by a wide enough margin to cover the cost of the package with room to spare, for $j > 0$, consumers in the aggregate are willing to pay its cost and have something left over. Inasmuch as the tax package compensates all losers and divides this net gain among all consumers, the decision χ_C receives unanimous agreement.

D.14. For a subset $\mathcal{Y} \subset \mathcal{Y}$ of packages, for $y_j \in \mathcal{Y}$ let RV_j^{i*} denote a *ranking variation*, where, for each $i^* \in \{1, \ldots, N\}$, the RV_j^{i*} satisfy the dual constraints $\sum_{j\in \mathcal{Y}} \mathrm{RV}_j^{i*} = 0$ and $\forall\, y_j, y_{j'} \in \mathcal{Y}$, $V^{i*}(\underline{x}_0{}^{i*} - \mathrm{RV}_j^{i*}; y_j) = V^{i*}(\underline{x}_0{}^{i*} - \mathrm{RV}_{j'}^{i*}; y_{j'})$.

Note that the sign convention for RV_j^{i*} reverses that of CV_j^{i*} and EV_j^{i*}. It adjusts one package by a portion of the CV_j^{i*} and adjusts the other package by a portion of the EV_j^{i*}, to a point where i^* is indifferent between the packages.

D.15. A *cardinal-ranking procedure* (CRP) ranks the members of a subset of packages $\mathcal{Y}^+$ on the cardinal scale whose value for each $y_j \in \mathcal{Y}^+$ is $\sum_{i*}\mathrm{RV}_j^{i*}$.

D.16. A *semi-compensated VCG mechanism* (SCVCG) imitates a CVCG using approximate information about consumer indirect utility functions $V^{i*}(\cdot;\cdot)$.

The CRP will form an integral part of the CVCG and of the SCVCG. However, it provides an intermediate step that by itself is insufficient to obtain a final ranking.

D.17. A VCG-related mechanism with choice function χ_μ is *decisive* iff, for every pair (y_j, y_0), $\forall\, \underline{x}_0$ and $\forall\, V^i$ derived from U^i that satisfy A.5-A.8, $\chi_\mu([y_j, y_0], \Delta T, \underline{x}_0) \neq \varnothing$.

D.18. A mechanism with choice function χ_μ is *fully decisive* iff, for every finite set $\mathcal{Y}$ of packages, $\chi_\mu(\mathcal{Y}, \Delta T, \underline{x}_0) \neq \varnothing$. The mechanism is *efficient* if, where $\chi_\mu(\mathcal{Y}, \Delta T, \underline{x}_0) = y_{j'}$, there is no y_j such that $\chi_\mu([y_j, y_{j'}], \Delta T, \underline{x}_0) = y_j$, except for random selection in case of ties.

A6.5.B.4 Precise and Approximate Lindahl Taxes and Transfers

When tax assessments to finance public goods packages are unrelated to household values of $\mathrm{w.t.p.}_j{}^i$, the VCG mechanism has unsatisfactory properties for packages with intangible attributes. Therefore we consider tax assessments that are less than or equal to $\mathrm{w.t.p.}_j{}^i$, presented in Chapter 2 as Lindahl taxes and transfers. For simplicity, assume at first that the population is partitioned into a number of homogeneous subgroups, within each of which all tangible and intangible values are identical.

D.19a. The voting population can be partitioned into a set of subgroups, each with multiple members who are identical with respect to wealth and preferences.

Suppose that there is an incentive-compatible mechanism to elicit the w.t.p.$_j^i$ of each member of an official legislature. The Election Commission must also learn the subgroup's wealth effect $d\mathrm{CV}/d\underline{x}_0$ for a proposed package. With this information, the Commission can design the desired set of Lindahl taxes and transfers.

Chapters 2 and 3 present an incentive-compatible mechanism to elicit w.t.p.$_j^i$ information from each member an official legislature. By construction, legislators have a strong incentive to provide accurate information. Using this information from official legislatures, the Election Commission will use a predetermined rule to set Lindahl taxes and transfers.

D.19b. The voting population can be partitioned into a set of subgroups, each with multiple members who are similar but not identical with respect to wealth and preferences, such that CVCG procedures for legislative information reduce the set of potentially winning packages to at most two packages.

If each population subgroup identified by their wealth and demographic characteristics does not have homogeneous valuations of a public good, a CVCG is impossible. In this case, when facing multiple packages the otherwise unmodified VCG mechanism could go astray. A set of taxes and transfers designed to imitate a CVCG will only approximately succeed if there is no way to identify values objectively within the group, that is, if there is no incentive-compatible way to subdivide the groups to make their valuations homogeneous. To choose the right public goods package requires information about every consumer's CV, even though those who oppose a package report their EV's rather than their CV's as w.t.p.$_j^{i'}$ in response to the mechanism. Therefore, the legislative procedure must estimate the difference between CV and EV for each such consumer. That is, the SCVCG must be used to approximate a CVCG.

In such cases the Election Commission needs information about variability within subgroups of w.t.p.$_j^i$ and of the 'income effect'—the effect of a change in wealth on each household's valuation of the public good. This information can be necessary for optimal decisions if the within-group variability is large enough to be a factor. The Statistical Advisory Committee can calculate the probability of error in the choice of the top two candidate packages by using standard statistical methods, as illustrated by Green and Laffont (1977a).

Using each subgroup of the legislature separately, the Statistical Advisory Committee must not only estimate the subgroup's wealth effect $d\text{CV}/d\underline{x}_0$ for each package, but also the covariance of this derivative with w.t.p.$_j^i$, among subgroup members. With these estimates, the Election Commission estimates $\text{CV}_j^{i'}$ for each consumer i' who opposes the package j, based on that consumer's stated w.t.p.$_j^{i'}$ to defeat j.

A6.5.B.5 Choice Among Multiple Packages

Suppose now that D.19a holds and that the Election Commission obtains w.t.p.$_j^i$ information, plus income effects, from the official legislatures. The Election Commission can establish a preliminary ranking of several alternative packages in each of several ways: for example, by comparing their sums of CV's, their sums of w.t.p.$_j^i$, or their sums of EV's. Inasmuch as changes in wealth can affect w.t.p.$_j^i$'s for different packages differently, these three sets of sums may disagree on the ranking. A set of rules about how the welfare gains conveyed by each package shall be distributed among households can generate its own ranking, which may disagree with all the preceding rankings. This apparent anomaly is a kind of index-number problem.

It is less of an anomaly than it seems at first sight. Precisely the same 'anomaly' is commonplace in the private sector. If enough opera lovers can afford to patronize it, they can support a local opera company, whereas if these patrons lose much of their wealth to patrons of Grand Ole Opry because one major local industry collapses while another flourishes, the opera company will disband or go elsewhere. One can easily compile a long list of such examples.

Therefore, the mechanism for package selection must take into account how the gains provided by a package will be divided among households. It can happen that when two packages are unanimously preferred to the status quo, the ranking of the two relative to each other will depend upon the division of the gains. Consequently, the mechanism must specify both how gains are to be divided and the manner in which it chooses among multiple packages. This division must be independent of the w.t.p.$_j^i$ reported in a referendum by taxpaying households, if the mechanism is to achieve incentive compatibility.

Now, before considering further the roles of the legislatures and of the voting households in the procedures, consider first the overall combined approach in broad outline. Suppose that D.19a holds. Then the first step, using legislative information to devise a set of Lindahl taxes and transfers for each public goods package, and applying the concept of the CVCG, divides the set of packages into a subset $\mathcal{Y}^+$ that all households prefer to y_0 and another subset $\mathcal{Y}^-$, containing packages compared to which all households prefer y_0 or are indifferent. However, this step will not generally produce unanimous preferences in the comparison of every pair of such packages. If there is disagreement among households about which package is best, the Election Commission adjusts some of the taxes and transfers to obtain a unanimously agreed best $y_{j'}$.

Although many tax-allocation rules are possible, for simplicity we will consider only one such rule, or collection of rules, to illustrate the structure of the CVCG.

D.20a. When D.19a holds and there are multiple packages for consideration, the mechanism finds taxes and transfers that separate the packages into the two subsets $\mathcal{Y}^+$ and $\mathcal{Y}^-$. The latter, inferior group of packages disappears from further consideration. For each superior public goods package $y_j \in \mathcal{Y}^+$, its initial set of taxes and transfers will have $\Delta T_j^{i'} = -\mathrm{CV}_j^{i'} - \varepsilon$ for each subgroup of consumers i' who have $\mathrm{CV}_j^{i'} > 0$, with arbitrarily small ε. The mechanism prorates the quantity $[u_j + \sum_{i'}(\mathrm{CV}_j^{i'} + \varepsilon)]$ as ΔT_j^i among other consumers i in proportion to their (negative) values of CV_j^i. We assume that $\mathcal{Y}^+ \neq \varnothing$.

D.21a. When D.19a holds, among the superior subset $\mathcal{Y}^+$ of packages the mechanism applies the CRP to various subsets of $\mathcal{Y}^+$, and makes further tax adjustments $\Delta' T_j^i$ in addition to those of D.20a, as needed, in order to achieve a unanimous ranking of all $y_j \in \mathcal{Y}^+$ by consumers. Section 6.A.5.D presents a procedure for obtaining this ranking.

D.20b. When D.19b holds, the Election Commission applies the taxes and transfers of D.20a and 6.A.5.D, using average values for each subgroup of consumers as if each were homogeneous.

D.21b. When D.19b holds, the CRP ranking identifies $\mathcal{Y}^{++}$, the top two candidate packages of $\mathcal{Y}^+$, which, by D.19b, are unambiguous. The mechanism then applies the CRP to these two packages as a binary choice, and assesses a VCG tax as specified by D.12.

Because the rules for division of welfare gains can affect the choice of best package, these rules leave no discretion to the Election Commission, and are neutral among the members of the subset $\mathcal{Y}^{++}$ of packages. They use Lindahl taxes and transfers that harmonize with the other procedures.

To illustrate the solution, consider first the case of a two-consumer economy with two candidate packages unanimously favored over the status quo, of which y_1 would preferred by consumer 1 and y_2 would be preferred by the consumer 2 if the taxes to pay for each were initially set according to D.20a. Using D.14 and D.15, we tentatively modify the tax or transfer for each consumer. For consumer 1 we increase the tax share of package y_1 and reduce the tax share of package y_2 by the same number of dollars—for each \$$K$ added to consumer 1's tax to finance y_1 we sweeten the y_2 package for consumer 1 by \$$K$. Then we find that value of K such that consumer 1 is indifferent between y_1 and y_2. In parallel, we modify the tax package for consumer 2 by increasing the tax to finance y_2 by \$$K'$ and sweeten the y_1 package by \$$K'$, choosing that value of K' such that consumer 2 is indifferent between the two packages. The larger of K and K' determines the better package.

Then, for example, if $K' > K$, so that y_2 is better, the mechanism modifies consumer 1's tax packages by the full \$$K$ of the tentative modifications, plus κ of reduced tax or additional transfer to go with the y_2 package. The mechanism increases the y_2 tax package to consumer 2 by \$$K+\kappa$, and sweetens the y_1 package by \$$K$, which by construction leaves consumer 2 with a welfare gain from our choosing y_2 rather than y_1, as measured by what $CV_2{}^2$ would be if $(y_1, \underline{x}_1)$ were the status quo, of $2K' - 2K - \kappa$.

For three (or more) candidate packages, and many subgroups of consumers, the same procedure is applied in multiple form. That is, we tentatively modify all taxes and transfers to find the equal-utility combination at which the sum of tax reductions equals the sum of tax increases for each subgroup of consumers. Then for each package we sum over all consumers the new tax changes. The list of values of these sums ranks the packages. Because the modifications sum to zero for each consumer's taxes and transfers, one can readily verify that these numerical values provide a cardinal ranking of the public goods packages, that is, a ranking that is transitive. However, this ranking is preliminary, in that the tax modifications that lead to a unanimous ranking, set out in Section A6.5.D, may induce changes in the ranking.

Consider now the division of procedural steps between the legislatures and the population of voting households. If the role of the legislative information is too limited, and if the mechanism depends too much on messages from voting households, the mechanism can sometimes be manipulated. This possibility follows from the dependence of the outcome on the way that welfare gains are divided. Consumers who anticipate correctly how the final ranking of the elements of set Υ^{++} would play out under truthful reporting could influence it to their advantage by misrepresenting their preferences.

Therefore, we attempt a division of procedural steps that controls the agenda for consumer messages, and assesses VCG taxes S^i, in such a way as to achieve incentive compatibility. In particular, the legislative information fully determines and restricts the referendum agenda under pre-determined rules, while messages from voting consumers confirm the final choice and the indirect utility functions that underlie it, and determine the VCG tax assessments.

D.22. (1) Under either D.19a or D.19b, using legislative information, the Election Commission estimates the relevant CV_j^{i*} and RV_j^{i*}, in order to determine the tax sets under D.20a that separate the public goods packages into the sets Υ^+ and Υ^-, and then modifies the tax sets of the packages in Υ^{++} as specified by D.21a.

(2) The two most-preferred adjusted packages that, according to the official legislatures, are most certain to win then go to a confirming referendum by taxpaying consumers. Consumers $i*$ are asked to rank the packages and to state their $\mathrm{w.t.p.}_j^{i*}$ to obtain each of the packages in preference to each of the other packages below it in their rankings, including y_0.

(3) If the ranking of the packages is unanimous, the mechanism chooses the agreed best package, and no VCG tax is assessed. If not, the mechanism uses the $\mathrm{w.t.p.}_j^{i*}$ information from the referendum, together with estimated values of $d\mathrm{CV}_j^{i*}/d\underline{x}_0$ from the official legislatures, to obtain corrected CV_j^{i*} and RV_j^{i*}, and determines the corrected ranking of the packages using the CRP. Let $y_{j'}$ be the best package.

(4) If the message from a consumer i' changes the mechanism choice to package $y_{j'}$ from the package y_j that the mechanism would have chosen without the consumer's message, the VCG tax $S^{i'}$ will be that specified by D.12 for this binary choice.

The referendum does not change the taxes and transfers, so that if the legislative information were misleading or incomplete in any way, the final choice might not be unanimous. If so, the mechanism substitutes estimated CV's for the reported w.t.p.$_j^{i'}$'s of consumers who oppose the final choice. This feature in fact helps insure incentive compatibility. As noted earlier, data from all parts of the referendum determine the incentive payments to the legislators. The multiple w.t.p.$_j^{i}$ messages verify legislative information about wealth effects on w.t.p.$_j^{i}$, and in addition provide a strong check on attempts by legislators to manipulate the outcome. The limited agenda, with no package that a population subgroup prefers to $y_{j'}$ provides no subgroup an opportunity to manipulate the outcome.

Section A6.5.D presents a proof that it is possible to rank the options and determine tax packages such that there is an option that the legislatures (and also entire population, if D.19.a rather than D.19.b holds) will prefer unanimously to all others.

A6.5.B.6 Preliminary Discussion

Assumption D.8, that public goods packages are normal goods, affects procedures and results only in the case where population subgroups are not homogeneous, that is, where exact Lindahl taxes and transfers are impossible. In that case the difference between CV and EV affects the optimality of the mechanism, and requires elaborate procedures to approximate optimality. This effect occurs whether a public good is an inferior good or a normal good, which affects only the direction of the required adjustments. Therefore we concentrate on the case of the normal good.

The public good that is on the borderline, having a w.t.p.$_j^{i*}$ for every consumer that is constant as the consumer's wealth changes, can be dealt with quickly. In the simplest case, the only effect of the public good is to change the incomes and wealth of consumers, without entering directly into a utility function U^i. If so, the w.t.p.$_j^{i*}$ of each consumer $i*$ is simply the change in wealth $\Delta\underline{x}^{i*}$ due to the public good. Furthermore, if this change in wealth is independent of the consumer's initial wealth $\underline{x}_0^{i*}$, evidently $CV^{**} = EV^{**}$, and the VCG mechanism will give optimal results because there is no 'income effect' to be concerned about. The same conclusion applies if the public good is a perfect substitute for wealth, in the sense that each consumer's w.t.p.$_j^{i*}$ for the good is independent of initial wealth. For such cases the CVCG and SCVCG mechanisms, with their elaborate procedures, are unnecessary, in the sense that these mechanisms would give the same outcomes as would the VCG mechanism, although one might prefer the CVCG because it avoids incidental wealth redistribution by public goods.

A6.5.C Analysis

As a preliminary to our analysis of binary-valued goods, we note again that public goods may have quantities that are continuous variables, or may take on only the binary values (0, 1). Consider the case where there are several of the former and a single public good y_h that can take on only the binary values (0,1). For each value of y_h, the existence proofs for public competitive equilibrium apply, so that a public competitive equilibrium exists. Moreover, if we add another binary-valued public good with an arbitrarily predetermined quantity, the same point applies. Therefore, equilibrium exists for each potential combination of public goods.

Given this finding, we may encompass all public goods of continuously variable quantity in y_0, in order to focus our attention on the problem of binary public goods. That is, the notation and concepts of Subsection A6.5.B.3 apply, and the selection of y_j uses a pivotal mechanism.

Then it follows that the amount of wealth each household would be willing to be taxed, to have its way on a choice of public goods, is a finite number.

Lemma 21. $\forall\ i \in \mathcal{I}$, $\forall\, j$, $\exists \underline{x}_j^{\,i} < \underline{x}_0^{\,i}$ such that $V^i(\underline{x}_j^{\,i}; y_j) = V^i(\underline{x}_0^{\,i}; y_0)$, and $\forall\ i' \in \mathcal{I}'$, $\forall\, j$, $\exists \underline{x}_{0j}^{\,i'} < \underline{x}_0^{\,i'}$ such that $V^i(\underline{x}_{0j}^{\,i'}; y_0) = V^i(\underline{x}_0^{\,i'} - \Delta T_j^{\,i}; y_j)$.

Proof: Immediate, by the continuity of indirect utility, and the monotonicity of utility in all goods. Assumption D.6 assures that both $\underline{x}_j^{\,i} > \underline{\underline{x}}^{\,i}$ and $\underline{x}_{0j}^{\,i'} > \underline{\underline{x}}^{\,i'}$. Because they have upper and lower bounds, $\underline{x}_j^{\,i}$ and $\underline{x}_{0j}^{\,i'}$ must be finite numbers. ■

Lemma 22: $\forall\, j$ and $\forall\ y_0$, $\underline{x}_0$, the VCG mechanism is decisive.

Proof: Immediate. The $\underline{x}_j^{\,i}$ and $\underline{x}_{0j}^{\,i'}$ are well-defined, bounded, single-valued real numbers. The criterion on the left-hand side of (A6.63a) and (A6.63b) is a sum of such numbers, and therefore is also a well-defined, bounded, single-valued real number. ■

In addition, we have

Lemma 23: For simple binary choice, regardless of the number of consumers, truth is the dominant strategy for every consumer i^* in reporting w.t.p.$_j^{\,i^*}$ to the VCG pivotal mechanism.

Proof: Each consumer's w.t.p.$_j^{i*}$ to obtain y_j or preserve y_0 is independent of what other consumers' w.t.p.$_j^{i**}$ values may be, by definition D.7 and the equalities in Lemma 21. What a consumer $i^* \in \{1, \ldots, N\}$ will be required to pay, by D.12, depends only on what other consumers report as their w.t.p.$_j^{i**}$ amounts, which are independent of that reported by consumer i^*. It follows that misreporting of w.t.p.$_j^{i*}$ can in no circumstance benefit consumer i^*. A false report when consumer i^* would otherwise be liable for tax either has no effect on the tax on consumer i^*, or, if it does, would reduce it to zero while reversing $\chi(y_j, y_0,\underline{x}_0)$, a result that would lower the utility of consumer i^*. A false report when consumer i^* would otherwise not be liable for tax either has no effect on this zero tax, or, if it does, would increase it to an amount in excess of the true w.t.p.$_j^{i*}$ while reversing $\chi(y_j, y_0, \underline{x}_0)$, a result that would also lower the utility of consumer i^*. That is, the incentives are the same for this case as when utility is separable. ■

This textbook proof does not depend on separable utility. Note, however, that by 'simple binary choice', we mean that there is only one y_j that is technically available other than y_0, so that consumers do not anticipate a subsequent binary choice involving another public good. The proof would fail in cases of multiple packages.

While some of our preceding remarks agree in spirit with the pessimistic result on the pivotal mechanism in the presence of income effects presented by Green and Laffont (1977b, Appendix), their claim is unsound. Lemmas 22 and 23 contradict the Green-Laffont result. The problem is due to two questionable steps they employed. First, the utility function in their example is discontinuous, which is to say irrational. Second, they inaccurately presented the VCG mechanism for this case as one that maximizes the sum of individual utility functions, a criterion valid only for the case of transferable utility. Otherwise, a sum of unobservable utility functions has no relation to a sum of w.t.p.$_j^{i*}$, which can be measured by revealed preference through an incentive-compatible mechanism.

Lemma 24. For simple binary choices, when D.19a holds the CVCG is incentive-compatible.

Proof: Immediate from Lemma 23, because when there are only two packages to consider (one being the status quo), a CVCG mechanism is a VCG mechanism with its tax structure specified by D.20a. ■

Lemma 25. For simple binary choices, the SCVCG is incentive-compatible.

Proof: Immediate from Lemma 23, as with Lemma 24. ■

Lemma 26. For the pair of packages $y_j, y_{j'} \in \Upsilon^{++}$, assume without loss of generality that the CVCG ranks $y_{j'}$ superior to y_j. Then there is no set of taxes and transfers for y_j such that all consumers prefer y_j to an unchanged package $y_{j'}$.

Proof: Every set of taxes and transfers must satisfy the budget constraint $\sum_i \Delta T_j^i = u_j$. Hence a set of taxes and transfers for the inferior package y_j that differed from that used by the mechanism would increase the taxes of some consumers and reduce the taxes of others. There is no set of taxes and transfers obtained in this way that can result in a package y_j that is unanimously preferred to the original package y_j, and hence there is none unanimously preferred to $y_{j'}$. ■

Lemma 27. When D.19a holds, every consumer prefers the package $y_{j'}$ chosen by the CVCG to every other package.

Proof: Because the indirect utility functions are continuous in wealth, a set of taxes and transfers can be found under the procedure of D.20a for each package y_j such that either $y_j \in \Upsilon^-$ or $y_j \in \Upsilon^+$. Similarly, adjusted taxes can be found under the procedure of D.21a for each package $y_j \in \Upsilon^{++}$, such that consumers unanimously prefer $y_{j'}$ to every other such y_j. That is, the procedures D.20a and D.21a always succeed. By construction, everyone prefers each such y_j to every other package $y_{j*} \notin \Upsilon^{++}$. ■

Lemma 28. When D.19a holds, the CVCG is fully decisive.

Proof: By Lemma 22, the CVCG is decisive for a pairwise decision between every pair $(y_j, y_{j''})$, because it is a VCG mechanism for each such decision. By construction, the packages in the subset $\Upsilon^{++} \subset \Upsilon^+$ contain the best package. The procedures in D.20a and D.21a rank packages in

$\mathbb{Y}^{++}$ unambiguously, apart from ties, so that they determine a best package. Consumer messages confirm this choice unanimously. ■

Lemma 29. Both the CVCG and the SCVCG are incentive compatible.

Proof: The sampling procedure provides information on the preferences of each subgroup of consumers, whose subsequent messages serve only to choose a best package from the fixed agenda, and to verify the information so as to set incentive payments for legislators. Because of the fixed agenda, households cannot manipulate the allocation of welfare gains by using false messages to change the selection of candidate packages under D.22. In the case of the CVCG, if a false report by consumer i could change the outcome, the new outcome would be one that i ranks as inferior to or at best no better than the otherwise chosen outcome. That is, each consumer's incentive to report w.t.p. between the best package and another package is the same as under the VCG. Hence the mechanism is incentive compatible for each consumer not in an official legislature. In the case of the SCVCG, limitation of the agenda to two items means that Lemma 25 applies. In both cases, each legislator i's wealth is substantially less than the expected compensation for accuracy, and less than the penalty for error, which therefore exceeds the legislator's w.t.p.^{i} for every package. Therefore, the dominant strategy for legislators is to give truthful information. ■

Theorem 6. For all utility functions satisfying A.5-A8, when D.19a holds the CVCG ranking of packages starting from a specified status quo is incentive compatible, is fully decisive, and is Pareto-efficient.

Proof: Immediate, from Lemmas 27, 28, and 29. Because the mechanism generates zero VCG tax assessments, all decisions being unanimous, its budget is balanced. Because of unanimity and the balanced budget, its outcome is Pareto Efficient. ■

Lemma 30. When D.19b holds and the SCVCG applies D.20b and D.19b to rank packages and to determine their accompanying set of taxes and transfers, there is no resulting package y_j that every consumer prefers to $y_{j'}$, the package ranked as best.

Proof: If there is an adjusted package y_j that every consumer prefers to $y_{j'}$, every legislator also prefers y_j to $y_{j'}$. By Lemma 29, the messages and legislative information report this preference. Then at stages D.21a and D.21b of the mechanism, y_j must be in the pair of final candidates for best package. When all consumers prefer y_j to $y_{j'}$, continuity of indirect utility assures that the CRP will rank y_j above $y_{j'}$ and that the VCG tax procedure will confirm this unanimous ranking. The tax adjustment procedures stop with no further adjustment at this point. This result contradicts the premise that the mechanism chooses $y_{j'}$ as best. ■

Lemma 31. When D.19b holds, the SCVCG is fully decisive.

Proof: The premise D.19b implies that the choice problem for the SCVCG is binary. Because at the point of final choice it is a VCG mechanism, the SCVCG is decisive for this choice, by Lemma 22. ■

Theorem 7. For all utility functions satisfying A.5-A.8, when D.19b holds the SCVCG ranking of packages starting from a specified status quo is incentive compatible, is fully decisive, and is Pareto-efficient if $\forall\ i^* \in (1, \ldots, N)$, $S^{i^*} = 0$.

Proof: Immediate, from Lemmas 29, 30, and 31.

Remarks:

1. Without the tax package adjustments set out here for the CVCG or SCVCG, the VCG mechanism can have cycles, and therefore is manipulable, in the presence of income effects. Furthermore, even without cycles, the w.t.p.$_j^{i'}$ of an alternative to a package is an EV$_j^{i'}$, not a CV$_j^{i'}$, so that a package chosen by the VCG could lack the potential to be a Pareto improvement.

2. The proofs of Lemmas 25, 29, 30, and 31 use only the two-package premise supplied by D.19b. When it holds, the roles of official legislatures are to approximate Lindahl taxes and transfers and to increase the likelihood that all $S^{i^*} = 0$. The Lemmas and Theorem 7 are valid, however, even if the legislatures provide no information other than satisfaction of the two-package premise.

3. The problem of a Pareto-nonoptimal budget imbalance if not all $S^{i^*} = 0$ remains unresolved, although some results indicate that there are ways to refund the budget imbalance consistent with Bayesian incentive compatibility. See d'Aspremont, Cremer, and Gerard-Varet (1990) and Section A6.3. The possibility of adapting these results to the decision problem considered here has not been explored.

4. If D.19b is not satisfied, so that the SCVCG would need to rank multiple packages in its final ranking stage, one can find examples such that a consumer could advantageously manipulate the final choice of package.

A6.5.D Procedure to Obtain a Unanimous Ranking of Packages

The procedure D.20a identifies a set of packages $\mathcal{Y}^+$, with associated tax packages, that consumers unanimously prefer to the status quo. Consumers may disagree, however, on the relative ranking of the packages in $\mathcal{Y}^+$, so that further steps must be specified to achieve unanimous rankings of all packages $y_j \in \mathcal{Y}^+$. Let $\underline{x}_j^i$ denote either $\underline{x}_0^i - \Delta T_j^i - \Delta' T_j^i$ or $\underline{x}_0^i - \Delta T_j^i - \Delta^* T_j^i$, according to the context, at the values of these variables at the step where $\underline{x}_j^i$ appears. The values of $\Delta' T_j^i$ and of $\Delta^* T_j^i$ are zero until they are otherwise set in this procedure.

Suppose that consumer i ranks package y_j higher than package $y_{j'}$, and that this ranking must be reversed to achieve unanimity, without disturbing a unanimous ranking of another package $y_{j''}$ relative to the pair y_j and $y_{j'}$. We will show that, given the continuity of indirect utility, this reversal can be obtained by raising i's tax share for y_j and lowering i's tax share for $y_{j'}$, with offsetting changes in the tax shares of other consumers. The procedure to obtain unanimous ranking is not unique, nor, for a given set of preferences, can one be sure that the ranking is unique. The following set of steps represents an algorithm that could be programmed to a computer, that is that leaves no discretion to the Election Commission. One can readily verify by summation that the tax adjustments of Steps 3 and 4 together, of Step 5, and of Step 6 have zero net change in the budget of each affected package.

Step 1. Determine whether $\mathcal{Y}^+$ can be divided into proper subsets $\mathcal{Y}_1, \mathcal{Y}_2, \ldots,$ such that $\forall\, y_j \in \mathcal{Y}_1$ and $\forall\, i$, if $y_{j'} \in \mathcal{Y}_k$, $k > 1$, $V^i(\cdot;\, \underline{x}_j^i;\, y_j) > V^i(\cdot;\, \underline{x}_{j'}^i;\, y_{j'})$. Find the maximum number of disjoint subsets $\mathcal{Y}_1, \ldots$ that meet this condition. If every such subset has only one package, stop. Otherwise, leave unchanged the tax package ΔT_j^i for every consumer i in a $\mathcal{Y}_k$ of only one member y_j, and renumber the $\mathcal{Y}_k$ so that only those with more than one member are numbered sequentially, starting from the highest as $\mathcal{Y}_1$.

Step 2. Apply the CRP to $\mathcal{Y}_1$. Inasmuch as the cardinal values of the packages sum to zero, either they are all zero or at least one is positive and at least one is negative. If not all cardinal values are zero, disregard the remainder of this step and apply Step 3. If all are zero, $\forall\, i$ and $\forall\, y_j \in \mathcal{Y}_1$, let $\Delta'T_j^i = \text{RV}_j^i$. Renumber each $\mathcal{Y}_k$ to be $\mathcal{Y}_{k-1}$ and repeat this entire step for the new $\mathcal{Y}_1$, if there is one. Otherwise, stop.

Step 3. For the package $y_{j'}$ with the highest cardinal ranking in $\mathcal{Y}_1$, that is with the highest value of $\sum_{i*} \text{RV}_{j'}^i > 0$, $\forall\ i$ such that $\text{RV}_{j'}^i < 0$, let the tax adjustment $\Delta'T_{j'}^i = \text{RV}_{j'}^i - \varepsilon$, for an arbitrarily small positive ε. Denote by $\mathcal{I}$ the subset of consumers i who receive this tax reduction.

Step 4. $\forall\ i' \notin \mathcal{I}$, let $k_{j'} = [\sum_{i'}\text{RV}_{j'}^{i'} + \sum_i \Delta'T_{j'}^i]/\sum_{i'}\text{RV}_{j'}^{i'}$, and let $\Delta'T_{j'}^{i'} = (1 - k_{j'})\,\text{RV}_{j'}^{i'}$.

Step 5. For each $y_j \in \mathcal{Y}_1$ such that $j \neq j'$, find that set of hypothetical tax adjustments $\Delta^*T_j^{i*}$ such that $\forall\ i^*$, $V^{i*}(\cdot;\ \underline{x}_j^{i*};\ y_j) = V^{i*}(\cdot;\ \underline{x}_{j'}^{i*};\ y_{j'})$. If there is a case with $\sum_{i*} \Delta^*T_j^{i*} > 0$, disregard the remainder of this step and apply Step 6. If for every $y_j \in \mathcal{Y}_1$ such that $j \neq j'$, $\sum_{i*} \Delta^*T_j^{i*} < 0$, $\forall\ j$ and $\forall\ i'$ such that $\Delta^*T_j^{i'} \geq 0$, let $\Delta'T_j^{i'} = \Delta^*T_j^{i'} + \varepsilon$, and $\forall\ i \neq i'$ let $\Delta'T_j^i = \Delta^*T_j^i(-\sum_{i'} \Delta'T_j^{i'}/\sum_i \Delta^*T_j^i)$. If $\exists j$ such that $\sum_{i*} \Delta^*T_j^{i*} = 0$, let every $\Delta'T_j^i = \Delta^*T_j^i$. Remove $y_{j'}$, and remove each other package y_j such that all consumers are indifferent between y_j and $y_{j'}$, from $\mathcal{Y}_1$. If the number of remaining members in $\mathcal{Y}_1$ is two or more, apply step 2. If there is only one remaining member, renumber each $\mathcal{Y}_k$ to be $\mathcal{Y}_{k-1}$ and apply step 2 to the new $\mathcal{Y}_1$, if there is one. Otherwise, stop.

Step 6. Let $\mathcal{Y}_1^+$ be the subset of $\mathcal{Y}_1$ such that step 5 obtains $\sum_{i*} \Delta^*T_j^{i*} > 0\ \forall\ y_j \in \mathcal{Y}_1^+$. Then $\forall\ y_j \in \mathcal{Y}_1^+$, $\forall\ i''$ such that $\Delta^*T_j^{i*} \leq 0$ let $\Delta'T_j^{i*} = \Delta^*T_j^{i*} - \varepsilon$. $\forall\ i \neq i''$ let $\Delta'T_j^i = \Delta^*T_j^i(-\sum_{i''}\Delta'T_j^{i*}/\sum_{i \neq i''} \Delta^*T_j^{i*})$.

With these tax adjustments, consumers unanimously prefer each such y_j to $y_{j'}$. If $\mathcal{Y}_1^+$ has only one member, apply Step 2 to the remainder of $\mathcal{Y}_1$ after removing y_j and $y_{j'}$ if this remainder has more than one member. If it has only one remaining member, renumber each $\mathcal{Y}_k$ to be $\mathcal{Y}_{k-1}$ and apply step 2 to the new $\mathcal{Y}_1$, if there is one. Otherwise, stop. If $\mathcal{Y}_1^+$ has more than one member, redesignate $\mathcal{Y}_1^+$ as $\mathcal{Y}_1$. Then in this case, if $\mathcal{Y}_1 - y_{j'} - \mathcal{Y}_1^+$ has more than one member, renumber it as $\mathcal{Y}_2$, renumber all $\mathcal{Y}_k$, $k > 1$, as $\mathcal{Y}_{k+1}$, and apply Step 2 to $\mathcal{Y}_1$.

By construction, the above procedure achieves the intended result, as the following tedious proof demonstrates.

Lemma A1. If in Step 2 the cardinal values $\forall\ y_j \in \mathcal{Y}_1$ are zero, then all consumers i^* are indifferent among all these y_j, given the values set by Step 2 of $\Delta'T_j^{i*}$.

Proof: Immediate, by the definition of RV_j^{i*}. ■

Lemma A2. If, in Step 5, $\forall\, y_j \in \Upsilon_1$ with $j \neq j'$, $\sum_{i^*} \Delta^* T_j^{i^*} < 0$, then after the step is completed consumers i^* unanimously prefer $y_{j'}$ to all other $y_j \in \Upsilon_1$.

Proof: By the definition of $\Delta' T_j^{i'}$ and by the monotonicity of V^i, $\forall\, i'$ we have $V^{i'}(\cdot\,; \underline{x}_j^{i'}; y_j) < V^{i'}(\cdot\,; \underline{x}_{j'}^{i'}; y_{j'})$ after Step 5. Now for small enough ε we have $\sum_{i'} \Delta' T_j^{i'} < -\sum_i \Delta^* T_j^i$, given the premise $\sum_{i^*} \Delta^* T_j^{i^*} < 0$. Therefore for each consumer $i \neq i'$, who prior to this step prefers $y_{j'}$ to y_j, $\Delta' T_j^i / \Delta^* T_j^i < 1$, so that $V^i(\cdot\,; \underline{x}_j^i; y_j) < V^i(\cdot\,; \underline{x}_{j'}^i; y_{j'})$ remains undisturbed by Step 5. ■

Lemma A3. If, in Step 5, there is $y_j \in \Upsilon_1, j \neq j'$, such that $\sum_{i^*} \Delta^* T_j^{i^*} = 0$, then after the step is completed consumers i^* are all indifferent between $y_{j'}$ and y_j.

Proof: Immediate, by the definition of $\Delta^* T_j^{i^*}$. ■

Lemma A4. If, in Step 5, for every $y_j \in \Upsilon_1$ with $j \neq j'$, $\sum_{i^*} \Delta^* T_j^{i^*} \leq 0$, then after the step is completed consumers i^* unanimously prefer $y_{j'}$ to each other $y_j \in \Upsilon_1$ to which they are not unanimously indifferent.

Proof: Immediate, by the proofs of Lemmas A2 and A3. ■

Lemma A5. After Step 6, when applicable, consumers i^* unanimously prefer all members of Υ_1^+ to $y_{j'}$.

Proof: The proof is the same as the proof of Lemma A2, with i'' replacing i', with signs and inequalities reversed except for the ratio $\Delta' T_j^i / \Delta^* T_j^i < 1$, and with 'Step 6' replacing 'Step 5'. ■

Lemma A6. When consumers i^* unanimously prefer $y_{j''}$ to all members of a set Υ_1 and unanimously prefer all members of Υ_1 to y_{j^*}, so that $y_{j''} \notin \Upsilon_1$ and $y_{j^*} \notin \Upsilon_1$, these unanimous preferences remain unchanged by the procedure applied to Υ_1.

Proof: By the premise of the lemma, prior to applying the procedure to Υ_1, $\forall\, y_j \in \Upsilon_1$ and $\forall\, i^*$ we have $V^{i^*}(\cdot\,; \underline{x}_j^{i^*}; y_j) < V^{i^*}(\cdot\,; \underline{x}_{j''}^{i^*}; y_{j''})$. For a consumer i who receives a positive transfer to the package $y_{j'} \in \Upsilon_1$, that is, for whom $\Delta' T_{j'}^i < 0$ at Step 3, $\forall\, y_{j'''} \in \Upsilon_1$ such that $\text{RV}_{j'''}^i > 0$ the resulting

$V^i(\cdot;\underline{x}_{j'}{}^i;y_{j'}) < V^i(\cdot;\underline{x}_{j'''}{}^i;y_{j'''})$, for sufficiently small ε, by the continuity and strict monotonicity of V^i, and by the definition D.14 of $\text{RV}_{j'''}{}^i$. Hence $V^i(\cdot;\underline{x}_{j'}{}^i;y_{j'}) < V^i(\cdot;\underline{x}_{j''}{}^i;y_{j''})$. Then $\forall\, y_j \in \Upsilon_1$ with $j \neq j'$, the $\Delta' T_j{}^{i*}$ applied in Step 5 when $\sum_{i*} \Delta^* T_j{}^{i*} \leq 0$ assures that $V^{i*}(\cdot;\underline{x}_j{}^{i*};y_j) \leq V^{i*}(\cdot;\underline{x}_{j'}{}^{i*};y_{j'})$, by Lemma A4. Hence when $\sum_{i*} \Delta^* T_j{}^{i*} \leq 0$, the completion of Step 5 leaves $y_{j''}$ unanimously preferred to $y_{j'}$, which in turn is unanimously preferred to or regarded as good as all other $y_j \in \Upsilon_1$. When Step 6 applies, if $\exists\, i''$ and y_j such that $\Delta^* T_{j'}{}^{i''} \leq 0$ then the value of $\Delta' T_{j'}{}^i$ implies that the resulting $V^{i''}(\cdot;\underline{x}_j{}^{i*};y_j) - V^{i''}(\cdot;\underline{x}_{j'}{}^{i*};y_{j'})$ is arbitrarily small, because of the continuity of indirect utility. Therefore we can assure that $V^{i''}(\cdot;\underline{x}_j{}^{i*};y_j) < V^{i''}(\cdot;\underline{x}_{j''}{}^{i*};y_{j''})$ remains unaffected, as required. By construction, if $\Delta^* T_j{}^{i*} > 0$ then $\Delta' T_j{}^{i*} > 0$, $\forall\, y_j \in \Upsilon_1{}^+$ and $\forall\, i^* \in \{1, \ldots, N\}$, so that the inequality $V^{i*}(;\underline{x}_j{}^{i*};y_j) < V^{i*}(\cdot;\underline{x}_{j''}{}^{i*};y_{j''})$ remains unaffected. That is, after Step 6 is completed, if necessary, consumers unanimously prefer $y_{j''}$ to every member of $\Upsilon_1{}^+$. All the above conclusions, plus Lemmas A1-A5, apply to every subsequent application of steps 2-6 to $\Upsilon_1{}^+$. Hence the lemma is proved for $y_{j''}$. Now consider y_{j*}. Steps 3, 4, 5, and 6 can give only non-negative transfers (that is, $\Delta' T_j{}^{i*} \leq 0$), to a package $y_j \in \Upsilon_1$ that a consumer ranks lowest among the members of Υ_1, so that the unanimous preference for y_j over y_{j*} will remain unaffected. At Step 3 $y_{j'}$ receives a positive or zero transfer, while after Step 4 $y_{j'}$ remains preferred to each consumer's lowest-ranked package, by the definition of the $\text{RV}_j{}^i$. Hence at the end, $V^{i*}(\cdot,\underline{x}_{j'}{}^{i*},y_{j'}) > V^{i*}(\cdot;\underline{x}_{j*}{}^{i*};y_{j*})$, $\forall\, i^*$. Then for $j \neq j'$ let $y_j \in \Upsilon_1$ be a package that consumer i ranked above lowest prior to the application of Step 5. If in Step 5 $\Delta' T_j{}^i \geq 0$, the resulting value of $V^i(\cdot;\underline{x}_{j'}{}^i;y_{j'}) - V^i(\cdot;\underline{x}_j{}^i;y_j) \geq 0$ is arbitrarily small, so that we still have $V^i(\cdot;\underline{x}_j{}^i;y_j) > V^i(\cdot;\underline{x}_{j*}{}^i;y_{j*})$. If in Step 5 or Step 6 $\Delta' T_j{}^i < 0$, then the relation $V^i(\cdot;\underline{x}_j{}^i;y_j) > V^i(\cdot;\underline{x}_{j*}{}^i;y_{j*})$ is of course undisturbed. If in Step 6 we have $\Delta' T_j{}^i > 0$, by Lemma A5 after this step $V^i(\cdot;\underline{x}_j{}^i;y_j) > V^i(\cdot;\underline{x}_{j'}{}^i;y_{j'})$.
■

Theorem A. The procedures of Steps 1-6 result, after a finite number of iterations, in a unanimous ranking of all packages $y_j \in \Upsilon^+$.

Proof: The set $\mathcal{Y}$ has a finite number of members, and therefore so has $\Upsilon^+ \subset \mathcal{Y}$. Each complete iteration of the steps either achieves a unanimous ranking of a subset $\Upsilon_1 \subset \Upsilon^+$ or separates it into two disjoint subsets, one of whose members consumers unanimously prefer to the members of the other. After iterations of the sequence from Step 2 fewer than the initial number of members of $\mathcal{Y}_1$, the procedure must result in a set of taxes and transfers such that consumers have a unanimous ranking of all members of $\mathcal{Y}_1$. By the lemmas, every unanimously agreed preference for a package or for a subset of packages relative to $\mathcal{Y}_1$, or for $\mathcal{Y}_1$ relative to a package, is unchanged by the steps. Therefore the number of iterations required to achieve a unanimous ranking of all $y_j \in \mathcal{Y}^+$ is finite. ■

A6.5.E Conclusions

The results in the theorems are promising, although one must note that all mechanism choices with both the CVCG and the SCVCG depend on the status quo $(\underline{x}_0{}^i, y_0)$. That is, with a different initial distribution of endowments or a different initial public goods package, the choice of a new public goods package may also be different. However, this apparent anomaly simply parallels the well known index-number problems that may arise for the private sector when the distribution of endowments changes.

At the close of the preceding section we noted that a SCVCG, like a VCG, can be manipulated when there are multiple packages. What could perhaps be fruitfully explored is the possibility of Bayesian incentive compatibility for this case. It would also be interesting to examine how this problem compares with similar problems arising under existing political systems. How a government mechanism that uses the concepts in this section would perform in practice depends on particulars of how divisive the issues are that it must address. That is, it is an empirical question, unless a better technical resolution is found for the remaining problems in these concepts.

7 Why Nash Solutions are Not Solutions

7.1 INTRODUCTION

Chapters 5 and 6, with the latter's appendix, complete the technical background needed to support the constitutional concepts of Chapter 3. Now, as a final technical note, we consider why a number of proposed mechanisms that have precise Lindahl taxes as Nash equilibria cannot deliver the promised outcomes. The sampling method we propose in Chapters 2 and 3 can realistically approximate Lindahl taxes for the voter population. Our object here is to explain why there is no better way to approximate them than by this proposal. A more technical treatment of this point appears in Roberts (1976). See also Groves and Ledyard (1987), pp. 65-68.

In widely cited papers, Hurwicz (1979) and Walker (1981) present mechanisms whose Nash equilibria yield 'Lindahl allocations' for the financing of a public good. Tian (1989) proposed a generalized mechanism, with a larger message space than those used by Hurwicz and by Walker, with the same outcome. That is, the transfers (tax payments) produced by these equilibria are Lindahl taxes. (Note that 'Lindahl taxes' are one-part taxes, which impose a uniform price per unit of public good on each taxpayer.) These authors recognized that Nash equilibria have less desirable properties than dominant-strategy equilibria; the former are not generally strategy proof, may not converge, and so on. Nevertheless, the results seem striking and may have led some to believe that a way had been found to implement Lindahl taxes. One may fairly conjecture that this impression is strengthened by the complex, opaque character of each of the mechanisms.

Under the Hurwicz mechanism, each individual (whom we shall call a 'player') sends a message consisting of a quantity and a price. The price message helps to determine the tax to be paid by two other players to finance the public good. If the outcome is not a Lindahl tax-quantity outcome, each player is liable for both a tax share of the public good and for a penalty. When the outcome is the Lindahl outcome, the penalties disappear and, under Nash behavior, the outcome is an equilibrium. Under the Walker mechanism each player sends a message consisting of only one number, which serves both as a quantity and a price. The mechanism is otherwise similar to the Hurwicz mechanism. Under the Tian mechanism each player's message consists of a vector: the player's private goods endowments, three prices or taxes for each public good, prices of private goods, quantities of private goods, and a parameter. Again, the Lindahl outcome is a Nash equilibrium for both these latter mechanisms.

On close examination, however, it turns out that we are no closer to having a way to implement Lindahl taxes than we were when Lindahl proposed them. The properties of the proposed mechanisms under manipulation are strictly equivalent to the properties of the Lindahl tax with an auctioneer, and are substantially equivalent to those of the Lindahl tax without an auctioneer. This finding is unlikely to be reversed by another, as yet undisclosed mechanism.

7.2 ALTERNATIVE MECHANISMS WITH EQUIVALENT RESULTS

We take as fundamental to the mechanism design problem the proposal by Hurwicz (1972) that an informationally decentralized social choice mechanism must require each participant to send messages that are consistent with a rational valuation function. This rule is enforceable, and without it the use and analysis of iterative mechanisms would be a shambles. Taking this Hurwicz consistency rule as given, we note the following facts.

Fact 1. A Lindahl tax with an auctioneer (wherein the auctioneer calls out a tax share for each player, whose message in reply is a quantity demanded of the public good) has a Nash equilibrium at the true Lindahl-Pareto optimum.

When the player assumes that the tax shares and the messages of other players will remain unchanged, the player's preferred message is the correct quantify demanded of the public good as derived from the player's true utility function. This fact was noted early on by Muench and Walker (1979); see also Foley (1970) and Groves (1979). Most remarkably, it was overlooked by Hurwicz in his otherwise insightful and comprehensive survey (1985), even though he took note of the auctioneer mechanism.

Fact 2. Whatever the iterative mechanism, non-equilibrium combinations of messages, being intermediate steps, appear in the extended form of the game but not in the normal form.

The specification of a strategy for the normal form need not spell out the message to be send in each contingency, so long as the specification can be used to infer each such message uniquely. For example, the strategy 'tell the truth' need only specify the utility function from which the messages at successive stages of the game will be derived. The game mechanism itself specifies the constraints under which the player optimizes, so that the mechanism plus the utility function together are sufficient to determine the message in every situation. This game concept is suggested for this type of problem by Muench and Walker (1979).

Fact 3. If a mechanism has a Nash equilibrium at the true Lindahl taxes, it has a manipulative Nash (MN) equilibrium at the apparent Lindahl taxes that correspond to a false utility function chosen by one player, for given utility functions of the other players.

If a player i with true utility function U^i is replaced by another player i' with true utility function $U^{i'}$, the correct Lindahl tax changes from T^i to $T^{i'}$. The outcome with $T^{i'}$ is of course a Nash equilibrium for a mechanism that always has a Nash equilibrium at the Lindahl tax. If, instead of replacing player i with another player, we have player i adopt the strategy of deriving messages from $U^{i'}$ instead of from U^i, the game will be the same as if player i' were there. Once the apparent Nash equilibrium is found, player i must accept it, because of the Hurwicz consistency rule referred to at the outset of this discussion. Thus the game will have its MN equilibrium at the tax $T^{i'}$, as *Fact 3* points out.

Given these facts, the following proposition is obvious.

Proposition. In normal game form, the Hurwicz (1979), Walker (1981), and the Tian (1989) mechanisms are strictly equivalent to the Lindahl tax mechanism with an auctioneer; and the Lindahl tax mechanism without an auctioneer is substantially equivalent to the other four.

We illustrate the game with the following public goods problem. In a two-good economy, the public good y can be produced from the private good x at constant unit cost: $y = w - x$, where w is the aggregate initial endowment. There are N players; player i has the utility function $U^i(x^i, y)$ with the customary properties, including diminishing marginal utility. The Lindahl optimum is $y^* > 0$, with player i paying T^i in tax. If all other players send messages derived from their true utility functions, player i's utility from truthful responses is $U^i(w^i - T^i, y^*)$. If instead player i sends messages derived from a free-riding utility function $U'^i(x^i)$, in which y has zero marginal utility, the quasi-Lindahl outcome is y^{**} and player i's utility will be $U^i(w^i, y^{**})$. For large N, where y^{**} is close to y^*, this latter utility is typically higher than that derived from responding truthfully, as has been pointed out in many textbook examples of free riding. The incentive to free ride will hold in every circumstance except where player i's response will have an appreciable effect on the amount of public good

Table 7.1 Payoff matrix for Lindahl mechanisms to finance production of a public good

Player i Reports	Payoffs			
	Number of Others Who Report Truthfully			
	0	E	$>> E$	$N-1$
$U^i(x^i, y)$	0	0	7	10
$U'^i(x^i)$	0	2	4	6

produced. Henceforward, for simplicity we will refer to basing responses on the true utility function as 'truthful reporting'.

Then the payoff matrix to the game appears as shown in Table 7.1, where we scale player i's utility so that $U^i(w^i, 0) = 0$ and $U^i(w^i, y^{**}) = 10$. When at most $E > 0$ players tell the truth, no public good is produced; the first column therefore shows zero payoff in both rows. When $E + 1$ players report truthfully, a positive amount of the public good will be produced, and those who do report truthfully will share the full cost of that amount. For player i, telling the truth increases the amount of public good produced enough to compensate for jumping from zero tax to i's share of the cost of the resulting amount. There must be at least one such integer $E < N$, because when there are N truth-tellers, $y^* > 0$. For at least the case where player i expects E players to tell the truth, the payoff to player i must be higher for truthful reporting than for free riding, because the tax is a Lindahl tax and marginal utility is diminishing. (Player i receives some net consumer surplus from helping to pay for the production of a non-zero y that would not otherwise occur.) With ingenuity, one can construct examples in which there are other columns in which truth has a higher payoff than has free riding; typically, however, there is only the one column for E as just described that has this truth-telling incentive.

Regardless of the details, this matrix is the same for the Hurwicz mechanism, the Walker mechanism, the Lindahl mechanism with an auctioneer, and the Lindahl mechanism without an auctioneer. In the first three of these mechanisms the details of the extensive form of the game (of which only part have been specified) imply that truth-telling is a Nash equilibrium. Therefore we may say that all three are equivalent in all material respects. The Lindahl mechanism without an auctioneer lacks this Nash equilibrium property. (Bagnoli and Lipman, 1992, show that there exists a truth-telling Nash equilibrium when the quantity of the public good is predetermined; they do not consider the case where the mechanism or game must determine the quantity.) Despite the lack of a corresponding result for the present problem, the payoff matrix is nevertheless the same for the original Lindahl mechanism, so that the lack of a truth-telling Nash equilibrium is inconsequential when players are willing to engage in manipulative behavior. Therefore, all four mechanisms are substantially equivalent, in that the players have the same set of strategy options in all four, with the same outcomes. For all four mechanisms, the Roberts (1976) result applies, namely that as N increases, the incentive to free ride increases. (See also Foley, 1970). Although Hammond (1979) claims to contradict this finding, his model is too specialized and restrictive to take seriously.

7.3 CONCLUSION

For the results just described, the decisive postulate is that each player's utility function is unknown to the central authority and to other players, so that the only restriction on reporting or message-sending is the Hurwicz (1972) restriction referred to at the outset. Whenever this postulate is used, each player is free to select a utility function for reporting or message-sending that yields the highest payoffs to that player. For a given set of utility functions, every mechanism that yields a Lindahl outcome will yield the same outcome, when (as under classical assumptions) that outcome is unique. Therefore, every mechanism will have the same payoff matrix for its normal form, as illustrated in the example used here. Consequently the listed Facts, the consequent Proposition, and the related explanation must necessarily apply to every mechanism designed to elicit the full Lindahl outcome, including its tax structure.

Notes

Notes to Chapter 1

[1] Forster (1972), p. 67.

[2] See Paper No. 10 in Hamilton, Madison and Jay (1961) pp. 77-84.

[3] Allen (1972), p. 221; Chagnon (1974), pp. 127-29; Chang (1986), pp. 245-49, 262-74, 309-16; Ferrill (1985), pp. 20-31; Gabriel (1990), pp. 23-30; Harris (1972), pp. 256-57; Neel (1970); Rowlands (1972); Service (1975), pp. 206, 209-10, 215-17.

[4] For a lengthy analysis of such data, see Bailey (1992), pp. 175-92.

[5] Bailey (1980), pp. 13-14, using data from Denison (1978), p. 26.

[6] Also reported in U.S. Bureau of the Census (1995), Table 384, and corresponding tables of previous years.

[7] Kneese (1984), pp. 102-103, scaled up to current prices using the CPI.

[8] Bailey (1989) has a discussion of force mix and of methods for improving budget control, together with the above rough estimates.

[9] Studies reported in Johnson (1991), p. 229, have more recent estimates that also fall in this range.

[10] My estimates are long-term estimates based on the model used Hufbauer and Elliott (1994). Hufbauer and Elliott kindly lent me their computer model for this purpose. Their estimates, which appear to be based on short-term elasticities, show a larger producer-labor gain relative and less waste than do mine. Our concern is with long-term effects, however.

[11] It also agrees with a public opinion survey in the U.S. on citizen perceptions of the level of waste in government. See Balz and Morin, (1991), in which they reported that according to a Post-ABC News survey in October, 1991, Americans believed that 49 cents of every tax dollar is wasted. Cited by Mueller (1996).

[12] Olson (1982), Ch. 3, elaborates at length on the proposition that special interest groups with disproportionate influence lower economic efficiency. See also Usher (1992).

[13] For a general discussion of interest group issues, with citations to other literature, see Mueller (1989), pp. 203-205, 307-310, and 453-57, and Sandler (1992).

[14] He cites a more extended treatment in Brennan and Lomasky (1993).

[15] For an elaboration and analysis of this point for different cases, see Aranson (1979), pp. 72-76.

[16] Besides the works already cited, see Anderson and Hill (1986); Buchanan and Faith (1987); Lowenberg and Yu (1992); Merville and

Osborne (1990); Mueller (1991); Ordeshook (1992); Spindler (1990); and Sunstein (1991).

17 For more cursory assertions of the same view, see also Breton (1993); Stigler (1992); and Thompson and Faith (1981).

18 In his subsequent work Ordeshook has conspicuously abandoned this earlier view. See Riker and Ordeshook, (1973), or Aranson and Ordeshook (1981).

19 See citations on pp. 17-19 and in notes 12-15 and 18. For a penetrating review article of Wittman's book, see Boudreaux, (1996). For a thorough and rigorous statement of the fundamental theory involved, see Sandler (1992), Chs.1-2 and throughout. For an alternative formulation emphasizing the participation decision and thereby casting doubt on Wittman's claims, see Dixit and Olson (2000).

20 In Becker (1985) he edges slightly toward the Wittman position, but clearly stops short of supporting it.

Notes to Chapter 2.

1 Bertrand Russell (1930), p. 83.

2 See also Auster and Silver (1979), Ch. 8, who outline constitutional plans bolder than Mueller's and similar in some ways to what follows here, but with inadequate analysis and without an integrated self-enforcing incentive structure. A less comprehensive plan can be found in Clarke (1980).

3 Saggs (1989), p. 30; Hoffman (1979), pp. 391-94; Service (1975), pp. 233-34. See also H. Weiss and others (1993) and Hodell, Curtis and Brenner (1995).

4 See, for example, Buchanan (1983).

5 For arguments supporting this rule, see Brennan and Buchanan (1980), pp. 190-92; Anderson and Hill (1986); Mueller (1991); and Lowenberg and Yu, (1992). Mueller discusses the point at more length in (1996), Ch. 16. Sunstein (1991) argues against it.

6 For an excellent discussion, see Mueller (1996), Ch. 15.

7 The Appendices to Chapter 6 have some advanced technical analysis of this mechanism, together with citations to key papers that deal with it. For a concise presentation of the mechanism for the main cases, see Varian (1992), pp. 426-29. The original papers that presented these ideas were Vickrey (1961), Clarke (1971) and Groves (1973). The clearest full exposition of their applicability to public goods appears in Tideman and Tullock (1976). See also Mueller (1989), pp. 124-34.

8 For a proof of this claim see Chapter 5.

[9] Calfee and Rubin (1992) develop the pertinent analysis for a logically equivalent problem.

[10] See, for example, Mueller et. al. (1972).

[11] This proposal is less unusual than that for random selection of legislators. For an economic analysis of the case for it, see Torsvik, (1994).

[12] Kiralfy, 2nd ed. (1956), pp. 153-60; 8th ed. (1990), pp. 129-34. See also Berman, (1983), pp. 268-69 for a philosophical and historical argument favoring such competition.

[13] The estimate assumes that taxpayers willingly pay for the transfer to foreign producers that the U.S. quota system provides. Otherwise the required compensation to consumers would be several times the amount of producer gains. The ratio reconciles well, either way, with the range of estimates for agriculture presented in Chapter I. My estimates are long-term estimates based on the model used by Hufbauer and Elliott (1994).

[14] Mencken (1929).

[15] For data and discussion on private charitable contributions other than to family members, see Rose-Ackerman (1996). See also Roberts (1984).

[16] See, for example, Bailey (1993) and the references cited there. For a more fine-grained treatment of altruism, see also Kingma (1989).

[17] For a more elaborate explanation of the underlying theory that leads us to disregard *y*, in a broader context involving other similar welfare calculations, see Harberger (1964), especially 61f.

[18] For a useful related perspective on the modeling of tastes, developed in another context, see Muth (1966).

[19] See, for example, Friar (1996), which reports sympathetically and without comment the following quote from Berrick (1996): 'Berrick sets out to debunk what she calls 10 myths concerning welfare. These include: "Welfare payments are too generous" (no state's welfare payments raise families above the poverty line; in California, AFDC pays a family of three $607 a month); . . .' As Friar and Berrick must have known, women on welfare can get food stamps, Medicaid, housing and nutritional assistance, etc., in addition to AFDC, bringing the typical total in California to the cash-flow equivalent of a job paying almost $2000 a month. See the discussion in Chapter I, 10-11 and the associated citations in note 17 of Ch. I.

Notes to Chapter 3

[1] Frost (1991), p. 29.

[2] See, for example, Mieszkowski and Zodrow (1989).

[3] For a helpful impromptu lecture on ancient Greek geography and politics, I am indebted to Robert Bauslaugh, Department of Classics, Emory University.

[4] For a description of these examples, together with a thorough analysis of the related economic theory, see Foldvary (1994).

Notes to Chapter 4

[1] Agar (1942), p. 225.

[2] His precise words were 'In this world of sin and woe, no one pretends that democracy is perfect or all-wise. Indeed, it has been said that democracy is the worst form of government, except all those other forms that have been tried from time to time.' *Hansard*, Nov. 11, 1947, col. 206-207.

[3] For an excellent article that dispels some wishful thinking on this point, see Sutter (1995).

[4] A recent exception is Mueller (1991) which has some more radical suggestions.

[5] As noted in Chapter 2, see Mueller (1996) and Auster and Silver (1979).

[6] For a full explanation of the conditions for full capitalization and of the effects of local public goods on the incomes of persons other than landowners when these conditions are not met, see Tideman (1993), pp. 137-44. In a framework of approximate Lindahl taxes, Tideman proposed using the VCG mechanism to determine the supply of local public goods, similarly to what we propose here but without most of our proposed framework.

[7] For a thorough discussion and analysis of this problem, mainly but not exclusively in relation to courtroom evidence, see Parker (1995). See also Foster, Bernstein and Huber (1993), Ch. 2 and *throughout*, and Huber (1991).

[8] For insightful discussions of this problem, see Anderson and Hill, (1986) and Merville and Osborne (1990).

[9] For a summary and for an up-to-date set of citations of applications of this method of analysis to other countries, see Kotlikoff (1995-96).

[10] Recall that Chapter I presents estimates of the inefficiency of most modern government programs of this kind.

[11] For more discussion, see the Appendix to Chapter 2. For a more thorough, though confusing, discussion, see Brubaker (1983); Tullock (1982); Margolis (1983). See also Tideman (1983) for a response to Margolis with regard to the meaning of individual valuations.

[12] Some examples that particularly deserve study are Arendt (1963), pp. 252-283; Dahl (1989), pp. 332-41, and Fishkin (1991), pp. 92-101.
[13] Estimate derived from the President's Commission On An All Volunteer Armed Force (1970), Tables A-11 and C-IV, 181-209.

Notes to Chapter 5
[1] See the mathematical appendix of Calfee and Rubin (1992).
[2] For a full development of this analysis for a logically equivalent problem, see the appendix of Calfee and Rubin (1992).

Notes to Chapter 6
[1] The necessary restriction for a more general strategy space is due to Hurwicz (1986).
[2] For a textbook presentation of this tax for the case of transferable utility, see Varian (1992), p. 429, or Tideman and Tullock (1976).
[3] For a survey of results relating to the general proposition, see Groves and Ledyard (1987), p. 65.
[4] Clarke (1971) and Tideman and Tullock (1976, 1977) explained informally why the budget surplus of the VCG tax declines relative to the size of the economy at the rate $O(1/N)$ as the economy grows large. Green, Kohlberg, and Laffont (1976) and Rob (1982) proved variations of this idea in probabilistic terms for binary choices. Green, Kohlberg, and Laffont (1976) also proved convergence on Pareto optimality in a large replicated economy, with a non-optimal distribution rule. d'Aspremont, Cremer, and Gerard-Varet (1990) provided important results and insights on Bayesian incentive-compatibility for some special cases involving transferable utility. Most notably, they elaborated on an earlier proof that there is a way to reconcile efficient outcomes, including exact budget balance, with Bayesian incentive compatibility. The results in Rob (1982) and in Green, Kohlberg, and Laffont (1976) deal only with the case of discrete choices, where they reasoned in probabilistic terms. Their results show convergence on optimality at the same rate as the rate of shrinkage of the VCG tax itself, so that the relationship between the incentive to misrepresent preferences and the incentive to participate seriously does not improve appreciably.
[5] This restriction is satisfied by the function $U^i(x^i, y) = A(y)x^i + B^i(y)$, used by Bergstrom and Cornes (1983) and by Conn (1983), where the function $A(y)$ is identical for all consumers.

Bibliography

H. Agar, *Time for Greatness* (Boston: Little, Brown & Co., 1942).

W. Allen, 'Ecology, Techniques and Settlement Patterns', in P. J. Ucko, R. Tringham, and G. W. Dimbleby (eds), *Man, Settlement And Urbanism* (London: Gerald Duckworth, 1972).

T. L. Anderson and P. J. Hill, 'Constraining the Transfer Society: Constitutional and Moral Dimensions', *Cato Journal* 6 (1986) 317-339.

P. H. Aranson, 'The Uncertain Search for Regulatory Reform', University of Miami School of Law, Law and Economics Center Working Paper No. 79-3 (1979).

P. H. Aranson, 'Rational Ignorance in Politics, Economics, and Law', *Journal des Economistes et des Etudes Humaines* 1 (Winter 1989-90) 25-42.

P. H. Aranson and P. C. Ordeshook, 'Regulation, Redistribution, and Public Choice', *Public Choice* 37 (1981) 69-100.

H. Arendt, *On Revolution* (New York: Viking Press, 1963).

K. J. Arrow, 'The property rights doctrine and demand revelation under incomplete information', in M. J. Boskin (ed.), *Economics and human welfare: Essays in honor of Tibor Scitovsky* (Academic Press: New York, 1979).

K. J. Arrow and F. H. Hahn, *General Competitive Analysis* (San Francisco: Holden-Day, 1971).

R. Auster and M. Silver, *The State as Firm* (Boston: Martinus Nijhoff, 1979).

M. Bagnoli and B. L. Lipman, 'Private Provision of Public Goods Can Be Efficient', *Public Choice* 74 (1992) 59-78.

M. J. Bailey, 'The Marshallian Demand Curve', *Journal of Political Economy* 62 (1954) 255-261.

M. J. Bailey, *Reducing Risks To Life* (Washington, DC: American Enterprise Institute, 1980).

M. J. Bailey, 'National Military Strategy and Force Structure', Unclassified Working Paper (June, 1989).

M. J. Bailey, *Studies In Positive And Normative Economics* (Aldershot, England: Edward Elgar, 1992).

M. J. Bailey, 'Note on Ricardian Equivalence', *Journal of Public Economics* 51 (1993) 437-446.

M. J. Bailey, 'Implementation of the Thompson Mechanism', *Public Choice*, 89 (1996) 231-243.

M. J. Bailey and P. H. Rubin, 'A Positive Theory of Legal Change', *International Review of Law and Economics* 14 (1994) 467-477.

D. Balz and R. Morin, 'Pessimism and Political Powerlessness Rises', *Washington Post* (Nov. 3, 1991) A1.

G. S. Becker, 'A Theory of Competition among Pressure Groups for Political Influence', *Quarterly Journal of Economics* 98 (1983) 371-400.

G. S. Becker, 'Public Policies, Pressure Groups, and Dead Weight Costs', *Journal of Public Economics* 28 (1985) 329-347.

B. Benson, *The Enterprise Of Law: Justice Without The State* (San Francisco: Pacific Research for Public Policy, 1990).

T. C. Bergstrom and R. C. Cornes, 'Independence of Allocative Efficiency from Distribution in the Theory of Public Goods', *Econometrica* 51 (1983) 1753-1765.

H. J. Berman, *Law and Revolution: The Formation of Western Legal Tradition* (Cambridge, Mass: Harvard University Press, 1983).

B. D. Bernheim, 'Ricardian Equivalence: An Evaluation of Theory and Evidence', in Stanley Fischer (ed.), *NBER Macroeconomics Annual 1987* (Cambridge, Mass: MIT Press, 1987).

B. D. Bernheim and K. Bagwell, 'Is Everything Neutral?', *Journal of Political Economy* 96 (1988) 308-338.

J. D. Berrick, *Faces of Poverty: Portraits of Women and Children on Welfare* (New York: Oxford University Press, 1996).

T. E. Borcherding, W. W. Pommerehne and F. Schneider, 'Comparing the Efficiency of Private and Public Production: The Evidence from Five Countries', *Zeitschrift für Nationalökonomie* 42 (Suppl. 2, 1982).

D. J. Boudreaux, 'Was Your High-School Civics Teacher Right After All?' *The Independent Review* 1 (1996) 111-128.

G. Brennan and J. M. Buchanan, *The Power to Tax* (New York: Cambridge University Press, 1980).

G. Brennan and L. Lomasky, *Democracy and Decision* (New York: Cambridge University Press, 1993).

A. Breton, 'Toward a Presumption of Efficiency in Politics', *Public Choice* 77 (1993) 53-66.

W. T. Brookes, 'The National Press and the Statist Quo', *Cato Policy Report* 15 (September/October 1993) 1-15.

E. R. Brubaker, 'On the Margolis "Thought Experiment" and the Applicability of Demand-Revealing Mechanisms to Large-Group Decisions', *Public Choice* 41 (1983) 315-319.

J. M. Buchanan, 'The Achievement and Limits of Public Choice in Diagnosing Government Failure and in Offering Bases for Constructive Reform', in H. Hanusch (ed.), *Anatomy of Government Deficiencies*

(New York: Springer Verlag, 1983) reprinted in J. M. Buchanan, *Explorations into Constitutional Economics* (College Station, Texas: Texas A&M University Press, 1989).

J. M. Buchanan, and R. L. Faith, 'Secession and the Limits of Taxation: Toward a Theory of Internal Exit', *American Economic Review* 77 (Dec. 1987) 1023-1031;

J. E. Calfee and P. H. Rubin, 'Some Implications of Damage Payments for Nonpecuniary Losses', *Journal of Legal Studies* 21 (1992) 371-411.

T. Carroll, 'The Real Price Tag of New York's Welfare Benefits' (Albany, New York: Empire Foundation and Change-NY, August 1994) cited by Tanner, Moore and Hartman (1995).

A. T. Carter, *An English History of the Courts*, 7th edn (London: Butterworth, 1944).

N. A. Chagnon, *Studying the Yanomamo* (New York: Holt, Rinehart, & Winston, 1974).

K.-C. Chang, *The Archaeology Of Ancient China*, 4th edn (New Haven: Yale Univ. Press, 1986).

E. H. Clarke, 'Multipart Pricing of Public Goods', *Public Choice* 11 (1971) 17-33.

E. H. Clarke, *Demand Revelation and the Provision of Public Goods* (Cambridge, Mass: Ballinger, 1980).

R. H. Coase, 'The Problem of Social Cost', *Journal of Law and Economics* 3 (1960) 1-44.

R. A. Collinge, 'A Creation of Markets for Market Power, Spillovers, and Public Goods', Unpublished Ph. D. dissertation, University of Maryland, 1983.

D. Conn, 'The Scope of Satisfactory Mechanisms for the Provision of Public Goods', *Journal of Public Economics* 20 (1983) 249-263.

R. Cornes and T. Sandler *The Theory of Externalities, Public Goods, and Club Goods* (New York: Cambridge University Press 1986).

R. A. Dahl, *Democracy and Its Critics* (New Haven: Yale University Press, 1989).

C. d'Aspremont, and L. A. Gerard-Varet 'On Bayesian Incentive Compatible Mechanisms', in J.-J. Laffont (ed.), *Aggregation and Revelation of Preferences* (New York: North Holland 1979).

C. d'Aspremont, J. Crémer and L. A. Gérard-Varet, 'Incentives and the Existence of Pareto-Optimal Revelation Mechanisms', *Journal of Economic Theory* 51 (1990) 233-254.

G. Debreu, *Theory of Value* (New York: Wiley, 1959).

G. Debreu, 'Smooth Preferences', in *Mathematical Economics: Twenty Papers of Gerard Debreu* (Cambridge, UK: Cambridge University

Press, 1983). Also: 'Smooth Preferences: A Corrigendum', in the same volume.

E. F. Denison, 'Effects of Selected Changes in the Institutional and Human Environment upon Output per Unit of Input', *Survey of Current Business*, 58 (1978) 26.

A. Dixit and M. Olson, 'Does Voluntary Participation Undermine the Coase Theorem?' *Journal of Public Economics*, 76 (2000) 309-335.

W. R. Dougan and J. M. Snyder Jr., 'Interest-Group Politics under Majority Rule', *Journal of Public Economics* 61 (1996) 49-71.

A. Downs, *An Economic Theory of Democracy* (New York: Harper & Brothers, 1957).

M. L. Eysenbach, 'Note on a Pareto-Optimal Decision Process', *Public Choice* 1 (1967) 105-107.

A. Ferrill, *The Origins of War* (New York: Thames and Hudson, 1985).

J. S. Fishkin, *Democracy and Deliberation* (New Haven: Yale University Press, 1991).

J. Floyd, *The Distribution Effects Of Farm Policy: A Comparison of The Experience of Canada and The United States in The Northern Great Plains*, unpublished doctoral dissertation (U. of Chicago, 1963).

F. Foldvary, *Public Goods and Private Communities* (Aldershot, Hants, UK: Edward Elgar, 1994).

D. K. Foley, 'Resource Allocation and the Public Sector', *Yale Economic Essays* 7 (1967) 45-98.

D. K. Foley, 'Lindahl's Solution and the Core of an Economy with Public Goods', *Econometrica* 38 (1970) 66-72.

E. M. Forster, *Two Cheers for Democracy* (London: Edward Arnold, 1972).

K. R. Foster, D. E. Bernstein and P. W. Huber (eds), *Phantom Risk: Scientific Inference and The* Law (Cambridge, Mass: MIT Press, 1993).

W. Friar, 'Exposing the Faces behind the Stats', Oakland Tribune, Feb. 20, 1996, p. CUE-1.

R. Frost, 'Mending Wall' in *A Boy's Will* and *North of Boston* (New York: Dover Publications, 1991).

R. A. Gabriel, *The Culture of War* (New York: Greenwood Press, 1990).

J. Green, E. Kohlberg and J.-J. Laffont, 'A Partial-Equilibrium Approach to the Free-Rider Problem', *Journal of Public Economics* 6 (1976) 375-394.

J. Green, and J.-J. Laffont, 'On the Revelation of Preferences for Public Goods', *Journal of Public Economics* 8 (1977) 79-93.

J. Green and J.-J. Laffont, 'Characterization of Satisfactory Mechanisms for the Revelation of Preferences for Public Goods', *Econometrica* 45 (1977) 427-439.

J. Green, and J.-J. Laffont, *Incentives in Public Decision-Making*, (New York : North-Holland, 1979).

T. Groves, 'Incentives in Teams', *Econometrica* 41 (1973) 617-631.

T. Groves and J. O. Ledyard, 'Some Limitations of Demand-Revealing Processes', *Public Choice* 29-2 (1977) 107-124.

T. Groves and J. O. Ledyard, 'Incentive Compatibility Since 1972', in T. Groves, R. Radner, and S. Reiter (eds), *Information, Incentives, and Economic Mechanisms* (Minneapolis: University of Minnesota Press, 1987).

A.. Hamilton, J. Madison and J. Jay, *The Federalist Papers* (New York: The New American Library, 1961).

M. H. Hansen, *The Athenian Democracy in the Age of Demosthenes*, translated by J. A. Crook (Oxford: Blackwell, 1991).

A. C. Harberger, 'The Measurement of Waste', *American Economic Review Papers and Proceedings* 54 (May, 1964) 58-76.

D. R. Harris, 'Swidden Systems and Settlement', in P. J. Ucko, R. Tringham, and G. W. Dimbleby (eds), *Man, Settlement And Urbanism* (London: Gerald Duckworth, 1972)

J. C. Hause, 'The Theory of Welfare Cost Measurement', *Journal of Political Economy* 83 (1975) 1145.

H. Houthakker, 'Revealed Preference and the Utility Function', *Economica* N. S. 17 (1950) 159-174.

H. M. Hochman, and J. D. Rodgers, 'Pareto Optimal Redistribution', *American Economic Review* 59 (1969) 1348-1362.

D. A. Hodell, J. H. Curtis, and M. Brenner, 'Possible Role of Climate in the Collapse of Classic Maya Civilization', *Nature* 375 (1995) 391-394.

M. A. Hoffman, *Egypt before the Pharaohs* (London: Ark, 1979).

P. W. Huber, *Galileo's Revenge: Junk Science in the Courtroom* (Harper Collins, 1991).

G. C. Hufbauer and K. A. Elliott, *Measuring the Costs of Protection in the US* (Washington, DC: Institute for International Economics, 1994).

L. Hurwicz, 'Outcome Functions Yielding Walrasian and Lindahl Allocations at Nash Equilibrium Points', *Review of Economic Studies* 46 (1979) 263-282.

L. Hurwicz, 'On Informationally Decentralized Systems', in C. B. McGuire and Roy Radner (eds.), *Decision and Organization*, 2nd edn (Minneapolis: University of Minnesota Press, 1986).

L. Hurwicz and M. Walker, 'On the Generic Non-Optimality of Dominant-Strategy Allocation Mechanisms: A General Theorem that Includes Pure Exchange Economies', *Econometrica*, 58 (1990) 683-704.

R. M. Jackson, *The Machinery of Justice in England*, 6th edn (Cambridge, UK: Cambridge University Press, 1972).

D. G. Johnson, *World Agriculture In Disarray*, 2nd edn (New York: St. Martin's Press, 1991).

D. G. Johnson, *Less than Meets the Eye* (London: Centre for Policy Studies, 1995).

R. A. Kessel, 'Price Discrimination in Medicine', *Journal of Law and Economics* 1 (Oct. 1958) 20-53.

B. R. Kingma, 'An Accurate Measurement of the Crowd-out Effect, Income Effect, and Price Effect for Charitable Contributions', *Journal of Political Economy* 97 (1989) 1197-1207.

A. R. Kiralfy, *The English Legal System,* 2nd edn (London: Sweet & Maxwell, 1956); 8th edn (1990).

A. V. Kneese, *Measuring the Benefits of Clean Air and Water* (Washington, DC: Resources for the Future, 1984).

A. V. Kneese and B. T. Bower, *Managing Water Quality: Economics, Technology, Institutions* (Baltimore, Md: Johns Hopkins University Press, 1968).

A. V. Kneese and C. L. Schultze, *Pollution, Prices, and Public Policy* (Washington, DC: Brookings Institution, 1975).

L. J. Kotlikoff, *Generational Accounting* (New York: The Free Press, 1992).

L. J. Kotlikoff, 'Generational Accounting', in *NBER Reporter* (National Bureau of Economic Research, Winter 1995-96), 8-14.

J.-J. Laffont, (ed.) *Aggregation and Revelation of Preferences* (New York: North Holland, 1979).

J.-J. Laffont and E. Maskin, 'A Differential Approach to Expected Utility Maximizing Mechanisms', in J.-J. Laffont (ed.), *Aggregation and Revelation of Preferences* (New York: North Holland, 1979).

Ledyard, J. O. 'Dominant Strategy Mechanisms and Incomplete Information', in J.-J. Laffont (ed.), *Aggregation and Revelation of Preferences* (New York: North Holland, 1979).

E. Lindahl, 'Just Taxation – A Positive Solution', translated by E. Henderson, in R. A. Musgrave and A. T. Peacock (eds), *Classics in the Theory of Public Finance* (New York: Macmillan, 1958) 168-176.

A. D. Lowenberg, and B. T. Yu, 'Efficient Constitution Formation and Maintenance: The Role of Exit', *Constitutional Political Economy* 3 (1992) 51-72.

T. R. Malthus, *First Essay on Population* (London: Macmillan, 1798).

H. Margolis, 'A Thought Experiment on Demand-Revealing Mechanisms', *Public Choice* 38 (1982a) 87-91.

H. Margolis, *Selfishness, Altruism, and Rationality* (New York: Cambridge University Press, 1982b).

H. Margolis, 'Reply to Brubaker and Tullock', *Public Choice* 41 (1983) 321-325.

H. L. Mencken, in *Baltimore Evening Sun*, Dec. 9, 1929.

L. J. Merville, and D. K. Osborne, 'Constitutional Democracy and the Theory of Agency', *Constitutional Political Economy* 1 (1990) 21-47.

P. Mieszkowski and G R. Zodrow, 'Taxation and the Tiebout Model', *Journal of Economic Literature*, 27 (1989) 1098-1146.

E. J. Mishan, *Cost-Benefit Analysis*, 4th ed. (New York: Routledge, Chapman & Hall, 1988).

H. Moulin, *Axioms of Competitive Decision Making* (New York: Cambridge University Press, 1988).

D. C. Mueller, *Public Choice,* 1st edn (New York: Cambridge University Press, 1979).

D. C. Mueller, *Public Choice II* (New York: Cambridge University Press, 1989).

D. C. Mueller 'Choosing a Constitution in Eastern Europe: Lessons from Public Choice', *Journal of Comparative Economics* 15 (1991) 325-348.

D. C. Mueller, *Constitutional Democracy* (New York: Oxford University Press, 1996).

D. C. Mueller, R. D. Tollison and T. D. Willett, 'Representative Democracy via Random Selection', *Public Choice* 12 (1972) 57-68.

R. A. Musgrave, *The Theory of Public Finance* (New York: McGraw-Hill, 1959).

R. F. Muth, 'Household Production and Consumer Demand Functions', *Econometrica* 34 (1966) 699-708.

J. V. Neel, 'Lessons from a "Primitive" People', *Science* 170 (1970) 815-822.

W. Nicholson, *Microeconomic Theory*, 6th edn (Fort Worth: Dryden Press, 1995).

M. Olson, *The Logic of Collective Action* (Cambridge, Mass: Harvard University Press, 1965).

M. Olson, *The Rise and Decline of Nations* (New Haven: Yale University Press, 1982).

P. C. Ordeshook, 'Constitutional Stability', *Constitutional Political Economy* 3 (1992) 137-175.

P. C. Ordeshook, 'Pareto Optimality in Electoral Competition', *American Political Science Review* 56 (1971) 1141-1145.

J. S. Parker, 'Daubert's Debut: The Supreme Court, the Economics of Evidence, and the Adversarial System', *Supreme Court Economic Review* 5 (1995) 1-56.

M. V. Pauly, 'Taxation, Health Insurance, and Market Failure in the Medical Economy', *Journal of Economic Literature* 24 (June 1986).

President's Commission on an All Volunteer Armed Force, *Report* (USGPO: Washington, DC 1970).

T. Rader, *Theory of Microeconomics* (New York: Academic Press, 1972).

W. H. Riker and P. C. Ordeshook, *Introduction to Positive Political Theory* (Englewood Cliffs, NJ: Prentice-Hall, 1973).

R. Rob, 'Asymptotic Efficiency of the Demand Revealing Mechanism', *Journal of Economic Theory* 28 (1982) 207-220.

A. W. Roberts and D. E. Varburg, *Convex Functions* (New York: Academic Press, 1973).

J. Roberts, 'The Incentives for Correct Revelation of Preferences and the Number of Consumers', *Journal of Public Economics* 6 (1976) 359-374.

R. D. Roberts, 'A Positive Model of Private Charity and Public Transfers', *Journal of Political Economy* 92 (1984) 136-148.

S. Rose-Ackerman, 'Altruism, Nonprofits, and Economic Theory', *Journal of Economic Literature* 34 (1996) 701-728.

M. J. Rowlands, 'Defense: A Factor in the Organization of Settlements', in P. J. Ucko, R. Tringham, and G. W. Dimbleby (eds), *Man, Settlement And Urbanism* (London: Gerald Duckworth, 1972).

P. H. Rubin and M. J. Bailey, 'The Role of Lawyers in Changing the Law', *Journal of Legal Studies* 23 (1994) 807-831.

H. W. F. Saggs, *Civilization before Greece and Rome* (New Haven: Yale Univ. Press, 1989).

P. A. Samuelson, 'The Pure Theory of Public Expenditures', *Rev. Econ. Stat.* 36 (1954) 386-89. Reprinted in K. J. Arrow and T. Scitovsky (eds), *Readings in Welfare Economics* (Homewood, IL: Irwin, 1969).

T. Scitovsky, 'A Note on Welfare Propositions in Economics', *Rev. Econ. Stud.* 9 (1941) 77-88. Reprinted in K. J. Arrow and T. Scitovsky (eds), *Readings in Welfare Economics* (Homewood, IL: Irwin, 1969).

T. Sandler, *Collective Action* (Ann Arbor: Univ. of Michigan Press, 1992).

E. R. Service, *Origins of the State and Civilization* (New York: W. W. Norton, 1975).

Z. A. Spindler, 'Constitutional Design for a Rent-Seeking Society', *Constitutional Political Economy* 1 (1990) 73-82.

G. J. Stigler, 'Law or Economics', *Journal of Law and Economics* 35 (1992) 455-468.

G. J. Stigler and G. S. Becker, 'De Gustibus Non Est Disputandum', *American Economic Review* 67 (1977) 76-90.

J. E. Stiglitz, *Economics of The Public Sector*, 2nd edn (New York: W. W. Norton, 1988).

C. R. Sunstein, 'Constitutionalism, Prosperity, Democracy: Transition in Eastern Europe', *Constitutional Political Economy* 2 (1991) 371-394.

D. Sutter, 'Constitutional Politics Within the Interest-Group Model', *Constitutional Political Economy* 6 (1995) 127-137.

M. Tanner, S. Moore and D. Hartman, 'The Work vs. Welfare Trade-Off', CATO Policy Analysis no. 240 (Washington, DC, 1995)

E. A. Thompson, 'A Pareto-Efficient Group Decision Process', in G. Tullock (ed.), *Papers on Non-Market Decision-Making* (Charlottesville, Va: University of Virginia Press, 1966) 133-140.

E. A. Thompson, 'A Reply', *Public Choice*.1 (1967) 109-112.

E. A. Thompson and R. Faith, 'A Pure Theory of Strategic Behavior and Social Institutions', *American Economic Review* 71 (1981) 366-380.

G. Tian, 'Implementation of the Lindahl Correspondence by a Single-Valued, Feasible, and Continuous Mechanism', *Review of Economic Studies* 56 (1989) 613-321.

T. N. Tideman, 'A Collective Conception of Collective Value,' *Perspectives on Local Public Finance and Public Policy* 1 (1983), 3-22.

T. N. Tideman, 'Integrating Rent and Demand Revelation in the Evaluation and Financing of Services', in H. Ohta and J.-F. Thisse (eds), *Does Economic Space Matter?* (New York: St. Martin's Press, 1993) 133-150.

T. N. Tideman and G. Tullock, 'A New and Superior Process for Making Social Choices', *Journal of Political Economy* 84 (1976) 1145-1159.

T. N. Tideman, and G. Tullock, 'Some Limitations of Demand-Revealing Processes: Comment', *Public Choice* 29-2 (1977) 125-128.

G. Torsvik, 'When Groups Contribute to a Public Good: The Importance of Institutional Framework for Making Collective Decisions', *Public Choice* 80 (1994) 41-54.

G. Tullock, 'More Thoughts about Demand Revealing', *Public Choice* 38 (1982) 167-170.

US Bureau of the Census *Statistical Abstract of the United States* (Washington, DC: USGPO, 1995).

US Council of Economic Advisors, *Economic Report of the President* (Washington, DC: USGPO, 1986).

US Department of Commerce *Survey of Current Business* (Washington, DC: USGPO, May 1995).

D. Usher, *The Welfare Economics of Markets, Voting and Predation* (Ann Arbor: Univ. of Michigan Press, 1992).

H. R. Varian, *Microeconomic Analysis*, 3rd edn (New York: W. W. Norton, 1992).

W. Vickrey, 'Counterspeculation, Auctions and Competitive Sealed Tenders', *Journal of Finance* 16 (1961) 8-37.

R. E. Wagner, 'Pressure Groups and Political Entrepreneurs', in Gordon Tullock (ed.), *Papers on Non-Market Decision-Making* (Charlottesville: University of Virginia, 1966) 161-170.

M. Walker, 'On the Nonexistence of a Dominant Strategy Mechanism for Making Optimal Public Decisions', *Econometrica* 48 (1980) 1521-1540.

M. Walker, 'A Simple Incentive Compatible Scheme for Attaining Lindahl Allocations', *Econometrica* 49 (1981) 65-71.

H. Weiss et al., 'The Genesis and Collapse of Third Millennium North Mesopotamian Civilization', *Science* 261 (1993) 995-1004.

K. Wicksell, 'A New Principle of Just Taxation', translated by J. M. Buchanan, in R. A. Musgrave and A. T. Peacock, (eds), *Classics in the Theory of Public Finance* (New York: Macmillan, 1958) pp. 72-118.

Wittman, D. 'Why Democracies Produce Efficient Results', *Journal of Political Economy* 97 (1989) 1395-1424.

Wittman, D. *The Myth of Democratic Failure* (Chicago: University of Chicago Press, 1995).

Index